Intersectionality as Critical Social Theory

Intersectionality
as Critical Social Theory

PATRICIA HILL COLLINS

DUKE UNIVERSITY PRESS *Durham and London* 2019

Designed by Matthew Tauch
Typeset in Minion Pro and Helvetica Neue Lt Std
by Westchester Publishing Services

Library of Congress Cataloging-in-Publication Data
Names: Hill Collins, Patricia, author.
Title: Intersectionality as critical social theory / Patricia Hill Collins.
Description: Durham : Duke University Press, 2019. | Includes
    bibliographical references and index.
Identifiers: LCCN 2018061091 (print) | LCCN 2019005395 (ebook)
ISBN 9781478007098 (ebook)
ISBN 9781478005421 (hardcover : alk. paper)
ISBN 9781478006466 (pbk. : alk. paper)
Subjects: LCSH: Intersectionality (Sociology) | Critical theory. | Social change. |
    Social justice.
Classification: LCC HM488.5 (ebook) | LCC HM488.5 .H56 2019 (print) | DDC 303.4—dc23
LC record available at https://lccn.loc.gov/2018061091

This book is dedicated to the memory of my parents,

Eunice Randolph Hill and Albert Hill

Contents

Acknowledgments

My time in the sociology department at the University of Maryland, College Park, was essential to my ability to write this book. I thank my colleagues George Ritzer and Laura Mamo, who welcomed me into our theory graduate specialization. Over the years, conversations with my faculty colleagues within sociology greatly enriched my thinking this project, among them Bill Falk, Feinian Chen, Harriett Presser, Stanley Presser, Sonalde Desai, Meyer Kestnbaum, Kris Marsh, Jeff Lucas, Rashawn Ray, and Dawn Dow. Special appreciation goes to Roberto Patricio Korzeniewicz, not only for his support of my scholarship but also for his fundamental fairness and humanity in relation to the issues in this book. What a gift that he was department chair as I finished this manuscript.

Because I worked on various aspects of this book during my entire tenure at the University of Maryland, I could not have completed various stages of this project without help from a mini-army of graduate students. My teaching and my service on dissertation committees in sociology, American studies, education, kinesiology, journalism, and women's studies greatly enriched the knowledge that I brought to this project. This intensive work with students as well as the contact I had with wonderful graduate and undergraduate students through my teaching and casual hallway conversations enriched this project. Now that the pain is behind all of us, I want to acknowledge the students whose dissertations in sociology I chaired or co-chaired: Tony Hatch, Michelle Corbin, Nazneen Kane, Paul Dean, Valerie Chepp, Margaret Austin Smith, Kendra Barber, Kathryn Buford, Michelle Beadle, Danny Swann, Rachel Guo, and Sojin Yu. I also acknowledge students whose dissertations inform important aspects of this book. Thank you to Emily Mann, Daniel Williams, Michelle Smirnova, Nihal Celik, Jillet Sam, Chang Won Lee, Aleia Clark, Les Andrist, Wendy Laybourn, Thurman Bridges, Christine Muller, Amy Washburn, Benli Shecter, Rod Carey, Laura Yee, Aaron Allen, Dina Shafey, Kristi Tredway, Allissa Richardson, and Kevin Winstead. I also thank students who are not mentioned above but who, through their service as research or teaching assistants or through unforgettable conversations, contributed to this project. Special thanks to Nicole de Loatsch, Zeynep Atalay, Carolina Martin, Beverly Pratt, Shanna Brewton-Tiayon, Melissa Brown, Anya Galli, Bill Yagatich, Dave Stroehecker, Kimberly Bonner, Bryan Clift, Joe Waggle, Heather Marsh, and the unforgettable Mehmet Ergun. I list you all because, while I could see the breadth and scope of the creativity that you brought to me, you often remained unaware of each other.

Over the years, my conversations with colleagues old and new have enriched my sense of intersectionality's current practices and future possibilities. I cannot name you all, but I am thankful nonetheless. Special thanks to Margaret Andersen, Sirma Bilge, Nira Yuval-Davis, Bonnie Thornton Dill, Kanisha Bond, Brittney Cooper, Ana Claudia Perreira, Djamila Ribeiro, Kristi Dotson, Evelyn Nakano Glenn, Angela Y. Davis, Angela Randolpho Paiva, Ângela Figueiredo, Laura Trout, Marcus Hunter, Colin Koopman, Waverly Duck, Kathryn T. Gines, Theresa Perry, Shawn Copeland, Juan Battle, Troy Duster, Erin Tarver, Beverly Guy-Sheftall, Elizabeth Higginbotham, Howard Winant, Kimberlé Crenshaw, Linda Tuhiwai Smith, Graham Hingangaroa Smith, Jessie Daniels, Catherine Knight Steele, and Emek Ergun.

I would like to thank all of the people who invited me to visit your campuses, conferences, and community settings. I work out my ideas via conversation, and the public forums you provided were invaluable to this project. I have far too many people to be able to mention you individually, but I hope you know how appreciative I am for the opportunity to contribute to your initiatives.

The team of people at Duke University Press who worked with me on this book showed professionalism and exceptional patience. This book would not have been possible without the careful and caring stewardship of Gisela Concepción Fosado, my editor. Our first conversation convinced me how much Gisela believed in this book, and her commitment to it was an important touchstone for me throughout its production. I thank the two anonymous reviewers who waded through an earlier, more convoluted version of this manuscript. I don't know how they did it, but they saw the promise of the argument and encouraged me to persist. The production team on this project has been first rate: special thanks to Andrea Klingler, the intrepid copyeditor who waded through the manuscript; as well as to Jessica Ryan, managing editor; Sara Leone, project editor; and Alejandra Mejía, editorial associate.

Finally, a full and balanced life is necessary to nurture the life of the mind and to provide support for a project of this magnitude. Thanks to my friends in tap, Zumba, and tai chi, past, present, and future, for reminding me of the need to move. My sister-friend Patrice L. Dickerson provided a good listening ear throughout this project. And as always, my family—Roger, Valerie, Lauren, Harrison, and Grant—provide much love and lots of laughter. They mean the world to me.

Introduction

Intersectionality came of age in the twentieth century during a period of immense social change. Anticolonial struggles in Africa, Asia, and Latin America; the emergence of a global women's movement; civil rights movements in multicultural democracies; the end of the Cold War; and the defeat of apartheid in South Africa all signaled the end of long-standing forms of domination. It was clear that deeply entrenched social inequalities would not disappear overnight, nor would the social problems that they engendered. What was different was a new way of looking at social inequalities and possibilities for social change. Seeing the social problems caused by colonialism, racism, sexism, and nationalism as interconnected provided a new vantage on the possibilities for social change. Many people came to hope for something better, imagining new possibilities for their own lives and those of others.

Intersectionality draws from and carries this legacy. What were once diffuse ideas about the interconnectedness of people, social problems, and ideas are now central to intersectionality as a recognized form of critical inquiry and praxis. Yet, as intersectionality has matured, both it and the world around it have changed. Decolonization has morphed into neocolonialism, feminism confronts a deeply entrenched misogyny, civil rights flounders on the shoals of a color-blind racism, Cold War thinking persists in proxy form in undeclared wars, and racial apartheid has reformulated both within and across national borders. Social inequality seems as durable as ever. Within these new social conditions, new social problems complement long-standing ones from the past. Change seems to be everywhere, yet not in the way that intersectionality's initial advocates imagined it would unfold. Democratic institutions that once offered such promise for realizing ideals of freedom, social justice, equality, and human rights are increasingly hollowed out from within by leaders who seem more committed to holding on to power than to serving the people. Such big ideals can seem less relevant now—quaint notions that were useful during past centuries but perhaps less attainable now. Given the scope and durability of social inequality and the social problems that it engenders, it's hard not to become disillusioned. How do people engage in social action during times of such change such as our own? Conversely, which ideas will prove to be most useful in shaping such actions?

This brings me to why I wrote this particular book, and why I decided to finish it now. I see important parallels between the challenges that confronted intellectual-activists who initially contributed to intersectionality's emergence and those of today. In *Intersectionality as Critical Social Theory*, I take the position that intersectionality is far broader than what most people, including many of its practitioners, imagine it to be. We have yet to fully understand the potential of the constellation of ideas that fall under the umbrella term *intersectionality* as a tool for social change. As a discourse, intersectionality bundles together ideas from disparate places, times, and perspectives, enabling people to share points of view that formerly were forbidden, outlawed, or simply obscured. Yet because ideas in and of themselves do not foster social change, intersectionality is not just a set of ideas. Instead, because they inform social action, intersectionality's ideas have consequences in the social world.

Intersectionality is well on its way to becoming a critical social theory that can address contemporary social problems and the social changes needed to solve them. But it can do so only if its practitioners simultaneously understand and cultivate intersectionality as a *critical* social theory. A form of critical inquiry and praxis, intersectionality has not yet realized its potential as a critical social theory, nor has it adequately democratized its own processes for producing knowledge. But the foundation is there. Intersectionality possesses a knowledge base; a series of ongoing questions; a mass of engaged, interdisciplinary practitioners; and traditions of praxis that collectively inform its theoretical possibilities. Intersectionality is poised to develop an independent theoretical space that might guide its ongoing questions and concerns. Yet without serious self-reflection, intersectionality could easily become just another social theory that implicitly upholds the status quo. If practitioners do not pursue intersectionality's critical theoretical possibilities, it could become just another form of, as a friend of mine put it, "academic bullshit" that joins an arsenal of projects whose progressive and radical potential has waned. It could become just another idea that came and went.

Critical social theory sits in a sweet spot between critical analysis and social action, with theories that can cultivate the strongest links between the two proving to be the most resilient and useful. Developing intersectionality as critical social theory involves two challenges. On the one hand, the time is right to look within the parameters of intersectionality with an eye toward clarifying its critical theoretical possibilities. On the other hand, time may be running out for advancing intersectionality as a critical social theory in the academy. If intersectionality does not clarify its own critical theoretical project, others will do so for it.

Why Critical Social Theory? Intersectionality at the Crossroads

In *Intersectionality as Critical Social Theory*, I use intersectionality as a lens for examining how critical analysis and social action might inform one another. I want to know how and why intersectionality might become a critical social theory that keeps critical analysis and social action in play. Within the academy, intersectionality is doing substantial work within research, teaching, and administration, yet without agreement about what it actually is. Within scholarly literature, intersectionality has been conceptualized as everything from a paradigm, concept, framework, heuristic device, and theory (Collins and Bilge 2016). In my assessment, this heterogeneity has thus far been a good thing, inviting participation in building intersectionality from many different perspectives, thereby signaling intersectionality's dynamic nature. The scope of work that now exists under the umbrella term *intersectionality* provides a promising foundation for specifying intersectionality's distinctive questions, concerns, and analyses.

At the same time, intersectionality's tenure in the academy has brought it face to face with academic gatekeeping practices concerning social theory. When it comes to social theory, much more is at stake for intersectionality within academic debates than as to whether Marxism is really dead or why poststructuralism is not critical enough. Social theory is not just about the ideas in an argument; it's also about the practices of theorizing that produce those ideas. The meaning of a particular social theory lies not just in its words but also in how its ideas are created and used. As a maturing field of study, intersectionality needs to evaluate the criteria and practices that inform its theorizing. Western social theories have long been placed in service to various systems of domination. It is important not just to read what theories say but also to understand how social theories work within society, especially if they claim to be *critical* social theories.

When it comes to critical social theory, intersectionality stands at a cross-roads. To me, characterizing intersectionality as a "social theory" without serious critical analysis of what that means is both premature and problematic. The increasing and seemingly cavalier characterization of intersectionality as a social theory within intersectional scholarship resembles the initial rush toward intersectionality itself. In the 1990s, many people took up the ideas of intersectionality within a relatively short period of time. This period of discovery was initially energizing. Yet as intersectionality as a form of critical inquiry and praxis has matured, and continues to be discovered by even more people, its advocates must become more self-reflective about intersectionality's objectives, analyses, and practices. Specifically, intersectionality needs to find ways to adjudicate often competing perspectives on what it is, what it should be doing, and why it should be doing it. Having so many people claim intersectionality and use it in such disparate ways creates definitional dilemmas for intersectionality (Collins 2015). Leaving the theoretical dimensions of intersectionality unexamined only heightens these dilemmas. Without analyzing how its own critical analyses and social actions are interrelated, intersectionality may become trapped in its own crossroads, pulled in multiple directions and drowning in ideas. Without sustained self-reflection, intersectionality will be unable to help anyone grapple with social change, including changes within its own praxis.

In this book, I take the position that social theory constitutes a particular kind of knowledge. Social theories aim to *explain* the social world, offering interpretations for how and why things are the way they are as well as what they might or might not become. Because theories explain the social world, they affect the social world, even though their influence may not be apparent. Some social theories have the power to oppress, and do so quite effectively, without most people realizing the power of theory in maintaining an unjust social order. Other social theories have sparked considerable social action, providing critical explanations of the social world that catalyzed rebellions small and large. Social theories justify or challenge existing social orders. Within this universe of social theory, critical social theory both explains and criticizes existing social inequalities, with an eye toward creating possibilities for change. Stated differently, critical social theories aim to reform what is in the hope of transforming it into something else.

Critical social theory is also a particular kind of knowledge because it focuses on the social world. The social world is one that is created by human beings and changed by us. For critical social theory, this focus on the social world informs a vocabulary of interrelated terms—namely, social inequality, social problems, social order, social justice, and social change. For all of these terms, it is important to remember that without people interacting with one another, there is no social world. For critical social theories, understanding and changing the social world is the primary object of investigation. These analyses deepen understanding of the social world but are not substitutes for it.

The distinction between critical social theory and theorizing is also important for this book. Understanding theorizing as a process of explaining the social world and social theory as the product of critical analysis democratizes knowledge creation. Elites are not the only ones who theorize. Many everyday people offer compelling explanations of their social worlds. For example, in previous work, I examined Black feminist thought as an example of critical social theory that did not come from elites (Collins 1998a; 2000). Educated academics are not the only ones who produce critical social theory, but they are the ones who are more likely to claim it and benefit from it. Yet wherever we work, both inside and outside academia, those of us with literacy, education, and opportunities cannot squander these scarce resources by seeing our intellectual production as our personal property to hoard for our own benefit. My experiences as a social studies teacher in primary and middle schools; as a college professor teaching Africana studies, sociology, and social theory; as a scholar writing about these issues over several decades and reading the exciting work by up-and-coming scholar-activists have convinced me of the importance of ideas, analyses, and critical social theory. Scholar-activists in Baltimore, Soweto, São Paulo, both Birminghams (U.S. and U.K.), Vancouver, Havana, Auckland, and Istanbul do intellectual work in very different environments. They may never meet one another face to face, yet they work on remarkably similar social problems. Significantly, they seek compelling, complex analyses of how colonialism, patriarchy, racism, nationalism, and neoliberal capitalism, either singularly or in combination, inform their realities. Intersectionality is a broad-based, collaborative intellectual and political project with many kinds of social actors. Its heterogeneity is not a liability, but rather may be one of its greatest strengths.

Overview of the Book

Intersectionality as Critical Social Theory introduces and develops core concepts and guiding principles of what it will take to develop intersectionality as a critical social theory. I do not detail what intersectionality as critical social theory actually is. Rather, I develop a set of conceptual tools for how we might move intersectionality closer to becoming a critical social theory. In other words, this book provides a provisional foundation for thinking about intersectionality as a critical social theory that is under construction.

I recognize that this book, like intersectionality, covers a broad range of material. In order to visualize the progression of my main arguments, I have included a detailed table of contents in the Appendix that shows the overall architecture of the book. I include this outline as a navigational tool for seeing how the argument is sequenced and to help you see the scope of the overall argument. Please return to this outline as you read; it should help show you where you are in the text. As you can see from the scope of the outline in the Appendix, you might be very familiar with some subjects and unaware of others. For example, you might be familiar with feminist theory but know little about American pragmatism, have solid grasp of epistemology but be unfamiliar with Black feminism, or be aware of the importance of critical thinking to cognitive psychology and education but be less familiar with the history of eugenics.

Many people find social theory to be off-putting, accusing it of being overly abstract and irrelevant. Whereas the theorist sees specialty language as important for explaining complex ideas, laypeople might experience such language as exclusionary. The issue is that theorists and laypeople alike possess specialty language that reflects complex experiences and different points of view. Recognizing this dilemma, I had to find a way to write for a broad readership. My solution is to teach you what I need you to know so that you can grasp the abstractions of the arguments in this book. That decision made this book extremely difficult to write, but necessary.

As you read the book, keep in mind that *Intersectionality as Critical Social Theory*, like intersectionality itself, includes a range of topics, themes, theories, and arguments that do not normally go together. This book requires a different way of reading, one where you imagine yourself as part of an interpretive community of people whose areas of expertise differ dramatically from your own. I've written chapters, and in some cases, sections of chapters, so that they can be read as freestanding essays that are accessible to readers from varying backgrounds. As you read, keep in mind that this book is written in the intersectional space of placing different ideas in dialogue. My goal is to speak to a heterogeneous readership without compromising the integrity of the arguments presented here. Working with intersectionality itself is like that.

Organizationally, *Intersectionality as Critical Social Theory* is divided into four parts that provide conceptual tools for intersectionality's theoretical construction. Part I identifies some basic vocabulary for bringing a range of social actors to the table of theory-building. A sense of the scope of what counts as intersectionality among its practitioners (chapter 1) and what counts as critical social theory among social theorists (chapter 2) introduces these often disparate interpretive communities to one another. Part II focuses on intellectual resistance, an important dimension of intersectionality's critical mandate. Intersectionality has ties to multiple resistant knowledges, many of which serve as the source of its ideas and practices (chapter 3), and it also must attend to how epistemic power affects the limits and possibility of its own intellectual resistance (chapter 4). Part III analyzes social action as a way of knowing as an important aspect of theorizing intersectionality. How to conceptualize experience and social action in the context of community (chapter 5) and how social action might inform intersectionality's definitional boundaries (chapter 6) constitute important dimensions of intersectional theorizing. Part IV tackles two taken-for-granted core constructs within intersectionality, arguing that intersectionality as critical social theory must self-reflexively analyze each one. Relationality is a core theme within intersectionality that needs critical analysis (chapter 7), and intersectionality's commitment to social justice can no longer be assumed—it must be constructed (chapter 8).

Make no mistake: *Intersectionality as Critical Social Theory* was challenging for me to write and it will probably be challenging for you to read. With so much at stake, especially during our current period of change, I see no better way to write it. I've done my best to make the complex arguments in this book accessible. You will have to do your best to interpret what the argument presented here means to you.

Part I: Framing the Issues—Intersectionality and Critical Social Theory

When it comes to intersectionality's theoretical contours, it is important not to conflate the *ideal* of intersectionality as critical social theory with its current reality. Intersectionality is one of those fields in which so many people like the idea of intersectionality itself and therefore think they understand the field as well. In actuality, intersectionality is far broader than most people imagine, including those of us who have studied it for some time. I have trouble wrapping my mind around the scope of what now appears from a simple literature search of the term *intersectionality*. The copious body of scholarship that uses this term and related terminology—such as *race, class,* and *gender*—provides a wide array of material for mapping intersectionality as a field of inquiry and praxis. When it comes to intersectionality's content, there's almost too much material to categorize. Sufficient scholarship now exists to clarify important dimensions of intersectionality's cognitive architecture for critical social theory (Collins and Bilge 2016).

Getting a better sense of intersectionality itself requires a closer look at intersectionality's internal dynamics. When scholars, activists, or practitioners say that their project is "intersectional" or that they are "doing intersectionality," what do they mean? In chapter 1, "Intersectionality as Critical Inquiry," I examine the cognitive underpinnings of intersectionality. I investigate three dimensions of how people *use* intersectionality to examine the social world—namely, as a metaphor, as a heuristic, and as a paradigm. I argue that these characteristic uses of intersectionality provide a conceptual foundation for intersectionality's theoretical development. My goal is to specify the critical thinking tools that underlie intersectionality's internal practices as a way to introduce intersectionality as a critical theory in the making. How might intersectionality's practitioners build on this cognitive foundation to develop intersectionality's theoretical potential? In chapter 1, I also introduce important premises concerning intersectionality as critical social theory, which I develop throughout the book. For one, because intersectionality's scope is so broad, it is situated in an ongoing tension between conceptions of social theory within the social sciences and within interpretive fields such as philosophy and the humanities. The broader understanding of social theory that people have in mind when they use intersectionality reflects these tensions. These distinctive understandings of social theory itself also influence people's perceptions of whether intersectionality is a social theory and their evaluation of its status. For another, there is a significant distinction between the content of social theory and the processes of doing social theory. Stated differently, social theory is a body of knowledge that explains the social world, and theorizing is a process or way of working that produces social theory. Developing intersectionality as a critical social theory requires attending to both.

These distinctions between how the humanities or the social sciences define social theory, and between the content of social theory and processes of theorizing that create that content are both important. Yet significantly, neither of these aspects of social theory is inherently critical. The humanities and the social sciences contain social theories that have alternately upheld the status quo, criticized it, or both. Similarly, there is nothing inherently critical about the content of any given social theory and the processes of doing it. As a critical social theory in the making, intersectionality has a stake in clarifying what being critical means for its own project. In chapter 2, "What's Critical about Critical Social Theory?," I analyze how varying perceptions of the meaning of being critical have similarly varied implications for intersectionality. I examine three particular sites of critical social theory from different national traditions and periods of time: critical theory of the Frankfurt school (1930s–1940s), British cultural studies (1970s–1980s), and strands of Francophone social theory (1950s–1960s). When it comes to critical social theory, no one model, template, recipe, or set of rules can be followed as inherently critical. Critical social theory emerges within a specific context and speaks to that particular context.

The analysis of these particular sites of critical social theory identifies two important aspects of being critical. The first is familiar: critical theory as criticism or as criticizing some idea, practice, or behavior. Criticizing something is a common meaning of being critical. But I also introduce a less familiar sense of being critical—namely, an entity that is essential, needed, or critical for something to happen. For example, water is critical in sustaining life, and love may be critical for human development. Can ideas such as intersectionality serve a similar critical purpose in the social world? I raise this question early in the book, but leave it unanswered.

Together, these opening chapters explore two important aspects of developing intersectionality as critical social theory: one involving intersectionality's internal dynamics and the other, intersectionality's relationship with established critical social theories. Looking within its own practices and to the practices of others frames the broader issues that inform intersectionality's critical inquiry. Moreover, not only do chapters 1 and 2 introduce intersectionality itself as well as selected theoretical traditions with academia; when read together, these chapters juxtapose the openness of intersectionality, as an emerging theoretical endeavor, to established traditions of theoretical canon-building in the academy. Just as there is not yet any agreed upon way of doing intersectionality, the traditions of critical social theory surveyed here illustrate that there is no one way of thinking and doing critical social theory. Yet they also trouble the academic landscape by illustrating how some critical social theories are more widely accepted than others. In essence, how critical or resistant can critical social theories be within the contours of academia if we continue to think of theorizing as a purely academic endeavor? What possibilities for resistant knowledge, especially critical social theory, are generated or precluded by this assumption?

Part II: How Power Matters—Intersectionality and Intellectual Resistance

Many intellectual histories overlook the importance of power relations in shaping the questions, assumptions, knowledge, and impact of a given social theory. In part II of the book, I analyze power relations not by emphasizing domination, but rather by developing the concept of intellectual resistance and exploring intersectionality's connections to it. Here I investigate intersectionality's ties to intellectual resistance as a two-pronged endeavor. Intersectionality itself can be seen as a knowledge project of resistance, one in which critical analysis underpins its intellectual resistance. Intersectionality also confronts epistemological challenges to its intellectual resistance. Particular knowledge projects are sites of intellectual resistance, and critical social theory is a particular form of intellectual resistance.

A far broader political and intellectual landscape shapes intersectionality's theorizing than that provided by academic social theories. Gender, race, ethnicity, nation, sexuality, ability, and age are not just categories designed to make intersectionality more user-friendly for academic research. Rather, these terms also reference important resistant knowledge traditions among subordinated peoples who oppose the social inequalities and social injustices that they experience. Such projects aim to address the deep-seated concerns of people who are subordinated within domestic and global expressions of racism, sexism, capitalism, colonialism, and similar systems of political domination and economic exploitation. Whatever the form of oppression they experience—race, class, gender, sexuality, age, ability, ethnicity, and nation—subordinated groups have a vested interest in resisting it.

Chapter 3, "Intersectionality and Resistant Knowledge Projects," examines how critical race studies, feminism, and decolonial knowledge projects illuminate different dimensions of intellectual resistance. Critical inquiry that begins within the assumptions of resistant knowledge projects often has access to a more expansive repertoire of critical ideas than that which originates within the framing assumptions of academic social theory. I selected these three sites of resistant knowledge production because they speak to important issues concerning critical theorizing, intellectual resistance, and intersectionality. All three projects have a presence both inside and outside the academy. All have histories of political activism that recognize the importance of theorizing via praxis. None by itself is a critical social theory in the sense of the critical theories in academia discussed in chapter 2. But by demonstrating varying forms of intellectual resistance, all three make important yet distinct contributions to intersectionality's theoretical project.

Critical race theory, broadly defined, has long challenged the racial theories manufactured within academic disciplines in Europe and North America, drawing primarily on Black diasporic and indigenous resistant knowledge traditions to do so. By advancing a hard-hitting critique of the gender bias within Western knowledge, academic feminism has made real headway in gaining visibility as a bona fide field of study. Yet while feminist theory has garnered increasing legitimation as a critical social theory, feminism writ large continues to confront deep-seated misogyny across many social institutions. Despite these challenges, feminism models a useful form of self-reflexive critical analysis about its own practices. Decolonial knowledge projects have become increasingly visible, especially as the critical edge of postcolonial studies has seemingly waned within the academy. Resistant knowledge projects of decolonization demonstrate a critical response to both the limitations of an academic discourse that seemingly represents them and the ongoing yet changing contours of contemporary neocolonial relationships.

In chapter 4, "Intersectionality and Epistemic Resistance," I examine how epistemic resistance is vital to opposing racism, sexism, class exploitation, and similar social phenomena. In making a case for the necessity of epistemic resistance for intersectionality, I focus on epistemology and methodology within academic venues. Together, epistemology and methodology influence different aspects of knowledge production. On the one hand, intersectionality is situated *within* broader epistemological frameworks that regulate definitions of what counts as theory and how theories will be evaluated. Through these definitional and evaluative processes, epistemologies exercise power in regulating social theories. Epistemology is implicated in power relations; it is not a passive bystander during the social construction of knowledge. On the other hand, intersectionality draws upon methodologies as conduits for critical theorizing that can uphold or upend epistemic power. But it cannot uncritically use existing methodologies; rather, it may need to develop its signature methods. Toward this end, I introduce dialogical engagement as a guiding framework for intersectionality's methodology, one that I also use throughout this book.

Together, these chapters examine various aspects of intellectual resistance. Understanding intersectionality as a critical social theory in the making requires a more expansive set of analytical tools that takes both its ideas and its practices into account. Within the academy, political and intellectual resistance occurs in the terrain of epistemology and methodology, areas long seen as unbiased and therefore apolitical. Yet epistemology and methodology both speak directly to intersectionality as a critical theory in the making. They do not stand outside politics but are directly implicated in developing or suppressing knowledges of resistance. How might intersectionality's social theories reflect its methodological practices and vice versa? The experience of doing intersectionality is praxis, and such praxis informs intersectional theorizing.

Part III: Theorizing Intersectionality—Social Action as a Way of Knowing

As the traditions of resistant knowledge surveyed in this book suggest, social action and experience have been important interdependent dimensions of theorizing advanced by subordinated groups. For people penalized by colonialism, patriarchy, racism, nationalism, and similar systems of power, experiences with oppression are often the catalyst for critically analyzing these systems and taking action within them. Experiences provide a reason why people are willing to take on the tough job of theorizing. Yet taking informed social action, the hallmark of analyzing experience, has also been an important dimension of critical theorizing. This notion of learning by doing suggests that thinking and acting are not separate endeavors, but rather are recursive. Moreover, experience and social action are both tied to social context—they constitute ways to ground theorizing within power relations, not as a reaction to power, but as social action in response to power relations.

Within Western social theory, social actions and the experiences they engender are often interpreted as data to be included within existing social theories or bias to be excluded from them. Experience is not a valued way of knowing, and theorizing through social action may not be seen as theorizing at all. These epistemological assumptions devalue important theoretical tools that catalyze and shape resistant knowledge itself. Groups that advance critical race studies, feminism, and decolonial studies, among others, confront accusations of being too particularistic both in invoking their own experiences in analyzing the world and in focusing on oppression and domination. Their actions to change the social world do not make them more knowledgeable but rather more biased. This epistemological framework has important implications for intersectionality. One outcome is that intersectionality has been criticized for being too closely associated with the ideas and interests of women, Black people, poor people, and people in subordinated groups. Another is that these criticisms work to limit intersectionality's theoretical possibilities because they constrain important tools for theorizing within resistant knowledge traditions. Moreover, these assumptions work to shrink the pool of people who are deemed credible to do social theory in the first place, as well as the ideas that such people bring to the process of theorizing.

Methodologically, intersectionality suggests something far more radical about the process of theorizing than quiet contemplation by a lone scholar who is removed from the social world. Rather than rejecting experience and social action as dimensions of its critical theorizing, I suggest that intersectionality would do better to redefine social action as a way of knowing that, because it valorizes experience, potentially strengthens intersectional theorizing. Developing an argument for how and why social action and experience constitute important dimensions of intersectionality's critical theorizing is the best way to respond to intersectionality's critics. Toward that end, I ask, What conception of social action as a way of knowing might intersectionality develop for its theoretical toolkit? How might experience enhance intersectional theorizing?

Chapters 5 and 6 provide different approaches to and different lenses on these connections among experience, social action as a way of knowing, and intersectionality's critical theorizing. In chapter 5, "Intersectionality, Experience, and Community," I place Black feminist thought and American pragmatism in dialogue in order to shed light on two current controversies confronting intersectionality. One concerns how experiences constitute an important, albeit overlooked, tool of critical theorizing. Because experiences occur in the social world, they are windows to that world. Experiences can be theorized just as thoroughly as books, movies, and texts. Individuals have experiences, yet the meaning they make of them stems from their placement within the families, groups, nations, and other collectivities that make up their social world. The texts of discourse analysis cannot talk back to theorists.

But people who are the subjects of study by researchers often do, drawing upon their experiences as a source of knowledge. The other controversy concerns the need for a vocabulary with which to analyze the social world as more than a constellation of individuals. Here, social action comes into play because the social world is always under construction both by individuals and by social groups. The construct of community as a way of understanding collective identity and collective action, especially within and across intersectionality's heterogeneous communities of inquiry, is especially helpful. Black feminism and American pragmatism are very different discourses, yet reading them together provides complementary perspectives on experience, on community, and, by implication, on social action as a way of knowing.

In Chapter 6, "Intersectionality and the Question of Freedom," I investigate how rethinking social action as a way of knowing might inform intersectionality's critical theorizing. The chapter examines the work of Simone de Beauvoir (1908–1986) and Pauli Murray (1910–1985), two important feminist intellectuals whose engagement with existentialism, African American social and political thought, or both provide distinctive standpoints on their understandings of freedom. Placing the ideas of two feminist intellectuals in dialogue illuminates how their respective analyses of oppression and freedom draw upon experience and social action as ways of knowing. Each intellectual's analysis of freedom has implications for intersectionality's emphasis on the recursive relationship of ideas and social action. Beauvoir is known for her existentialist analysis of freedom, yet despite being familiar with oppressions of race, gender, class, and sexuality, Beauvoir never advanced an intersectional analysis of oppression or freedom. Murray's life course and intellectual production took a different path. Her increasingly sophisticated analyses of oppression and freedom were honed within a recursive space between analysis of and struggles for freedom. Murray's intellectual and political work illustrates the process of working dialogically over time with race, class, gender, sexuality, and nation in crafting an intellectual and political agenda. Because Murray's intellectual framework did not come finished, her engaged social action suggests a sustained intellectual journey that serves as a template for intersectional theorizing.

Together, these two chapters reiterate two important methodological dimensions of intersectionality that are introduced in earlier chapters and run throughout the book. One theme concerns the significance of dialogical engagement for intersectional theorizing: for chapter 5, placing Black feminist thought and American pragmatism in dialogue to rethink experience and social action, and for chapter 6, placing the ideas of Beauvoir and Murray in dialogue as a pathway to theorizing oppression and freedom. Together, these chapters demonstrate the importance of dialogical engagement for intersectional theorizing.

The other methodological theme concerns the importance of broadening intersectionality's context of discovery by making sure that intersectionality builds inclusive communities of inquiry. In earlier chapters, I looked to discourses that are outside intersectionality's canon—namely, recognized critical social theories and resistant knowledge projects—in search of ideas that might contribute to intersectionality's theoretical development. In chapters 5 and 6, by bringing Black feminist thought and Pauli Murray as a Black feminist intellectual-activist to the center of analysis, I demonstrate the potential benefits of broadening intersectionality's context of discovery and its communities of practice.

Part IV: Sharpening Intersectionality's Critical Edge

Intersectionality has flourished because its practitioners share certain core constructs and guiding premises. But can it continue to flourish without sustained self-reflection on its own foundational ideas and practices? Intersectionality as a critical social theory in the making cannot take any of its previous accomplishments for granted. Upon its entry into the academy, intersectionality had a strong critical edge, one that reflected its ties to resistant knowledge projects and its commitment to decolonizing knowledges within academic venues. Yet how critical is intersectionality now? It's no longer sufficient to proclaim that intersectionality advances cutting-edge critical analysis. As a maturing discourse, intersectionality must begin to specify the terms of its own practice, not defensively in response to its critics, but affirmatively via sustained self-reflection about its paradigmatic premises and methodological practices. Sharpening intersectionality's critical edge requires developing agreed-upon understandings, however provisional, of its core constructs and guiding principles.

Relationality and social justice constitute two core constructs that uncritically circulate within intersectionality. Because they are ever-present and taken-for-granted assumptions, they are not necessarily analyzed or critically evaluated; rather, they shape scholarship in and the practice of intersectionality.

Relationality is an essential core construct for intersectionality itself. There would be no intersectionality without relationality: focusing on relationships *among* entities constitutes a defining feature of intersectionality.

Yet what kind of relationality does intersectionality as critical social theory need? Thinking about relationality also has important implications for intersectionality's working hypothesis of the relational nature of power relations. The premise that race, gender, class, and other systems of power mutually construct one another now functions as a taken-for-granted truism within intersectionality. Yet where is the evidence that intersectionality yields better explanations of power relations than other social theories? The theme of relationality also weaves throughout this book, appearing alternately as a framework for dialogical engagement among discourses and communities of inquiry, and as a methodological strategy for doing intersectional theorizing. Yet this claim itself is hegemonic. Where is the evidence that relational analyses of social phenomena yield better explanations of the social world than other types of analyses?

In Chapter 7, "Relationality within Intersectionality," I examine this challenging issue of conceptualizing the dynamics of relationality within intersectional inquiry. I ask, How might intersectionality develop a substantive, theoretical argument that explains the relational processes that lie at its very core? To address this question, I sketch out three modes of relational thinking within intersectionality—namely, relationality through addition, articulation, and co-formation. To me, systematizing the relational logic that informs intersectionality's scholarship and activism offers a promising first step for clarifying the contours of relationality itself. Because relational thinking through addition, articulation, and co-formation constitute starting points, not end points, for analyzing relationality, they offer one way of organizing the thinking tools that people take into varying intersectional projects.

In chapter 8, "Intersectionality without Social Justice," I analyze the taken-for-granted assumptions that social justice is inherently a part of intersectionality and that doing intersectional scholarship is somehow the same as doing social justice work. I do so by placing intersectionality in dialogue with eugenics, a once normal science that has been closely associated with ultra-nationalism. I argue that eugenics lacked a commitment to social justice, yet its effectiveness relied on a relational logic that bears striking resemblance to that of intersectionality. Significantly, eugenics drew upon understandings of race, gender, class, nation, age, ethnicity, sexuality, and ability in ways that made its core premises intelligible and that simultaneously generated support for its political goals. What lessons might intersectionality draw from the case of eugenics concerning the significance of an ethical commitment within scholarship? What is the place of ethics within intersectionality writ large and within intersectionality as critical social theory in particular?

Together, these two chapters aim to sharpen intersectionality's critical edge. But they raise more questions than they answer, leaving it to readers to decide whether these are the issues that intersectionality needs to examine, and if so, how to go about doing so. In this sense, chapters 7 and 8 invoke the spirit of the entire book, one of raising questions and trying to answer them, recognizing that because intersectionality is fundamentally dialogical, no one person or group can have all of the answers. Developing intersectionality as a critical social theory that is not just ideas is a collective, collaborative endeavor.

I realize that *Intersectionality as Critical Social Theory* raises more questions than it answers, but perhaps that is the purpose of doing critical social theory. Critical theorizing means taking a position while recognizing the provisional nature of the positions we take. It means being self-reflexive not only about other people's behavior but also about one's own praxis. To create a foundation for this internal and external self-reflexivity, throughout *Intersectionality as Critical Social Theory* I explore how epistemological and political criteria shape both intersectionality's contours as a resistant knowledge and its status as a critical social theory. I place epistemology front stage in ways that show how ways of understanding truth frame knowledge projects in general and intersectionality in particular. Because truth is so intertwined in political concerns, I also place far more emphasis on power and politics in this book than is standard in intellectual histories of social theory. In doing so, my goal is to provide a complex, expansive, yet not overly complicated way of moving into and through intersectionality's theoretical issues and controversies.

....

No one book can be all things to all people, and this book is no exception. *Intersectionality as Critical Social Theory* is a labor of love that brings an additional lens to my ongoing intellectual activism (see, e.g., Collins 2013). It builds on and extends dimensions of my long-standing engagement with intersectionality. Across a series of books and articles, I've been painstakingly making my way through distinct bodies of scholarship on race, gender, class, sexuality, nation, and age, among other categories of analysis. A few examples illustrate how the understanding of intersectionality that I bring to you in this volume reflects my serious study of race, gender, class, sexuality, nation, ethnicity, and age, both singularly and in varying combinations, over an extended period of time. In *Black Feminist Thought: Knowledge, Consciousness, and the Politics of Empowerment* (2000), I provided an intersectional analysis of African American women's intellectual production, arguing that Black feminism constituted an independent knowledge project that took a distinctive standpoint on and engaged in a distinctive politics in response to oppression. In *Black Sexual Politics: African Americans, Gender, and the New Racism* (2004), I examined racism, sexism, and heterosexism as mutually constructing systems of power, arguing that African American political struggle needed to take all into account. *From Black Power to Hip Hop: Racism, Nationalism, and Feminism* (2006) developed a framework that incorporated nationalism as a system of power into my intellectual work, focusing both on the ideologies of racism, nationalism, and feminism as well as on public policies and political activism that ensued. Through nine editions of *Race, Class, and Gender: An Anthology*, Margaret Andersen and I reviewed emerging scholarship on race, class, gender, sexuality, ethnicity, nation, and age, effectively mapping the field every three years by surveying what people were publishing. By selecting articles that reflected intersectional analysis and identifying persisting limitations within intersectionality (the treatment of social class) as well as new areas of inquiry (sexuality and transnationalism), we were able to trace, in real time, how the field developed (Andersen and Collins 2016). Collectively, these and other publications laid a sociological foundation for engaging the thematic content, characteristic practices, and theoretical contours of intersectionality. I detail my involvement in intersectionality to illustrate that I am serious about this material. It is not a fad for me, and as my own intellectual trajectory illustrates, there are no shortcuts to intersectionality.

This is a big book full of big ideas. Much is at stake in getting intersectionality right within our current social, intellectual, and political contexts. Intersectionality emerged in the mid-twentieth century during massive social changes that were catalyzed by and reflected in a range of social movements. If contemporary intersectionality embraces this legacy and develops critical tools that can deal with the challenges of our times, it holds similar potential now. Intersectionality is now far bigger than its mid-twentieth-century history. It has taken on a life of its own in arenas as diverse as human rights, public policy, social media, and social movements. Significantly, it has also made its way into academia and has taken root there, showing admirable staying power. Intersectionality's reach goes beyond the groups who initially advanced its claims through their critical ideas and actions. Intersectionality has not been business as usual—it has proven itself to be scrappy and resilient under difficult conditions. Many people have found intersectionality to be an important intellectual, political, and ethical tool for empowerment. What will it take for it to remain so? That is the subject of this book.

PART I Framing the Issues

Intersectionality and Critical Social Theory

1

Intersectionality as Critical Inquiry

So much has happened since the 1990s that the case *for* intersectionality no longer needs to be made. A surprising array of academics, activists, policy-makers, digital workers, and independent intellectuals recognize intersectionality as an important form of critical inquiry and praxis (Collins and Bilge 2016). Both within and outside the academy, administrators, teachers, social workers, counselors, and public health professionals have increasingly used intersectional analyses to shed light on important social problems concerning education, health, employment, and poverty (Berger and Guidroz 2009; Dill and Zambrana 2009). Grassroots community activists, social media activists, and social movement participants continue to draw upon intersectionality's ideas to shape their political projects. In the United States, for example, intersectional ideas reappear within the social justice movements of African Americans; women; undocumented immigrants; lesbian, gay, bisexual, transgender, queer (LGBTQ) groups; poor people; and religious minorities (see, e.g., Terriquez 2015). Ironically, white nationalists also draw upon a variation of intersectional analysis in defending their claims that white, working-class American men constitute a neglected minority. Intersectionality's reach is not confined to the United States. In a global context, grassroots and human rights advocates find that intersectionality's focus on the interconnectedness of categories of race, class, gender, sexuality, ethnicity, nationality, age, and ability sheds new light on how local social inequities articulate with global social phenomena (Collins and Bilge 2016, 88–113).

Since the 1990s, intersectionality has increasingly influenced scholarship, research, and curricular choices in colleges and universities. A copious body of scholarship within the humanities and the social sciences now self-identifies as intersectional, with anthologies emphasizing different aspects of intersectionality itself as well as various configurations of intersectionality's core categories of analysis (Grzanka 2014; Dill 2002; Lutz, Vivar, and Supik 2011; Berger and Guidroz 2009; Andersen and Collins 2016). Scholarship informed by intersectionality can now be found within both interdisciplinary fields and more traditional academic disciplines (Collins 2017a; Lutz, Vivar, and Supik 2011; May 2015). However imperfectly conceptualized and applied diversity requirements may be within colleges and corporations, they constitute one outcome of intersectionality's impact. Scholars of intersectionality have generated several monographs that explore these and other aspects of intersectionality as a field of inquiry and praxis (Carastathis 2016; Collins and Bilge 2016; Hancock 2016; May 2015; Wiegman 2012).

Intersectionality seems to be here to stay, at least for now. Yet the speed and spread of intersectionality, and the heterogeneous forms it now takes, point to new definitional dilemmas concerning intersectionality's current status and future prospects (Collins 2015). Intersectionality cannot rest on its past accomplishments and current status. Instead, the time seems right to analyze what intersectionality is, what it is not, and what it might become. Current debates within intersectionality provide much-needed critical commentary about its definitional dilemmas. Just as intersectionality is broad and complex, critical commentary about intersectionality within scholarly venues, the popular press, and digital spaces is similarly diverse. Here areas of discussion encompass varying perspectives on intersectionality's origins, the partiality of intersectionality's growing list of categories, whether intersectionality is a theory or a methodology, intersectionality's ties to social justice work, and even whether we are in or should move into a post-intersectionality phase. Given intersectionality's broad scope, consensus among its practitioners is likely to remain elusive. Instead, identifying important avenues of investigation within intersectionality that can accommodate heterogeneous points of view may prove to be more productive.

Thinking through intersectionality's theoretical contours constitutes an important next step in its development. Because intersectionality straddles traditions of social action and academic scholarship, it is uniquely positioned to develop critical theoretical analyses of the social world. Intersectionality can develop a critical social theory that reflects the wide array of ideas and actors that currently fall under its expansive umbrella. Yet it cannot do so without thinking systematically about the contours of critical social theory as well as its own theoretical knowledge and theorizing practices. As a work in progress, intersectionality is a critical social theory in the making, one that may already be doing substantial theoretical work without being recognized as such.

In this chapter, I investigate how intersectionality's practitioners conceptualize and use intersectionality's ideas. I am less concerned with the content of intersectional knowledge than with ways of thinking that people use in creating such knowledge.[1] Using this approach, I identify important thinking tools that provide a cognitive foundation for intersectionality as a critical social theory in the making. Cho, Crenshaw, and McCall (2013) provide a useful starting point for identifying these tools. They characterize intersectionality as an analytical sensibility whose meaning emerges through use. They contend that "what makes an analysis intersectional is not its use of the term 'intersectionality,' nor its being situated in a familiar genealogy, nor its drawing on lists of standard citations. Rather, what makes an analysis intersectional . . . is its adoption of an intersectional way of thinking about the problem of sameness and difference and its relation to power" (795). This definition suggests several important questions that inform the arguments in this book. What exactly is an "intersectional way of thinking"? Does this mean that intersectional scholars use special cognitive tools? Or that they use conventional forms of critical analysis in new ways or toward different ends? Is the issue of sameness and difference essential to intersectionality? Significantly, how do power relations inform intersectionality's theoretical content and the processes used to develop that knowledge?[2]

I explore these questions throughout this book, yet in this chapter, I lay a foundation for examining them by discussing the use of metaphoric, heuristic, and paradigmatic thinking within intersectionality as a field of inquiry.[3] I first examine how the metaphoric use of intersectionality facilitates a new view of social relations as interconnected entities. The metaphor of intersectionality is simultaneously a new way of conceptualizing power relations and a thinking tool that draws upon the power of metaphors in the process of theorizing. Next, I examine intersectionality's heuristic thinking—namely, how using intersectionality as rule of thumb or shortcut for thinking provides an important tool for problem solving. Intersectionality aims to explain the social world, and heuristic thinking provides an accessible route for people who utilize intersectionality to address specific social problems. I move on to examine how intersectionality's core constructs and guiding premises contribute to paradigm shifts concerning power and social inequality. These discussions explore the thinking tools or processes that people use to produce intersectionality itself. Metaphoric, heuristic, and paradigmatic thinking map the ways that people enter into, respond to, and shape intersectionality as a form of critical inquiry. Collectively, they describe a conceptual foundation or cognitive architecture for developing intersectionality as a critical social theory.

Intersectionality as a Metaphor

Kimberlé Crenshaw had no way of knowing that she was naming intersectionality as a form of critical inquiry and praxis when, in the early 1990s, she published her two groundbreaking articles on intersectionality (Crenshaw 1989, 1991). Crenshaw's scholarly articles constitute an important turning point in the shifting relationships between activist and academic communities (see, e.g., Collins and Bilge 2016, 65–77). Social movements in the mid-twentieth century pushed for institutional transformation in housing, education, employment, and health care. Transforming educational institutions and the knowledge they embodied was central to these initiatives. Indigenous peoples, African Americans, women, LGBTQ people, Latinos/as, and similarly subordinated groups challenged both the substance of knowledge about their experiences and the power arrangements within primary schools, high schools, colleges, and universities that catalyzed such knowledge. Many such groups produced oppositional or resistant knowledge that was grounded in their own experiences and that challenged prevailing interpretations of them (see chapter 3). Higher education was an important site for social transformation. Calls for transforming curricular practices within the academy stimulated an array of programs that embarked on a similar mission of institutional transformation (Collins and Bilge 2016, 77–81; Dill and Zambrana 2009). Crenshaw's naming of intersectionality tapped into these important processes of institutional transformation with the academy.

Within contemporary neoliberal sensibilities, the commitment to the idea of social transformation within mid-twentieth-century social movements can be hard to understand. Yet a broader understanding of the meaning of resistance to subordinated people suggests that Black people, indigenous peoples, women, Latinx, LGBTQ people, differently abled people, religious and ethnic minorities, and stateless people continue to see transforming social institutions as necessary. Claims for social transformation can seem to be idealistic and naive, yet with hindsight, aspirations for social transformation in prior eras inform contemporary realities. Specifically, many of the visible changes within colleges and universities over the past several decades reflect prior efforts at institutional transformation (Dill 2009; Mihesuah and Wilson 2004; Parker, Samantrai, and Romero 2010).

In a 2009 interview, two decades after publishing her signature articles, Crenshaw reflected on the experiences that led her to use the term *intersectionality* within the broader social conditions of the times. For Crenshaw, her activism in college and law school revealed the inadequacies of both antiracism and feminist perspectives, limitations that left both political projects unable to fully address the social problems that each aimed to remedy. There seemed to be no language that could resolve conflicts between antiracist social movements that were, in Crenshaw's words, "deeply sexist and patriarchal," and feminist activism, where "race reared its head in a somewhat parallel way" (Guidroz and Berger 2009, 63). For Crenshaw, informed social action within both movements required new angles of vision. This particular social problem propelled Crenshaw's search for provisional language that she could use to analyze and redress the limitations of mono-categorical thinking regarding both race and gender. Crenshaw describes what she had in mind when she introduced the term *intersectionality*:

> That was the activist engagement that brought me to this work. And *my own use of the term "intersectionality" was just a metaphor* [italics added]. I'm amazed at how it gets over- and underused; sometimes I can't even recognize it in the literature anymore. I was simply looking at the way all these systems of oppression overlap. But more importantly, how in the process of that structural convergence rhetorical politics and identity polities—based on the idea that systems of subordination do not overlap—would abandon issues and causes and people who actually were affected by overlapping systems of subordination. I've always been interested

in both the structural convergence and the political marginality. That's how I came into it. (Guidroz and Berger 2009, 65)

For Crenshaw, intersectionality named the structural convergence among intersecting systems of power that created blind spots in antiracist and feminist activism. Crenshaw counseled that antiracist and feminist movements would be compromised as long as they saw their struggles as separate and not intertwined. Significantly, racism and sexism not only fostered social inequalities, they marginalized individuals and groups that did not fit comfortably within race-only, gender-only mono-categorical frameworks. Women of color remained politically marginalized within both movements, an outcome that both reflected the harm done by racism and sexism, and limited the political effectiveness of both movements. Crenshaw's understanding of the term *intersectionality* is important for subsequent use of the term. Her work suggests that, from its inception, the idea of intersectionality worked in multiple registers of recognizing the significance of social structural arrangements of power, how individual and group experiences reflect those structural intersections, and how political marginality might engender new subjectivities and agency (Collins and Bilge 2016, 71–77).

By now it is widely accepted that *intersectionality* is the term that has stuck. Of all the words that Crenshaw could have selected, and of all the idioms that might have resonated with intersectionality's adherents, why did this specific term resonate with so many people when Crenshaw first used it? Crenshaw's comment that her use of the term *intersectionality* was "just a metaphor" provides an important clue.

Many people think of metaphors as literary devices that are confined to fiction and essays. Yet metaphors are also important in shaping how people understand and participate in social relations. People from all walks of life use metaphors every day. As a foundation of thinking and action, metaphors help people understand and experience one kind of thing in terms of another. A metaphor can spark an instant sense of understanding, fostering an immediate sense of the formerly unknown in terms of the known.[4] In essence, the capacity to think and act is metaphorical in nature (Trout 2010, 3). As metaphor, intersectionality named an ongoing communicative process of trying to understand race in terms of gender, or gender in terms of class. Rather than following the chain of metaphors (race is like and unlike gender), the metaphor of intersectionality provided a shortcut that built on existing sensibilities in order to see interconnections.

Cultural theorist Stuart Hall provides another clue as to why intersectionality as a particular metaphor travelled so quickly. In an article published in the 1990s, Hall argues that metaphors are often linked to social transformation, ways that people can move from the familiar to imagining the unfamiliar. Hall posits that metaphors of social transformation must do at least two things: "They allow us to imagine what it would be like when prevailing cultural values are challenged and transformed, the old social hierarchies are overthrown, old standards and norms disappear . . . and new meanings and values, social and cultural configurations begin to appear. However, such metaphors must also have analytic value. They must somehow provide ways of thinking about the relation between the social and symbolic domains in this process of transformation" (Hall 1996b, 287).

As a metaphor of social transformation, intersectionality invokes both elements. It arrived in the midst of ongoing struggles to resist social inequalities brought about by racism, sexism, colonialism, capitalism, and similar systems of power. The metaphor of intersectionality could move among and through these forms of domination, providing a snapshot view of their sameness and difference as a way to see their interconnections. Intersectionality as metaphor did not proscribe what social transformation would look like, or even the best way of getting there. Instead, using intersectionality as a metaphor provided analytic value in linking social structures and the ideas that reproduce them—in Hall's terms, the ties between the social and symbolic domains of social change. For people who, like Crenshaw, were interested in social transformation, the metaphor of intersectionality expressed the aspirations of the time.

Crenshaw's metaphor was recognizable to many people because it invoked the tangible, spatial relations of everyday life. Everyone is located in physical space, and everyone has had to follow a path or move through an intersection of some sort. People could pick up the metaphor, imagining different kinds of pathways and crossroads, and use intersectionality as a metaphor to understand very different things. The idea of an intersection where two or more pathways meet is a familiar idea in physical, geographic space. The roads or pathways need not be straight or paved to invoke this sense of a spatial intersection. All cultures have intersections or places where people cross paths, whether superhighways or barely marked paths in a forest. Moreover, the places where people cross paths are often meeting places, spaces where different kinds of people engage one another. Being in an intersection or moving through one is a familiar experience. This spatial metaphor also invokes the idea of seeing several possible pathways from the vantage point within the intersection, and being faced with the decision of which path to take. In this sense, the spatial metaphor itself is open-ended and subject to many interpretations. Intersectionality as a metaphor worked so well because it was simultaneously familiar yet highly elastic.

This spatial metaphor that could be seen in the material world implicitly advanced a more abstract theoretical claim about social structure—namely, that the places where systems of power converged potentially provide better explanations for social phenomena than those that ignored such intersections. Racism and sexism may be conceptualized as distinctive structural phenomena, yet examining them from where they intersect provides new angles of vision of each system of power as well as how they cross and diverge from one another. Politically, the idea of intersectionality also worked. The term *intersectionality* encapsulated the convergence of multiple social justice projects and long-standing critical practices within academia.

Crenshaw's use of the term *intersectionality* as a metaphor for structuring her argument tapped into this power of metaphor to provide a snapshot view of complex social relations during a time of considerable social change. Significantly, Crenshaw's metaphor was not confined to explaining racism, sexism, and similar systems of power. The metaphor of intersectionality emerged in the context of solving social problems brought on by multiple and seemingly separate systems of power. In her careful reading of Crenshaw's signature articles on intersectionality, philosopher Anna Carastathis (2014) examines how Crenshaw used intersectionality as a "provisional" concept to frame her argument about resistance to oppression. For those involved in activist projects, intersectionality enabled those who used the term to understand, for example, a familiar racism in terms of an unfamiliar sexism, or a familiar violence against women of color as individuals in terms of a less familiar analysis of state-sanctioned violence of colonialism. Using intersectionality as a metaphor provided a ready-made yet open-ended framework for making meaning of the social world. In this sense, intersectionality as metaphor offered an invitation to an array of social actors who were thinking about similar things within different social locations and from varying vantage points.

The significance of this particular metaphor lies in using these familiar ideas about physical space in order to apply to broader, less visible symbolic understandings of race, class, gender. Using intersectionality as a metaphor provided new angles of vision on each system of power, how they cross and diverge from one another, as well as political possibilities that were suggested by this new analysis. In this sense, the metaphor of intersectionality as a crossroads works well as a mental map that encourages people to look toward particular intersections in order to guide their intellectual work and political practice. It also fosters a new view of the social world that can be seen from working within particular intersections. It encompasses ideas about human agency and intentionality in a space of indecision.

When Crenshaw dismissed intersectionality as just a metaphor, she could not foresee the impact of this particular metaphor in informing critical inquiry and social change. Instead, Crenshaw's use of intersectionality seemingly provided the right metaphor at the right time. As intersectionality has grown, the importance of its metaphoric thinking has become clearer. Crenshaw's use of intersectionality as a metaphor was not incidental to intersectionality's subsequent development, but rather proved to be a fundamental pillar within intersectionality's cognitive architecture and critical thinking.

Why Metaphors Matter

If naming the ideas that intersectionality invokes were as simple as choosing from a predetermined array of terms that had already undergone academic scrutiny, it would make sense to debate intersectionality's merits in this universe of alternative terms. Intersectionality may not be the best metaphor for explaining social phenomena, but it is the one that has persisted. Some scholars recognize the significance of intersectionality as metaphor, yet offer alternatives to it that seemingly do a better job of explaining social reality. For example, Ivy Ken's (2008) use of sugar as a metaphor aims for a more historically grounded, fluid understanding of intersectionality. Mapping how sugar as idea and product weaves throughout historical and contemporary relationships of capitalism, racism, and sexism, Ken's metaphor of sugar is an innovative, alternative entry point into the constellation of ideas referenced by intersectionality. Sugar may be a better fit for the ideas that intersectionality invokes, but pragmatically, would it have worked as well?

The puzzle to be explained here concerns why the *term* intersectionality continues to resonate with so many people as a preferred way of conceptualizing an amorphous set of *ideas*. Can sugar as metaphor do the same metaphoric work as intersectionality? Conceptual metaphor theory helps explain why intersectionality as a metaphor persists.[5] For one, intersectionality as metaphor provides a cognitive device for thinking about social inequality within power relations. It asks people to think beyond familiar race-only or gender-only perspectives in order to take a new look at social problems. For another, intersectionality as metaphor provides a framework for drawing upon what people already know about racism to learn about sexism and vice versa. Significantly, as metaphor, intersectionality suggests that racism and sexism are connected, the first step in establishing conceptual correspondences between these two constructs. In this sense, using intersectionality as a metaphor breaks down mono-categorical analyses to focus on the conceptual correspondences or relationships among racism and sexism. And this process need not end with just race and gender. Crenshaw's article named a starting point for developing conceptual correspondences.

Intersectionality may not have started out as a core conceptual metaphor for understanding social inequality, but over time, it has increasingly functioned as one. Significantly, the use of metaphor has been a crucial part of social theorizing itself. Just as creating social meanings in everyday life relies upon metaphors, theoretical knowledge also relies in some fashion on metaphorical thinking in constructing knowledge. In her classic work *Whose Science? Whose Knowledge?*, feminist philosopher Sandra Harding examines how metaphors have played an important role in modeling nature and in specifying the appropriate domain of a theory (1991, 84–85). Harding points out that metaphors are important dimensions of doing social theory, the case, for example, of imagining society in metaphorical terms—society as a machine, an organism, or a computer—and by implication, changing the core metaphor of a field changes its theoretical orientation to the social world. Originally offered in the context of critical science studies, this critical perspective advanced within feminist philosophy preceded more recent attention to metaphors as an important dimension of social theorizing (Abbott 2004; Swedberg 2014). For example, in his volume *The Art of Social Theory*, Richard Swedberg remarks on these connections between metaphors in everyday life and within the sophisticated process of theorizing: "Metaphors abound in everyday language, in the arts as well as in the sciences. Their power can be immense, as evidenced by the metaphor of the brain as a computer. This metaphor is generally seen as having helped cognitive science come into being" (2014, 89). In this sense, Crenshaw's reflection that intersectionality is *just* a metaphor underestimates the power of conceptual metaphors for critical analysis.

Intersectionality's metaphor of the connectedness of different systems of power has proven to be an important one for theorizing power relations and political identities. For example, Norocel's (2013) study of the radical right populist movement in Sweden provides an important example of an explicit use both of conceptual metaphor theory and of intersectionality as a metaphor. Norocel examines how the radical right used the idea of *Folkhem* (the home of [Swedish] people) as a conceptual metaphor to ground their political project. As a metaphor, *Folkhem* helped structure radical right masculinities, specifically heteronormative masculinities, at the intersection of gender, class, and race. Norocel identifies the significance of conceptual metaphor theory for this project: "The choice of a certain conceptual metaphor in a specific social context . . . has a crucial impact on how we structure reality, determining what is explained and . . . what is left outside this framework of intelligibility, thereby highlighting the various power relations at work in that particular discourse . . . . In other words, the analysis of metaphors needs to be undertaken whilst bearing in mind the very discourse in which they are embedded" (9). In Norocel's study, the idea of gender, class, race, and sexuality provided a framing metaphor that could be extended to explain a political phenomenon in a specific national context.

Feminist theorist Chela Sandoval also recognizes the significance of metaphors for theorizing power relations. In a section titled "Power in Metaphors" in her signature book *Methodology of the Oppressed* (2000), Sandoval describes how different metaphors highlight important distinctions between hierarchical and postmodern understandings of power. Imagining power relations as a hierarchical pyramid differs dramatically from imagining power relations through a flat, spatial metaphor of centers and margins. Sandoval notes that the shift away from a hierarchical, "sovereign model" of power enables power to be figured as a force that circulates horizontally:

> As in the previous, sovereign, pyramidal model of power, the location of every citizen-subject can be distinctly mapped on this postmodern, flattened, horizontal power grid according to attributes as race, class, gender, age, or sexual orientation, but this reterritorialized circulation of power redifferentiates, groups, and sorts identities differently. Because they are horizontally located, it appears as if such politicized identities-as-positions can equally access their own racial-, sexual-, national-, or gender-unique forms of social power. Such constituencies are then perceived as speaking "democratically" to and against each other in a lateral, horizontal—not pyramidal—exchange, although from *spatially* differing geographic, class, age, sex, race, or gender locations. (72–73)

This metaphoric shift has important implications for intersectionality (Collins 2018). Intersectionality as a core conceptual metaphor has travelled well, stimulating much innovative work within intersectionality. Yet the use of metaphoric thinking for intersectional analysis raises several questions. Do some aspects of intersectionality as metaphor work better in addressing certain social problems and less well with others? What experiences would people need to bring to the metaphoric use of intersectionality for it to have meaning?

Critics raise a valid point about the limits of intersectionality as a metaphor when used to invoke the image of a literal crossroads. In her signature book *Borderlands/La Frontera: The New Mestiza* (1987), Chicana feminist writer Gloria Anzaldúa expands upon the metaphor of intersectionality as a literal crossroads managed by traffic cops to that of the borderlands as a meeting place. The borderlands is simultaneously a place, reflecting the social relations of the physical border that influenced Anzaldúa's experiences growing up in south Texas. In this sense, borderlands are structural places that reflect hierarchical power relations and lie outside acceptable categories of belonging (Yuval-Davis 2011). Borderland spaces show the working of hierarchical power relations, or the sedimented effects of, in Sandoval's words, a "sovereign, pyramidal model of power." But Anzaldúa's borderland is simultaneously a way of describing the experiences of navigating marginal, liminal, and outsider within spaces that are created by multiple kinds of borders. This is the potential for "democratic" exchanges within borderland or intersectional spaces.

Anzaldúa's work illustrates the possibilities and limitations of spatial metaphors of power. As AnaLouise Keating points out, Anzaldúa is generally defined as a "Chicana lesbian-feminist" author, but Anzaldúa described herself more broadly as being on various thresholds, simultaneously inside and outside multiple collectivities. Anzaldúa both maintains multiple allegiances and locates herself in multiple worlds:

> "Your allegiance is to La Raza, the Chicano movement," say the members of my race. "Your allegiance is to the Third World," say my Black and Asian friends. "Your allegiance is to your gender, to women," say the feminists. Then there's my allegiance to the Gay movement, to the socialist revolution, to the New Age, to magic and the occult. And there's my affinity of literature, to the world of the artist. What am I? A *third world lesbian feminist with Marxist and mystic leanings.* They would chop me up into little fragments and tag each piece with a label. (Keating 2009a, 2)

Anzaldúa uses her experiences with multiple groups as the foundation of her analysis, yet she is less interested in finding freedom by extracting herself from multiple groups in order to find herself, but rather in understanding how her sameness and difference across multiple groups fosters new experiences of self. As Keating describes this positioning, "Although each group makes membership contingent on its own often exclusionary set of rules and demands, Anzaldúa refuses all such terms without rejecting the people or groups themselves" (2009a, 2). For Anzaldúa, the borderlands suggests a place not simply to house experiences but also a way of working, both politically and intellectually.[6]

Intersectionality may be the metaphor that has taken hold as the descriptor to describe the field itself, yet the spatial metaphor of the borderland also deepens understandings of intersecting power relations. Anzaldúa's work links experiences, spatial metaphors, power, and political engagement, signaling an important approach to critical theorizing. In discussing the significance of Gloria Anzaldúa's work within intersectionality, Patrick R. Grzanka describes Anzaldua's "borderland" metaphor as signifying a geographic, affective, cultural, and political landscape that cannot be explained by binary logic (black/white, gay/straight, Mexican/American, etc.) or even the notion of liminality, that is, *the space between*. For Anzaldúa, the borderlands are a very *real* space of actual social relations that cannot be captured within existing social theory. Grzanka describes the connections between the metaphor of intersectionality and that of the borderlands: "Anzaldúa's work exemplifies the concept of intersectionality perhaps better than the traffic intersection metaphor so central to the field and to Crenshaw's initial articulation of the concept, because Anzaldúa denies any logic that presumes there were ever discreet dimensions of difference that collided at some particular point: in the borderlands, mixing, hybridity, unfinished synthesis, and unpredictable amalgamation were always already happening, and are forever ongoing" (2014, 106–107). In this sense, the concept of the borderlands illustrates the power of metaphor that, in this case, not only complements but also deepens intersectionality's metaphoric posture.

As metaphors, neither intersectionality nor the idea of the borderlands provide coherence, consistency, or closure. Both travel, sometimes working in tandem for some projects and apart in others. They illustrate that when a concept is structured by a metaphor, it is only partially structured and can be extended in some ways but not in others (Trout 2010, 13). Metaphors provide a holistic mental picture of interrelated phenomena as well as new insights into and angles of vision on social relations. Heuristics offer tools for investigating the ideas that emerge through intersectionality's metaphoric thinking. Heuristics provide thinking tools that are typically used to solve problems. They are versatile and can be applied to an array of specific questions and concerns.

Intersectionality's Heuristic Thinking

Heuristics are techniques for social problem solving, learning, and discovery. As such, heuristic thinking informs how people approach old and new puzzles, be they social problems in the social world or puzzles of how to do better scholarship. In their everyday use, heuristics include techniques such as using a rule of thumb, making educated guesses, and relying upon common sense. This use of heuristics draws from everyday experiences with an eye toward shaping action strategies in everyday life. In its more technical sense, heuristics also provide a set of assumptions or provisional lenses that can be used to solve social problems within an academic discipline or field of study. According to Abbott, "heuristics is the science of finding new ways to solve problems" (2004, 81).

In essence, the metaphoric use of intersectionality facilitates new angles of vision on many topics. It suggests that shifting from seeing social phenomena as separate and distinct to seeing their interconnections would be beneficial. In contrast, using intersectionality as a heuristic points toward action strategies for *how* to move forward in solving social problems and in grappling with existing puzzles. Heuristics inform the questions for a particular study, for a plan of political action, and for solving problems in everyday life. Heuristics offer guidance, as rules of thumb or common practices, for social action. The common sense, taken-for-granted rules of intersectionality as a heuristic thus provide a preliminary vocabulary for intersectionality's scholarship and praxis.

Using intersectionality as a heuristic has facilitated the rethinking of existing knowledge—namely, social problems such as violence, social institutions such as work and family, and important social constructs such as identity. Kimberlé Crenshaw's classic article "Mapping the Margins: Intersectionality, Identity Politics, and Violence against Women of Color" (1991) illustrates the heuristic use of intersectionality for rethinking existing knowledge concerning violence as a social problem. Crenshaw's immediate concern lay in analyzing violence against women of color, with the goal of strengthening grassroots and legal responses to it. Lacking the term *intersectionality*, Crenshaw draws upon the existing heuristic of race/class/gender as interconnected phenomena as a starting point for problem solving concerning violence. In this regard, her approach illustrates the use of intersectionality (the race/class/gender heuristic) as a way to generate usable knowledge for social science as an instrument for "social problem solving" (Lindblom and Cohen 1979, 4).

Yet, in the context of using the race/class/gender heuristic, she recognizes its limitations for her particular project and adapts it for her specific context. Crenshaw kept the idea of intersectionality, yet incorporated categories that were a better fit for the women of color under consideration. Specifically, Crenshaw underemphasizes class as an explanatory category that explains violence against women of color. Instead, she includes the category of "immigrant status," itself a construct invoking discourses of nation (citizenship status) and ethnicity (culture as proxy for color, race, and often religion). Via this adaptation, Crenshaw argues that the provisional combination of race, gender, and immigrant status better fit the experiences of the group in question as well as the social problems with violence that they encountered. Yet neither the existing race/class/gender framework nor the new framework that emphasizes race, gender, and immigrant status was by itself sufficient. Crenshaw then offers the term *intersectionality* as a way to respond to the challenge of solving social problems that could not be incorporated within the race/class/gender rubric. This shift from race/class/gender to intersectionality illustrates the utility of heuristics—ironically, in this case, in naming intersectionality itself.

Certainly analyses of violence, as well as the intersectional categories that have been used to study it, have expanded tremendously since Crenshaw's signature article. Because violence against women has been such a powerful catalyst for intersectionality itself, intersectional analyses of this topic are not only widespread but have also informed political activism and public policy (Collins and Bilge 2016, 48–55). Analyses of violence that draw upon intersectionality reappear across a wide array of topics, such as the nation-state violence of militarism and war (Peterson 2007), the treatment of sexual violence and ethnicity in international criminal law (Buss 2009), and hate speech itself as part of relations of violence (Matsuda et al. 1993). Solutions to violence against women remain unlikely if violence against women is imagined through mono-categorical lenses such as the gender lenses of male perpetrators and female victims, or racial lenses that elevate police violence against African American men over domestic violence against African American women. Viewing violence through an intersectional lens potentially creates new forms of transversal politics to confront it (Collins 2017b).

Using intersectionality as a heuristic has facilitated the rethinking of social institutions such as work, family, the media, education, health, and similar fundamental social institutions through what seem to be fairly straightforward heuristic approaches. One strength of heuristic thinking concerns its ease of use for criticizing existing knowledge and posing new questions.

For example, when it comes to the study of work, asking simple questions such as, "Does this apply to women?" or "Is slave labor included in the definition of work?" or "Why are white male workers the focus of studies of work?" identifies areas of overemphasis and underemphasis in understandings of work. The experiences of a particular group of working-class, white, male industrial workers or middle-class, white, male corporate managers and executives have garnered the lion's share of scholarly attention. What are the effects of treating findings on this particular group as universal on work-related scholarship? The effectiveness of heuristic thinking lies in its simplicity—its use shifts established perspectives on scholarship and practice. The heuristic of asking how an intersectional framework would shift what is considered to be fixed, and fix what has been in flux, signals a sea change in how to do scholarship.

The greatly changed scholarship on work within sociology after the introduction of intersectionality illustrates this process. First and foremost, the paid work of a particular group of men working in specific jobs within Western societies is no longer assumed to be coterminous with the meaning of work. Intersectionality has opened the door to redefining work. Specifically, work constitutes one important concept that contains highly nuanced scholarship on how labor market organization, occupational segregation, work/family balance, and aspects of paid and unpaid reproductive labor underpin complex social inequalities. These topics have provided an especially rich terrain for intersectional scholarship from the race/class/gender period through contemporary analyses of global capitalism (Ong 1999). Reflecting the social movement origins of race/class/gender studies, intersectional scholarship on work in the 1980s examined segmented labor markets and the ways in which women and people of color were shunted to bad jobs and dirty work (Amott and Matthaei 1991). Building on analyses of capitalism that examined how the good jobs and bad jobs of labor markets were organized using social inequalities of gender, race, and economic class, studies of domestic work in particular opened the door to showing how work was central to the exploitation of women and men of color (Glenn 2002; Hondagneu-Sotelo 2001; Rollins 1985). This foundational scholarship on work foreshadowed important directions within contemporary social science research, such as intersections of race and gender in the labor market (Browne and Misra 2003), how workplace desegregation has proceeded in the private sector (Tomaskovic-Devey and Stainback 2012), the status of African American professional men in the workplace (Wingfield and Alston 2012), and the emerging contours of paid reproductive labor (Duffy 2007).

Using intersectionality as a heuristic has also proven to be especially valuable in rethinking the important social constructs of identity and subjectivity. The now commonsense idea that individual identity is shaped by multiple factors whose saliency changes from one social context to the next owes much to intersectionality's ease of use as a heuristic. On a basic level, an individual need no longer ask, "Am I Black or am I a woman or am I a lesbian first?" The answer of being *simultaneously* Black *and* a woman *and* a lesbian expands this space of subjectivity to encompass multiple aspects of individual identity. Rather than a fixed, essentialist identity that a person carries from one situation to the next, individual identities are now seen as differentially performed from one social context to the next (Butler 1990). The process of crafting a unique sense of self that rests on multiple possibilities generated new questions about how those identities were interconnected and co-forming, rather than how they were or should be ranked.[7]

Intersectionality is not a theory of identity, but many scholars and intellectual activists understand it through this lens primarily because the heuristic use of intersectionality as applied to the topic of identity is commonplace. Given the inordinate attention devoted to identity and its seeming association with intersectionality, returning to Stuart Hall's work, written about the same time as Butler's, may be helpful. Unlike Butler, Hall contends that the performative nature of identity and the frameworks of social structures *both* matter: "Identity is not a set of fixed attributes, the unchanging essence of the inner self, but a constantly shifting process of *positioning*. We tend to think of identity as taking us back to our roots, the part of us which remains essentially the same across time. In fact identity is always a never-completed process of becoming—a process of shifting *identifications*, rather than a singular, complete, finished state of being" (Hall 2017, 16). Other scholarship examines identity in relation to social inequality and political action, such as the possibilities of identity categories as potential coalitions (Carastathis 2013), or case studies on how attending to intersecting identities creates solidarity and cohesion for cross-movement mobilization within participatory democracies (Palacios 2016).

Using intersectionality as a heuristic not only has facilitated the rethinking of existing knowledge—violence and similar social problems, work and similar social institutions, as well as identity and similar social constructs—it has also brought new systems of power into view. Intersectional analysis now incorporates sexuality, ethnicity, age, ability, and nation as similar categories of analysis (Kim-Puri 2005). Specifically, increased attention to the themes of nation, nationalism, nation-state, and national identity has aimed to align the power relations of nation with structural analyses of racism, capitalism, and patriarchy (Yuval-Davis 1997). Literature on the nation-state and its citizenship policies has benefited from intersectional frameworks, the case of Goldberg's (2002) analysis of the racial state, or Evelyn Glenn's (2002) study of work, American citizenship, and nation-state power. Intersectional frameworks have also deepened understandings of nationalist ideologies, as evidenced in Joane Nagel's (1998) analysis of masculinity and nationalism, or George Mosse's (1985) classic work on nationalism and sexuality. The political behavior of subordinated groups as they aim to empower themselves has also garnered intersectional analysis, for example, Ana Ramos-Zayas's (2003) ethnographic study of Puerto Rican identity within a Chicago neighborhood that illustrates the benefits of incorporating nationalism in studies of local politics. Intersectional analyses of nation-state power have expanded to consider transnational processes, for example, placing analyses of transnational tourism within intersectional processes of erotic autonomy, decolonization, and nationalism (M. J. Alexander 1997, 2005a).

The heuristic use of intersectionality has generated a tremendous amount of new knowledge, far more than any one individual or group of individuals can examine. As of this writing, some fields of study have accumulated sufficient scholarly evidence to examine the patterns of intersectional scholarship within their own areas of inquiry. The heuristic use of intersectionality within sociology, history, anthropology, education, social work, and similar established disciplines certainly has led to considerable published research. Yet these communities of inquiry bring their own interpretive frameworks and scholarly conventions to the content of intersectional knowledge created within their parameters. Using intersectionality as a heuristic potentially fosters disciplinary reform. In contrast, interdisciplinary fields of inquiry such as women's, gender, and sexuality studies; ethnic studies; Black studies; media studies; American studies; and cultural studies enjoy similar heuristic use of intersectionality yet face fewer disciplinary barriers. These interdisciplinary fields typically offer more intellectual latitude, but often at the cost of less institutional support. They too are limited to postures of reform, this time not of their own frameworks and practices, but rather those of the universities that house them.

At some point, one bumps up against the limitations of heuristic thinking. In this sense, the ways in which race/class/gender studies have unfolded since the 1980s can serve as a cautionary tale for the vast amount of data that is currently being produced by the heuristic use of intersectionality. Race/class/gender studies laid substantial groundwork for intersectionality's metaphoric and heuristic use. Scholars and activists working in race/class/ gender studies, and similar interdisciplinary endeavors routinely used the phrase "race, class, and gender" for a wide array of projects (Andersen and Collins 2016; Collins and Bilge 2016). The heuristic use of "race, class, and gender" as a provisional, placeholder term across the myriad projects that sprang up within and across academic disciplines catalyzed considerable scholarship. Viewing race, class, and gender as interconnected phenomena seemingly shared a loose set of assumptions: (1) race, class, and gender referenced not singular but intersecting systems of power; (2) specific social inequalities reflect these power relations from one setting to the next; (3) individual and collective (group) identities of race, gender, class, and sexuality are socially constructed within multiple systems of power; and (4) social problems and their remedies are similarly intersecting phenomena. Each of these assumptions served as jumping off points for a range of projects. Intersectionality drew from and expanded the heuristic use of these assumptions that underlay race/class/gender studies.

Race/class/gender studies and intersectionality both rely on heuristic thinking, yet while it may seem that they are interchangeable, they do have distinctive approaches to social problem solving. Using the framework of race/class/gender analysis reminds researchers to attend to race, class, and gender as *particular* categories of analysis. Either singularly or in combination, the categories of race, class, and gender identify distinctive structural foundations for social inequalities, for example, the racism of white supremacy, the class exploitation associated with capitalism, and the sexism inherent in patriarchy. Race, class, and gender not only reference specific systems of power; each category has its own storied traditions of scholarship and activism done by interpretive communities that developed around each category. Ironically, the particular history of the field itself was seen as getting in the way of its universal possibilities. The field was seen as being too particular because it confined analysis to race, class, and gender. Some users erroneously assumed that these particular concepts, when taken literally, must be present in every analysis, and that the absence of any one category compromised the integrity of race/class/gender studies. Because it was deemed to be too closely associated with the particular, subordinated social groups that were central to its creation and growth, the field of race/ class/gender was also seen as having another kind of particularity problem. "Race" meant Black people, "gender" meant women, and "class" meant poor people. Yet race/class/gender never argued that its concepts were confined to subordinated people—it was perfectly capable of studying privilege within the categories of race, class, and gender. Similarly, race, class, and gender were never meant to be used as a fixed list of entities that applied in all times in all places. Rather, race/class/gender was a heuristic that pointed toward other combinations that not only were possible but were better suited for a range of particular issues and contexts.

The heuristic use of intersectionality provides different strengths and limitations. Because intersectionality does not specify the configuration of categories, or even the number of relevant categories for a particular analysis, it seemingly offers more flexibility than race/class/gender studies. By providing a new term that was elastic enough to incorporate the particularities of race/class/gender studies yet expand them to include additional particular concepts, intersectionality ostensibly solved the particularity problem of race/class/gender. Yet intersectionality's quest for universality—and this is important for its status as a social theory in the making—meant that it need not attend to its own particular history. Using intersectionality as a heuristic by referring to a *generic* intersectionality without attending to particulars of the categories themselves, or to the social issues that catalyzed both race/class/gender studies and intersectionality, created new problems. The rapid uptake of intersectionality by adding even more categories suggests a parallelism among these categories, one that implies that each system of power is fundamentally the same. Stated differently, if the categories of race, class, and gender, among others, are equivalent and potential substitutes for one another, then the systems of power that underlie intersectionality are similarly equivalent. Understanding one means understanding the others.

This assumption of equivalence and interchangeability may facilitate intersectionality's ease of heuristic use, but it simultaneously limits intersectionality's theoretical potential. For example, the category of class has been often mentioned within intersectionality yet less often treated as an analytical category that is equivalent to race and gender. Moreover, the categories of nation, sexuality, ethnicity, age, religion, and ability resemble one another but cannot be collapsed into one another under the heading of a generic intersectionality. Each is an analytical category that cannot be simply added together and combined with the others. The relationships among these categories lie in their particulars—they must be empirically studied and theorized, not simply assumed for heuristic convenience. This brief comparison of race/class/gender and intersectionality suggests that if a heuristic device is applied uncritically, more as a formula than as a tool of invention for critically engaged social problem solving, it may no longer be able to spark innovation.[8]

How might intersectionality make sense of itself, especially in relation to its potential as a critical social theory in the making? Intersectionality offers a window into thinking about the significance of ideas and social action in fostering social transformation. The metaphor of intersectionality puts a name and a face to a common project of using more holistic frameworks to explain and address social problems. Intersectionality as a heuristic offers provisional rules of thumb for rethinking a range of social problems as well as strategies for criticizing how scholarship studies them. In this sense, intersectionality's metaphoric and heuristic thinking provides important conceptual tools for problem solving. These strategies remain important, yet their use should not be conflated with theorizing.

Intersectionality stands in a meeting place of its own making, one where the knowledges and practices catalyzed by its metaphoric and heuristic practices converge and grow. The effects of intersectionality are far-reaching—it has catalyzed significant changes within academic disciplines concerning some of their cherished frameworks, such as the aforementioned case of sociology and work. Intersectionality has also influenced the contours of women's, gender, and sexuality studies; media studies; and similar interdisciplinary fields of inquiry. Intersectionality's knowledge and practices stemming from how its practitioners use it might have catalyzed a wealth of new knowledge across many fields of study. To me, intersectionality has reached an important milestone in its own journey, a place where it has catalyzed paradigm shifts across many fields of study, but one where it also must spend time examining its own paradigmatic thought. Stated differently, attending to intersectionality's *paradigmatic thinking* adds another dimension to its cognitive architecture.

Intersectionality and Paradigm Shifts

Paradigms provide frameworks that describe, interpret, analyze, and in some cases explain both the knowledge that is being produced as well as the processes that are used to produce it. Paradigmatic thinking involves having a model or provisional explanation in mind, a typical pattern of something, a distinct set of concepts or thought patterns. Such thinking is often difficult to recognize as such, because paradigms are often implicit, assumed, and taken for granted. For example, for some time, assumptions about biology and the natural world exerted enormous influence on research on gender and sexual identities, on public policies that understood citizenship through binaries of fit and unfit bodies, as well as on broader evolutionary explanations of the natural and social worlds. The reliance on biological explanations seemed more like the truth itself, rather than just one paradigm among many.

When the paradigmatic thinking in a field changes, the ideas and social relations within that field can also change quite dramatically. Thomas Kuhn's (1970) description of how paradigm shifts occur in the natural sciences provides a useful rubric for understanding intersectionality's effects on existing fields of study. Ironically, Kuhn analyzed the way that paradigms changed within the natural sciences as an implicit critique of the social sciences; he wanted to demonstrate how paradigms in the natural sciences provided certainties for scientific disciplines—certainties that the social sciences seemingly lacked. Yet this dimension of his work has been overshadowed by how rapidly the concept of a paradigm shift travelled into the social sciences, as well as into everyday language.[9]

A paradigm shift is a change not just in ideas, but also in how a field of study reorganizes its practices to facilitate its problem-solving objectives. When fields encounter anomalies, or puzzles that can no longer be solved within the conventions of their dominant paradigm, they shift, often rather dramatically. The old paradigm can disappear rapidly, with a new one emerging to take its place. A paradigm shift occurs along three dimensions: the new paradigm (1) convincingly resolves previously recognized problems; (2) has enough unresolved problems to provide puzzles for further inquiry; and (3) attracts enough specialists to form the core of new, agreed upon provisional explanations for the topic at hand. When applied to intersectionality, the concept of a paradigm shift suggests that intersectionality convincingly grapples with recognized social problems concerning social inequality and the social problems it engenders; that its heuristics provide new avenues of investigation for studying social inequality; and that it has attracted a vibrant constellation of scholars and practitioners who recognize intersectionality as a form of critical inquiry and praxis. This newly formulated, heterogeneous community of inquiry both resonates with the metaphor of intersectionality as a collective identity and relies on heuristic thinking for social problem solving.

This concept of a paradigm shift is especially useful for thinking through the changes that intersectionality has engendered within disciplinary and interdisciplinary fields. Kuhn's argument is targeted toward changes within the natural sciences, where paradigms consist of shared assumptions within an *existing* field of study, subfields within a particular discipline, or both. Yet when uncoupled from the assumption that paradigm shifts occur primarily within existing fields of inquiry, Kuhn's basic argument concerning paradigm shifts also applies to broader interpretive frameworks. Paradigm shifts are significant because they describe what happens when traditional frameworks no longer sufficiently explain social realities and thus become ineffective. In this sense, the concept of a paradigm shift is especially important for intersectionality as a critical social theory in the making, because a paradigm shift identifies a significant turning point when established social theories lose their critical edge and when other social theories displace them.

Intersectionality has certainly contributed to paradigm shifts in thinking about how mutually constructed power relations shape social phenomena. Across academic disciplines, traditional paradigms approached racial inequality and gender inequality, for example, as distinct, separate, and disconnected phenomena. Because race, class, gender, sexuality, age, ethnicity, nation, and ability were conceptualized as separate phenomena, their interactions remained invisible because no one thought to look for them. Using intersectionality as a metaphor fundamentally challenged this taken-for-granted assumption, and using intersectionality as a heuristic developed new knowledge as evidence for intersectional claims. In this sense, intersectionality was not just an adjustment to business as usual. It pointed toward a fundamental paradigm shift in thinking about intersecting systems of power and their connections to intersecting social inequalities.

Thinking through how intersectionality has fostered paradigm shifts within existing fields of study raises one fundamental question: Is intersectionality itself emerging as a paradigm in its own right? Using intersectionality as a metaphor did not specify its content. That's part of what made it so easy to use and to take up. Similarly, using intersectionality as a heuristic means applying its rule-of-thumb strategies to specific topics and problems. In contrast, exploring intersectionality's paradigmatic thinking means turning the analytical lens back onto intersectionality itself. It requires a sustained, self-reflexive analysis of intersectionality's internal ideas and practices.

In the following section, I sketch out selected core constructs and guiding premises of intersectionality that are drawn from my readings of intersectional inquiry as well as my understandings of intersectional practice. When

TABLE 1.1

Intersectionality's Paradigmatic Ideas

CORE CONSTRUCTS	GUIDING PREMISES
Relationality	(1) Race, class, gender, and similar systems of power are interdependent and mutually construct one another.
Power	
Social inequality	(2) Intersecting power relations produce complex, interdependent social inequalities of race, class, gender, sexuality, nationality, ethnicity, ability, and age.
Social context	
Complexity	(3) The social location of individuals and groups within intersecting power relations shapes their experiences within and perspectives on the social world.
Social justice	
	(4) Solving social problems within a given local, regional, national, or global context requires intersectional analyses.

combined, these core constructs and guiding premises provide a provisional template for analyzing intersectionality's ideas and practices. My goal is to address some ideas of intersectionality's paradigmatic use—namely, the core constructs and guiding premises within intersectionality's critical inquiry.

Table 1.1 provides a provisional schema of the paradigmatic ideas that form the content of intersectionality's critical inquiry. These ideas come from its metaphoric, heuristic, and paradigmatic uses. This schema distinguishes between the core constructs that reappear across intersectionality and guiding premises that inform intersectional analysis.

Intersectionality's core constructs routinely appear within intersectional inquiry, either as topics of investigation or as methodological premises that guide research itself. They are (1) relationality; (2) power; (3) social inequality; (4) social context; (5) complexity; and (6) social justice (Collins and Bilge 2016, 25–30, 194–204). For example, when it comes to social science research, intersectionality requires attending to complexity, whether in the questions asked, the methods used in a study, or the interpretation of findings. Intersectional analyses are by nature complex and complicated.

Intersectionality's guiding premises are working hypotheses or assumptions that inform intersectionality's inquiry and praxis. These ideas inform specific scholarly and political projects. These guiding premises are recognizable to intersectionality's practitioners. Just as biologists or human rights professionals know that, by working within their field, they share certain assumptions about biology and human rights with others in their field, people who see themselves as doing intersectional inquiry would share common questions, approaches, and rationales for why they do intersectionality in the first place. Together, intersectionality's core constructs and guiding premises are foundational to intersectionality's critical inquiry because they constitute building blocks for the content of intersectionality as critical social theory and processes of critical theorizing that might characterize intersectionality's praxis.

Core Constructs and Guiding Premises

Intersectionality's core constructs constitute one important dimension of intersectionality's paradigmatic thinking. The themes of relationality, power, social inequality, social context, complexity, and social justice reappear across intersectionality as a form of critical inquiry and practice (Collins and Bilge 2016, 25–30, 194–204). When it comes to scholarship, these themes are not all present in a given work, the treatment of them varies considerably across research traditions, and the relationship among them is far from coherent. My goal here is to identify intersectionality's core constructs that, either singularly or in combination, reappear within intersectional scholarship. Significantly, none of these themes is unique to intersectionality in the academy. They also appear across diverse projects with little apparent connection to intersectionality. In this sense, intersectionality often shares terminology and sensibility with similar projects but is not derivative of them. Identifying these core constructs constitutes a promising first step in sketching out intersectionality's paradigmatic use in scholarship. Significantly, how these constructs are used within intersectionality offers a window into intersectionality's critical inquiry.

Relationality constitutes the first core theme that shapes heterogeneous intersectional projects (Phoenix and Pattynama 2006, 187). This emphasis on relationality shifts focus away from the essential qualities that seemingly lie in the center of categories and toward the relational processes that connect them. The idea of relationality is essential to intersectionality itself. The very term *intersectionality* invokes the idea of interconnections, mutual engagement, and relationships. Race, gender, class, and other systems of power are constituted and maintained through relational processes, gaining meaning through the nature of these relationships. The analytic importance of re-lationality in intersectional scholarship demonstrates how various social positions (occupied by actors, systems, and political/economic structural arrangements) necessarily acquire meaning and power (or a lack thereof) in relation to other social positions.[10]

The significance of *power* constitutes a second core theme of intersectionality's critical inquiry. Intersecting power relations produce social divisions of race, gender, class, sexuality, ability, age, country of origin, and citizenship status that are unlikely to be adequately understood in isolation from one another. Non-intersectional scholarship assumes that race, class, and gender are unconnected variables or features of social organization that can be studied as singular phenomena—for example, gender or race as discreet aspects of individual identity, or patriarchy or racism as mono-categorical systems of power. Intersectionality posits that systems of power co-produce one another in ways that reproduce both unequal material outcomes and the distinctive social experiences that characterize people's experiences within social hierarchies. Stated differently, racism, sexism, class exploitation, and similar oppressions may mutually construct one another by drawing upon similar and distinctive practices and forms of organization that collectively shape social reality.

Third, intersectionality has catalyzed a rethinking of *social inequality*. Within the academy, prevailing frameworks explained social inequalities as separate entities, for example, class inequality, racial inequality, gender inequality, and social inequalities of sexuality, nation, ability, and ethnicity. The causes of social inequality often lay in fundamental forces that lay outside the particulars of race, class, gender. Yet treating social inequality as a result of other, seemingly more fundamental social processes suggested that social inequality was inevitable because it was hardwired into the social world, into individual nature, or into both. Intersectionality rejects these notions that normalize inequality by depicting it as natural and inevitable. Instead, intersectionality points to the workings of power relations in producing social inequalities and the social problems they engender.

A fourth core theme within intersectionality's critical inquiry stresses the significance of *social context* for knowledge production. This theme is especially important for understanding how interpretive communities, both academic and activist, organize knowledge production. This premise applies to the internal dynamics of a given interpretive community, for example, how sociologists or women's studies scholars go about their work; to the relationships among interpretive communities, such as how sociology and Africana Studies within academia develop different interpretations of race and racism; as well as to how communities of inquiry are hierarchically arranged and valued, for example, how Western colleges and universities rank the sciences over the humanities. Social context also matters in understanding how the distinctive social locations of individuals and groups within intersecting power relations shape intellectual production.[11]

Managing *complexity* constitutes a fifth core theme of intersectionality's critical inquiry. Intersectional knowledge projects achieve greater levels of complexity because they are iterative and interactional, always examining the connections among seemingly distinctive categories of analysis. Complexity is dynamic—intersectionality's categories of race, class, gender, and sexuality, among others, are a useful starting point for inquiry. Bringing multiple lenses to intersectional inquiry facilitates more complex, comprehensive analyses. Managing complexity also speaks to intersectionality's methodological contours. Complex questions may require equally complex strategies for investigation.

Social justice constitutes another core construct that underlies intersectionality's critical inquiry. The construct of social justice raises questions about the ethics of intersectional scholarship and practice. Within contemporary academic venues, the significance of social justice as a core theme within intersectionality is increasingly challenged by norms that place social justice, freedom, equality, and similar ethical issues as secondary concerns within acceptable scholarship. Viewing theory and practice in binary terms not only fosters a division between truth and power within intersectionality; it also challenges intersectionality's long-standing ethical commitment to social justice. Historically, social justice was so central to intersectionality that there was little need to examine it or invoke it. Currently, many intersectional projects do not deal with social justice in a substantive fashion, yet the arguments that each discourse makes and the praxis that it pursues have important ethical implications for equity and fairness.

I've introduced relationality, power, social inequality, social context, complexity, and social justice as discrete categories, but in actuality these core concepts inform one another. Varying intersectional projects place varying degrees of emphasis on each one. In fact, examining how scholars and practitioners use the core constructs within their projects provides a useful way of mapping intersectionality over time, which is the case, for example, of the waning influence of social justice within intersectionality. Similarly, the growing influence of complexity studies as well as developments within intersectionality itself signal new ways of thinking about intersectionality and complexity (Walby 2007). Rather than using these core constructs as a checklist to see which boxes a particular project checks off, it may be more useful to investigate how and in what ways these concepts reappear, either singularly or in combination, within intersectional inquiry.

How might these core constructs within intersectionality's critical inquiry shape it? Some concepts are so fundamental to intersectionality itself that removing them would compromise the very meaning of intersectionality. Relationality constitutes one core construct. It is reflected in the name of the field itself, it shapes the methodological premises of intersectional projects, and it describes the content of intersectional knowledge. The very question of the connections *among* intersectionality's core constructs is fundamentally one of relationality. In contrast, other core themes are more contingent. For example, intersecting systems of power as well as social inequalities of race, class, gender, and similar categories of analysis occupy prominent positions within intersectionality. Yet, does the absence of a particular category of analysis within intersectional inquiry somehow lessen its value? Similarly, some intersectional scholarship is inattentive to power relations or ethical standards of social justice. Does this absence make these projects less authentically intersectional? Some core constructs are differentially contingent. They can be used to structure a study itself, the case of attending to social context, or they can be used to evaluate outcomes; for example, is a particular study stronger because intersectionality has fostered greater complexity?

This brings me to another important dimension of intersectionality's critical inquiry—namely, my provisional list of guiding premises that distinguish intersectional scholarship (see Table 1.1). Such premises should be recognizable to intersectionality's practitioners in the ways that those of any field of inquiry are to its researchers, teachers, and students. These guiding premises synthesize the assumptions that intersectionality's practitioners take into their projects in order to guide their work: (1) Race, class, gender, and similar systems of power are interdependent and mutually construct one another. (2) Intersecting power relations produce complex, interdependent social inequalities of race, class, gender, sexuality, nationality, ethnicity, ability, and age. (3) The social location of individuals and groups within intersecting power relations shapes their experiences within and perspectives on the social world. (4) Solving social problems within a given local, regional, national, or global context requires intersectional analyses.[12] Together, these core constructs and guiding principles provide a vocabulary for describing intersectionality's paradigm shift. This shift raises important questions about how intersectionality's cognitive architecture might inform intersectional theorizing. This framework

FIGURE 1.1 Intersectionality's cognitive architecture.

DIMENSIONS OF CRITICAL THINKING		
	CORE CONSTRUCTS	
METAPHOR	Relationality	**GUIDING PREMISES**
....	Power	Race, class, and gender as systems of power are interdependent
HEURISTIC	Social inequality	
	Social context	Intersecting power relations produce complex social inequalities
....		
	Complexity	Intersecting power relations shape individual and group experiences
PARADIGM	Social justice	Solving social problems requires intersectional analyses.

of core constructs and guiding premises also offers a way of seeing the limits of paradigmatic thinking and the possibilities of the beginnings of theorizing. How might intersectionality's core constructs inform the guiding premises within the field of intersectionality itself? Conversely, how might these guiding premises shed light on the meaning of intersectionality's core constructs?

Figure 1.1 organizes the dimensions of intersectionality's cognitive architecture—namely, the thematic content of intersectionality as social theory and the processes of how intersectionality might theorize the social world. These core constructs and guiding premises provide tools for mapping the specific content of intersectional knowledge. In the case of intersectionality, because its core constructs are shared by many other projects, specifying what is meant by these constructs and how they will be used within intersectional inquiry constitutes an important, ongoing challenge. Similarly, the guiding premises constitute a starting point for identifying the shared assumptions that organize intersectionality's knowledge base. Metaphoric, heuristic, and paradigmatic thinking constitute the critical thinking tools that surround the process of doing social theory. Figure 1.1 identifies the dimensions of critical thinking that potentially inform theory within intersectionality's current use. Paradigmatic thinking is most closely aligned with theorizing because it does specify core concepts and guiding premises. Yet scholarly literature is unclear about whether social theories are housed within paradigms, the case where a scientific discipline has one overarching paradigm that houses several theories that work within its parameters; or whether paradigms are housed within social theories, the case where philosophy or literary criticism provides an overarching social theory of poststructuralism that houses lesser explanatory frameworks or paradigms. The difference might be semantic, one of parsing words to fit different disciplinary and interdisciplinary realities. My sense is that, because intersectionality itself encompasses a constellation of different projects that draw from both the social sciences and the humanities, intersectionality as critical inquiry might house multiple paradigms to guide its discovery and analysis.

Either way, paradigm shifts matter because they mark the moment when traditional frameworks become ineffective, and when existing social theories no longer sufficiently explain social realities. In this sense, the idea of a paradigm shift is especially important for developing a social theory generally and a *critical* social theory in particular, because paradigm shifts identify especially rich possibilities for critical theorizing. Stuart Hall describes these connections between paradigm shifts and doing social theory, suggesting that "if paradigms are closed . . . new phenomena will be quite difficult to interpret, because they depend on new historical conditions and incorporate novel discursive elements. But if we understand theorizing as an open horizon, moving within the magnetic field of some basic concepts, but constantly being applied afresh to what is genuinely original and novel in new forms of cultural practices, and recognizing the capacity of subjects to reposition themselves differently, then you needn't be so defeated" (Grossberg 1996, 138). In other words, intersectionality moves toward an "open horizon" suggested by its use of metaphor, heuristics, and paradigms, recognizing how its core constructs and its guiding premises constitute a paradigm shift. In this sense, intersectionality's paradigmatic use via this current constellation of core themes and guiding premises, as described here, constitutes more a starting point for developing a critical social theory, and not the end point of intersectionality as critical inquiry.

Intersectionality, Social Theory, and Theorizing

The seemingly cavalier characterization of intersectionality as a social theory within intersectional scholarship is one reason I decided to write this book. Every time I encounter an article that identifies intersectionality as a social theory, I wonder what conception of social theory the author has in mind. I don't assume that intersectionality is already a social theory. Instead, I think a case can be made that intersectionality is a social theory in the making. But what kind of social theory, toward what ends, and using what tools?

Commonsense understandings of social theory and theorizing provide a good starting point for answering these questions. Sociologist Richard Swedberg, for example, contends that "theory is . . . *a statement about the explanation of a phenomenon*. And theorizing, from this perspective, is *the process through which a theory is produced*" (Swedberg 2014, 17; italics in original). Here Swedberg introduces the important distinction between social theory as a body of knowledge that explains a phenomenon, and social theorizing as the process used to create that body of knowledge. Within this framework, intersectionality as a social theory would need to *explain* a given social phenomenon, not simply describe it. And intersectional theorizing would be the *process* or methodology used in developing those explanations.

This definition provides a useful starting point, but it also obscures some fundamental differences in how different disciplines and fields of study conceptualize social theory as well as the processes they use to generate it. Intersectionality needs to navigate some significant differences that distinguish how social sciences and the humanities understand and produce social theory. Western social sciences rest on a specific view of social theory. Within sociology, political science, economics, geography, and anthropology, theorizing emerges in explaining the truths of the social world. The social world itself is not simply an accumulation of individuals. Rather, the social world has social structures that can be uncovered via scientific processes. Social theories rely on empirical data to buttress their explanations, but the truth of social theories lies in whether they can be reliably tested. A scientific truth is not an absolute, but rather is the best explanation for empirical evidence. Within social science, a social theory is an explanation for a social phenomenon, and methodology describes the process of arriving at that truth. The scientific method is a paradigm that guides the process of theorizing.

The humanities take a different approach. Philosophy, literary criticism, and history, as well as interdisciplinary fields such as cultural studies and media studies that have been influenced by the humanities, do not seek absolute or even provisional truths about the social world, but rather investigate the meaning of the human condition. Theorizing about broad philosophical topics such as democracy, inequality, freedom, social justice and love stems from efforts to make sense of human life and experience. There are no right or wrong arguments, no absolute truths, only narratives or stories that are more or less relevant to the search for meaning. Because intersectionality encompasses both social sciences and humanities, it can be conceptualized alternately as a social theory that guides the search for truth and as a social theory that guides the search for social meaning.[13]

Not only is intersectionality not yet a social theory, if it were to be one, how would it navigate these varying perspectives on truth and meaning as fundamental to social theory? Intersectionality can easily become polarized around these different understandings of social theory. In response to this threat, rather than introducing intersectionality through the lenses of often contentious debates between scientific and narrative traditions, I have entered these debates by examining what already is within intersectionality. My interest lies in existing practices that can provide a foundation for intersectional theorizing. The cognitive architecture of metaphors, heuristics, and paradigms discussed in this chapter not only provide a roadmap for, as Cho, Crenshaw, and McCall (2013) put it, an "intersectional way of thinking," they also provide a vocabulary for analyzing intersectional theorizing. Metaphors, heuristics, and paradigms collectively constitute different aspects of intersectionality's cognitive architecture that are part of the toolkit of intersectional theorizing in both the social sciences and the humanities. The metaphor provides a concept, an idea that marks the visibility of the field. Heuristics provide orienting strategies for getting things done, premises or working hypotheses from or for social action, or both. Paradigms provide frameworks for analyzing and often explaining both the knowledge that is being produced as well as the processes that are used to produce it. There is no inherently linear progression in how individuals actually use or should use these aspects of intersectional analysis. Intersectionality is a collective endeavor, and individuals enter the field at different times, in different places, and through various projects. No intersectional theory is waiting for them when they arrive. Rather, intersectional theorizing or theory-building for intersectionality emerges through the critical thinking made possible by how individuals and groups use these critical thinking tools.

In this volume, I take the position that social science and narrative approaches to social theory and theorizing already coexist within intersectionality, and that this coexistence can be a strength for intersectional theorizing. Because intersectionality draws on both the search for truth that underpins the social sciences and the search for meaning that characterizes the humanities, preserving the existing creative tension between these two understandings of social theory is important.

The distinctions between social theory and theorizing as the process of generating social theory, the distinctions between social scientific and narrative approaches to theory and theorizing, and intersectionality's metaphoric, heuristic, and paradigmatic uses provide a vocabulary for intersectionality as a social theory in the making. In my investigation of intersectionality as a social theory in the making, I rely on this vocabulary throughout the book. But I also contend that intersectionality is neither an academic fad nor an immature social theory. Instead, I see intersectionality as a different kind of social theory in the making, whereby its association with social justice movements adds another dimension to its theorizing. Intersectionality has been associated with aspirations for social transformation and social change.

By following well-established procedures for theorizing, intersectionality can certainly become a social theory in the traditional sense, as understood within the social sciences and the humanities. Yet would this represent a maturing of intersectionality or an attenuation of its possibilities? At its heart, intersectionality is a set of ideas that is critical of the established social world. What processes lie at the heart of *critical* theorizing? What would it take for intersectionality to develop a *critical* social theory about the social world? As I discuss in the next chapter, simply labeling a theory critical doesn't make it so. How might academic social theories that are already recognized as critical illuminate the meaning of being critical for intersectionality?

2

What's Critical about Critical Social Theory?

Contemporary academia seems awash in the term *critical*. Books, journals, symposia, and several fields of study use the term *critical* to distinguish themselves from something that they are not. For example, critical race studies, critical realism, critical ethnic studies, and critical science studies use the term *critical* to differentiate themselves from their more traditional counterparts.[1] Yet using *critical* as a prefix sidesteps the definitional challenge that fields of inquiry speak for themselves on their own terms. Significantly, these ambiguities that surround the meaning of being critical are especially important for critical social theories as well as for the processes of theorizing that they engender. Within the academy, new social theories aim to make their mark by criticizing and trying to unseat their more mainstream predecessors. The more hard-hitting and adversarial an argument seems to be in upending conventional wisdom, the more critical it is assumed to be. In what can turn into a struggle for dominance among social theories, a paradigm shift can install the formerly outsider theory as the new established theory, one waiting for a new critic to knock it from its throne.

Within academic contexts, theoretical ideas are rarely inherently and forever progressive or conservative. Rather, such ideas are repeatedly reinterpreted in response to changing social contexts. The meaning of how critical (or not) a social theory is deemed to be reflects spatial and temporal dimensions—namely, where it is located and when it occurs. For example, feminist theories of patriarchy were long marginalized within the disciplinary practices of Western academic institutions, thereby defining feminist theorizing as a perpetual critique of the gender bias within established social theories. Such criticism may be necessary, but it also offers a narrow understanding of the meaning of being critical for critical social theory. In this case, women's studies scholars and feminist philosophers also developed a parallel form of criticism that went beyond calls of trying to be heard within Western knowledge. By centering on feminist analyses of the social world as essential to their project, feminist thinkers garnered visibility and acceptance for feminist theory. As a result, feminist theory has become increasingly mainstream, often positioned as the established critical social theory that others criticize as part of their understanding of being critical. In these settings, the meaning of being critical is not simply a matter of intellectual debate about theoretical understandings of gender. It also emerges within the changing political relationships between what is established and what is not.

Intersectionality faces similar issues. Many of its practitioners pride themselves on being defenders of critical analysis, conflating their criticism and seeming rejection of mainstream discourse with the meaning of being critical. Yet how critical is intersectionality? Intersectionality's genealogy certainly provides more opportunities to develop an expansive understanding of critical inquiry and praxis. Intersectionality is situated at an intellectual crossroads where multiple knowledge projects meet, with similarly diverse critical perspectives on established knowledge. Intersectionality has a foot in two interrelated worlds. On the one hand, its placement within academic contexts provides access to the rich history of the theorizing traditions of the social sciences and the humanities. Yet on the other hand, because intersectionality also includes activists, artists, practitioners, and intellectuals whose work crosses academic borders, its political and intellectual context is far broader than academia itself. Intersectionality's reach is intentionally broad and inclusive, with little consensus on what it means to be critical.

This chapter investigates how varying perceptions on the meaning of being critical have similarly varied implications for intersectionality. In chapter 1, I pointed out how ongoing tensions between conceptions of social theory within the social sciences and within interpretive fields inform intersectionality's social theory and theorizing processes. Significantly, neither of these distinct understandings of social theory is inherently critical. Yet as a *critical* social theory in the making, intersectionality has a stake in clarifying what being critical means for its own project. As sociologist Craig Calhoun points out, "the idea of critique is obviously an old one in philosophy, but also a hard one to pin down" (1995, 13). Keeping this difficulty in mind, I examine three distinct traditions of critical social theory within Western social theory that provide different lenses on the meaning of being critical. And their perspectives have varying implications for intersectionality as a critical social theory in the making as well as for intersectionality's critical theorizing.[2]

I begin with the critical theory developed at the Institute for Social Research at the University of Frankfurt in Germany (the Frankfurt school). This interdisciplinary project is often presented as a point of origin for and predecessor of contemporary critical social theory (see, e.g., Bohman 2016; Calhoun 1995; Held 1980). In this volume I capitalize Critical Theory to distinguish the specific discourse of the Frankfurt school as a specific school of thought. In contrast, I use the phrase *critical social theory* to refer to range of theoretical projects that self-define or might be classified as critical. Significantly, Frankfurt school scholars explicitly tried to meld the scientific and philosophical understandings of social theory into the very definition of critical social theory.[3]

Next, I examine British cultural studies as a self-reflexive critical theoretical project whose ideas have also influenced contemporary understandings of critical social theory. I focus on British cultural studies at the Centre for Contemporary Cultural Studies (CCCS) at the University of Birmingham in the U.K. because it was an explicitly critical project. British cultural studies highlighted many familiar themes within contemporary social theory— namely, marginality, exile, refugee status, citizenship, and related questions of belonging within national identity—and has a big footprint concerning the contours of contemporary critical analysis.

Finally, I investigate Francophone social theory in the 1950s and 1960s, an important period when the relationships among multiple strands of Western social theory were in flux. I treat this case in detail because, unlike criti-cal social theory of the Frankfurt school or cultural studies of the Birming-ham school, the critical contours of French postmodern social theory that became dominant in academia in the 1990s draws from this earlier period. Moreover, many academics who were trained in the 1990s often are unaware of the earlier debates within Francophone social theory and see poststruc-turalism as simultaneously normative and critical. I provide context for this particular understanding of the meaning of being critical.[4]

The Critical Theory of the Frankfurt School

For many philosophers and social theorists in Europe and North America, the Critical Theory of the Frankfurt school serves as a starting point for a genealogy of Western critical social theory (Bohman 2016; Calhoun 1995; Held 1980).[5] Most histories of critical social theory place its origins in the Critical Theory that was advanced in the 1930s by a group of philosophers, sociologists, social psychologists, and cultural critics who were affiliated with the Institute for Social Research at the University of Frankfurt in Germany. Collectively known as the Frankfurt school, Max Horkheimer, Theodor Adorno, Eric Fromm, Herbert Marcuse, Walter Benjamin, and other intellectuals at the Institute drew upon continental European philos-ophy to develop a critical posture toward established social theory (Held 1980). Yet their theoretical work and by extension their understanding of the meaning of being critical was not done in the safety of academic seclusion. Instead, despite being scholars and not activists, they worked in a social context where expressing the wrong ideas could be dangerous.

Because the scholars of the Frankfurt school worked in Europe during the period leading up to World War II, they could not ignore the threat the newly installed Nazi regime posed to Europe and to their own safety (Held 1980; Kim 2005). Because Horkheimer, Adorno, Fromm, Marcuse, and Ben-jamin were all members of a well-established European intellectual elite, they were well grounded in continental philosophy. They understood how important German intellectual traditions were to Western knowledge. Yet their intellectual work occurred in the specific social context of an explic-itly fascist government that was intent on eliminating Jews, Roma people, homosexuals, political dissidents, mixed-raced people, and other ostensibly undesirable people from the German nation-state. Moreover, as intellectuals who were knowledgeable about the contributions of Jewish intellectuals to

European theory, these scholars were also well aware of the deep roots of anti-Semitism in Europe. As individuals, the degree to which they claimed a Jewish identity was less important than the anti-Semitic policies of an increasingly fascist German nation-state. Many scholars became refugees, facing the same challenges as contemporary scholars, journalists, and intellectuals who flee dictatorships. The status of the Institute for Social Research also speaks to the precarious nature of intellectual work done by Frankfurt school scholars. While it is associated with its tenure in Frankfurt, the Institute relocated several times. It was founded in 1924; Max Horkheimer became its director in 1929 and recruited many of its scholars. As the situation deteriorated within Europe, the Institute moved to Geneva in 1933. Two years later it moved again, this time to New York, where it became affiliated with Columbia University.

How did the scholars of the Frankfurt school manage to do critical analysis within these precarious conditions? Critical thinking, the hallmark of theoretical work, was discouraged within fascist environments. Being openly critical of the government was highly risky. Working under these conditions required members of the Frankfurt school to be clear about the goals for their scholarship as well as the processes that they used in doing it. The themes that they emphasized and the arguments that they advanced reflect their attentiveness to the processes of theorizing. They had to be clear about their intended audiences, as well as the potential impact of their scholarship on actual people, including themselves.

The thematic content of the Critical Theory of the Frankfurt school is expansive, but here I briefly sum up the treatment of culture as one important theme. The scholars of the Frankfurt school identified the rise of mass culture as one of their core concerns. In *Dialectic of Enlightenment*, Horkheimer and Adorno (1969) posited that technological developments enabled cultural products such as music, film, and art to be distributed on a mass scale, reaching all who were connected by technology in society. Technology seemingly generated a sameness in production, in shaping the content of cultural frameworks. But it also fostered a sameness of cultural experience in that a mass of people could passively consume cultural content rather than actively engage one another. They argued that these new cultural formations fostered political passivity. Mass culture suppressed critical thinking and the social action that it might engender.

From contemporary vantage points, Horkheimer and Adorno's arguments about mass culture may seem fatalistic. Horkheimer and Adorno advanced an implicit criticism of fascism in a social context when it was dangerous to do so. Fascism required political passivity, and mass media was an increasingly important mechanism for reproducing it.[6] Yet the main idea here lies less in the substance of their argument and more in how they were able to advance, under extremely difficult conditions, compelling critical analysis that has largely withstood the test of time. Understanding the processes of theorizing within a given social context is crucial for understanding the content of any social theory. Horkheimer and Adorno's analysis of mass culture illustrates how critical theorizing typically reflects the possibilities and constraints that face intellectuals within specific social contexts. For many thinkers who confront censorship, the issue is often whether the story can be told at all and, if so, how it can be told.

Culture was one of several themes within Critical Theory. But as suggested thus far, the Frankfurt school's approach to critical theory also required a distinctive process of theorizing. Working in a precarious environment and being dedicated to critical analysis within that setting highlighted the significance of self-reflexivity as part of the process of theorizing. As critical theorists working in a dangerous social context, members of the Frankfurt school had to be politically savvy and self-reflexive about their theoretical praxis. Toward this end, they sought to distinguish their aims, methods, theories, and forms of explanation from traditional understandings in the natural and the social sciences, and they used the term *critical* to signal these distinctions. The founders of the Frankfurt school chose the name Critical Theory to signal their approach to social, political, and cultural problems that aimed to join theory and empirical research (Calhoun 1995, 13). In this sense, they looked beyond the instrumental goals of science to support "'human emancipation' in circumstances of domination and oppression" (Bohman 2016, 1–2).

Horkheimer's Definition of Critical Theory

In his classic essay, "Traditional and Critical Theory," Max Horkheimer (1982 [1937]) provides a rubric for distinguishing Critical Theory from its traditional counterpart. In this essay, originally published in 1937, Horkheimer sketches out what he sees as important distinctions among social theories that alternately claim and reject the status of *critical*. Horkheimer's understanding of traditional theory rested on his understanding of the promise of Western science as bringing potential benefit to the world. Using science as a prototype for his understandings of traditional social theory, Horkheimer refused to reject the conceptual tools or methodologies of science writ large.

Despite the spread of eugenics as normal science (see chapter 8), Horkheimer respected the capacity of science to bring about social good, and he valued its calls for objectivity and the reasoned use of evidence.

Horkheimer also drew upon Marxist social theory to highlight the missing dimensions of traditional social theory. The historical materialism of Marxist social thought emphasized narrative traditions of history and philosophy, traditions that investigated the meaning of social phenomena. Yet because Marxist social thought itself advanced structural explanations of social phenomena, and drew upon the same reasoned evidence of traditional social theory, it could be seen as an alternative science of society rather than as a distinctive philosophical tradition. The Frankfurt school intellectuals neither comprised a Marxist school of thought nor aimed to extend Marxism as a philosophy or politics. Instead, Marxist social theory was a visible and important dimension of continental European philosophy, and they adapted this critical theoretical framework for their own project.

Horkheimer's essay reflected these creative tensions between scientific and narrative traditions. He seemed unwilling to relinquish either, choosing instead to draw from their shared promise of bringing informed scientific knowledges, one traditional and the other critical, to bear on important social issues. Horkheimer embraces the positive benefits of reason for bettering society—a shared dimension of traditional and critical theory—yet rejects traditional theory's tendency to naturalize and thereby justify existing forms of social organization.

Horkheimer built his notion of Critical Theory upon an idea of theory that differed from the ordinary use of the term. Horkheimer's thesis that Critical Theory is a dialectical theory of society speaks both to social theory as a product and to theorizing as a process. Yvonne Sherratt describes this distinction, noting that for Horkheimer, "'theory' was not about developing a string of connected statements that represented the nature of the world around us. He did not believe that the word 'theory' should simply refer to a static set of propositions. In contrast, he thought that theory referred to a kind of *activity* generated within a particular social context. For him *theory* meant in essence what you and I would normally take *theorising* to mean" (2006, 198). Moreover, Horkheimer was quite clear in spelling out what he meant by the term *critical*:

> The critical attitude of which we are speaking is wholly distrustful of the rules of conduct with which society as presently constituted provided

each of its members. The separation between individual and society in virtue of which the individual accepts as natural the limits prescribed for his activity is relativized in critical theory. The latter considers the overall framework which is conditioned by the blind interaction of individual activities (that is, the existent division of labor and the class distinctions) to be a function which originated in human action and therefore is a possible object of planful decision and rational determination of goals. (1982, 207)

Here, Horkheimer clearly rejects blind faith in rules that societies aim to inculcate in their members. When science or traditional social theories uncritically produce knowledge that naturalizes and normalizes the social order, they disempower people. Thinking critically about such rules enables people both to unmask societal rules that foster passivity and to refuse to accept them. Horkheimer identifies the rules that regulate labor as fostering a passivity that convinces people to accept the "blind interaction of individual activities." When Horkheimer argues in favor of a "planful decision and rational determination of goals," he sees the benefits of rationality as modeled by science for criticizing the social norms that produce class inequalities and the social problems that ensue.

Horkheimer identifies several core elements of Critical Theory that distinguish it from its traditional counterparts: (1) a distinctive *theory of how social change has been and might be brought about*; (2) adherence to an *ethical social justice framework* that aspires to better society; (3) engagement in *dialectical analysis* that conceptualizes critical analysis in the context of socially situated power relations; and (4) *reflective accountability concerning critical theory's own practices*. Horkheimer's discussion of Critical Theory provides a useful starting point for specifying the contours of critical social theory in general. It also provides an important set of ideas for conceptualizing the meaning of critical inquiry for intersectionality.

First, as part of its overall goal, Critical Theory advances a distinctive theory of how *social change* has been and might be brought about. As Horkheimer describes it, "theory has a historically changing object which, however, remains identical amid all the changes" (1982, 239). Critical Theory views change as inherent to society; it also posits that societies all contain certain core principles that remain the same even though they may change form and expression. Change may be vital for Critical Theory, but the question is, which aspects of the changing same merit critical social theory's attention?

Building on Horkheimer's logic, an intersectional argument would explain the *changing same* of power relations as shaped by human agency across multiple, co-forming systems of power. Social inequality is the social problem that needs to be changed. Yet an intersectional analysis that attends to power relations would also see multiple and co-forming expressions of social inequality—economic inequality, racial inequality, gender inequality, and sexuality inequality, for example—as simultaneously particular in their organization and effects, yet universal in their material reality. Making social change the focus of critical social theory inevitably raises questions of what needs changing.

Second, this emphasis on explaining change suggests that Critical Theory has explicitly ethical or normative aspirations—it aims to better society by *both* understanding *and* working to change it. In his 1937 essay, Horkheimer mentions social justice, pointing to critical social theory as a potential site of resistance to injustice: "For all its insight into the individual steps in social change and for all the agreement of its elements with the most advanced traditional theories, the *critical theory has no specific influence on its side, except concern for the abolition of social injustice*" (Horkheimer 1982, 242; italics in original). Horkheimer suggests that grappling with social injustice is a central activity of critical theory: "But the transmission will not take place via solidly established practice and fixed ways of acting but via concern for social transformation. Such a concern will necessarily be aroused ever anew by prevailing injustice, but it must be shaped and guided by the theory itself and in turn react upon the theory" (241). Because social theories can be marshaled for oppressive or emancipatory purposes, questions of ethics permeate all scholarship.

Unfortunately, social injustice has persisted despite Horkheimer's attention to this moral, ethical theme. Since the 1930s, the globe has weathered several genocides, ongoing wars, and the intractability of poverty and the social problems that accompany them. It has also created some entirely new problems, or at least has come to realize that they exist. The environmental degradation brought on by climate change that is now becoming evident has roots in the Industrial Revolution. Activists often call upon critical social theories to take public stances in relation to social injustice. Yet the carefully calibrated analyses of the Frankfurt school's Critical Theory suggest that critical social theories are often better served by more nuanced and thoughtful responses to social injustice. Scientific norms of objectivity militate against such ethical stances as introducing partisanship and bias into scholarship. This aspect of Critical Theory has important implications for intersectionality. Social justice was once a central, guiding assumption of its critical inquiry, but since its naming in the 1990s, it is more often a question to be examined (see chapter 8).

Third, Horkheimer contends that Critical Theory is a dialectical theory of society, originating not in the "idealist critique of pure reason," but rather in a dialectical process that is critical of the ways that the political economy is organized (1982, 206). Because social relations are inherently power relations, Critical Theory engages in a *dialectical analysis* that is cognizant of both structures of power as well as its own relationship to them. By implication, this dialectical approach criticizes the outcomes of current social arrangements—for Horkheimer's time, the social injustices that were associated with the growth of fascism in Italy and Germany. This framework of critical thinking rejects the epistemological stance of traditional theory—that science operates as a mirror of the world—in favor of a dialectical conception of knowledge whereby what counts as theories, facts, or both is part of an ongoing historical process in which the way we view the social world (theoretically or otherwise) and the structures of the social world are reciprocally determined.

Horkheimer's construct of dialectical analysis resembles what I discuss in subsequent chapters as intersectionality's commitment to dialogical engagement (see chapters 4 and 7). But it also differs in significant ways. Contemporary, commonsense understandings of dialogical engagement conceptualize dialogues as conversations that are designed to shed light on differences and ideally reach some sort of consensus. The very idea of intersectionality invokes the idea of relationality generally and dialogical engagement in particular. Yet Horkheimer's focus on dialectical processes reminds us that power relations shape all dialogues, challenging the assumption that dialogues occur among equals. The notion of a dialectic invokes two or more different positions on a given topic, two or more perspectives on a specific entity, that may be opposed and irreconcilable. Dialectical engagement among multiple perspectives is a continual negotiation that is marked by phases of consensus and conflict. When it comes to understanding how epistemic oppression and epistemic resistance influence intersectional theorizing, this construct of dialectical analysis may be especially useful.

Finally, within Horkheimer's rubric, Critical Theory expresses a *reflective accountability* concerning its own practice. In other words, Critical Theory critically assesses its methodology and holds itself accountable for effects that its knowledge may have. On the surface, critical and traditional social theory potentially share this core value. Yet what is included in the scope of accountability matters. Because traditional theory brackets out the effects of power relations on its own practices, it holds itself to a narrower set of evaluative criteria. The scientific method for reducing bias in empirical research illustrates the ways in which epistemologies and methodologies elevate certain forms of self-reflexivity within predetermined paradigms and simply eliminate self-reflexivity about other aspects of the research process. Specifically, the source of research questions reflects a narrow context of discovery whereby themes that already concern scholars are prescreened for acceptability. In contrast, for critical social theory, accountability matters—there is no knowledge for knowledge's sake whereby a scholar can produce knowledge and remain unconcerned about how it is used. Critical Theory demonstrates reflexivity about *both* its own practices *and* how its social location within power relations shape those practices. Reflexivity is part of critical practice, especially when knowledge has potential effects on people's lives.

My understanding of intersectionality is that this idea of reflexive accountability lies at intersectionality's core. In essence, one purpose of this book is to stimulate reflexive accountability about intersectionality writ large, and intersectionality as critical social theory in particular. Chapter 1's discussion of intersectionality's cognitive architecture provides critical thinking tools for the kind of reflexive accountability that I see as essential to intersectionality as a critical social theory in the making. In particular, I introduced four guiding premises that characterize intersectional practice as part of my discussion of intersectionality's paradigmatic thinking. I also presented relationality, power, social inequality, social context, complexity, and social justice as core constructs within intersectionality's paradigmatic thinking (see chapter 1, figure 1.1). Intersectionality already has within its theory and practice an expansive set of ideas and practices that enable it to be self-reflexive and accountable. But how self-reflexive are intersectionality's practitioners about their own inquiry and praxis? Moreover, given the exponential growth of material that self-identifies as intersectional, where does one begin in building a self-reflexive critical analysis of intersectionality? This cognitive architecture provides a provisional set of tools to examine the ways in which Horkheimer's understanding of Critical Theory has and might inform intersectionality. But the task of theorizing intersectionality itself is ongoing and extensive.

The Critical Theory advanced by Frankfurt school scholars provides an important benchmark for subsequent discussions of critical social theory. Other perspectives build on its foundation, identifying various aspects of the concerns of Frankfurt school scholars as foundational to critical social theory writ large (Agger 2013; Bohman 2016; Calhoun 1995; Held 1980). For example, sociologist Craig Calhoun (1995) identifies poststructuralist and feminist theory in such fashion, interpreting their preoccupation with the idea of difference as the core object of investigation for contemporary critical social theory. Agger (2013) takes a similar position, identifying feminist theory and cultural studies as archetypal critical theoretical projects for critical social theory. Bohman lumps a variety of critical projects together, observing that "any philosophical approach with similar practical aims could be called a 'critical theory,' including feminism, critical race theory, and some forms of post-colonial criticism" (2016, 2).

Building on this assumption that these theories are *already* critical, defining critical social theory becomes a straightforward project of extrapolating universal criteria for critical social theory from the particulars of these pre-selected cases. Yet this tendency to use a short list of existing social theories that have a priori been defined as "critical" archetypes for critical social theory itself directs attention away from critical social theory as an ongoing intellectual project. The body of scholarship produced by Frankfurt school theorists is clearly important. To its credit, Critical Theory takes the issues of its own practice seriously. But the Frankfurt school's understanding of critical social theory is also one perspective among many. Can elevating any one or even a short list of social theories as the model for all others ever be sufficient? What other critical theoretical traditions exist within Western social theory that shed light on the meaning of being critical?

Critical Analysis and British Cultural Studies

British cultural studies provides a rare opportunity to trace the trajectory of an academic field of study that placed critical analysis at the center of its unfolding praxis.[7] From its inception in the 1960s, the Birmingham School of Cultural Studies, alternately referred to here as British cultural studies, was inherently critical of the class, national, and imperial politics of Great Britain. It also built self-reflexivity into its own internal practices as a field of critical inquiry. The Centre for Contemporary Cultural Studies (CCCS) at the University of Birmingham was founded in 1964, with Richard Hoggart as the first director. In 1969, Stuart Hall became acting director of CCCS and remained in this position until 1979.

Under Hall's leadership much of CCCS's work was collaborative, interdisciplinary, and focused on investigating specific social problems within

British society.[8] The intellectuals who were attracted to CCCS in the 1960s and 1970s were young, at the early stages of their careers, and included racial and ethnic scholars as well as women. Because the Birmingham school was interdisciplinary, CCCS accommodated heterogeneous theoretical perspectives within its institutional setting.

One noteworthy dimension of British cultural studies concerned its commitment to the collaborative nature of intellectual production. CCCS's organization illustrated a different way of working that was far more collaborative than that within traditional academic environments. CCCS attracted a heterogeneous constellation of intellectuals who, because they were engaged in interdisciplinary critical inquiry, could not rely on prevailing disciplinary paradigms to guide their scholarship. Their scholarship aimed to criticize prevailing paradigms about class and nation within Great Britain and, via their critical inquiry, catalyze paradigm shifts. Stuart Hall's analysis of metaphors of social transformation describes these paradigmatic shifts. Social transformation requires challenging and transforming prevailing cultural values and overthrowing old social hierarchies. In their place, new meanings, values, and cultural configurations appear (Hall 1996b, 287).

The intellectuals at CCCS created new interdisciplinary organizational structures, yet they also needed to identify new conceptual frameworks to guide their critical inquiry. Their intellectual work needed some sort of conceptual center that could pull their various projects together, making their individual knowledge projects recognizable to one another. At the same time, this conceptual center needed to provide space for the individual innovation and experimentation that would enable the field to grow.

Culture provided this kind of anchor—it was simultaneously amorphous and particular. In this sense, culture constitutes a dynamic core of the work of the Centre that was elastic enough to hold the varying interests and perspectives of its intellectuals. At CCCS, British cultural studies expanded understandings of culture by redefining it as a crucial institutional location for social structural inequalities. Going beyond Marxist analyses that often conflated culture with political ideology, or commonsense notions of mass culture as an entity that produced false consciousness, cultural studies highlighted the critical possibilities of cultural analysis. A critique of capitalism provided the backdrop for analyses of social problems within British society by Hall and others at CCCS (Hall 1996c, 1996d). The historical materialist roots of Marxist social theory examined people as workers, theorizing about how work constituted one essential dimension of capitalism.[9] CCCS scholars also presented an understanding of culture that drew from both social science and narrative traditions of theorizing. Many aspects of culture could be analyzed as social texts where meanings were not free-floating and detached from social interests, power relations, and material life.

Culture thus redefined stimulated several rich areas of investigation within British cultural studies. One important avenue of investigation involved a revitalized interest in the connections of popular culture and social inequality. For example, in the 1990s, several scholars examined how culture was used to enforce social norms that reproduced social class relations. But the work of cultural studies scholars did not look solely to top-down uses of culture. Their work was groundbreaking in examining how subordinated groups (or classes) also used popular culture to resist their subordination. For example, Paul Gilroy's "There Ain't No Black in the Union Jack": The Cultural Politics of Race and Nation (1987) and Kobena Mercer's Welcome to the Jungle: New Positions in Black Cultural Studies (1994) both analyze Black popular culture as a site of political engagement. Specifically, the cultural production of Caribbean and African working-class youth in music, dance, film, and the arts offered critical analyses of differential policing policies and similar practices. Many were born in Britain but experienced significant discrimination despite their British citizenship.[10]

Another core avenue of investigation examined the connections between this more robust analysis of culture and British national identity. Cultural studies took on the question of how cultural analysis shed light on a British national identity whose colonial history was central to its domestic national history. Migration from British colonies greatly changed the demographics of Britain, with important implications for who was considered British. Many members of CCCS were themselves migrants or children of migrants. Their differential treatment as citizens was often displaced onto their foreignness, a cultural interpretation. First- and second-generation migrants to the U.K. from elsewhere in the British empire came to a growing awareness that race and ethnicity tempered the meaning of what it meant to be British. Debates about Black British identity, as constructed from the common experiences of migrants and long-term residents, took many forms in the 1990s. This reflects, in part, the significance of national identity within the British empire, Europe's history with nationalism during World War II, as well as the growing influence of migration from Britain's former colonies on British domestic politics.

Critical analyses of these constructs of class and nation constituted core theoretical concerns of British cultural studies, yet over time, collaborative work among British cultural studies scholars illuminated additional categories of analysis that were also germane to the expansive understanding of culture. Rather than turning inward and specializing in class and nation, British cultural studies expanded its internal self-reflectivity by incorporating new ideas. Of particular note, British cultural studies took on questions of empire and how a global context shaped the domestic concerns of Britain (see, e.g., Gilroy 1993). The CCCS's commitment to self-reflexive analysis about its own theorizing catalyzed its ability to incorporate ethnicity, race, and gender as categories of analysis, often in response to criticisms within the field.

As a result of this openness to incorporating new ideas, British cultural studies has a rich history of critical analysis concerning the meaning of categories of class, nation, race, ethnicity, and gender, as well as their intersections. Race and ethnicity provided important critical tools for assessing ideas of British national identity as dependent on colonialism and the inability of class analysis to provide a universal framework for economic justice.[11] The Centre's signature publication, *The Empire Strikes Back: Race and Racism in 70s Britain* (1982), was both groundbreaking in presenting a racial analysis of class and nation of Britain, and in illustrating the Centre's commitment to collaborative intellectual work. Subsequent scholarship, such as the Centre's work on Black youth, the state, and police, all drew upon a robust conception of culture as an important analytical tool.[12]

Grounded in this expansive understanding of culture, and given the collaborative nature of CCCS's structure among a heterogeneous group of scholars, over time the Centre's scholarship demonstrated a sustained critical engagement with some aspects of capitalism, nationalism, decolonialism, racism, and patriarchy. I read the history of British cultural studies as an intersectional paradigm that did not occur under the term *intersectionality*.[13] In this sense, British cultural studies and intersectionality express similar histories, yet the trajectories that they followed in moving through varying categories of analysis emphasize different areas that point to the effects of national and intellectual contexts on similar knowledge projects. In some ways, British cultural studies is both an inspiration and a cautionary tale for intersectionality.

Stuart Hall and Articulation

Stuart Hall's involvement in British cultural studies provides a window not only on Hall as an exemplary albeit overlooked intellectual within critical social theory, but also on some family resemblances between British cultural studies and intersectionality. Hall was an expansive thinker; his intellectual work during the various phases of his career returned to how aspects of class, nation, race, ethnicity, and gender shaped the critical inquiry within British cultural studies.

As director of CCCS, Hall solo-authored few books of critical social theory, instead choosing to work collaboratively with his colleagues at CCCS. Hall also published numerous essays on a range of topics (see Morley and Chen, 1996). Currently, Hall is being rediscovered by scholars with sufficient clout to bring his ideas back (see, for example, volumes by Hall [2017] and Mercer [2017b]). Stuart Hall is a top-notch critical social theorist, one whose work informs this book, but his placement within a field that was critical of traditional knowledge as well as his demographic profile as Black and a migrant has fostered the erasure of his ideas.[14]

Hall was a synthetic thinker whose critical theorizing traversed many intellectual traditions. Situated at a convergence of many intellectual streams, Hall synthesized many seemingly disparate influences within his intellectual work. He was especially well versed in both Marxist social theory and poststructuralism, and he was clearly attentive to postcolonial theory. His familiarity with Marxism grounded his work in material conditions; culture was not merely a set of ideas but rather constituted a set of social relations. Hall drew upon and adapted poststructuralist conceptions of decentering, deconstruction, and difference to his own specific projects. He also contributed to and drew from concepts of migration, diaspora, and exile from postcolonial and decolonial studies. The range of topics in his published essays is impressive. Hall's ideas have traveled into many fields, often without attribution. Hall's significance as a critical social theorist has been underemphasized outside of cultural studies venues, an ironic erasure given the so-called linguistic turn within poststructuralism and its insights concerning culture.[15]

The rediscovery of Stuart Hall only scratches the surface in analyzing his critical social theory, but this rediscovery provides a window into British cultural studies as a discourse that resembles intersectionality but followed a different trajectory. Some of the similarities are evident. British cultural studies and intersectionality share similar content—both investigate power relations of race, class, gender, sexuality, nation, and ethnicity. The different emphases that they place on varying intersections, those of race and nation or of class and gender, for example, reflect the specific social contexts of the U.S. and the U.K. British cultural studies reflects intersectionality's core concepts of relationality, power, social inequality, social context, complexity, and social justice, often refracted through different terminology and particular circumstances. Significantly, by making British national identity central to its discourse, British cultural studies emphasized the importance of national political concerns for its knowledge project. In comparison, the workings of American national identity are far more muted in intersectionality, enabling it to minimize the influence of American political concerns on its genealogy.

The comparisons between the critical analyses of class, nation, race, ethnicity, and gender within British cultural studies and intersectionality's understanding of these same categories are suggestive. Intersections of class and nation were more prominent within the formative years of British cultural studies, with race and gender serving as categories of critique of ongoing cultural studies praxis. In contrast, the trajectory of critique within intersectionality in the U.S. differed: intersections of race and gender influenced intersectionality's early years, with sexuality, ethnicity, and nation providing critique later on. Significantly, unlike intersectionality, investigating the relational nature of these categories was not the primary object of investigation for British cultural studies. Instead, by using these same categories differently, British cultural studies provides a distinctive model of critical analysis that, while drawing from a different national and intellectual context, sheds light on different patterns of emphasis and underemphasis of these same ideas within intersectionality.

Comparing British cultural studies and intersectionality highlights the utility of identifying similarities and differences. But here I want to focus on a space of intellectual convergence between the two fields of inquiry. Hall's concept of articulation provides an important point of contact for the critical theorizing of each project. In one of his later works, Hall himself comments on how the idea of articulation resembles the concept of intersectionality. In *Familiar Stranger* (2017), published posthumously, Hall discusses articulation in relation to plantation society in Jamaica. He argues that the factors that shape such a society are always misaligned such that "one can never be matched to another, or read from one another in a neat, stylized choreography" (91). Rather, they perpetually displace and draw upon one another. The challenge is to examine how they are articulated, recognizing that they are always in motion. Hall then extrapolates from this case of plantation society to discuss the meaning of race:

> A virtue of this approach is that it accords a degree of social determinacy: it is exactly on this ground that, for example, the idea of race in Jamaica was (and is) organized. This never works as a given, or as an absolute;

it's the consequence of contingent, discursive struggles . . . race can be understood as a decisive element in the business of determination, despite the various contingencies in play. Race, colour and class did not seamlessly translate into one another. It was more a case of what feminist theorists like Kimberlé Crenshaw, Avtar Brah, Gail Lewis and others call *intersectionality* [italics added], emphasizing their intimately related, but at the same time incommensurable, awkward and unsettled fit. (2017, 91)

When it comes to the question of the nature of intersecting power relationships, Hall identifies how varying ideas articulate within the category of race to give it an unstable yet recognizable meaning. He then acknowledges a family resemblance between his understanding of articulation and intersectionality's core idea of relationality. This is a dual articulation: articulation of race, color, and class *within* the category of race; and race as a category within intersectionality—that articulates with gender and class.[16]

Hall's analysis of articulation provides theoretical and methodological tools not only for managing the various critiques that were internal to cultural studies, but also for providing guidance in how to conceptualize the relationships among intersectionality's categories of race, class, and gender, among others. On the one hand, articulation can be understood as a theoretical way of characterizing a social formation (Slack 1996, 112). Hall presents a relational analysis of how one entity comes to stand for another, making representation central to how intersecting power relations operate: "Race/colour really does work as the principle of articulation across society as a whole: as the means by which multiple forms of oppression interconnect and take on meaning. Race, whatever it may signify, cannot be seen except through its appearances, while skin colour is only too visible. So it is tempting for one to stand in for—*to represent*—the other" (Hall 2017, 103). Broadening this perspective beyond race and color, Kobena Mercer points out how Hall's conception of power rests on the "relational mode in which Hall has always conceptualized race, ethnicity, and nation" (2017a, 8). In other words, race, color, ethnicity, and nation take meaning from one another, and this process of mutual construction characterizes the social formation writ large.

On the other hand, articulation suggests a methodological framework for understanding what a cultural study does—namely, providing strategies that give a social context for analysis (Slack 1996, 112). Hall's interpretation of articulation illustrates how, within British cultural studies, dialogical engagement across different disciplines of training and political perspectives was a stimulus for creativity. Placing critical analysis of class, nation, ethnicity, race, and gender in dialogue provides a rich interpretive context that was not just interdisciplinary but also intercategorical (McCall 2005). Rather than simply arguing in the abstract in favor of relational engagement among multiple social theories and theorizing traditions, articulation points toward dialogical engagement as crucial for critical theorizing.

The ideas of the many intellectuals who developed British cultural studies, including Stuart Hall, reappear within contemporary scholarship, often without attribution. The ideas of British cultural studies have taken root in many places, often among intellectuals and activists who remain unaware of the institutional history of British cultural studies. But when it comes to being critical, it is important to remember that the intellectuals and activists who develop a critical analysis within academic contexts can expect few guarantees. Their ideas may live on while they remain largely forgotten, overlooked, or frozen in time as icons for critical analysis.

The Contested Terrain of Francophone Social Theory

Poststructuralism became prominent in the academy in the 1990s, yet the foundation for its ascendency was laid much earlier within Francophone social theory.[17] In post–World War II France, it was virtually impossible for French intellectuals to ignore anticolonial liberation struggles and their demands for freedom. During the 1950s and 1960s, the question of freedom was not simply a theoretical abstraction. Instead, the terms of France's participation in World War II coupled with Third World liberation struggles sorely tested France's stated commitment to the universal ideals of the Enlightenment. Navigating the contradictions raised by the ideal of freedom and its imperfect practice was not a new question for French national identity. France's national identity as a republic, one grounded in a belief in *liberté, egalité, fraternité*, had been repeatedly challenged by the legacy of anti-Semitism within France and by French colonialism. French collusion with the Nazis during World War II suggested that anti-Semitism was not a historical artifact but an ongoing dimension of French society. Similarly, France had repeatedly encountered challenges to its sense of national identity within colonies where the contradictions between the lofty rhetoric of equality and the realities of colonialism were painfully evident. Haiti, Vietnam, and Algeria were separated by culture, continent, and time, yet all three colonies launched rebellions against France. Despite declarations that all people in the French empire were "French," colonial subjects belied this national myth.

In this context of social change, many French intellectuals found themselves with social theories that did not fit the events around them. No longer could intellectuals speak for and about colonial subjects without consequences. Colonial subjects increasingly spoke for themselves as part of liberation struggles, bringing French intellectuals face-to-face with a series of existential questions. How might France come to terms with its involvement in World War II, specifically its legacies of resistance to and collusion with the Nazis? How should France respond to the demands of its colonial subjects, many of whom were engaged in liberation struggles in its colonies? What might be the role of French intellectuals in negotiating these concerns?[18]

Taking a closer look at Francophone intellectual production during this period highlights the unacknowledged significance of intellectuals from French colonies to anticolonial liberation struggles during decolonization as well as to the directions of Francophone social theory itself. The work of Frantz Fanon, a psychiatrist from Martinique who trained in France and who became involved in the liberation struggle in Algeria, highlights important tensions within Francophone social theory. Mainstream interpretations of Fanon's intellectual work typically emphasize his ties with existentialism, focusing on his affiliation with French philosopher Jean-Paul Sartre. But this approach misreads the radical potential of Fanon's critical theorizing, effectively making Fanon just another easily forgotten French thinker.[19]

Fanon is best known for his books *The Wretched of the Earth* (1963) and *Black Skin, White Masks* (1967), both written in the context of anticolonial social movements. For example, in the *Wretched of the Earth*, Fanon analyzes the psychological dimensions of liberation struggles, explaining how violence among subordinated peoples emerged as a response to state-sanctioned violence of colonial institutions. Significantly, Fanon also looked beyond the liberation struggles that surrounded him, analyzing how the same national culture that was essential to liberation struggles could become a problem for new nation-states. As a psychiatrist, Fanon was also sensitive to the psychic violence of racism and colonialism, exploring in *Black Skin, White Masks* the psychological costs of oppression to people of African descent. In these and other works, Fanon was adamantly focused on the needs of subordinated people, from the perspective of subordinated people. His scholarship criticized practices that fostered domination, both by colonial powers as well as among oppressed peoples themselves.

When it came to social change, Fanon saw the limits of reform. Decolonization required social transformation of social institutions, of human relationships within culture, and of everyday ideas. Not being born into French intellectual circles, Fanon's distinctive path to intellectual work had an important effect on the contours of his critical analysis. Frantz Fanon came of age during post–World War II decolonization, a social context that contributed to his development as an independent critical thinker.[20] Neither the virtuosity of his intellectual production nor his incisive critical analysis of colonial relationships stemmed from his aspirations to be assimilated into philosophy or into French intellectual circles. Fanon's critical analysis was less concerned with reforming French social theory, although such reform might constitute a step in the right direction, and more with theorizing the transformational possibilities of liberation struggles. His work was simultaneously critical *of* the status quo, in this case, the damage done by colonialism and racism, and critical *for* oppressed people in diagnosing the harms of oppression and healing from it.

Fanon was a seminal figure during the period of dismantling formal colonial structures. Yet a broad and diverse global network of scholar-activists who also worked before, during, and after the period of formal colonialism were devoted to Third World liberation struggles. Collectively, these scholar-activists aimed to decolonize colonial relations, abolish slavery, and resist the Western knowledge that upheld unjust power relations. Such projects spanned the Francophone world, but they also characterized decolonial projects in British, Dutch, and Portuguese colonies.

The list of critical intellectuals who have contributed to liberation theory is long, with many remaining anonymous. Historically, intellectuals from subordinated groups whose critical theoretical work sustains direct ties to subordinated populations have been overlooked and often maligned within European and North American social theory. Intellectual production such as Fanon's is taken seriously when its ideas could be appropriated or its impact could not be ignored. For example, William E. B. Du Bois has recently received long overdue recognition within the discipline of sociology for his groundbreaking research (Morris 2015). Yet the corpus of Du Bois's work as a scholar and as an activist reached far beyond this one field (Lewis 1995). Individual scholars may gain recognition within Western social theory, but the entire corpus of intellectual production that aimed to decolonize Western knowledge itself simply does not appear in theory texts, including renditions of critical social theory (see, e.g., Agger 2013; Calhoun 1998).

Fanon is an important figure for determining what makes critical social theory critical, because his work can be read as an important critical social theory that both catalyzed substantial energy among oppressed people and that also broke through into Western social theory on its own terms. Fanon could not be demoted to the category of a street intellectual, a misappropriation of Italian theorist Antonio Gramsci's important construct of the organic intellectual, one with street smarts yet little formal education (Gramsci 1971). Significantly, Fanon's writings provided core texts for liberation struggles on the African continent and beyond, competing directly with more conservative, reform-oriented perspectives, including those of the French intelligentsia.

This brings me to Fanon's affiliation with Jean-Paul Sartre, and how Fanon's critical theory was received within Francophone social theory. Because Sartre's affiliation with Frantz Fanon is perhaps better known within some segments of mainstream social theory, I use it to point to the tenuous position of Fanon and similar intellectuals from subordinated groups who often are only received within academia when they have an important theoretical patron. Such provisional acceptance requires walking a fine line between two choices: on the one hand, assimilating within traditional social theory and by implication, upholding the status quo; and on the other hand, accommodating watered-down versions of critical social theory and by implication, joining an inherently reformist project. Within such settings, there apparently is no third choice of social transformation. Yet intellectuals who manage to occupy a border space between dominant knowledges and resistant knowledge traditions can produce innovative social theory with far-reaching impact. This seems to be what Fanon accomplished.[21]

Frantz Fanon, Liberation Theory, and Existentialism

Positioning Fanon's intellectual work as engaged in dialogue with traditions of anticolonial liberation theory and existentialism provides an alternative understanding of the meaning of critical theorizing. Take, for example, the differences in how Fanon's theoretical analyses of colonial oppression and the challenges of national liberation have been received by intellectuals and activists within global liberation struggles and by privileged intellectuals within Europe and North America. Fanon is often positioned within the Francophone intellectual context via a strategy of framing his interest in existentialism from the perspective of France's social problems of grappling with the realities of losing colonial power. Within this narrative, Sartre facilitates

Fanon's visibility within French intellectual circles by establishing ties be-tween Sartre's own abstract understandings of freedom within existential-ism and the tangible freedom struggles of decolonization. Fanon becomes interesting to other prominent French intellectuals primarily because he was affiliated with Sartre and they could neither appropriate nor ignore his work. Yet this positioning does not do justice to Fanon, nor to a much broader community of intellectual activists whose critical theorizing emerges from liberation struggles and not from within the interests of colonial powers.

The question for me is less why French intellectuals such as Sartre would be interested in Fanon's work, but rather, why Fanon and other scholar-activists, most of whom were familiar with Marxist social theory, found *existentialism* especially compelling for their emancipatory projects. My sense is that intellectual activists who, like Fanon, were engaged in liberation strug-gles found theoretical work that spoke to issues of freedom useful. Against the backdrop of the Algerian War (1954–1962), when Fanon's work was pub-lished, the term *liberation* travelled widely and was taken up by intellectuals who worked in quite different social contexts. During subsequent decades, the power of the term *liberation* and its association with freedom resonated beyond this case of Fanon and Algerian independence.[22] In a global context, intellectuals who were affiliated with, if not leaders of, anticolonial and an-tiracist projects also advanced strong claims for human freedom, not in the abstract, but their own liberation. Other social movements took inspiration from these anticolonial and antiracist struggles, among them calls for the women's liberation and the gay liberation movements.[23]

Within this mix, existentialism's emphasis on human freedom aligned with these particular political projects for liberation. Existentialist thinkers had long been preoccupied with the question of human freedom (Marino 2004; Crowell 2015). Jean-Paul Sartre, Simone de Beauvoir, Albert Camus, and other post–World War II Francophone intellectuals took diverse and often conflicting perspectives on the question of freedom, an especially crit-ical issue in the context of the Algerian War (Le Sueur 2008; Schalk 2005). Sartre is widely credited with developing the main ideas of French existen-tialist philosophy in the post–World War II period.[24] Sartre made an effort to work in dialogue with intellectuals from subordinated groups. For example, he wrote the preface to the first edition of *The Wretched of the Earth* (1963), a significant show of support for a book that to this day remains controversial.

During this period, Marxism, existentialism, and poststructuralism within French intellectual circles were three distinctive sites of social theory that had varying relationships to Fanon's liberation theory. Interestingly, existentialism and Marxism waned in influence in these circles in the decades following the 1950s and 1960s. In contrast, structuralism and poststructuralism rose in prominence. Despite substantial differences in personnel, form, content, and genealogy, both existentialism and Marxist social theory contained explicit analyses that directly addressed the kinds of social change fostered by liberation struggles. In contrast, poststructuralism had far less to say about liberation and freedom.[25]

When it came to explaining liberation or freedom struggles, no one theory had all the answers. Existentialism's emphasis on existential freedom valorized individual consciousness and human agency, yet lacked a comparable analysis of collective behavior that could analyze the existential challenges facing a group or community of people. Marxist social theory analyzed social structures under capitalism and the collective social action of class relations, but its valorization of class over race, ethnicity, and similar categories of analysis limited its potential.[26] Poststructuralism was by far the most conservative of the three theoretical perspectives described here. When it came to political activism, poststructuralism was propelled by neither an aspirational vision such as freedom (existentialism) nor a hard-hitting structural analysis of how to bring it about (political solidarity via class struggle). Instead, its proponents sidestepped both philosophies, criticizing freedom as a shopworn Enlightenment ideal inherited from the grand narratives of modernity. They also rejected socialist revolutions that aspired to bring about freedom by criticizing Marxism as a failed political project.

The debates among French intellectuals concerning the Algerian war for liberation reveal poststructuralism's implicit rejection of liberation theory. Because anthropologist Pierre Bourdieu has had a major impact on contemporary social theory, with his ideas taken up across multiple fields of study, here I explore some of his ideas on freedom and liberation.[27] A careful read of the corpus of Bourdieu's ideas from this pivotal period in Francophone social theory provides a more complex picture of the critical contours of Bourdieu's social theory. For example, Bourdieu thought that Sartre's and Fanon's perspectives on Algeria were dangerous. The evidence for this claim comes from a surprising source: James D. Le Sueur's *Uncivil War: Intellectuals and Identity Politics During the Decolonization of Algeria* (2008). In this volume, Le Sueur presents a view of French intellectual life that is highly sympathetic to Bourdieu. Bourdieu even wrote a foreword for Le Sueur's volume. This is one reason why I found the following passage to be so jarring. Le Sueur reports: "In a 1994 interview with me Bourdieu put it this way: Fanon's *The Wretched of the Earth* and Sartre's preface to it were not only inaccurate about Algeria, they were hazardous because they used 'Parisian' ideas to explain Algeria. Sartre's preface, Bourdieu said, is 'a completely irresponsible text'" (2008, 282). Le Sueur continues, now quoting directly from Bourdieu's actual words, who asserts:

> "[what] Fanon says corresponds to nothing. It is even dangerous to make the Algerians believe the things he says. This would bring them to a utopia. And I think these men contributed to what Algeria became because they told stories to Algerians who often did not know their own country any more than the French who spoke about it . . . [T]he texts of Fanon and Sartre are frightening for their irresponsibility. You would have to be a megalomaniac to think you could say just any such nonsense. It is true, of course, that I do not have a lot of admiration for these two . . . even when they are right, it is for bad reasons" (282).

Bourdieu's dismissive vitriol goes beyond a gentlemanly difference of opinion with either Fanon or Sartre. Bourdieu blames these intellectuals, who were associated with existentialism, for the troubled aftermath of a liberation struggle that, at the time, was staunchly resisted by the French military. Perhaps Bourdieu misspoke or his meaning was lost in translation when he states, "it is even dangerous to make the Algerians believe the things he says." Bourdieu's words suggest that Algerians are apparently incapable of reason—they are subject to beliefs imposed upon them by others, in this case, Fanon as an outside agitator.[28]

Despite Pierre Bourdieu's surprisingly candid hostility to existentialism and, by implication, liberation theory, his ideas as well as those of French philosophers have shaped the trajectory of poststructuralism within Western social theory. By the 1990s, the analytical tools of postmodern social theory were already well established. Postmodern social theory's three orienting strategies of decentering, deconstruction, and difference provided an important set of tools for social criticism. By themselves, these strategies offered useful tools for critical analysis. Yet when uninformed by political and ethical considerations, these same tools of decentering, deconstruction, and difference can uphold dramatically different projects (Collins 1998a, 124–154).[29] For example, Critical Theory brings a self-reflective political and ethical analysis to theorizing, applying rules of accountability to its own praxis. Postmodern social theory has no such commitment. Similarly, British cultural studies contains an implicit social justice ethos, anchoring its critical tools in a knowledge project guided by a commitment to social transformation. Postmodern social theory eschews ethical commitments such as these. Accountability for the effects of its critical analysis on actual people or politics was optional. Poststructuralism's deconstructive tools became effective weapons of critique, yet did not necessarily express political or ethical accountability.

Given this brief history, identifying poststructuralism as *inherently* critical seems shortsighted. How the ideas of a particular social theory or a social theorist are used within a particular project illuminate the ways in which a social theory is critical. In this book, I draw on many arguments advanced by Michel Foucault, an important figure in philosophy and Francophone social theory. I draw on his ideas concerning the relationship of knowledge and power (Foucault 1980), the construct of disciplinary power (Foucault 1979), the distinctions he makes between archaeologies and genealogies of knowledge (Foucault 1994), and his groundbreaking analyses of sexuality (Foucault 1990) not because they are inherently critical but because they contribute to the critical dimensions of this project. Just as no one social theory has all the answers, no one social theorist has them either. Foucault avoided dealing with racism and colonialism in these classic works, only returning to these issues in his later writings (Foucault 2003; Stoler 1995). Would we have gotten such groundbreaking analyses of knowledge and power had Foucault written his analysis of sexuality, not in relation to French society, but in relation to the realities of Algerian decolonization struggles?

My point here is not to praise Foucault or castigate Bourdieu, but rather to question the contemporary uses of postmodern social theory. Poststructuralism has become a dominant and seemingly hegemonic discourse whose legitimacy as critical social theory is taken for granted. For many junior scholars who were trained in poststructuralism but remain unaware of its history, the meaning of critical theorizing is often synonymous with using deconstructive tools that criticize anything and everything without consequences.

What are we missing when the notion of what it means to be critical emanates from such a short list of people, within such a small body of work, that occurred during a particular time, and within a particular nation-state? One could easily read my rendition of French intellectual history as a case of epistemic oppression wherein poststructuralism worked to contain the radical potential of postcolonial theory by displacing liberation theory with the ostensibly critical analysis of endless deconstructionist critique (see chapter 4's discussion of epistemic oppression and resistance). The vanishing history of existentialism points to a bigger question: *Why* did the narrative of poststructuralism (which ironically claims not to be a coherent social theory even though it is often used as such) advanced by elite French intellectuals become such a dominant if not hegemonic narrative within academic social theory, ironically, often serving as the standard bearer for critical social theory itself?

The contested terrain of Francophone social theory presented here highlights the connections between the social and political contexts in which theorizing occurs and the social theory that ensues. Consider how working within Western assumptions about the intended audiences of critical theory can compromise a given theory's critical intent. In *Discourses on Liberation: An Anatomy of Critical Theory*, Kyung-Man Kim (2005) evaluates the critical theories of Jürgen Habermas, Pierre Bourdieu, and Anthony Giddens, three important contemporary social theorists. Rather than assuming that their work is inherently critical because academic communities of inquiry designate them as critical theorists, Kim evaluates their scholarship in relation to the goal of fostering liberation. Through a close read not only of what these theorists say but also what they don't say, Kim identifies questions that they asked yet were inadequately answered, as well as important questions that they failed to ask.

Kim concludes that their theoretical analyses were compromised by the assumptions that these particular theorists made about their intended audiences. Significantly, Habermas, Bourdieu, and Giddens write primarily to and for readers whom they imagine as being like themselves, if not people whom they already know within their academic networks. These theorists do not see the general public as their primary audience and as a result, offer idealized perspectives on the relationship between themselves as theorists and the laypeople whose interests their critical theories seemingly address. Lee contends that this failure to engage the ideas of lay actors who are most affected by their theories creates blind spots in their theoretical analyses. Habermas, for example, argues that "understanding lay people's self-description of their own activities and institutions . . . is not a discovery but a *dialogic process* in which both theorists and lay actors work together to bring about an institutional change by building up a new framework of meaning" (Kim 2005, 124; emphasis added).

Working dialogically is a powerful idea, one that has entered into many fields, and one that I take up throughout this volume. Yet Habermas's notion of a dialogic process seems methodologically undercut by an assumption that everyday people constitute objects and not agents of knowledge. How exactly would Habermas suggest that laypeople engage dialogically with his version of critical theory? In this sense, Habermas's methodology undermines his own dialogical ideal, one of allowing laypeople to "participate in the social-scientific discourse only to the extent that they conform to his own rationality criteria" (Kim 2005, 124). This imagined relationship illustrates how the concept of dialogical engagement, absent a power analysis, can reproduce existing social hierarchies. Habermas imagines himself and laypeople as committed to the same project on paper, yet dialogical engagement that occurs within unequal power relations fosters unequal participation in knowledge production (Dotson 2011).

Taking other social theorists to task for the same conceptual blind spots, Kim wonders whether social theorists who cannot communicate across differences in power can create liberatory discourses for laypeople. He ends *Discourses on Liberation* with a hard-hitting criticism: "Turning toward one another, and engaged in a dialogue with those ideas and texts that have been consecrated in previous interaction ritual chains, critical theorists experience collective effervescence and create new objects for worship . . . In attempting to consecrate their own intellectual offspring, members of the intellectual community aim to reorganize the intellectual network around their ideas. Their main concern after all is not whether they can make the lay audience interested in what they say" (Kim 2005, 126).[30] In essence, the content of any given critical social theory can be undermined by the processes that are used to create it.

Reform, Transformation, and Critical Social Theory

For intersectionality as a critical social theory in the making, the distinction between reform and transformation as goals of critical social theory provides a frame for teasing out the critical dimensions of intersectionality. Reformist projects fundamentally see existing social conditions as amenable to improvement. Within reformist projects, a social problem is a particular issue that can be solved in ways that leave a social system intact. For example, gender violence against women as a social problem can be remedied by incremental changes within a given system, such as tightening sexual harassment policies in universities or treating hate crimes as special crimes. Over time, such measures can make systems more humane. In contrast, transformative projects see specific social systems themselves as both the cause of specific problems and problems in their own right. For example, gender violence is a symptom of broader structural problems of sexism and heterosexism. Yet gender violence is unlikely to disappear without transforming the social relations that house it. In essence, the goals of social reform and social transformation influence the critical discourse that arises in order to move toward those goals. Moreover, the possibilities and limits of a given social context also influence the meaning of being critical in a particular social context.

Reform and transformation are often seen as expressing different aspects of critical analysis, with transformation conceived as the more radical and therefore more critical construct and reform cast as a lesser form of critical analysis. Because critical social theory incorporates both the content of social theories (theoretical knowledge) and the processes used to produce them (theorizing), this evaluation works better in the abstract than in actual social contexts. Understanding theorizing as a process of explaining the social world and social theory as the product of informed analysis broadens the possibilities for being critical. The critical nature of a social theory can lie in its words without having much direct effect on the processes that shape the world that surrounds it. The Frankfurt school intellectuals certainly wished that their Critical Theory might transform the society in which they worked, but for that group, even reform lay out of reach. The critical nature of a social theory can lie in its actions—namely, the practices that it uses to get its work done. British cultural studies certainly made important contributions to transformative knowledge, but could this knowledge have been so transformative without the collaborative organization of how knowledge was organized at CCCS? The three knowledge projects surveyed here provide three distinctive perspectives on how the critical content and processes of social theory reflected the possibilities for reform and transformation within their respective social contexts.

Frankfurt school scholars aimed to reform Western social theory by drawing on the best of Western philosophy and social science. Individuals or even the scholars as a group may have desired social transformation (it's hard to imagine that they saw reforming Nazi Germany as a viable option), but the circumstances under which they worked limited their project to reformist objectives. Ironically, while they may not have transformed or even reformed the theories or practices of their time, a close reading of how Critical Theory conceptualized its own project and practice offers an important legacy for contemporary intersectionality. Critique and analysis lay at the center of their projects, but these same tools can uphold both reformist and transformative objectives. Rather than trying to reform or transform society, their methodological approach to critical social theory identified important conceptual tools that could contribute to such transformation.

By criticizing practices within British society that fostered social problems, British cultural studies produced empirical work that contributed to important reformist projects. There will always be room for scholarship that aims to improve people's lives concerning jobs, housing, education, health, and the environment. A fair amount of intersectionality's own scholarship stimulated by heuristic thinking aims not to transform society, but to see reform as important in its own right. Via its empirical work, the Birmingham school aimed to build a new British society that took seriously the heterogeneity that already characterized British national identity. Yet it's also important to point out that theoretically, the overarching project of British cultural studies was informed by a theoretical commitment to social transformation. They aimed to transform economic and social relations of race and class, not reform them. British cultural studies faced a dilemma that routinely confronts similarly aspirational projects. Arguing in favor of social transformation within one's own academic institution requires confronting the particular organizational culture. How does one sustain a project that is explicitly dedicated to social transformation within an institution that has minimal interest in that expressed outcome? British cultural studies had to navigate these tensions between its reformist realities and its transformative ideals.

The contested theoretical debates among Francophone social theorists highlight how the relationships among several projects that coexisted in the same interpretive space influenced analyses of reform and transformation. Frantz Fanon's liberation theory had little interest in reforming colonialism by making it more humane. Liberation theory aimed for social transformation. The existentialists aimed to look beyond the here and now, grounding an understanding of freedom in human consciousness. In the aftermath of World War II and in the midst of the dismantling of colonialism, existentialism aimed to contribute to social transformation. Despite varying interpretations and failed political projects, the idea of social transformation lay at the heart of Marxist social theory. With these heterogeneous and explicit approaches to social transformation, how did poststructuralism prevail, with corresponding effects on the meaning of being critical? The answer to this question may lie less in the substance of the ideas of these various discourses and more in the political relationships among them.

Regardless of its critical content, when one social theory becomes dominant or hegemonic, the politics of what it took for it to get there are erased. In this sense, the emphasis on reform or transformation within a given social theory is not hardwired into its arguments, logic, or evidence but rather is socially constructed via dialogical engagement with other social theories as well as how it is situated within power relations. The meaning of being critical lies not solely in the methodology of theorizing (the Frankfurt school) nor in the expressed content of a field of study (the Birmingham school), but also in the dialogical engagement among discourses within a particular social context. As Foucault points out, subjugated knowledges that never rise to the level of social theory—or, in the case of Francophone social theory, critical theoretical discourses that seemingly disappeared—constitute the absence that frames what's in the center. When it comes to critical social theory produced within the academy, the lion's share of attention has focused on the forms that critical analysis takes within established social theories, many of which were already known as critical social theories. I had no problem finding scholarship on the Critical Theory of the Frankfurt school, poststructuralism, existentialism, Marxist social theory, and cultural studies either as critical discourses in their own right, or as providing a critical lens for some other established theory. Because these and similar social theories provide a conceptual landscape for intersectionality within academic venues, they provide different models of what it means to be critical within Western social theory.

What would it mean to theorize the social world *from the perspective of people who are subordinated* within intersecting power relations? Studying the critical theorizing of people of color, women, poor people, immigrant populations, and indigenous peoples, especially when such knowledge occurs outside academic venues or within the context of social movements, requires casting a far wider net. This shift in perspective brings the question of resistance into view. Such groups have a vested interest in opposing the political domination that fosters their subordination. Such groups develop resistant knowledge projects that also pivot on this distinction between social reform and social transformation as central to their theoretical ideas and practices. In what ways might shifting the center from established social theories such as those surveyed in this chapter to knowledge projects of resistance inform intersectionality as critical social theory?

PART II How Power Matters

Intersectionality and Intellectual Resistance

3

Intersectionality and Resistant
Knowledge Projects

I often wonder how differently understandings of critical social theory might have unfolded within European and North American academic institutions had other narratives provided starting points for analysis. In *Southern Theory*, Raewyn Connell (2007) entertains this claim by looking to the Global South for other ways of theorizing. Many intellectuals with ties to the Global South identify particular social problems, raise distinctive questions in response to those problems, and bring new angles of vision to their theoretical projects. Liberation theory, for example, reflects the aspirations of people who were involved with decolonization struggles in Africa and Latin America, thereby offering a dramatically different analysis of colonialism and how it might be resisted (Fanon 1963; Mendieta 2016). Describing theories from the African diaspora, philosopher Lucius Outlaw Jr. (2017) sees Black intellectual production as "philosophizing born of struggles." By focusing on resistance, such work brings alternative understandings of critical analysis to theorizing.[1]

Theorizing resistance has been essential to the knowledge projects of oppressed peoples. Such projects aim to address the deep-seated concerns of people who are subordinated within domestic and global expressions of racism, sexism, capitalism, colonialism, and similar systems of political domination and economic exploitation. Despite differences in form, strategies, duration, or visibility, these knowledge projects of resistance, described here as resistant knowledge projects, grapple with the existential question of how individuals and groups who are subordinated within varying systems of power might survive and resist their oppression. Whatever the form of oppression they experience—race, class, gender, sexuality, age, ability, ethnicity, and nation—subordinated groups have a vested interest in resisting it.[2]

As a resistant knowledge project, intersectionality bundles together ideas drawn from quite disparate knowledge projects with varying histories of critical theorizing. Critical Theory, British cultural studies, liberation theory, existentialism, Marxism, poststructuralism, and similar social theories constitute important sources of ideas for intersectionality's critical analysis. Yet intersectionality has a far broader conceptual landscape than that provided by academic social theories. In its move toward critical social theory, intersectionality also draws from feminist, antiracist, decolonial, and similar political projects in which theorizing resistance is tied to praxis. Within such projects, gender, race, class, ethnicity, nation, sexuality, ability, and age are not just categories designed to make intersectionality more user-friendly for academic research. Rather, these terms also signify important resistant knowledge traditions among subordinated peoples whose resistant knowledge criticizes the social inequalities and social injustices that they experience.

In this chapter, I examine critical race theory, feminist theory, and post-colonial theory as three forms of critical theorizing with ties to broader resistant knowledge projects. Because the distinctive genealogies of the cases surveyed here provide unique angles of vision on the politics of theorizing through praxis, they shed light on the question, What's critical about critical social theory?[3] Critical race theory, broadly defined, has long drawn upon African diasporic knowledge traditions for its antiracist theorizing. By challenging the racial theories within academic disciplines in Europe and North America that have been central to reproducing racism, critical race theories have offered a sustained antiracist critique. Despite the longevity of critical analyses of racism, antiracist scholarship has faced an uphill battle in eliminating racial assumptions from Western knowledge. Because faculty and students of color have also been systematically excluded from Western colleges and universities, sustaining criticism over time has been especially difficult. In contrast, feminist scholars have advanced well-established critiques of gender bias within Western knowledge, in part because of the large number of women who have graduated from universities with advanced degrees. Significantly, the broader scope of feminism provides to feminist scholars more opportunities to criticize gender inequities inside and outside the academy. As a field of inquiry within the academy, feminist studies faces political and intellectual criticisms from its constituencies. Despite its small footprint, postcolonial theory has had far more visibility in the academy as a critical discourse on Western knowledge. Yet its respectability within elite Western academic institutions seems strangely divorced from the very issues that were central to its creation. Contemporary knowledge projects of decolonization that aim to decolonize contemporary cultural practices, material realities, and political relationships offer new challenges to postcolonial theory.

Critical social theories cannot be defined solely by what they opposed in the past; rather, they also have to make the case for what they are for, and why that matters now. In this regard, each of the three cases in this chapter brings a different lens to the common challenge of critical theorizing in relation to social change. Such critical theorizing requires that they evaluate the merits of their theoretical explanations for racism, sexism, and colonialism, as well as how such systems might be resisted. But it also requires analyzing how praxis within a knowledge project requires ongoing self-diagnosis or self-reflexivity about the utility of one's own critique. When it comes to critical theorizing, the cases examined here illustrate different dimensions of these interdependent processes of external critical theorizing that looks outward and internal critical theorizing that looks inward.[4]

Antiracism and Critical Race Theory

The term *critical race theory* refers to a specific set of theories and practices advanced in the 1990s primarily by African American, Latino, and Asian American legal scholars (Bell 1992; Crenshaw et al. 1995; Matsuda et al. 1993). As an interdisciplinary endeavor that drew from and reached beyond legal scholarship, critical race theory advanced antiracist analyses of late twenty-first-century racial practices. It tracked the change from color-conscious forms of racial rule—the case of racial segregation and South African apartheid—to a color-blind system that ostensibly eliminated racism. Social scientists in particular developed a substantial body of scholarship that explained the institutional contours of color-blind racism, its effects on social interaction, and how ideologies of color-blindness and postraciality uphold racial hierarchy (Bonilla-Silva 2003; Brown et al. 2003). New fields such as whiteness studies reconfigured whiteness as an unmarked racial category (Lewis 2004). The practices of color blindness not only were insufficient in resisting racism, they constituted a new form of racial rule, one that permeated major social institutions.

During the 1990s, the disciplinary location of scholars shaped the forms that critical race theory took. Legal scholars, for example, conceptualized law as a tool of social change that was essential to antiracist practices. This disciplinary location shaped the kinds of projects they undertook, for example, focusing on hate speech and how the narratives of the law upheld social injustices (Matsuda et al. 1993), and analyses of mass incarceration as a new form of Jim Crow (M. Alexander 2010). Being located within academia influenced the kinds of critical analysis they advanced. Significantly, because critical race theory was initially advanced by legal scholars, practitioners, and activists, it drew upon dual theoretical traditions of structural analyses of the social sciences—namely, the culpability of legal institutions as part of state-sanctioned racial discrimination—as well as narrative traditions of the humanities, namely, the testimonial authority of storytelling. Cheryl Harris's (1993) analysis in "Whiteness as Property" and Mari Matsuda's (1989) "Public Responses to Racist Speech: Considering the Victim's Story" illustrate the theoretical syncretism within critical race legal scholarship.

Yet this understanding of critical race theory as an academic endeavor of the past several decades ignores a much broader framework of antiracist discourse within the United States and antiracist theorizing globally, the case, for example, of Africana philosophy as "philosophizing born of struggles" (Outlaw 2017).[5] Critical race theory broadly defined includes ever-evolving, heterogeneous explanations of resistance to global racism. Within the U.S., for example, this broad view of critical race analyses encompasses diverse resistant knowledge projects of historically subordinated groups, among them Chicanos/as, Puerto Ricans, Haitians, Muslims, Chinese, Japanese, Korean, and Vietnamese immigrant populations; indigenous peoples; and immigrants from Jamaica, Cuba, and Nigeria. Each of these groups has been differently racialized at varying points in U.S. history, and each has crafted a distinctive response to the racial subordination that they confronted (Takaki 1993). This rich tapestry of racial scholarship that is explicitly resistant to racism is only now being recovered and appreciated.

The way that race has been studied within Western academic disciplines has long been the target of critical race projects, theoretical and otherwise. Take, for example, how the study of race has been farmed out across academic disciplines, providing a fragmented analytical framework for studying race. As a construct, race has an elasticity that transcends disciplinary boundaries, an important critical thesis provided by sociologist Michael Banton's (1998) categorization of conceptions of race—namely, race as designation, lineage, type, subspecies, status, class, and construct. Philosopher David Goldberg (1993, 2002) offers a similar analysis of racial order that points more directly to how racism takes form within nationalism and Western culture. These works illuminate the nature of race, yet the fragmented social location of racial scholarship within particular disciplines limits their theoretical impact. Racial theory's peripheral position within individual disciplines may have masked the importance of racial theory, especially antiracist theory writ large.

The social location of racial knowledge shapes scholarly approaches to race, racism, and antiracism. Much social science research has been overly preoccupied with explaining the existing racial order. Whether deeply entrenched past practices of scientific racism or contemporary color-blind assumptions of contemporary genetics, Western disciplines have been deeply implicated in defining racial boundaries and in assigning meaning to the racial categories that ensue (Tucker 1994; Wailoo, Nelson, and Lee 2012). Yet this seemingly benign, ostensibly objective racial social science also helped to reproduce racism by its very silence on the topic of antiracism.

Racial theory has long occupied a peculiar position in Western knowledge. Despite the ubiquitous use of race in empirical social science, some theorists argue that race and racism have been underemphasized within the *theoretical* concerns of Western social theory.[6] Yet the seeming absence of racial analysis within social theory, including critical social theories, does not mean that Western social theories lack a racial analysis. Racial theorizing operates not only through what is present in a given discourse but also through what is absent. For example, practices such as studying race as a decontextualized concept and examining the durability of the racial order need not explicitly discuss racial concerns to express a racial analysis. The omission of race, racism, and antiracism within ostensibly universal Western social theories signals the worth of these themes. In this sense, despite the visibility of race itself, racial theory seems to be everywhere within Western scholarship, typically without being recognized as such.

Antiracist critical social theory that aims to theoretically intervene into these practices has been constrained by the organization of knowledge within the academy. Significantly, racial theory seems to be absent because neither critical racial theory nor intellectuals of color fit comfortably within Western conventions. Privileged white men have long dominated social theory within European and North American intellectual production, enjoying easier access to the epistemic power granted to theorists than African Americans, whose very intellectual abilities remain suspect (see chapter 4's discussion of epistemic oppression, epistemic injustice, and epistemic resistance). Significantly, intellectuals of color have been denied entry into the academy, with only a select few gaining access to faculty and research positions, and with even fewer obtaining positions as philosophers or social theorists. African Americans constitute one group among many who have experienced these exclusionary practices. Yet carrying the racial stigma of intellectual inferiority has raised a high barrier against Black intellectuals finding work within the academy. Because African Americans as a collective have experienced forms of virulent racism, Black intellectuals have launched critical analyses of racism.

Political and intellectual contexts have shaped the contours of African American social and political thought in general, as well as the contours of critical race theory in the U.S. context. Intellectual traditions of antiracist theorizing have long criticized racial theories within Western academic disciplines, both by criticizing how science and the humanities explain Black disadvantage and by offering alternative narratives that point to racial discrimination and structural oppression. Such theorizing has straddled academic and activist borders, placing knowledge about racism and antiracist strategies in dialogue with the racial analysis of traditional academic scholarship. In essence, even though these traditions still remain ignored, misunderstood, and often dismissed—even by scholars who claim to be experts on racial theory—these intellectual traditions of antiracist theorizing have been central to the resistant knowledge projects of African Americans.[7]

Working both inside and outside academia, many Black intellectuals have taken critical postures toward the corpus of what counts as racial knowledge (both empirical and theoretical) as well as the epistemological practices that produce such knowledge. For example, at the turn of the twentieth century, William E. B. Du Bois, Anna Julia Cooper, Alain Locke,

Ida B. Wells-Barnett, and similar African American intellectual-activists developed antiracist analyses that continue to influence contemporary critical race theory (see, e.g., A. Cooper 1892; Lewis 1995; Molesworth 2012). Yet these intellectuals have only recently gained visibility as theorists within academic venues (see, e.g., L. Harris 1999; May 2007; Morris 2015). Such thinkers were often clearly cognizant of how Western knowledge projects helped reproduce racial hierarchy by controlling both the definitions of social theory and who would be allowed to do it. Black scholars were often put in subordinate positions, working for white scholars who drew upon their expertise in theorizing race. For example, *An American Dilemma: The Negro Problem and Modern Democracy*, Gunner Myrdal's classic analysis of American race relations, relied on the expertise of African Americans who worked on the project (Morris 2015, 198–215). In *The Scholar Denied: W. E. B. Du Bois and the Birth of Modern Sociology*, Aldon Morris describes how Myrdal's choice to head this important scholarly project reflects the politics of racial knowledge production: "Myrdal, though he diverged from white American scholars in arguing that social science . . . should play an interventionist role in addressing the race problem, [he] did agree . . . on a crucial matter: race was the white man's burden, and blacks, because of racial inferiority, did not possess the agency to address their own oppression" (214).[8]

This broader social, political, and academic context influenced the contours of antiracist analysis, which in turn influenced the trajectory of critical race theory in the academy. Black intellectuals who do manage to find a niche in the academy may produce groundbreaking critical social theory, but it may not be recognized as such. In this context, collaborative intellectual production has often been the requirement for Black intellectuals to be heard—the case of Fanon and Sartre comes to mind (chapter 2). Despite these power differentials, which affect the internal dimensions of collaborative work, collaborative intellectual production itself constitutes an important form of critical theorizing. Racial formation theory is important in this regard because, while it is not the progeny of Black intellectuals, it has been widely received by intellectuals of color as an important critical theoretical perspective for both critical race theory and for intersectionality as critical social theory.

Racial formation theory offers an important theoretical vocabulary for analyzing the significance of antiracist resistant knowledge projects in opposing racism (Omi and Winant 1994; Winant 2000).[9] Within racial formation theory, ideas matter, not simply as hegemonic ideologies produced by elites, but also as tangible ideas in action or actions in ideas that are advanced by specific interpretive communities. For example, the resurgence of white nationalism in the United States and Europe constitutes a *racial project* whereby one segment of white people, primarily young white men, believes that racial, ethnic, or immigrant groups, or all three, are the source of their problems. Hip hop also can be seen as a racial project of disenfranchised youth in a global context, one where Black and brown youth claim a voice within popular culture. The form that critical race theory took among legal scholars in the 1990s is also a racial project, one that made legal scholarship central to its project to advance a multicultural, antiracist initiative. Intersectionality also constitutes a racial project, albeit not one that is explicitly organized around race, but rather one where race forms an important site of contestation within it. Because groups aim to have their interpretations of race, racism, and antiracism prevail, knowledge lies at the heart of racial projects.

Racial formation theory contends that social relations take specific historical form because an array of interest groups advance racial projects that provide competing and overlapping interpretations of race. The actual racial formation does not result from incremental, evolutionary, and natural changes. Rather, racial formations reflect the sedimented human agency of past practices refracted through contemporary racial projects. For example, racial segregation is a particular racial formation wherein racial projects that upheld strict separation between so-called races prevailed. Racial apartheid in South Africa, de facto and de jure racial segregation in the United States, and the ghettoization of Black people and Latinos in urban neighborhoods illustrate racial segregation. But racial segregation goes beyond these familiar spatial practices. It applies to occupational categories that identify some jobs as suitable for whites and others as the domain of Black people, or tracking within schools that disproportionately assigns white students to classes for gifted learners and Black and Latino students to special education. Racial segregation can permeate many areas of social life, creating social distance that articulates with spatial segregation.

Racial formation theory also applies to color-blind racism that accompanies racial integration. Within a color-blind racial formation, people misrecognize racial hierarchy, fail to see racial discrimination, and, by choosing to remain "blind" to racism, perpetuate it. Because laws and ideology ostensibly forbid or censure racial discrimination, it seems easy to assume that racism either never existed nor does not currently exist. Brazil and France provide suggestive cases of how color-blind racism persists against racialized groups in countries that historically lacked formal racial categories.

What racial segregation accomplished by law, color-blind racism accomplishes by customized micro-aggressions and culture. One racial formation did not displace the other, nor is one intrinsically more "racist" than the other. Rather, racial formation theory examines how broader historic contexts structure racially disparate outcomes.

The strength of racial formation theory lies in how it links historically constructed power relations of racism with specific racial projects that are associated within those formations. Racial formation theory privileges race as its object of investigation, but its analysis of how and why social change occurs travels far beyond race. Through its analysis of racial projects, racial formation theory explains social change as the outcome of human agency. It studies how different groups within a racial formation advance different racial projects that uphold or resist racial hierarchy, such as the aforementioned differences between a segment of young white men in white nationalism and youth of color in hip hop. Racial projects that self-identify as racial are relatively easy to recognize. Black liberation theorists and white nationalists advance antithetical racial projects. But any given racial formation also contains projects that participate in reproducing or resisting the racial order in less visible ways. The aforementioned treatment of racial theory within Western disciplines can be seen as a racial project that is advanced by specific scholars, whether or not they see their ideas and actions as having racial intent. In this sense, racial formation theory examines the relationships among racial projects, the substance and style of racial projects, and the social changes that ensue when some projects achieve dominance. Significantly, the theory itself takes no normative position on the merits of various racial projects—white nationalism, black feminism, scientific racism, and color-blind racial ideologies are all racial projects.[10]

When it comes to critical theorizing about race, racial formation theory poses important questions: What kind of racial projects appear and disappear across specific racial formations and why? Specifically, why have racial projects of ultranationalism emerged within contemporary racial formations of color-blind ideology? Rather than assuming that white nationalism is an essential psychological characteristic of an imagined white racist, these questions investigate the emergence of ultranationalism among many white people as tied to specific racial projects authored by particular social actors. Similarly, how has the visibility of Black feminism in this same color-blind racial formation catalyzed Black women's intellectual-activism? Racial formation theory grants agency to multiple groups within a given racial formation and assigns accountability to groups for the effects of their ideas. As such, it accommodates the heterogeneity of multiple interpretive communities as well as styles of critical theorizing that accompany this heterogeneity.[11]

I spend time explaining racial formation theory in part to refute thinking within the academy that critical race theory does not exist or that if it does exist, it is derivative of other theories or unimportant because it is confined to the special case of race. Instead, racial formation theory provides an important set of conceptual tools for thinking about gender, class, and similar categories of analysis as knowledge projects within particular social formations. Use of these tools positions intersectionality as a resistant knowledge project that confronts this book's core question: What kind of critical social theory might intersectionality become? My approach thus far of looking to group-based initiatives that create and use knowledge relies on the notion of knowledge projects. Moreover, viewing intersectionality as a *resistant* knowledge project highlights the political dimensions of knowledge. Just as critical race theory as a resistant knowledge project aspires to resist racism, intersectionality as a knowledge project may aspire to resist the social inequalities within intersecting systems of power. Moving beyond race situates intersectionality within a similar albeit expanded set of intersecting power relations. Just as racial projects come and go, tested by the effects of their critical analysis of racial formations, intersectionality can change its form and function in response to the challenges it faces.

Racial formation theory sheds light on the importance of critical theorizing for critical race theory's external battles against antiracism. Critical racial theory has criticized academic racial theory. But tight intellectual space for critical race theory in the academy has meant far less space *within* critical race theory's interpretive communities for the kinds of internal critical analysis that it needs. Historically, critical race theory, with the space to experience internal dissent and difference as an unaffordable luxury, has often shown more solidarity to the external world than existed within its own project. Internal dissent and criticism may have existed, but they lacked viable outlets for expression and often remained dormant.

Negotiating this balance between criticizing factors that are external to a racial project and those that are internal to its practice has been an important dimension of critical race theory writ large. African American social and political thought highlights this theme. Black feminism in the U.S., for example, emerged within the broader antiracist project of African American social and political thought. Its trajectory within an antiracist discourse that itself struggled for survival within a racial formation of racial segregation shaped the contours of Black feminist thought, both the ideas it expressed (intersectionality) and the political means that it pursued in developing those ideas (flexible solidarity). Traditions of radical, antiracist analysis have long characterized African American social and political thought. Such thought has always existed, providing a rich set of ideas for critical race theory (Davis 1978; Kelley 2002; Marable 1983b; Taylor 2016; Van Deburg 1997). At the same time, in the context of the dangers of racial segregation, such thought has had to negotiate a narrow interpretive space within the contours of African American social and political thought. This confined space for radical, antiracist analysis within African American and similarly racialized communities has fostered different forms of silencing within such communities. Long-standing silences among Black women and Black LGBTQ people about gender and sexual inequities within African American communities suppressed critical analyses of Black sexual politics (Collins 2004). But over the course of intersectionality's development, the contours of critical analysis within Black social and political thought have changed markedly.

In a climate where identity politics has been redefined as a form of self-serving, particularistic politics, the courage that it took for Black women and Black LGBTQ people to openly express dissent within African American communities is easily misunderstood. A 1975 position paper by the Combahee River Collective marks an important moment when Black women created a critical analysis of racism, class exploitation, sexism, and homophobia outside Black communities that linked these systems of power to similar social relations within Black communities (Combahee River Collective ([1975] 1995). This important document marks an important milestone within intersectionality's genealogy, but its significance goes beyond the content of the statement. The Combahee River Collective broke a long-standing taboo within African American social and political thought: they criticized practices within Black communities and within wider society. The Collective saw scant contradiction between the particularities of Black women's needs and changes that needed to occur in wider society. Particularity was not presented as opposite to universal issues. Instead, the kind of identity politics advanced by the Combahee River Collective was far more expansive than its subsequent recasting in later years.[12]

The discourse on gender and sexuality within Black communities after Combahee illustrates a deepening of Black feminist thought as a critical posture on both U.S. society and the practices within African American communities. This criticism of U.S. social institutions is most often how Black feminist thought is framed for the general public, for example, as a criticism of representations of Black women in the media or discrimination in school-ing, housing, and employment. But Black feminism has also advanced a sus-tained and incisive criticism of power relations within African American communities. In this sense, gender and sexuality have served as important correctives to dynamics of race, class, gender, and sexuality within African American communities (Collins 2004). For example, contemporary Black feminist criticism builds on earlier analyses of the politics of respectabil-ity, a political strategy that was advanced by middle-class Black women for reasons of protection, but one that simultaneously sought to suppress the agency of working-class and poor Black women. Policing Black women's respectability drew upon gender and sexuality as tools of enforcement (B. Cooper 2017). The burgeoning of contemporary scholarship on homopho-bia within African American communities illustrates the emergence of a much broader critical discourse on sexuality (C. Cohen 1996; Cohen and Jones 1999).

The need to cultivate self-reflexive practices within antiracist resistant knowledge projects is essential. One dimension of white racism is its belief that all antiracist analysis should be targeted to white people. This is part of a race relations framework that subordinates Black interests to the needs of whites. It also fits within broader social norms of service whereby Black people should view their own interests as secondary to those of white people. Yet here I've presented a brief view of Black social and political thought that certainly criticizes practices within broader society but that also must care-fully calibrate criticism within its own resistant knowledge project. In this context, critical race theory faces distinctive challenges to ensure that its contributions to antiracism remain critical.

Feminist Politics and Feminist Theory

Within feminism as a broad-based social movement, feminist scholarship in the academy constitutes a resistant knowledge project dedicated to ad-vancing gender equity and gender justice. Within colleges and universities, women's studies scholars have developed a rich tradition of feminist criti-cism within both traditional disciplines and interdisciplinary fields of study. On many U.S. campuses, the interdisciplinary field of women's, gender, and sexuality studies provides an important intellectual site for scholarship on gender and sexuality. One would be hard-pressed to find a field of study in the humanities, the social sciences, and professional fields that does not take gender into account. Moreover, this institutional visibility has facilitated the emergence of feminist theory. Feminist scholars have been hard at work defining feminist theory and explaining its trajectory in monographs, edited volumes, and textbooks. Mainstream scholars often categorize feminist theory as already being sufficiently critical, an appellation that places it on a short list of critical social theories (Agger 2013; Bohman 2016).

In the U.S., this ongoing incorporation of gender scholarship within academic venues raises important questions for feminism generally and for feminist theory in particular. Because gender scholarship has been so widely received in the academy, how might feminism as a political project sustain its critical edge within the academy? Feminist theory can operate much as any academic social theory. Its very presence offers an implicit critique of the widespread practices of exclusion and bias that characterize Western scholarship on gender and sexuality. Yet feminism as a social movement has been far less interested in reforming knowledge in the academy than in addressing social issues such as reproductive rights, sexual harassment, wage disparities, family policies, and violence against women. Garnering academic recognition for feminist theory has been important in the academy, but how might this recognition affect feminism as a resistant knowledge project? In this context, it seems reasonable to ask, For whom is feminist theory critical, and in what ways?

As part of the incorporation of gender scholarship into academic venues in the 1980s, feminist scholars upended traditional discourses of gender and sexuality. Feminist philosophers in particular looked beyond proving the exclusion of knowledge about women or the bias in knowledge that did exist. Instead, they examined the epistemological foundations of Western knowledge itself, arguing that those foundations constituted an important arena of feminist critical theorizing. In doing so, feminist philosophers provided a rich theoretical vocabulary for understanding the gendered logic that underlay the theory and praxis of Western knowledge production. For example, Simone de Beauvoir's much quoted claim in *The Second Sex* that "one is not born, but rather becomes, [a] woman" ([1949] 2011, 283) argued that gender was socially constructed and not biologically determined. This was a radical idea for its time, one that laid a foundation for gender and sex based not in women's biology but in how society interpreted such biology. Beauvoir's contribution to feminist philosophy was immense—her analysis of women's oppression constituted a fundamental theoretical shift in theorizing about women's oppression and about the roots of gender inequality. Writing several decades before the emergence in the 1990s of

French poststructuralism as a dominant theoretical framework and of Judith Butler's groundbreaking analyses of sex and gender in the 1990s, Beauvoir laid an important foundation for the social construction of sex and gender within feminist theory.[13]

In *Gender Trouble*, Butler (1990) accepts the paradigmatic assumption of the social construction of gender to explore the female subject. As she counsels, "Feminist critique ought also to understand how the category of 'women,' the subject of feminism, is produced and restrained by the very structures of power through which emancipation is sought" (5). Butler deconstructs gender, and by implication all that seemingly results from gender, via an analysis of sexuality. In her retrospective 1999 Preface, Butler describes her argument as being quite simple. For her, the text asks, "How do non-normative sexual practices call into question the stability of gender as a category of analysis? How do certain sexual practices compel the question: what is a woman, what is a man?" (xi). In essence, sex and gender are recursive, whereby under conditions of normative heterosexuality, "policing gender is sometimes used as a way of securing heterosexuality" (xii). This view of gender and sex as inextricably linked brings theoretical heft to the analysis of sexuality, making important contributions to queer theory.

Judith Butler's impact on feminist theory continues, yet her arguments reflect how the humanities approach social theory. When it comes to the social sciences, another stand of feminist philosophy also criticized Western knowledge, in particular the logic of science as itself a process of social construction. Gender and sex were socially constructed, but so too were the social institutions that were sites of constructionism. Feminist philosophers criticized the categorical logic of binary thinking, narratives of evolutionary progress, and Western taxonomies of the Great Chain of Being as socially constructed ideas that naturalized and normalized hierarchies. Significantly, their emphasis on standpoint epistemology and power relations provided an important foundation for contemporary analyses of epistemology and of social justice (Harding 1986; Hartsock 1983; Young 1990). They focused attention on social structures of gender inequality and on how knowledge itself was part of relations of rule. The connections between epistemology, theory, methodology, and methods within feminist scholarship, and by implication, critical inquiry itself, has had an important and far-reaching effect on subsequent feminist scholarship (see, e.g., the essays in Mohanty 2003).

Feminist theory flourished in academia, in part because of the contributions of feminist philosophers suggested by this brief discussion of poststructuralist analyses of sex and gender, and because of the critical analysis of science as also a site of social construction. These approaches may seem to be different, but they both reject a notion of biological determinism. In other words, feminist theory's core premise that sex and gender are socially constructed articulates with its incisive analysis of how the logic of Western science underpins such constructions.

As a resistant knowledge project, feminism had a particular advantage in the academy itself that was unavailable to either critical race scholars or postcolonial scholars. The sizable number of women students and faculty who entered the academy and who supported women's studies programs provided a visible group of advocates for feminist scholarship. Moreover, women students were often white and middle-class, a status that highlighted the significance of gender. These women brought educational and financial resources with them, and they also could recruit men from their social circles as potential allies. Each woman need not be the representative of her gender. This context of a growing women's presence on campuses, coupled with the paradigmatic shifts catalyzed by feminist theory, fostered a broad political and intellectual space for critical theoretical work.

Where might contemporary feminist theory fit within a narrative of feminism as a resistant knowledge project? Into the 1990s, feminist theory took up issues that were directly relevant within feminist politics. Understandings of feminist theory as somehow informing feminist politics were commonplace. Yet contemporary feminist scholars cannot rest on this prior work, assuming that contemporary feminist theory is inherently critical or resistant. The seduction of academic recognition can mute the critical potential of feminist criticism. Instead, the contemporary challenge lies in tracing feminist theory's continued effectiveness in criticizing academic discourse, in generating critical theoretical analyses of contemporary issues, and in cultivating dialogues with feminist projects outside the academy. In essence, while it is tempting to produce feminist theory through traditional means, how critical will that theory actually be?

Critical internal self-reflection is even more necessary for contemporary feminist criticism in the academy, especially because feminist theory is categorized as *already* being a critical social theory. I see criticism that aims to strengthen feminism itself as healthy and necessary for feminist theory to flourish. There is no lack of criticism of feminism, and much of it comes from mass media sources outside feminism. Because feminism is so vast, with so many different opinions on what feminism is and what it should be doing, I focus here on three interconnected dialogues in feminism that are part of its internal self-reflexive analysis: critical analyses of sexuality emerging from queer theory, critical analyses of race and nation within the intellectual production of women of color, and intersectional analyses offered within queer of color critique. These three sites of internal critical dialogues spurred different outcomes within academic feminism.

Queer theory offered new challenges to the treatment of sexuality within Western scholarship in ways that simultaneously embraced and challenged feminism's gender analysis. Feminist theory had an implicit critical analysis that challenged how sexuality was central to women's subordination. Even though they had overlapping participants, queer theory and feminist theory were distinctive discourses with different histories. Queer theory challenged how the construction of sexuality affected men and women. Lesbians provided internal criticisms within each tradition, pointing to the male bias within queer theory and the straight (heterosexual) bias within feminism. Yet the growing acceptance of poststructuralism within both feminist theory and queer theory challenged identities of all sorts as a site of politics. For example, in the early pages of *Gender Trouble*, Butler rejects an important strand of feminist politics: "The political assumptions that there must be a universal basis for feminism, one which must be found in an identity assumed to exist cross-culturally, often accompanies the notion that the oppression of women has some singular form discernible in the universal or hegemonic structure of patriarchy or masculine domination" (1990, 6). Butler criticizes feminism's reliance on woman-as-subject as untenable and, by implication, criticizes identities themselves as the site of politics. This theoretical shift had important implications for lesbian identity politics and for other political projects in which subjectivity or identities were central. Butler's theory of performativity as a theory of the construction of identifications provided an important and influential vocabulary for theorizing gender and sexuality. The possibilities of performativity for feminist politics remained more uncertain.[14]

Feminist criticism could not avoid the difficult questions raised by queer theory and has largely accommodated its framing vocabulary.[15] Politically, queer theory is associated with the categories lesbian, gay, bisexual, and transgender, and indicates opposition to identity-based categories. It also signals a strong antipathy for heteronormativity—namely, the taken-for-granted social and sexual arrangements in a heterosexual-centered worldview. Intellectually, queer theory references theoretical work that, like Butler's, aims to deconstruct heteronormative ideology (Bettcher 2014, 5). Feminist theory incorporated queer theories of gender and sexual subjectivities into the feminist canon (Mann 2012, 211–255). Within feminist theory, gender oppression and sexual oppression increasingly became conceptualized as interconnected entities. Queer theory seemingly facilitated a paradigm shift within feminist theory in the academy, theorizing gender and sexuality as intimately and inextricably linked.[16]

This strand of feminist criticism incorporated critical analyses of sexuality within a broader gender project in ways that changed understandings of both gender and sexuality. Queering these gender binary categories of male/female and sexual binaries of straight/gay constituted an important political strategy for theorizing gender and sexuality as co-forming categories of analysis for individuals. The more expansive and fluid understandings of subjectivity (identifications) did create more interpretive space for individuals and did catalyze an expansive literature on subjectivities. Yet, despite the emergence of the term *heteropatriarchy*, which seemingly signaled a new overarching framework for intersectional analyses of gender and sexuality as systems of power, this kind of structural analysis was not a primary focus within queer theory.

In essence, feminist theory and queer theory cross-fertilized each other intellectually, but the political effects of these theoretical trends were far more difficult to see. Politically, movements for gender and sexual equality increasingly came under attack, raising important questions about the connections of feminist theory and queer theory as forms of resistant knowledge. Movements for gender and sexual equality both confronted structural policies that aimed to regulate gender conformity and heteronormativity in schools, jobs, family structures, and public policy. Feminist theory and queer theory both offered compelling theoretical explanations of the meaning of these structural policies. But they seemed far less relevant in addressing the specific social issues faced by people who were affected by the conversion of these policies. In this regard, the emergence of trans politics challenged social constructionism as a framing assumption of both feminist and queer theory. Trans politics refocused attention on the body, not solely as an entity for imposing social norms, but also as a physical entity with certain biological imperatives. People who were born male or female but felt that they were in the wrong body turned to medicine for biological guidance. The term *transsexual* refers to "individuals who use hormonal and/or surgical technologies to alter their bodies to conform to their gendered sense of self in ways that may be construed as being at odds with their sex assigned at birth" (Bettcher 2014, 3). Gender nonconformity was most certainly a response to pressures to perform normative sexuality and gender, but it also had biological dimensions.[17]

A second strand of criticism analyzed the treatment of race and nation within feminist inquiry. Women of color were especially vocal in criticizing Western feminism's long-standing focus on the experiences of white, Western, middle-class women. In launching their critiques, women of color often drew upon the antiracist, anticolonial, and decolonial resistant knowledge projects with which they were most familiar. Bringing a racial frame into feminism challenged the false universal of whiteness as a normalizing standard that was used to explain the experiences of all women. Racism, colonialism, imperialism, and nationalism, as well as the people who were most negatively affected by those forms of domination, were not seen as being central to feminist theories of gender or sexuality. Feminist analyses are more cognizant of how race, ethnicity, culture, and citizenship status shape both feminist praxis and feminist theory.

Many of the same people who were involved in antiracist projects and in intersectional projects also criticized the claim that feminism was for white women only. Yet the term *woman of color* contains the seeds of its own critique. Latina feminism highlights some of the issues of bringing a critique to feminism within the category of women of color. The ideas of Latina feminism are prominently represented within feminism. In their introduction, the editors of *Chicana Feminisms* posit that Chicana feminist writers have provided original analyses of many themes that affect Chicanas via processes of theorizing and documenting intersections of class, race, gender, and sexuality (Arredondo et al. 2003, 5). Many of these themes have been incorporated within feminism, for example, analyses of *mestizaje*, hybridity, and the borderlands (Anzaldúa 1987); reflections of the continuum of color, phenotype, and privilege; and ideas about oppositional consciousness, practice, methodology, and oppression (Sandoval 2000). Yet these and other forms of critical analysis become subsumed under the heading "women of color," a homogenizing move that positions all women who are categorized as women of color as critics of traditional feminism. The critique is incorporated within feminism, with far-reaching effects on feminist theory and practice. The ideas suggested by Chicana feminist theory are incorporated, with less attention to the particularities of issues of the women who developed those ideas.

Reflecting the influence of decolonial projects, the ideas of Latina feminism are also more closely aligned with those of transnational feminism, another discourse that is positioned as a critical perspective *within* the frameworks of Western feminism. Transnational feminists developed important critiques within Western feminism that influenced the directions of the field. In their classic edited volume, *Feminist Genealogies, Colonial Legacies, Democratic Futures*, M. Jacqui Alexander and Chandra Talpade Mohanty (1997) offer a critical feminist analysis of transnational processes. The connections among women of color in the U.S. and transnational feminists, who often become women of color when they are in the United States, is noteworthy. For example, like Gloria Anzaldúa, Mohanty also engages questions of borders, but in response to the hopes and disappointments of decolonization. In her introduction to *Feminism Without Borders*, Mohanty suggests that, while borders can signal containment and safety, women often pay a price to claim integrity, security, and safety of their own bodies. As she notes, "I choose 'feminism without borders,' then, to stress that our most expansive and inclusive visions of feminism need to be attentive to borders while learning to transcend them" (Mohanty 2003, 2). In *Pedagogies of Crossing*, M. Jacqui Alexander (2005b) uses the metaphor of a border crossing as a site of political and intellectual complexities.

Queer of color critique catalyzed a third strand of self-reflexive analysis that draws from and criticizes critical race theory, feminism, and queer theory. Despite challenges by women of color, critical race theory remains wedded to heteronormative gender ideology that privileges men of color. This politics of sexuality and gender limit its antiracist politics (see Collins 2004). Feminism remains limited by its genealogy of whiteness and its class politics, a criticism raised by women of color and shared by queer of color critiques. The politics of class, race, and gender shape queer theory such that it disproportionately benefits middle-class white men. In this way, queer of color critiques may be aimed at feminism, primarily because feminism is a large discourse, but its criticisms are fundamentally intersectional. Queer of color critiques constitute one effective way of expanding the framework for understanding the fluidity of gender, sexuality, race, class, and ethnicity together. Positioned at the intersection of gender, sexuality, and race, queer of color critiques became increasingly visible both within and outside feminism in part because feminism's critical analysis of gender, sexuality, and race is ongoing (Battle et al. 2002; C. Cohen 1996; Cohen and Jones 1999; Ferguson 2004).

Queer of color analyses criticized feminism for being overly concerned with the issues that affected white, middle-class people. For example, marriage equality seems to be a universal issue that might unite queer people regardless of race, gender, and sexual orientation. Queer of color critiques pointed out that the combination of racial and economic disparities meant that people of color would gain less from this victory. Similarly, workplace protections for LGBTQ people would be less valuable for Black trans people who experience extremely high rates of violence and murder. The vulnerability of trans youth of color pointed to the significance of age as a system of power. In essence, queers of color called for a more intersectional analysis of feminism itself in ways that recognized intersections of gender, sexuality, race, nation, class, and age.

When it comes to intersectionality, self-reflexive critique within feminism demonstrates a recursive relationship among gender, sexuality, and race that reflects the varying strands of self-reflexive critical inquiry about its own praxis. The strength of feminism lies in its ability to manage multiple criticisms of its theories and its praxis, trying to address, for example, the heterogeneous analyses of LGBTQ and trans people, those advanced by women of color and transnational feminists, and increasingly criticisms of both of these strands within scholarship on or by queers of color (C. Cohen 1996; Ferguson 2004; Petzen 2012; Somerville 2000). Yet when it comes to queer of color critiques, there is also an ironic twist to this self-reflexive analysis within contemporary feminism. Many of the core ideas of feminism itself were shaped by the ideas of queer Black and Latina feminists, among them Audre Lorde (1999), Gloria Anzaldúa (1987), June Jordan (1992), Barbara Smith (1983), Cheryl Clarke (1995), and the Combahee River Collective (1995). The tendency of valorizing particular queer women of color at the founding moments of a discourse while ignoring the ongoing presence of queer women of color within feminism itself speaks to persisting pressures within academia to whitewash knowledge.

This ongoing internal critical analysis within feminism is noteworthy, yet as a resistant knowledge project, feminism illustrates the difficulties of sustaining critical analysis with such a broad goal of women's empowerment and emancipation within academia and within wider society. The criticisms by LGBTQ people, trans people, U.S. women of color, transnational feminists, and queers of color concerning sexuality, race, transnational processes, and intersectional analyses have taken different forms with different outcomes, in part because these groups have been differentially situated in relation to feminism. As a result, they draw upon different intellectual traditions and theoretical frameworks. Lesbians were central to modern feminism's growth and success, and were already positioned within feminist projects as leaders with a stake in what feminism should become. Moreover, LGBTQ and trans people certainly supported feminism, but they often came to feminism through independent projects for sexual freedom. These groups were connected, but they were not the same. The initiative of bringing gender and sexuality into closer alignment could be led by social actors who belonged to both communities of inquiry.

In contrast, the whiteness of Western feminism, which in the U.S. followed patterns of racial/ethnic segregation in housing, schools, employment, jobs, and religious institutions, meant that, until the late twentieth century, African American women, indigenous women, Latinas, and Asian American women developed feminist sensibilities in the context of their racially/ethnically segregated communities. A similar system of segregation organized through discourses on citizenship and sovereign nation-states characterized the global context. Significantly, by pointing out the need for more intersectional analyses within feminism, queers of color navigated and claimed a borderland space among various resistance projects.

These internal critiques raise important challenges to feminist theory. The need for critical social theory that analyzes gender inequality and gender injustice within the academy persists. But how might these self-reflexive criticisms that are internal to feminism shape feminist theory? Feminism and intersectionality are closely aligned, but they are not synonymous. These distinctive strands of self-reflexive criticism within feminism illustrate how being differentially positioned within feminism itself fosters different outcomes. For gender and sexuality, the intersectional task lay in bringing two discourses into alignment to the point where the two constructs are often thought of as one theoretical unit. In contrast, for gender, race, and nation, the intersectional task lay in incorporating difference into preexisting feminist frameworks. Here, if difference becomes the surrogate for differences of race, ethnicity, and nationality, then intersectionality, with its seemingly seamless approach to difference, ostensibly solves feminism's difference problem (K. Davis 2008). Within this logic, intersectionality acknowledges but does not unsettle the differences that already exist within feminism itself. Moreover, incorporating into feminism a static understanding of intersectionality that conceptualizes intersectionality as a prepackaged bundle of racial, ethnic, and national differences means that feminism need not attend to the messy histories of racism and so on. Intersectionality has taken care of that.

There are no quick fixes for these historical patterns of exclusion from and biases within Western feminism. Intersectionality may seem to solve this problem of past exclusionary practices. Within feminist projects that lack historical specificity, intersectionality can serve as a benchmark for all the other "others" who were not acknowledged within a racially segregated feminism before the more enlightened intersectional feminism of today. Yet without sustained critical vigilance, intersectionality could become yet another empty racial signifier that masks how contemporary feminism has yet to move beyond prior racial exclusions.

Decolonization and Postcolonial Theory

By the turn of the twenty-first century, cracks in the credibility of postcolonial studies in the academy seemed increasingly evident. In a particularly scathing 2002 essay, Benita Parry took postcolonial theory to task for its "modes of postcolonial criticism where the politics of the symbolic order displaces the theory and practice of politics" (67). Parry identifies two trends in earlier postcolonial criticisms of colonial discourse—namely, textual reinterpretation of the ways in which key texts of Western knowledge were essential to colonialism, and explication of the varying ways in which colonized subjects had resisted and opposed such knowledges. She posits that as postcolonial theory retreated into a textual analysis that was overly influenced by postmodern analyses, it became hostile to aspects of liberation theory, viewing such theory as naive (78). In her assessment, "a turn from a rhetoric disparaging the master narratives of revolution and liberation, and a return to a politics grounded in the material, social, and existential, now appears urgent" (77).

Many intellectuals and activists seemingly have come to the same conclusion. The term *postcolonial* seems to be falling out of favor, with terms such as *decolonial, decoloniality,* and *decolonizing* taking their place. In the introduction to a special issue of *Feminist Studies* devoted to generating a conversation between decolonial and postcolonial feminisms, the editors summarize the main ideas in the debates (Ramamurthy and Tambe, 2017). They point out that while both postcolonial and decolonial scholars have been committed to "critiquing the material and epistemic legacies of colonialism," they find the distinctions that are often drawn between the two disquieting (504). One distinction is of postcolonialism as being passé and only about the past. Disagreeing with Parry, Ramamurthy and Tambe contend that "the depiction of postcolonial feminism as a deconstructive, abstract, elite theory confined to the ambit of modern colonial knowledge systems overlooked the important quandaries that postcolonial feminism raised about how to present marginalized people ethically and, indeed, how to understand the very desire to represent the marginalized—whether or not we claim belonging to them" (504).

The other distinction between postcolonial and decolonial feminism involves what they describe as the "spatial markings of decolonial and postcolonial feminisms" (504). Decolonial feminism is often associated with indigenous scholars from the Americas, and postcolonial feminism, with scholars from South Asia, Africa, and the Middle East. While others may disagree with these regional distinctions—indigenous peoples are not an American phenomenon—they claim that decolonial feminism insists on engaging with the history of settler colonialism, land disputes, and a global gendered racial capitalism. Ramamurthy and Tambe seek insight into the workings of the distinctions between postcolonial feminism and decolonial feminisms as a contemporary example of how these debates are unfolding.

I am comfortable with assuming that postcolonial feminism and decolonial feminism exist in the same time, making different contributions to the broader project of decolonization. It also is reasonable that postcolonial and decolonial scholars need not live and work in designated places that are designated for formerly colonized peoples. The spatial histories of colonialism are real, as are the epistemological ties of indigenous peoples to particular places (B. Cohen 2001; Hokowhitu et al. 2010). Rather, the issue here lies in exploring the theoretical contributions of postcolonial theory and decolonial knowledge projects to the broader shared agenda of decolonization. Postcolonial theory does have theoretical legitimacy in the academy, a status that it shares with feminist theory. The challenge for postcolonial theory lies in seeing how its critical theorizing does and might conform to decolonial resistant knowledge projects. Here I refer to a broad array of projects that the terms *decolonial, decoloniality*, and *decolonizing* signify as resistance projects of decolonization. The projects themselves are quite different from one another. Intellectuals, artists, activists, academics, and ordinary people seem to be involved in an ongoing struggle to save their homes, their land, their children, and their own bodies. Decolonization signifies dismantling the legacy of formal colonialism and imagining its replacement. Because knowledge has been pivotal to colonial rule and postcolonial explanations of it, the struggle over knowledge itself constitutes an important site of resistance. The title of Boaventura de Sousa Santos's edited volume signals a sea change in perspective: *Another Knowledge Is Possible: Beyond Northern Epistemologies* (2007).

This tension between postcolonial theory as an established field of academic study and a broader and more unruly constellation of resistant knowledge projects of decolonization references something far deeper than a semantic difference. Instead, this distinction signals a fundamental difference in theoretical framing of the same set of social forces as a result of being differently located within them. Using the framework of post-colonial theory can mean adhering to reified notions of the end of formal colonialism and the beginning of the new phase of postcoloniality. Given the durability of colonial knowledge within the academy, one that resembles durable racial knowledge in the academy, postcolonial theory is unlikely to exhaust possibilities for much-needed critical analysis. Working within the disciplinary assumptions of where postcolonial theory is located in the academy means using accepted methodological tools.[18] This approach views projects that grapple with the contested legacy of colonialism as just that—a legacy of trying to understand the past in order to complete the postcolonial project of the death of colonialism.

The perspective from resistance projects of decolonization is quite differ-ent. Whereas formal colonialism certainly ended, the political, economic, and cultural relations that characterized colonialism have not. The past is in the present, but the significant feature of the present is building a new future that might be appropriately called postcolonial one day. But that day is far in the future. From the perspective of ongoing projects of decolonization, postcolonial theory constitutes one discourse among many that presents one angle of vision on decolonial initiatives. Ironically, because elite institu-tions have housed prominent postcolonial scholars, whether intentionally or not, the social location of postcolonial studies can function as a colonial discourse in relation to the aspirations of people who aim to move "beyond Northern epistemologies" (Santos 2007; Santos, Nunes, and Meneses 2007). Significantly, projects of decolonization both analyze colonial relationships and resist them.

The distinctions between these two perspectives—namely, formal postco-lonial theory and heterogeneous decolonial knowledge projects—potentially illuminate different aspects of critical social theory. As a named discourse in the academy, postcolonial theory has a specific history, set of practitioners, and series of debates. Like critical race theory and feminist theory, postco-lonial theory assumes a critical posture toward dominant knowledge, in this case, colonial knowledge. A wide-ranging roster of prominent intellectuals has laid an important foundation for postcolonial theory's critical analysis: Frantz Fanon, Amilcar Cabral, Gayatri Spivak, Homi Bhabha, Edward Said, Arjun Appadurai, Stuart Hall, Paul Gilroy, and others have greatly enriched academic debates about a range of topics and have all been influenced by postcolonial discourse in some fashion. Within the array of intellectuals who have contributed to this field, Edward Said, Gayatri Spivak, and Homi

Bhabha constitute the three main figures who are consistently mentioned within a postcolonial theory canon.[19]

It is important to point out that, during the development of postcolonial theory in academia, its guiding intellectuals provided ideas that were simultaneously literary and metaphoric. For example, ideas such as borders, migration, exile, home, marginality, and the concept of the "other" had material implications for intellectuals who were exiled from their home countries or marginalized within their new ones. Borders presented a tangible challenge to people who were brown, or of a derogated religion, or from a nation-state with few protections for free speech. When Gloria Anzaldúa wrote of the borderlands, she invoked the meaning of a physical place, for example, the U.S.-Mexico border, as well as a form of identity that belonged to no one place or group, but that was making its way in a new space. The issue was less the substance of the ideas themselves than the shifting emphasis within postcolonial theory that decoupled its ideas from actual political struggles and substituted texts as the primary object of investigation.

Institutional location in the academy sheds light on these shifting emphases. Postcolonial theory has consistently overemphasized certain questions and concerns and underemphasized others, reflecting its legacy of being housed in the humanities. Relying on literary criticism of close readings of selected texts is a standard methodological approach in the humanities. It's no surprise that particular disciplinary practices influence postcolonial theory. Yet this approach to theorizing via textual analysis assumes a high degree of literacy, not to mention familiarity with the particular texts that form the core of any argument. This focus on deconstructing colonial literature constituted an important first step for dismantling the knowledge base of formal colonialism. Many intellectuals who are associated with seminal works in postcolonial theory generated incisive critical social theory within these parameters and via the strategies of critique.

Palestinian intellectual Edward Said's bold ideas not only criticized prevailing academic wisdom but shaped the contours of postcolonial theory. *Orientalism*, Said's groundbreaking volume that was published in 1978, advances a powerful critique of Western knowledge itself. He defines Orientalism as an imagined construct of the West that underpinned material, economic, and cultural domination. Said is clear to point out that Orientalism is not just a set of ideas, wherein "were the truth about them to be told, would simply blow away" (1978, 6). Instead, he argues, "any set of ideas that can remain unchanged as teachable wisdom (in academies, books, congresses, universities, foreign-service institutes) from the period of Ernest Renan in the late 1840s until the present in the United States must be something more formidable than a mere collection of lies. Orientalism, therefore, is not an airy European fantasy about the Orient, but a curated body of theory and practice in which, for many generations, there has been considerable material investment" (6). This tactic of reinterpreting classic texts as a window into colonial discourse is the bread and butter of literary criticism.[20]

The situation of exile constitutes a recurring theme within the work of postmodern intellectuals, taking special form in the work of postcolonial theorists. Edward Said is best known for his analysis of Orientalism, yet many of the themes that run through his work reflect his experiences as a Palestinian intellectual in exile. In *Orientalism*, Said (1978) analyzes how the Western creation of an imagined East represented the needs of the West and not the realities of the East. In *Culture and Imperialism*, Said (1993) deepens this analysis beyond the case of the so-called Orient to examine how Western imperialism ruled through cultural forms. Said is also quite clear about the difficulties of doing intellectual work that aimed not to produce liberatory programs for oppressed people, but rather to analyze the epistemological foundations that made imperialism and domination possible (Said 1994). Said was a privileged intellectual in the West, but he was also an intellectual in exile, and this made a difference in what he saw, what he wrote, and who he counted among his audience.[21]

By the 1990s, when postcolonial studies was taking hold, Said was no stranger to academic pushback. Said's thesis of Orientalism was highly controversial, and it remains so. In his 1994 volume *Representations of the Intellectual*, Said examines the challenges that face intellectuals who advance ideas that are critical of prevailing wisdom. Many of these intellectuals are in political exile from their home countries and are often persecuted there; others become stateless people because they have no home countries and are marginalized within Britain, France, the U.S., and similar destination countries. The politics of doing intellectual work in this social context cannot be dismissed as a benign background factor.

As an academic discourse, postcolonial theory has housed a series of debates about gender, race, and nation that resonate with the ideas of intersectionality.[22] Take, for example, Meyda Yeğenoğlu's 1998 volume, *Colonial Fantasies: Toward a Feminist Reading of Orientalism*. Identifying how "Orientalism" stimulated a distinctive strand of gender analysis, Yeğenoğlu criticizes how sexual difference has been relegated to a subfield within colonial discourse. Instead, her study focuses on the "unique articulation of sexual and cultural difference as they are produced and signified in the discourse of Orientalism" (Yeğenoğlu 1978, 1). Using the veiled women of the Orient, Yeğenoğlu analyzes the persistent Western fascination with the veiled woman as a site of fantasy, nationalist ideology, and discourses of gender. Yet both Orientalism and feminism insufficiently explain this complexity. Yeğenoğlu's intent in writing her book grew from her concern that Orientalist discourse required reformulation.

Yeğenoğlu's project illustrates a common strategy within intersectional analyses of taking a particular topic and criticizing how its absence within dominant narratives, its treatment within such narratives, or both, compromises them. In this case, Yeğenoğlu provides a critical reading of an important critical social theory that also criticized Western discourse. She wrote a critique of a critique. Significantly, she was able to do so from the social location of working within a Turkish university, itself a site that was influenced by the same Orientalist frameworks that merited resistance. Criticism such as hers has been an important tool within postcolonial theory. As a topic of scholarly inquiry, much critical analysis advanced within postcolonial theory has expanded critical understandings of colonialism and nationalism, often specializing in deconstructing narratives that uphold colonialism and that reproduce postcolonial relations.

While there may be a need for such criticism, postcolonial theory may be undercut by its social location in the academy. Its affiliation with the humanities and with literary and cultural criticism produced a highly specialized language of terms and conventions that make some of this work inaccessible. This raises the question of who the intended audience for such work might be. Postcolonial theory's specialized knowledge seemingly circulates more easily among postcolonial scholars than among academics in the social sciences or among a broader set of readers. Kyung-Man Kim's (2005) criticism of critical theory surveyed in *Discourses on Liberation: An Anatomy of Critical Theory* may be apt here. Rather than assuming that postcolonial theory is inherently critical because academic communities of inquiry recognize its prominent critical theorists, Kim evaluates critical scholarship in relation to the goal of fostering liberation, or in this case, decolonization. Kim saw Habermas as advocating dialogical engagement in his theory yet unable to have such dialogues with laypeople across differences in power. Unfortunately, postcolonial theory can read as the kind of social theory that laypeople imagine theory to be—elite, abstract, incomprehensible, and somehow "theoretical" because it cannot be easily understood. But the limits of postcolonial theory may go beyond academic politics and disciplinary conventions. The term *postcolonial* has lost its critical edge.

Certainly, the issues that catalyzed postcolonial studies in the 1990s have not abated. In fact, they have intensified. The term postcolonial itself no longer speaks to the realities of a new generation of intellectuals and activists for a reason.[23] The term *decolonial knowledge project* seemingly invokes a resistant dimension of postcolonial theory with closer ties to political action. Prior generations of intellectuals saw the need to consider the utility of all ideas for broader projects of liberation from colonialism, racism, and sexism. Postcolonial studies scholars have drawn inspiration from Frantz Fanon and Mahatma Gandhi, intellectuals who illustrate this kind of intellectual and political involvement (Caygill 2013, 69–76; Gandhi 1998, 17–22). Ideas matter for criticizing colonial relations. Ideas also matter for political strategies that might dismantle colonial relations. For Fanon, ideas also mattered in imagining the promise and perils of liberation itself. Fanon's expansive critical knowledge project spoke to the moment of political liberation. His was a resistant knowledge project of liberation in which the ties between knowledge and power, or between critical analysis and actions, were evident. Gandhi emphasized a different philosophy for dismantling colonialism, but the connections between his analysis and his political actions also had far-reaching repercussions.

What about now? People who have been affected by deeply entrenched colonial legacies are more likely to advance knowledge projects that reflect their experiences within and critical analyses of neocolonialism; those projects may also reflect the interests of those who are disproportionately harmed by neocolonial relations. The assumption that emancipation, freedom, or the end of formal rule brings about the end of colonial relationships is erroneous. Decolonial knowledge projects take many forms and exist in many places: intellectuals and activists in South Africa, Brazil, and New Zealand all use the terminology of decoloniality. They seemingly share a similar purpose of resisting the material, political, and cultural dimensions of colonialism's legacy. Decolonization involves engaging all aspects of colonial relationships—ones that rest on economics, politics, and culture. Materially, decolonization contains economic analyses and strategies for relieving human suffering. Politically, decolonization and empowerment go hand in hand. The lesson learned within neocolonialism is that national liberation does not ease material suffering. Decolonizing processes of knowledge production is essential. This is why decolonizing methodology is so important to resistant knowledge projects (see, e.g., L. Smith 2012). Criticizing and reforming dominant knowledge production practices is essential, but imagining new alternatives for transformation is equally essential.

Because they focus on the cultural as well as the material and political aspects of the process of decolonization, intellectuals who participate in decolonial knowledge projects, especially when they straddle academic borders, can be responsive to contemporary issues and concerns. Postcolonial studies provided a critical analysis of classic texts that created and upheld colonialism. Yet such texts represent the past; by themselves, they cannot speak to the present and the future. In decolonial knowledge projects, critical analysis and critical theorizing are often more directly connected to the expressed needs of particular groups, for example, the ongoing critical analysis of indigenous peoples in Brazil's Amazon basin, or that advanced by the many indigenous and immigrant groups in Canada whose different experiences with colonialism and ongoing experiences with neocolonialism cannot be legislated away, or the distinctive patterns of identity and resistance of indigenous peoples (Hokowhitu et al. 2010).

The sophisticated political and epistemological knowledge projects of Maori peoples in New Zealand provide a window into the scope and depth of such projects. In describing the purpose of her book, Linda Tuhiwai Smith identifies the significance of methodology itself: "*Decolonizing Methodologies* is concerned not so much with the actual technique of selecting a method but much more with the context in which research problems are conceptualized and designed, and with the implications of research for its participants and their communities. It is also concerned with the institution of research, its claims, its values and practices, and its relationship to power" (2012, ix). Smith's view of methodology has important implications for intersectionality.

Neocolonialism is not necessarily a racial project unique to indigenous peoples and people of African descent, nor is it something that temporally comes after formal colonialism has ended. Neocolonial relationships are more elastic. For example, formal colonialism required conquest, pacification, and domination of foreign populations. But these same strategies can affect so-called domestic populations. The discourse on internal colonialism posits that groups within the borders of a colonial power or sovereign state also experience a form of colonization. This notion of internal colonialism reframes standard national narratives, as in the case of Ireland as an internal colony of Britain, and internal colonialism of entirely new populations.[24]

It is important to point out that projects for decolonizing knowledge have not disappeared from academia. Rather, such projects face the challenge of sustaining their critical edge in the context of changing academic environments. Criticizing other resistant knowledge projects can be difficult within epistemic environments that define criticism purely through the lens of adversarial debate. Carving out a space within the academy for vibrant critical engagement can be risky. But many models exist of how to do it. Like Yeğenoğlu's critique of Edward Said's *Orientalism*, such projects may originate within academic institutions that are outside the West; but unlike Yeğenoğlu's project, they are broader than criticizing discourses in the academy. Such projects may draw from critical analyses on postcolonialism, yet are not contained by academic discourse. Instead, critical analysis is part of a larger project of political engagement.

Intersectionality and Resistant Knowledge

This chapter examines critical race theory, feminist theory, and postcolonial theory as forms of critical theorizing with ties to broader resistant knowledge projects of antiracism, feminism, and decolonialism. Beginning critical analysis in a different place potentially has important implications for intersectionality's critical inquiry. Prematurely lumping together resistant knowledge projects as well as the forms of critical theorizing they engender within intersectionality misreads the significance of heterogeneous approaches to resistance for intersectionality's critical theorizing. Instead of homogenizing resistant knowledges as minority studies and then interpreting their value as a critique of what is already assumed to be true, here I center my analysis on the complexities of three selected resistant knowledge projects. This cursory analysis of selected resistant knowledge projects has several implications for intersectionality.

First, critical inquiry that begins within particular resistant knowledge projects—for example, focusing on race, gender, or class—typically pursue questions that differ from those of traditional and critical social theory in the academy. Projects of antiracism, feminism, and decolonialism are called resistant knowledge projects for a reason. For such projects, the guiding question is less whether to resist prevailing power arrangements and more what forms such resistance might take. Intersectionality shares much with resistant knowledge projects of race, gender, and decoloniality. Because each area of inquiry provides a distinctive angle of vision on the meaning of critical theorizing for resistance, each reveals different aspects of critical theoretical engagement. Critical inquiry that begins within the assumptions of a particular resistant knowledge project often provides an expanded repertoire of critical ideas that might inform similar projects. In this case, putting critical race theory, feminist theory, postcolonial theory, and intersectionality in conversation potentially enriches the critical theorizing of each discourse. Such engaged dialogues promise to contribute to intersectionality's own potential as a critical social theory.

Critical theorizing for knowledge projects that specialize in resistance—the case of antiracism, feminism, and decolonization—facilitate critical social theories. People who are harmed by racism, heteropatriarchy, and colonialism have a vested interest in better understanding these systems of power. But they also have a vested interest in developing critical social theories that foster resistance projects of antiracism, feminism, and decolonization. Such critical theorizing is unlikely to emerge within the prevailing questions and concerns of contemporary Western social theory. Poststructuralist social theory, for example, has not expressed much interest in resisting its own source of power and authority. Why would it? Western social theories place far more emphasis on explaining social order than they do in explaining political resistance, let alone aspiring to generate it. In this context, specialty knowledges that have made resistance central to their actions take the lead in critical theorizing about social injustices as well as the forms that resisting such injustices might take.

Second, critical theorizing within resistant knowledge projects is open to more expansive methodologies as part of its theoretical project. Some critical theories, like critical race theory and feminist theory, demonstrate some sort of commitment to praxis—namely, the recursive relationship between actions and ideas. Within this framework, ideas do not drive actions—the case of theories as ideas that are tested through action, or actions as behaviors that are uninformed by analysis. Rather, praxis creates a more expansive space for critical theorizing, precisely because it is not confined to a discrete act at one moment in time, but rather can inform the entire ethos of a project. The forms of critical theorizing discussed here all recognize the significance of praxis within their respective knowledge projects, even though they express, for varying reasons, different sensibilities in relation to it.

This emphasis on critical theorizing via praxis has methodological implications for intersectionality's move toward becoming a critical social theory. The resistant knowledge projects surveyed here are more likely than mainstream social theories to entertain the possibility that using experiences and taking social actions constitute appropriate methods for analyzing resistance. Within traditional social theory, experiences and social action may provide data for existing theoretical frameworks, but these ways of knowing are unlikely candidates for raising the kinds of questions that interest theorists or for developing explanations for social phenomena. In contrast, in part because they have ties with constituencies that are affected by their knowledge, the critical theorizing projects of critical race theory, feminist theory, and postcolonial theory are more likely to value experience as a rich source of insight, and taking social action as a way of theorizing. Ideas matter, but when it comes to social inequality, critical theorizing is not just about ideas. There is a distinction between critical analysis that originates within academic assumptions that knowledge for knowledge's sake will somehow contribute to social change, and critical analysis that has the practical intent of fostering social change.

Third, the critical theorizing that informs resistant knowledge projects often questions what counts as critical social theory, precisely because their familiarity with praxis catalyzes a critical analysis of traditional social theory and its ties to power relations. In this chapter, I highlight the theoretical dimensions of resistant knowledge projects of antiracism, feminism, and decolonization, precisely because specializing in resistance is framed as activist and nontheoretical. Reducing them to activist endeavors, or as critiques of what already exists, misreads critical theorizing advanced by women and people of color as simple criticism, reactions from the margins of assumed theoretical truths. In contrast, I see these projects as doing critical theory that is more sophisticated than simple criticism, especially when such projects produce critical theoretical content through critical theorizing processes. Praxis encourages intellectuals within resistant knowledge projects to theorize differently, drawing upon multiple sources of expertise and asking different questions than those within traditional social theory.

When it comes to praxis in the academy, intersectionality has much to learn from critical race theory, feminist theory, and postcolonial theory concerning the challenges of epistemic resistance in the context of epistemic oppression. Because intersectionality also has a strong academic presence, yet one that is so decentralized, the issue of epistemic resistance takes on added importance for intersectionality. Epistemic resistance, or resisting the rules that govern what counts as knowledge, constitutes an important dimension of critical theorizing in academic venues. Intersectionality certainly has been inspired by multiple resistant knowledge projects that border it, as well as by a plethora of Western social theories. Yet the organizational practices of academia routinely limit critical analyses of resistance, not simply through ignoring resistance as a topic of investigation, but also through forms of epistemic power that organize intellectual work (chapter 4). If intersectionality is, in fact, as Vivian May contends, "a form of resistant knowledge developed to unsettle conventional mindsets, challenge oppressive power, think through the full architecture of structural inequalities and asymmetrical life opportunities, and seek a more just world" (2015, xi), it faces a formidable opponent within academic venues. Yet such venues also create opportunities to create knowledge that fosters social change.

Fourth, because the distinctions *among* resistant knowledge projects are rarely clear-cut, they face varying and overlapping challenges in remaining critical. These projects are interconnected, with practices in one area influencing those in another. Conceptually, no sharp definitional boundaries distinguish these fields within the academy; they often share intellectuals who can be alternately categorized as race theorists, feminist theorists, or postcolonial theorists. Yet politically, the treatment of intellectuals within each area, perceptions of the theoretical heft of each area, and ties that these knowledge projects have to political projects differ dramatically. In this chapter, I emphasized differences in critical inquiry in the three areas surveyed. Feminist theory offers valuable insight into feminism, yet it faces the challenge of its own success. Because feminist theory is recognized as being a critical social theory, unlike critical race theory, it need not fight the fight of epistemic acceptance. Critical race theory continues an uphill battle to be heard within traditional academic disciplines, a status that makes attending to its own praxis within academia essential.[25] As the changing relationship between postcolonial feminism and decolonial feminism suggests, critical theorizing within the resistance project of decolonizing knowledge and power relations is under construction. Critical race theory, feminist theory, and postcolonial theory illuminate the different challenges and varying critical responses to the particular set of social problems that each faces in its critical theorizing.

Viewing projects such as these as interconnected knowledge projects that specialize in resistance enriches their respective discourses. But when it comes to intersectionality, this interdependence of distinctive resistance traditions points toward dialogical engagement among critical social theories as an essential dimension of critical theorizing itself. Stated differently, critical theorizing for intersectionality rests on dialogical engagement with and among various knowledge projects. The boundaries among critical race theory, feminist theory, and postcolonial theory, for example, are blurred, with intellectuals who cross boundaries using ideas from many areas to inform their work. Moreover, because resistant knowledge projects of antiracism, feminism, and decolonization transcend academic borders, they illustrate how ideas themselves, especially critical ideas, defy political, social, and epistemic containment. Moreover, it is important to remember that when it comes to their intellectual production, many intellectuals who are associated with various aspects of intersectionality draw ideas from disparate knowledge traditions, have been differentially claimed (or not) by different academic disciplines, and criticize more than one discourse. For intersectionality, the task ahead lies in placing multiple resistant knowledge projects in dialogue, with an eye toward pooling intellectual resources on the meaning of resistance within intersectionality's critical theorizing.

Finally, uncritically defending or celebrating intersectionality or any other form of critical theorizing as a finished critical social theory undercuts its critical potential. Instead, each resistant knowledge project must develop its own internal mechanisms for building consensus and accommodating dissent within its distinctive cognitive architecture. For intersectionality, this means subjecting dimensions of its critical thinking—namely, its core constructs and guiding premises—to sustained scrutiny (figure 1.1 in chapter 1). Each resistant knowledge project must also evaluate its strategies for crafting coalitions with other like-minded projects, for example, how feminist theory and queer theory became more closely aligned within feminist scholarship. In contrast, postcolonial theory faces the challenge of redefining itself in relation to decolonial resistant knowledge projects. For intersectionality as a critical social theory in the making, cultivating these ties with like-minded projects means remaining open to patterns of consensus and dissent among critical race theory, feminist theory, postcolonial theory, and its own praxis.

Critical race theory, feminist theory, postcolonial theory, and intersectionality all aspire to shift paradigmatic thinking about social inequalities and social injustice. Yet, because intersectionality places the ideas of so many discourses, critical and otherwise, in dialogue, its critical theorizing is especially complex. For intersectionality, strategies of internal critical analysis as well as strategies for putting resistant knowledge projects in dialogue both constitute important strategies for sustaining critical inquiry. Such strategies provide a firewall against the growing tendency to collapse distinctive resistant knowledge projects into one overarching project and label it intersectional. Intersectionality could easily become a discourse in which resistance is hollowed out, primarily because it fails to attend to the particulars of resistant knowledge projects within its own genealogy and whose futures inform its own.

4

Intersectionality and Epistemic Resistance

When Kimberlé Crenshaw used the term *intersectionality* in the early 1990s, she had no way of knowing that the idea she saw as being just a metaphor would have such a sweeping impact within activist and academic communities. Crenshaw's contributions to intersectionality are important, but not in the way they have typically been interpreted within academia. Dominant narratives of intersectionality routinely cite two of Crenshaw's articles (1989, 1991) to support their claim that she "coined" the term *intersectionality*.[1] These narratives identify Crenshaw's initial use of the term *intersectionality* within academia as its point of origin. For many academics, the story of intersectionality begins (and in some cases ends) with a few ideas plucked from Crenshaw's early work (1989, 1991). Naming intersectionality seemingly started the academic clock on what kind of story would and could be told about intersectionality itself within academia.

This origin story inserts intersectionality into a familiar colonial narrative that positions Crenshaw as the intrepid explorer who, because she discovers virgin territory, gets naming rights. Yet from the perspective of the colonized, such colonial narratives also signal power relations of domination that begin with discovery, move on to conquest, and end with ongoing pacification.[2] Identifying intersectionality's narrative with its moment of academic discovery assigns value to when its explorers brought home something of interest to colonists. Given this context, who gets to tell intersectionality's story? And what story will they tell?

These questions point to the significance of epistemology as a dimension of critical theorizing. Epistemology is the study of the standards used to assess knowledge or *why* we believe what we believe to be true. Those who get to tell intersectionality's story wield epistemic power over intersectionality's history, borders, core questions, and goals. On some level, subordinated groups know that epistemology has never been neutral, and that epistemic power is part of how domination operates. For indigenous peoples, Black people, women, poor people, LGBTQ people, religious and ethnic minorities, and differently abled people, the concept of epistemic resistance provides an important conceptual tool for critical analysis. Some subordinated groups have built epistemic resistance into the fabric of their critical analyses, whereas for other groups, the idea of epistemic resistance is quite new. Despite this need for epistemic resistance, gaining access to the closed interpretive communities of Western social theory has made it difficult to challenge the epistemological contours of such communities from outside colleges and universities. This kind of epistemic resistance best comes from within.

Epistemology is important for determining what counts as critical social theory. Intersectionality is situated *within* broader epistemological frameworks that constrain fundamental definitions of theory and how theories will be evaluated. Different epistemologies advance different standards for defining social theory, thereby exercising different authority in regulating social theories. Within academia, methodology provides rules of conduct for producing knowledge within the framing assumptions of a particular epistemology. Surprisingly, despite the significance of epistemology and methodology for intersectional theorizing, with few exceptions (see May 2015 and Tomlinson 2013), both are routinely minimized within analyses of intersectionality itself. In this chapter, I examine epistemology and methodology as two important dimensions of intersectional theorizing. Intersectionality is not just about ideas and not just about power; rather, its critical inquiry taps the recursive relationship of knowledge and power as organized via epistemology and methodology. On the one hand, intersectionality is situated *within* broader epistemological frameworks that regulate definitions of what counts as theory, as well as how theories will be evaluated. On the other hand, intersectionality draws upon methodologies as conduits for critical theorizing that can uphold or upend epistemic power. Through these definitional and evaluative processes, epistemologies and the methodologies they uphold exercise power in regulating social theories. Epistemology shapes discourse itself—namely, who gets to tell intersectionality's story—and methodology determines what counts as a plausible story.

Who Gets to Tell Intersectionality's Story?

In researching this book, I regularly surveyed patterns in journal articles, book chapters, and books that self-identify as intersectional in some fashion. Over time, I came to see a pattern in the emerging literature on intersectionality about how intersectionality came into being. The most common narrative credits Kimberlé Crenshaw as introducing intersectionality by "coining" the term. Why did so many scholars, I wondered, repeat some variation of the term *coined* in their brief overview of intersectionality? Significantly, what were the effects of so many scholars repeating this narrative, often verbatim, as a taken-for-granted way of depicting intersectionality itself?

My concern with this particular narrative of intersectionality's genealogy concerns the effects of its circulation. The problem with the uncritical repetition of the "coining" narrative is not with what Crenshaw actually said, which, as philosopher Anna Carastathis (2016) reminds us, is far more complicated and sophisticated than mere naming. Rather, via its repetition, the coining narrative creates a familiar truth that enables prevailing academic genealogies of intersectionality to emphasize certain themes and neglect others. Specifically, this telling of intersectionality's story reinforces longstanding Western narratives of colonialism and capitalism.

The coining narrative melds well with colonial relations of discovery and exploration. When Crenshaw seemingly discovered the virgin territory of intersectionality, she gained naming rights over it. Within a colonial framework, Crenshaw is recognizable as an explorer who seemingly reflects the best of both worlds: her educational credentials demonstrate her mastery of the conventions of Western intellectual inquiry, and her access to native cultures provides special insight and experiences about places where academics could not previously go. She's a trustworthy translator within the space between two different ways of knowing.

The "coining" story also fits within capitalist narratives of expansion in search of new materials and markets, and the need to extract value from natural resources as part of that expansion. Such resources are of no value until they are removed from their natural settings and incorporated into capitalist marketplace relations. Within narratives of consumer capitalism, Crenshaw brought something of value into the academy—a natural resource that could be developed into a profitable academic commodity. The repetitive nature of the coining metaphor across diverse publications is noteworthy. Like narratives that assume the inevitability of capitalism itself, repeating the coining narrative often enough turns it into a taken-for-granted truth that needs no further explanation.

Yet this "coining" version of intersectionality's genealogy is one of many narratives that could be told about it. My intent is neither to set the story of intersectionality straight (Collins and Bilge 2016, 63–87), nor to defend intersectionality from commodification by academic poachers. Rather, my goal is to offer an alternative telling of intersectionality's story that is more closely aligned with the critical traditions of resistant knowledge projects. Within my narrative, Crenshaw's scholarly articles constitute less a point of origin for intersectionality itself and more an important turning point that highlights the shifting relationships among activist and academic interpretive communities under conditions of decolonization and neoliberalism. Crenshaw's signature work on intersectionality was published during a significant juncture when subordinated groups challenged not just the power arrangements of the academy that excluded them from literacy, education, and jobs, but also the epistemological authority of scholarly arguments that had long held sway in explaining the experiences of subordinated people.

For Crenshaw, naming intersectionality aimed not to seek some higher theoretical truth but rather to address how the specific social problem of violence affected people of color, women, and immigrant groups. In this regard, her work was aligned with antiracist, feminist, and decolonial resistant knowledge projects. In describing her use of the term *intersectionality* as a metaphor, Crenshaw notes that antiracist and feminist political projects often worked at cross-purposes, leaving women of color vulnerable to falling through the cracks (Guidroz and Berger 2009). By centering on the experiences of women of color in building her argument, Crenshaw saw the theoretical value in taking the experiences of women of color seriously. Crenshaw's use of *intersectionality* to name this space of contestation and possibility reflects her awareness of the challenges of accommodating the conflicting standards of distinctive resistant knowledge projects that share a common space.

Crenshaw was well positioned to see how, in the 1970s and 1980s, the backlash against social justice gains of prior decades might play out within antiracist and feminist communities in the U.S. On the one hand, anticolonial struggles, feminism, and similar mid-twentieth-century social movements had generated an expansive array of resistant knowledge projects that valorized self-reflectivity, experience, and creative social action as part of a search for social justice. Often influenced by the critical traditions of liberation theory, Marxism, and similar critical analytical traditions, these movements pushed for social change. Many of these projects understood how important it was to criticize existing scholarly practices. While there were many such projects, law and critical legal scholarship—Crenshaw's primary social location—was one important site for social change.[3]

On the other hand, during this same period and in response to social movement demands, colleges and universities were well into projects to desegregate their campuses. A cottage industry of diversity professionals sprang up within academia; these people were tasked with managing the interpersonal dynamics of desegregation. Legal protections granted formal equality to individuals, yet students, faculty, staff, and administrators dragged the baggage of their experiences within segregated social relations of race, gender, class, and sexuality with them. The desegregation of women, African Americans, Latinas/os, LGBTQ people, and other groups that had been marginalized within academia paralleled a similar decolonization of knowledge. African Americans, Latinos/as, women, and other historically excluded groups challenged curricular offerings and the truth of traditional scholarship itself. Calls to move beyond curriculum reform to curriculum transformation grew from a broader project to decolonize the knowledge that was produced within academia. Decolonizing academic knowledge from *within* academia, and within more heterogeneous scholarly communities of inquiry, raised new challenges within colleges and universities.

Gaining a name within academic communities signaled an important transition within intersectionality's genealogy, one that simultaneously granted it greater legitimacy as it was incorporated into academic venues but also presented new challenges when it arrived. As a named entity within Western academic discourse, intersectionality was no longer anonymous— it could be seen and increasingly heard. Epistemological challenges accompanied its naming. Before the 1990s, an array of resistant knowledge projects grew within a fluid borderland space that spanned activist and academic communities. Yet naming intersectionality revealed its ties to both communities, as well as the epistemological distinctions between them.

Significantly, acquiring a name highlighted the epistemological fault lines between activist and academic communities of inquiry. Such communities held different epistemological standards concerning the appropriate role of politics and ethics within intellectual work. Resistant knowledge projects with ties to activism criticized racism, heteropatriarchy, class exploitation, and colonialism from the perspectives of people who were harmed by such systems. Many resistant knowledge projects reflected an implicit if not explicit normative commitment to work for social change when confronted by socially unjust conditions under these systems of power. For such projects, there was neither a need to defend the social justice mandate of social action nor to explain why political action was necessary. In contrast, despite their commitment to critical analysis as a pathway to truth, traditional academic disciplines, especially the sciences and the social sciences, eschewed explicit commitments to social justice and similar normative standards. For fear of being judged as biased, they avoided political involvement. Individual intellectuals could embrace political causes, but politics and ethics could not be central to fields of study, save as topics of investigation. Norms of objectivity viewed ethics and politics as epistemologically suspect.

Within an alternative narrative that aligns intersectionality with the legacy of mid-twentieth-century social movements, being named constituted a turning point for intersectionality's genealogy as a resistant knowledge project. Once named, understandings of intersectionality that had flourished within the unnamed border spaces between activism and academia came under more sustained scrutiny concerning politics and ethics. Moving into academic venues and encountering epistemic power firsthand also raised new questions about the contours of epistemic resistance.

Epistemic Power and Critical Theorizing

Within academic contexts, the question of who gets to tell intersectionality's story reflects how epistemic power shapes critical inquiry. Epistemic power is deeply intertwined with political domination, and exercising epistemic power is a form of politics. Conversely, epistemic resistance is deeply intertwined with political resistance. Engaging in epistemic resistance is important for political resistance. Because epistemic power flows from the specific configurations of intersecting power relations in any given context, such power structures but does not predetermine the dynamics of intellectual work. Significantly, these ties between epistemic and political power are often hidden in plain sight. Whether traditional social theory or critical social theory, these ties between epistemic power and political power form the taken-for-granted background of theorizing.

Because intersectionality has long been associated with social justice, if not assumed to be inherently committed to social justice (see chapter 8), the question of how social theorists of intersectionality understand epistemic power becomes especially important for intersectional theorizing. In essence, social injustice can be just as hardwired into the practices of producing academic knowledge, including intersectionality itself, as it is within wider society. Understandings of epistemology that situate it outside of and above power relations mask how epistemology itself contributes to reproducing or challenging social inequality.[4] As philosopher Jose Medina points out, "a narrow conception of epistemology restricted to issues of justification of knowledge claims . . . is impotent, ineffectual, and always arrives too late" (Medina 2013, 253). A broader understanding of epistemology points to not only how social inequalities are reproduced in the application of seemingly objective rules, but also how the substance of the rules themselves foster social injustice. This concept of epistemology as an active participant in organizing power hierarchies has been fertile ground for intersectional analysis. Barbara Tomlinson (2013) analyzes how a dominant racial frame that suppresses the conceptual tools for analyzing racism contributes to a colonization of intersectionality. Vivian May (2015, 6–9) explores an intersectionality backlash wherein critiques of intersectionality draw upon deeply entrenched ways of thinking, even as intersectionality scholars have criticized these same tools as fostering misrepresentation, erasure, and violation.

Hiding in plain sight, epistemic power generates ever-present frameworks that identify, for theoretical and methodological projects, which topics are worthy of investigation as well as the best strategies for investigating what's worth knowing. Moreover, epistemic power shapes the organization of communities of inquiry that rely on these standards. Academic departments, fields of study, areas of specialization, curricular offerings, and classroom practices all constitute particular interpretive communities. Belonging to communities of inquiry and enjoying the privileges of membership often rests on a willingness to adhere to its assumptions and to play by its rules. Epistemology takes form within specific communities of inquiry, all of which have distinctive understandings of what counts as legitimate knowledge for them. Such communities provide a context of justification for what a particular community finds reasonable, true, and useful.

In this regard, intersectionality must consider how the demographics of interpretive communities and the epistemic standards that characterize those communities influence its own critical inquiry. As I examine in earlier chapters, intersectionality is situated at the crossroads of multiple interpretive communities that are characterized by diverse histories, concerns, and epistemic standards. Social theory catalyzes a particular kind of community of inquiry. When it comes to contemporary social theory in the academy, theoretical communities of inquiry are often tight-knit, located in elite institutions and with high barriers for entry.

Privileged intellectuals within academia can typically take their unrestricted access to the world of ideas for granted. Working within such homogeneous communities of inquiry, and theorizing from within such locations, can affect the critical analysis of even the most gifted thinkers. I doubt that Pierre Bourdieu or Judith Butler, for example, paid serious attention to how their social location as privileged intellectuals shaped what they were able to see as well as what they could say about it. Ideas such as Bourdieu's *habitus* or Butler's performativity seemingly come solely from their individual brilliance. Yet gifted as these thinkers may be, they were able to advance these ideas only in a context where they were already empowered to do so and where their ideas were welcome. Bourdieu, Butler, and a long list of Western intellectuals have espoused liberal if not progressive ideas as personal causes. But the goodwill of individuals is not the point here. Rather, belonging to privileged communities of inquiry grant members considerable epistemic power.

For privileged academics, the power hierarchies that underpin their scholarship typically constitute minor concerns and not major barriers to their intellectual production. Such intellectuals can simply accept jobs to which they feel entitled and arrive in their universities with the expectation that they will be able to say and do what suits them. Their legitimacy as social theorists is rarely in doubt. Philosopher Jose Medina's discussion of "active ignorance and the epistemic vices of the privileged" (2013, 30–40) describes this sense of what can be taken for granted and what can remain unexamined among social theorists. More credence is routinely granted to the ideas of established social theorists, especially if their analyses support the status quo. Yet privilege is seductive. How can intellectuals who work within homogeneous theoretical communities develop innovative ideas by talking only to each other?

In contrast, social theorists who are aligned with resistant knowledge projects do not theorize from positions of privilege, but instead work within often formidable institutional constraints. Significantly, their ties to activist projects that go beyond academic borders often energize their intellectual production as well as their willingness to persist within academic settings. Gloria Anzaldúa, Stuart Hall, Frantz Fanon, William E. B. Du Bois, Angela Y. Davis, and many of the intellectuals discussed in this book had to create the conditions that made their intellectual work possible. Some, like Ida B. Wells-Barnett and Pauli Murray, never found steady work and are only being acknowledged posthumously for their theoretical analyses. Even those intellectuals who find academic jobs confront uncertain futures. Some intellectuals, such as Hannah Arendt, Zygmunt Bauman, and Edward Said, who are rendered stateless by war or who leave their homelands in response to political unrest do manage to land on their feet. Intellectuals who criticize colonialism, racism, sexism, and capitalism, especially if they are affiliated with projects of resistance, often have no guarantees that either they or their intellectual work will endure.

In this context, the language of *epistemic oppression*, *epistemic injustice*, and *epistemic resistance* within philosophy provides an important vocabulary for analyzing the challenges intersectionality faces as a critical social theory in the making (see, e.g., Kidd, Medina, and Pohlhaus 2017; Medina 2013). Terms such as *epistemic oppression* and *epistemic injustice* provide a more nuanced understanding of how epistemology constitutes a structuring dimension of social injustice beyond the actual ideas of racism, heteropatriarchy, and colonialism as ideological systems (Dotson 2014; Kidd, Medina, and Pohlhaus 2017). Providing a language for how epistemic power influences various aspects of scholarly practice makes it possible to move beyond "bad apples" arguments about biased individuals. Instead, epistemic oppression and epistemic injustice name the structural dimensions of epistemic power as organized through the aforementioned interpretive communities that are essential to knowledge production.

Intellectual work in the academy is often imagined through the lens of epistemic equality. Within interpretive communities with a stated commitment to fairness and equality, all members ostensibly have equitable access to being treated equally, speaking freely, and being heard (Dotson 2011). Within such idealized communities, conversations among group members aim to build theoretical consensus by making sure that all ideas are debated and the best ideas are accepted as truth. Perhaps members of the Frankfurt school or the Birmingham school were able to develop this form of collegiality. Yet even under the best of conditions, collaborative intellectual work is rarely fair and equitable, especially when epistemic power remains unnamed and unexamined. Collaboration is much easier to achieve within homogeneous interpretive communities where a form of group think often masquerades as consensus. This kind of homogeneity and theoretical gatekeeping can keep the peace at the expense of suppressing innovative and often controversial ideas.

Within colleges and universities, the belief that everyone's ideas are equally valuable and entitled to be heard often bears little resemblance to actual academic practices. Instead, academic communities of inquiry draw upon taken-for-granted ideas about race, class, gender, sexuality, and similar categories to evaluate ideas in light of the people who raise them. These categories do not determine privilege and disadvantage, yet they align with prevailing hierarchies that privilege and derogate entire categories of people as capable of doing social theory. Most groups rely upon an agreed-upon form of epistemic oppression that suppresses the *epistemic agency* of some members of the group while elevating that of others. Stated differently, through their epistemic practices, interpretive communities regulate and reproduce relationships of unequal epistemic agency *among* their members. Yet despite ideological commitments to equality, inclusivity, and belonging, interpretive communities have hardwired practices that, whether intentional or not, replicate existing social hierarchies.[5]

Doing critical theorizing in these settings is difficult, especially if this work is critical of epistemic power itself. Yet critical analysis must take epistemic power seriously. How could Frantz Fanon theorize liberation without taking the epistemic assumptions of Francophone social theory into consideration? Criticizing such theory was part of the challenge of liberation; assuming that mainstream social theory was fair and impartial would irreparably compromise the critical dimensions of Fanon's arguments. Whether explicitly acknowledged or implicitly affirmed, intellectuals bring dominance structures with them into knowledge production processes. Intersecting power relations that privilege and penalize people with markers of race, class, gender, sexuality, ethnicity, age, and ability do not stop at the seminar room's door or wait patiently outside editorial board meetings. Epistemic power organizes not just the visible, formal structures of collective inquiry but also the backstage, typically anonymous practices of evaluation.

When it comes to critical social theory in the academy, intersectionality faces a conundrum. Its legitimation and success privilege some intellectuals over others, the case, for example, of academics who excel at manipulating Western theories or methodologies and who are housed at prestigious institutions. Without a structural analysis of how power is organized, intersectionality can easily replicate existing social hierarchies within its own practices whereby the seemingly naturalized and normalized inequalities *within* academia result from structures of power that lie outside. These same epistemic practices can increasingly marginalize and subsequently silence people *within* intersectionality who, ironically, are more closely aligned with the very resistance traditions that catalyzed intersectionality in the first place. In the absence of self-reflexivity about how differences in epistemic agency are themselves a reflection of power relations, it becomes less likely that intersectionality's critical posture can progress.

If epistemology itself is implicated in reproducing or resisting social inequality, or both, exactly *how* does this happen? Epistemic power operates not just through the content that is validated within taken-for-granted epistemological frameworks, in this case, making intersectionality's story via familial narratives of colonization and capitalism. Epistemic power also relies on specific strategies that differentially value intellectuals as social theorists as well as the worth of their theoretical arguments. These same relationships shape epistemic resistance.

Epistemic Resistance and Testimonial Authority

The case of Anita Hill during the 1992 Senate Judiciary Committee hearings of Supreme Court nominee Clarence Thomas illustrates the significance of claiming testimonial authority as a form of epistemic resistance (Collins 2000, 126). In this watershed case, Anita Hill shared graphic details of how her former boss Clarence Thomas had sexually harassed her before a committee composed of white men. Thomas also testified before the same committee, denying Hill's accusations and claiming that he was the victim of a "high-tech lynching." The committee believed Thomas's testimony and disbelieved Hill's.

These hearings were a watershed event in shaping the ideological composition of the U.S. Supreme Court as well as highlighting the significance of race and gender in U.S. politics.[6] Here I focus on the epistemological implications of the hearings. The optics surrounding the hearings provide a highly visible, public glimpse of what is often the private workings of epistemic power. In this case, the Senate Judiciary Committee drew upon ostensibly objective, established rules and ways of proceeding to weigh the merits of different stories. Yet the fact that the committee was comprised of wealthy white men provided a taken-for-granted frame for ascertaining truth. Individual senators may have held different opinions, yet they all participated in a homogeneous interpretive community that shared common experiences that accrued to them as powerful white men. The senators were comfortable judging the truthfulness of African American stories. This case stood out because a committee of white males judged the veracity of the testimony of two African Americans with similar biographies but who differed primarily by their gender. The committee was tasked with evaluating two different versions of the same events, in essence, deciding whose testimony held more authority for them. Because truth could not be determined by other means—there were no cell phones or hidden recording devices to capture the events on camera—the committee was asked to believe one narrative over the other. In this case, because Hill and Thomas were both African American, gender proved to be the significant factor.

These hearings showcase how epistemic power worked in one highly public and important venue to grant testimonial authority to one person's story at the expense of another's. And in this case, the stakes were high for both parties. They often are in any situation that aims to adjudicate different understandings of the same set of events. Whether interaction among students within classrooms or the more diffuse weighing of scholarly explanations in the practices of a scholarly discipline, less visible judges determine whose story is more believable. Testimonial authority organizes evaluation of scholarship itself, deeming certain topics worthy of consideration and leaving others unheard. The members of the Senate Judiciary Committee had names and faces and therefore could be held accountable for their assessments. In contrast, epistemic power within scholarly communities is more diffuse, with judgment itself rarely resting in any one judge or even a jury, but rather in the epistemological rules that bind community members together.

In this sense, the testimonial authority of any one individual within a given interpretive community reflects the interactions among its members. And community members in turn regulate their interactions within an epistemological framework of the agreed-upon rules. As interpretive communities, classrooms, courtrooms, and faculty meetings rely on similar processes. Testimonial authority within a given interpretive community rests on the ability of a person both to speak and to be heard (both Hill and Thomas spoke but were differently heard). But it also rests on interactions among the listeners who decide the degree to which the testimony put forward fits within the epistemological rules of the community (Thomas's version was a better fit than Hill's story). Intersecting power relations calibrate these interactions such that hierarchies of race, gender, sexuality, class, and citizenship empower some members both to speak and to be heard (the senators). Structured power relations also disempower others who remain differentially heard even when they speak; Hill and Thomas both testified, yet could their testimony be fully heard by the senators? In essence, testimonial authority rests within the epistemic power relations of a particular interpretive community to determine the rules of truth.

This case illustrates broader issues of how people who are harmed by the practices of racism, heteropatriarchy, capitalism, and nationalism struggle to tell their stories in public. The criticism that breaks through within structures of epistemic power constitutes a form of epistemic resistance, regardless of the merits of the content of such criticism. In essence, testimonial authority that challenges epistemological rules concerning who has the authority to testify and how their testimony fits within taken-for-granted knowledge is a form of epistemic resistance. Imagine how differently those hearings might have gone had Thomas and Hill both been white and privileged, or if Thomas was poor and Hill affluent. Yet as Hill's case suggests, when stories that criticize taken-for-granted knowledge do reach public venues, such stories are often ignored, disbelieved, or rewritten.[7]

Some scholars have interpreted this tendency to disbelieve the stories of subordinated individuals as a form of epistemic violence. Just as interpersonal and state-sanctioned violence underpin intersecting power relations by policing the borders of race, class, gender, sexuality, and similar forms of power, tactics of epistemic violence operate *within* interpretive communities to police the cherished ideas of any given group. As philosopher Kristie Dotson (2011) points out, epistemic violence operates through practices of silencing. Yet remaining silent does not signal consent; instead, it often results from being silenced. Because academics neither are equal in their ability to give testimony nor receive testimony in the same way, speaking from less powerless positions takes more skill and effort than speaking from the top. Anita Hill's experiences in the Senate confirmation hearings illustrate the difficulties of exercising testimonial authority in a situation where African American women had been silenced. Disbelieving Hill effectively silenced those who followed.

Dotson (2011) identifies the silencing strategies of testimonial quieting and testimonial smothering as forms of epistemic violence that are used to suppress the ideas of subordinated people. Both strategies illuminate how and why claiming testimonial authority is especially important for intersectionality as a resistant knowledge project. Testimonial quieting fundamentally silences less powerful people by ignoring what they have to say: "A speaker needs an audience to identify, or at least recognize, her as a knower in order to offer testimony. This kind of testimonial oppression has long been discussed in the work of women of color" (Dotson 2011, 242). This silencing certainly affects the face-to-face interactions of people within a given interpretive community. Numerous studies have documented the ways in which women students and faculty members are routinely ignored or their ideas dismissed in meetings. Yet this idea of testimonial quieting as a form of epistemic violence need not apply to face-to-face interaction. Interpretive communities that suppress ideas that criticize taken-for-granted norms also reinforce this form of silencing.

Testimonial smothering constitutes another silencing strategy of epistemic violence that is especially important for intersectionality. Testimonial smothering describes the internal self-censorship of people who understand that what they have to say may not be welcome. The interpretive community effectively smothers an idea before it is expressed. Within a face-to-face interpretive community, such smothering occurs when a person waters down her ideas to make them more palatable. If a Latina scholar who finds Gloria Anzaldúa's borderland analysis important assumes that her academic colleagues devalue her scholarly work, why should she continue to speak? The costs to individual scholars of repeatedly advancing arguments that one's colleagues either cannot or refuse to try to understand are exhausting. Moreover, it may not be worth the risk when confronted by individuals who wield inordinate testimonial authority over their subordinates. Self-censorship is often the cost of being heard at all.

The internal self-censorship of testimonial smothering has important consequences for members of dominant groups who lack exposure to alternative analyses that already lie within their group. For example, Gloria Anzaldúa's intellectual work is wide-ranging, cutting across many disciplines and using multiple languages and literary devices. Anzaldúa's published and unpublished work over thirty years illustrates a breadth and depth of analysis, with her poetry, prose, essays, and interviews constituting important foundational scholarship for intersectionality (Keating 2009a). Yet Anzaldúa remains less known outside Latino/a and women's studies, in part as a result of testimonial quieting that dismisses knowledge claims about her work and in part because of the testimonial smothering of individuals who fail to speak up. The outcome of such silencing is that each new generation must discover Anzaldúa anew.

Silencing and self-censorship go hand in hand—people who are repeatedly ignored quickly learn the protections of seeming acquiescence. Yet because ideas are not shared freely, these practices harm the quality of knowledge itself and foster ignorance among dominant group members concerning what subordinate group members actually think. Such communities "quiet" dissident voices and by doing so "smother" good ideas of their members.

Epistemic resistance occurs by rejecting these silencing strategies of testimonial quieting and smothering. The corpus of Kimberlé Crenshaw's work in developing intersectionality as a form of critical inquiry and praxis demonstrates multiple expressions of testimonial authority. Few scholars have been as diligent as philosopher Anna Carastathis in respecting Crenshaw's testimonial authority (Carastathis 2016). Rather than cherry-picking ideas from Crenshaw's work that best suited her preconceived notions of what she thought Crenshaw meant or said, Carastathis, through a close reading of Crenshaw's often-cited signature articles as well as her other scholarship, renders a careful and holistic interpretation of what Crenshaw actually said. Carastathis aims neither to celebrate or castigate Crenshaw's work, and certainly not to commodify it to boost her own career prospects. Instead, by taking Crenshaw's work seriously, she affirms Crenshaw's testimonial authority. So often scholars invoke the intellectual production of women of color such as Crenshaw without ever having read much of their work at all.[8]

Intellectual work, especially that of social theorists, often rests on a trajectory of scholarly inquiry, sometimes over a lifetime.[9] Academics who present themselves as knowing the work of a given scholar on the basis of a cursory reading of a small sample of work would be suspect. When it comes to the intellectual work of women of color and similarly subordinated groups, this treatment shows a disregard for our work. In the case of intersectionality's story, uncritically circulating the coining narrative silences and ignores Crenshaw's deepening theoretical understanding of intersectionality throughout her intellectual corpus. Instead, by ignoring Crenshaw's subsequent accomplishments, the coining narrative simply stops the clock. Decades' worth of intellectual activism disappears, thus suppressing the epistemic agency of many Black women and anointing Crenshaw as intersectionality's designated academic spokesperson. This is a stunning example of testimonial quieting—simply ignoring the historical record and letting it drop from sight to allow other issues to come to the forefront.

Crenshaw has been far from alone in contributing to intersectionality as a resistant knowledge project. But the breadth of her intellectual activism illustrates multiple forms of epistemic resistance. Crenshaw has continued to publish, working collaboratively with colleagues to produce material for the burgeoning field of critical race studies (Crenshaw et al. 1995) and to edit a special issue of a journal on intersectionality (Carbado et al. 2013). Crenshaw has also been active in advancing the ideas of intersectionality within domestic and global venues. In this regard, she also rejects the self-censorship of testimonial smothering. As a founding member of the Center for Intersectionality and Social Policy Studies at Columbia University, Crenshaw has been involved in building an interdisciplinary institute. The Center for Intersectionality is devoted to bringing intersectional analyses to theorizing about violence; such theorizing draws on social action for discovering intersectionality's questions, methods, and purpose (Collins and Bilge 2016, 50–51). Crenshaw's involvement resembles that of the intellectuals at the Frankfurt school of Critical Theory, who saw the need for an interdisciplinary institute to respond to the threats posed by European fascism, and that of members of the Birmingham school of cultural studies, who needed an institutional presence for critical analysis of postcolonial British national identity. Crenshaw's involvement in global human rights initiatives also speaks to the significance of theorizing in the context of praxis (Collins and Bilge 2016, 90). In this sense, by refusing to commodify her fame as the explorer who discovered intersectionality, Crenshaw rejects the impetus to reframe intersectionality as solely a product of academia.

Identity Politics and Standpoint Epistemology

As individuals, Anita Hill and Kimberlé Crenshaw relied on testimonial authority as a form of epistemic resistance. But when it comes to advancing intersectionality and similar resistant knowledge projects as collective endeavors, epistemic resistance is often a collective undertaking. Identity politics and standpoint epistemology constitute two important dimensions of epistemic resistance for subordinated groups. Identity politics valorizes the experiences of women, people of color, poor people, LGBTQ people, and similarly subordinated people as a source of epistemic agency. By claiming the authority of experience, standpoint epistemology defends the integrity of individuals and groups in interpreting their own experiences. Standpoint epistemology posits that experiences and creative social action provide distinctive angles of vision on racism, heteropatriarchy, and capitalist class relations for people who are differentially privileged and penalized within such systems. Given the significance of identity politics and standpoint epistemology in the epistemic authority of people of color, women, poor people, and new immigrant populations, understanding how criticisms of these practices undermine the epistemic resistance of subordinated groups is important. Overall, identity politics and standpoint epistemology increasingly came to be recast as flawed testimonial strategies (Collins 1998a, 201–228).

Women, Black people, and similarly subordinated groups routinely advance political claims in terms of the experiences that accompany negative identities. Yet experience as a way of knowing is routinely dismissed as mere opinion rather than informed testimony that illuminates the truths of being silenced and subordinated.[10] As I discuss in chapter 5, Black feminist thought rests on a deep-seated analysis of experience that has been essential to intersectionality. Misinterpreting the robust understanding of identity politics expressed within Black feminism by recasting these ideas as simple-minded (essentialized, and thereby lacking complexity) and self-serving (particularistic and lacking an appreciation of higher principles beyond one's own self-interest) not only misreads the intent of critical theorizing itself; it undercuts an important source of epistemic agency for individuals within oppressed groups. What sense does it make for a group that is oppressed by intersecting identity categories of race and gender to refuse to organize its political responses using the very categories that oppress it?[11]

Ironically, Crenshaw's 1991 signature article on intersectionality, the same article that has been claimed as a classic of intersectional literature, contains an extensive critical analysis of identity politics. In the article, titled "Mapping the Margins: Intersectionality, Identity Politics, and Violence Against Women of Color," Crenshaw offers an important, incisive analysis of identity politics, not to jettison them, but rather to suggest that interrogating the strengths and limitations of identity politics for social action by and on behalf of women of color would benefit from an intersectional analysis. Crenshaw was attentive to the needs of women of color as individuals as well as how those needs required *collective* agency within political projects. Crenshaw was also well aware of the robust framework of identity politics that the Combahee River Collective (1995) and others developed within Black feminism. In fact, her criticism suggested that the forms of identity politics that ignored women of color violated the identity politics of the Combahee River Collective by not being intersectional enough.

This contradiction—namely, claiming intersectionality yet rejecting the identity politics of the intellectual-activists who advanced the ideas of intersectionality—seemed to signal, "we want your theoretical ideas" (intersectionality), "but we don't want your identity politics" (its political implications).[12] Crenshaw's nuanced and critical analysis of group-based identity politics, one advanced by the same figure who is widely recognized as naming intersectionality itself, focused on the significance of collective identity for effective social action. Identity was an important site of intellectual engagement precisely because it was always under construction, as were the politics it engendered. Crenshaw was arguing for more inclusionary politics within group-based identity politics, not for identity politics as a form of exclusionary politics. Yet this was not the direction that subsequent academic discourse on identity politics took.[13]

Over time, identity politics became increasingly recast as an exclusionary, particularistic discourse that suppressed the subjectivity of the individual. Within epistemic norms of objectivity and nonpartisanship, this seemingly particularistic form of identity politics was harmful to the individuals who claimed it. Collective identities themselves became suspect, as did the collective identity politics they might engender. Recasting identity in this fashion overlooks antiracist and feminist politics that relied upon collective identity as a form of political mobilization. Intersectionality's emphasis on *identity* could then be criticized as problematic.

The issue here is not that the ideas of women of color and similarly subordinated groups were bankrupt, but rather that the people who initially advanced ideas of identity politics no longer controlled the narrative. The story of identity politics was no longer their story to tell. The shifting interpretations of identity and of identity politics illustrate the workings of epistemic power. The trends and patterns to deauthorize identity politics reflect the historically sedimented patterns of quieting and smothering that have upheld the dominant group's own identity politics. Ironically, dominant groups had long used identity politics and standpoint epistemology to advance what were in essence their particular interests. This usage drew little attention when it was masked by assumptions of universality. Yet these same strategies looked different within desegregated academic settings where everyone's expertise supposedly carried equal merit.

Yet losing testimonial authority over the term *identity politics* does not mean losing control of the ideas themselves. When it comes to its own identity politics, intersectionality must guard against replicating within its own discourse practices of testimonial quieting and smothering of epistemic power. Whatever it may be called, identity politics still has a place as a form of epistemic resistance. For example, Latina scholars have advanced a different criticism about the telling of intersectionality's story—namely, that it neglects the work of Gloria Anzaldúa and similar Latina thinkers. Recognizing the significance of Anzaldúa's ideas to many fields of study, as well as the rich contours of Anzaldúa's theorizing, Latina scholars in particular have exercised epistemic resistance by studying and advancing many of her signature ideas. While influenced by Anzaldúa, this scholarship has achieved a depth and breadth that both informs intersectionality and draws upon it. Chicana feminism has received considerable scholarly attention (Alarcón 1999; Arredondo et al. 2003; Blackwell 2011; Roth 2004), with contemporary Latina scholarship influenced by varying dimensions of Chicana theorizing (see, e.g., Garcia 1997; Moya 2001). Some scholars identify how Anzaldúa's ideas circulate as important philosophical constructs, for example, Anzaldúa's borderland/new mestiza framework and key ideas in phenomenology (Ortega 2001), and Chicana feminism and postmodernism (Moya 2001). I read this burgeoning intellectual production among Latina scholars as a form of collective identity politics that refuses self-censorship and silencing. Work like this suggests that democratizing the identity politics that already exist within intersectionality's borders is more productive than sanctioning identity politics itself.

Criticisms of standpoint epistemology reflect similar epistemic moves of avoiding direct confrontation with Black women, Latinas, indigenous women, and similar members of subordinated groups that have been prominent with intersectionality's genealogy. Yet wielding epistemic power here illustrates a different path of epistemic deflection. Standpoint epistemology rests on claiming the integrity of theorizing from one's own experiences. This means seeing one's own knowledge as situated within social contexts. For subordinated groups, intersecting systems of power organize those social contexts. In this sense, claiming a situated standpoint is also a form of epistemic resistance. Claiming situated standpoints, especially group-based standpoints, and theorizing from those social locations can be a form of empowerment for subordinated groups. Resistant knowledge projects illustrate this dimension of epistemic resistance. Yet situated standpoints are not a form of exclusionary identity politics. Rather, standpoint theories claim that bringing multiple standpoints to bear on what counts as truth can democratize the process of doing social theory. This is empowering for those who have been silenced within processes of theorizing. Within standpoint epistemology, the process of constructing truth is part of a dialogical relationship among subjects who are differently situated within interpretive communities (Stoetzler and Yuval-Davis 2002, 315).

Criticizing standpoint epistemology functions as a surrogate for criticizing unpopular and seemingly overly politicized knowledge claims. Criticisms of standpoint epistemology deflected attention away from how theorizing from situated standpoints served the interests of subordinated groups. Again, as was the case with identity politics, such criticisms avoided direct confrontation with African American women, Latinas, and women of color who were so central to intersectionality's inception. How do you criticize the ideas of a group of epistemic agents whose standpoints were so central to the formation of a field itself? At intersectionality's inception, it was obvious that the people who brought intersectionality to the forefront of academic consciousness were necessary participants. There would have been no intersectionality without them. Moreover, during intersectionality's academic incorporation, such direct attacks would mean that privileged academics would be open to counter-criticisms of their own group-based standpoints.

Instead of analyzing the ideas of the standpoints brought forth by subordinated groups—for example, the substance of Black feminism or Latina feminism—critics took aim at the integrity of the construct of a standpoint itself. The fundamental criticism of standpoint epistemology is that it is too particularistic and insufficiently universal. It could only produce multiple and partial perspectives on truth because it lacked mechanisms to correct for its own bias. Yet the purpose of standpoint epistemology was never to become a theory of truth. Rather, standpoint epistemology is a dimension of theorizing that recognizes the significance of power relations in producing knowledge. Significantly, intersectionality provided a space that could bring these separate resistant knowledge projects into closer alignment. Because the situated standpoints were not amenable to dominant group appropriation or control, the entire endeavor of having standpoints at all had to be discredited.

Women, people of color, and other social actors who bring the testimonial authority of experience (identity politics) or who cite resistant knowledge projects as providing viable epistemic alternatives to seemingly fair and impartial epistemic oppression (standpoint epistemology) face being silenced within established epistemic rules of conduct. In this sense, these individuals confront the challenge of exerting epistemic agency within intersectionality's communities of inquiry, communities that are far more heterogeneous across differences in power than they were prior to intersectionality's naming. Significantly, this diversity of community also means that people bring different sources of epistemic authority to the common project of intersectionality. This presents an important challenge for intersectionality in building inclusive interpretive communities across epistemic differences.

What explains these patterns? It's no secret that African American women, Latinas, and similar social actors have been central to intersectionality's story. Intersectionality broke through the traditional organization of epistemic power, arriving as a story that was told *by*, and not about, subordinated people. Within segregated settings, Black women, Latinas, and others could share their experiences, but they exercised minimal testimonial authority within wider society to explain or analyze their own experiences. Intersecting power relations of race, class, gender, sexuality, nationality, age, and ability fostered the views of people who were subordinated within such power relations as *objects* of knowledge for academic inquiry. Within intersectionality, these very same populations became *agents* of knowledge, offering expert testimony on their own lives and those of the people who had subordinated them. The content of their knowledge claims certainly threatened the status quo, but the process of challenging epistemic injustices was far more fundamental.

Within these newly desegregating settings, African American women and Latinas, among others, experience a formal equality of testimonial authority concerning their right to belong in the context of sedimented epistemic power relations that questioned their actual testimonial practices. Speaking from experience threatened epistemic norms, not just because the content was unflattering to elites, but more importantly, because doing so rejected the norms themselves. Discrediting the testimonial authority of historically subordinated groups could no longer be accomplished through tactics such as excluding them from educational opportunities, tracking them into less desirable jobs, or simply ignoring them. The Anita Hills of academia could not simply be disbelieved and summarily dismissed. Claiming testimonial authority by speaking from experience was far more difficult to discredit by using direct attacks on the interpretations of the experiences themselves. Everyone had experiences with racism, heteropatriarchy, capitalism, and nationalism; disputing the testimony of those brought new analyses of long-standing power relations to the forefront and was doomed to be a failing strategy. Assumptions of equity mean that all experiences with racism are equivalent. But as the flood of new perspectives on racism, heteropatriarchy, capitalism, and nationalism that rested on the testimonial authority of experiencing these systems from the bottom suggested, experiences may have been separate, but they were not equal.

Discrediting people of color as epistemic agents came less through attacks on their actual arguments (e.g., informed experience) and more through targeting the epistemic assumptions that underlay the process of legitimation. These epistemic attacks needed a continued commitment of equality, fairness, and objectivity to remain intact as a way of protecting the integrity of intellectual work. But they also aimed to erode the testimonial authority of subordinated people to analyze the social injustices examined within intersectional inquiry. Instead of saying, "We disagree with your intersectional arguments about racism," the polite response became, "We disagree with the foundations on which your arguments are premised. Your self-serving identity politics limit your ability to see beyond your own standpoint. Your testimonial authority that is grounded in experience lacks objectivity. How can you support the greater good of equality and fairness using these strategies? Therefore, because you do not play by our epistemic rules, why should we believe you?"

We seem to have come a long way from Anita Hill's experiences in exercising testimonial authority. But when it comes to intersectionality as a critical social theory in the making, is this really the case? Within academia, the task ahead for intersectionality's interpretive communities lies in applying these analyses of testimonial quieting and testimonial smothering to their own practices.[14] Intersectionality's trajectory within the academy resembles that of any resistant knowledge project that is deemed to be too threatening.[15] Epistemic resistance constitutes a worthwhile goal for intersectionality's critical theorizing, but what does this mean in practice? What are the processes that ground epistemic resistance itself? Epistemic resistance moves from being a theoretical construct, an aspirational goal for what should happen, by attending to the processes used to create knowledge. In this sense, methodology matters for intersectionality because it is a vehicle for producing intersectionality itself.

Why Methodology Matters for Intersectionality

Within academic settings, the role that epistemology plays in critical theorizing is often overshadowed by the emphasis placed on methodology. Each academic discipline has its own way of doing things, stressing the importance of adhering to academic conventions by following specific disciplinary rules. Conceptualizing research as a technical process ignores the significance of power relations in shaping research itself. Knowledge production is more than methodology, and methodology itself reflects the epistemological frameworks in which it is produced. Epistemic resistance makes the relationships of epistemology, methodology, and power relations more transparent.

In *Decolonizing Methodologies*, Linda Tuhiwai Smith (2012) describes the need to move beyond academic debates that criticize traditional research practices as well as criticisms by nonacademic actors who often reject scholarly research as irrelevant. Instead, Smith argues that her book "attempts to do something more than deconstructing Western scholarship simply by our own retelling, or by sharing indigenous horror stories about research. In a decolonizing framework, deconstruction is part of a much larger intent. Taking apart the story, revealing underlying texts, and giving voice to things that are often known intuitively does not help people to improve their current conditions. It provide[s] words, perhaps, an insight that explains certain experiences—but it does not prevent someone from dying" (2012, 3). Smith demands more from critical inquiry than mere criticism, questioning how useful a methodology may be to subordinated populations if it merely offers explanations of the existing social order that ignore important social problems. Research certainly matters for the careers of academics. By arguing that research should matter greatly for indigenous peoples for what they need in their own lives, Smith also criticizes methodologies that are used to study indigenous people but that take scant notice of the effects of knowledge.

Linda Tuhiwai Smith's call for decolonizing methodology requires thinking through the existing relationships between epistemic power, intersectional theorizing, and methodology. Methodology reflects the epistemological rules that govern scholarly inquiry. Because methodologies work within unexamined assumptions of epistemic power, standard approaches to methodology underemphasize the significance of power relations within intellectual inquiry. Instead, methodology is typically understood as an apolitical, objective approach or technique being taken in a particular study, or the reasoning for selecting a set of methods (Smith 2012, ix). Prevailing epistemic power places methodological concerns outside the boundaries of power relations. Within this logic, calls for decolonizing methodology are seen as calls to introduce a politicized bias into what is assumed to be a fair, objective, and apolitical endeavor.

Thus far in this book, I have argued that intersectionality is not just ideas, and to tell its story without attending to power relations misreads its purpose and undermines its practice. I have suggested instead that intersectionality is inherently a critical discourse, one whose origins reflect different theorizing processes that have important implications for methodology. Many scholars have raised a clarion call for resistant knowledge projects to decolonize knowledge, and Smith's focus on decolonizing methodologies brings significant theoretical insight to this endeavor. Moreover, one strength of Smith's analysis is that she suggests that while the tools of critical analysis may be apolitical, the ways in they are used are not. Metaphoric, heuristic, and paradigmatic thinking that have been so central to intersectionality's growth are standard critical thinking tools that can and have been used in many ways. The reasoning that informs the choice of methodology is the issue here, not the particular tools of methods of critical analysis.

One way of conceptualizing intersectionality is to see it as a methodology for decolonizing knowledge. If intersectionality can figure out a way to cultivate a democratic methodology within its own praxis, that would be radical. All knowledge produced within existing Western epistemologies becomes suspect precisely because the validity of such knowledge rests on exclusionary, nondemocratic methodologies. But again, it's not enough to simply criticize this situation. How would intersectionality go about generating new knowledge that would reflect inclusionary, democratic methodologies? Cultivating critical perspectives from a wide array of people and knowledge projects and figuring out methodological strategies for managing those heterogeneous perspectives is essential. In this endeavor, honing skills for informed dialogue not only constitutes an important intellectual challenge but also is a political necessity.

Working Dialogically Across Differences of Power

Dialogical engagement is a core construct not only for intersectionality but also for the organization of this book.[16] Rather than making an abstract case for dialogical engagement as a core premise of intersectionality, thus far I have taken a more pragmatic approach. I have situated intersectionality within a deeply textured critical theoretical landscape that highlights its multiple dialogues with disparate knowledge projects. Critical Theory, feminism, poststructuralism, liberation theory, critical race theory, British cultural studies, and decolonial knowledge projects all have distinctive understandings of the meaning of resistance. In this sense, these varying understandings of the meaning of critical analysis provide a rich set of ideas for intersectionality as a critical social theory in the making.

The organization of chapters thus far illustrates my epistemic commitment to dialogical engagement. I've been interested in mapping the many influences on intersectionality's understanding of the meaning of being critical. I've organized these dialogues by making an analytical distinction between critical theoretical knowledge projects that are inside the academy and resistant knowledge projects that transcend academic borders. Intersectionality in the academy encounters a conceptual landscape of theoretical projects that cannot be ignored because they are already assumed to be critical. Yet as I argue, such projects engage in epistemic gatekeeping concerning the meaning of critical theorizing as well as who gets to ask and answer that question. These projects wield epistemic power within academic settings in part because they are already assumed to be critical, and in part because of the stature of their advocates.

Considering the ways in which intersectionality is or might become a critical social theory requires casting a wide net for ideas and if available, knowledge projects that shed light on the meaning of critical analysis. Here intersectionality's conceptual landscape within academia provides much guidance. I've analyzed the critical dimensions of select broader philosophical and theoretical projects of Western social theory that are part of intersectionality's academic landscape. Some explicitly aim to be critical; others do not. Marxist social theory, the Critical Theory of the Frankfurt school, existentialism, liberation theory, and British cultural studies all have a critical impetus at their core. Other projects may carry the mantle of critical social theory, as in the case of postmodernism and poststructuralism, yet they might be more wedded to criticizing society than to reforming or transforming it. Despite this heterogeneity, knowledge projects such as these lend ideas to critical inquiry. Because intersectionality in the academy encounters these discourses, it can draw from a rich repository of ideas and reconfigure them for its own purposes.

Intersectionality also participates in broader social justice projects that are also part of its conceptual landscape. By including a chapter on resistant knowledge projects of race, gender, and colonialism, I question a core premise that social theorizing is primarily a Western academic endeavor. Resistant knowledge projects also have a presence within academia, but their inquiry and praxis are rarely confined to academia. For this reason, they may not be seen as sufficiently critical to merit the term *theory*, yet they are essential for intersectionality. These heuristic distinctions between critical inquiry that is already deemed to be a critical social theory and that which is not enabled me to explore varying understandings of the meaning of critical inquiry.

Intersectionality's understanding of the meaning of critical inquiry has also been informed by dialogues with and among the many resistant knowledge projects that transcend academic borders. This broader conceptual landscape contains a wide array of resistant knowledge projects that are closer to intersectionality than the ostensibly universal communities of inquiry of traditional disciplines. Often organized by people who experience domination, these knowledge traditions are often devoted to theorizing resistance with an eye toward catalyzing political action. These resistant knowledge projects concerning race, class, gender, sexuality, age, ability, ethnicity, and nation typically identify resisting oppression, domination, or social injustice as central to their critical engagement. Having varying historical and contemporary expressions, this constellation of knowledge projects is more eclectic. Some are exclusively found in the academy; others are not. Some straddle academic borders, thereby maintaining ties with academic and activist communities. Regardless of location, many have traditions of theorizing, yet the forms their theorizing takes are varied and many not be recognizable as theory. While not typically seen as sites of theorizing or as critical theories in their own right, these projects provide different lenses on the meaning of critical inquiry.

Summing up thus far, I have argued that, because intersectionality already has a broad albeit unrecognized context of discovery, finding ideas to develop intersectionality as a critical theory in the making is not a problem. The issue is not just how intersectionality will identify ideas that can be placed in dialogue with one another within its own practice, but also how intersectionality will manage dialogical engagement with other knowledge projects. Whether dialogical engagement among social theories and resistant knowledge projects, or among individuals within them, grappling with the contours of dialogical engagement is a fundamental methodological question that confronts intersectionality. It is especially important to craft a methodology that can incorporate multiple expressions of epistemic resistance within a broader context of epistemic power.

In essence, it's difficult to put new ideas into old epistemologies and methodologies with the expectation that the result will be more critical than before. To address Linda Tuhiwai Smith's (2012) call for decolonizing methodologies, dialogical engagement can be the glue that catalyzes both new knowledge and a new political praxis. Recognizing the breadth of intersectionality's current context of discovery is important for continuing to bring together an array of people, perspectives, and ideas needed for such dialogues. In some ways, intersectionality itself *is* a metaphor for interactions among disparate individuals, communities of inquiry, and knowledge projects. Yet dialogical engagement is not just a theoretical idea. It is also a methodological practice.

Working dialogically, however, always occurs across differences in power. Power relations shape all social relations, including the impetus to work dialogically. Even the most homogeneous communities contain considerable differences in power—those distinguishing the old from the young, women from men—the very categories of analysis that have been core to intersectionality itself. Naming the silencing strategies of epistemic violence within groups shows how epistemic power works in them. But these same strategies influence relationships *between* groups. Such tools illuminate the ways in which epistemology operates as a silent partner in research that facilitates both the power differentials and the practices they engender. That said, how might this idea of dialogical engagement generate methodological possibilities for intersectionality?

The Case of Abductive Analysis

Theoretically, dialogical engagement is commensurate with intersectionality's core theme of relationality.[17] Dialogical engagement may be a worthwhile goal, one with theoretical heft. But dialogical engagement is also an abstraction that often remains unspecified in practice. Practically, how might such relationships look? What does working dialogically mean for intersectionality's critical inquiry?

Here the idea of abductive analysis constitutes a useful framework for fleshing out the methodological contours of dialogical engagement.[18] Abductive analysis is a methodology that can inform both theoretical and empirical research. As an iterative methodology of working with multiple and often disparate sources of data, it doesn't require specific content, theories, or particular methods. Rather, within abductive analysis, inquiry constitutes a way of proceeding, of doing intellectual work within a set of critical assumptions concerning how it should be done. A common concern would lie at the center of a particular knowledge project, for example, in the case of intersectionality, understanding social inequality, intersecting power relations, and social change. An abductive approach does not decide on the front end which social theory is the best and then try to fit others into its framework. Instead, all social theories are in play and come into dialogue with one another and with the social theory in question in relation to their common object of investigation. Such theories do not compete for dominance in trying to be the best fit for explaining the topic. Instead, ongoing conversations should produce the best explanations.

Because abduction is a philosophical construct in its own right (Douven 2017), one way to see how abduction might work methodologically is to examine how its ideas influence already established research methodologies (Tavory and Timmermans 2014). Ethnographic methods within social science research provide a framework for seeing abduction in action. Specifically, ethnographic methodology that is informed by abduction sheds light on how social theories might be used differently within intersectionality.[19]

One common approach to ethnographic research is to advise researchers to enter a field of study without any preconceived theoretical frameworks. Through fieldwork, a researcher aims to observe and get a feel for the ideas and social organization of a particular social group from the perspective of members of that group. The researcher aims not to impose his or her theoretical frameworks on the people being studied, returning to social theories only after the field research is complete and the researcher is back in his or her home institution. This linear organization of theory—namely, using theoretical ideas *before* fieldwork in order to shape a study's guiding questions and paradigms, and *after* fieldwork is complete—effectively eliminates theorizing from the fieldwork itself. As a way to reduce bias, this process basically eliminates from the fieldwork site dialogical engagement between theory and data.

In contrast, abductive analysis in ethnographic research does not bracket theory from data gathered in the field, but rather includes theoretical analysis within actual fieldwork. A researcher can move back and forth between what he or she finds in the field and existing social theories while he or she is actually in the field (Tavory and Timmermans 2014). When the data in the field do not fit the theories, the researcher sets out in search of other theories, some of which may not seem to be relevant to the research project at all. This iterative process of moving among theories and data sparks new analyses while changing the course of the fieldwork as it progresses in the field. One need not wait until the end of fieldwork to test one's data against established theories. Theorizing itself emerges in the process of doing the fieldwork. There are certainly limitations to this approach—it matters who sets out to do fieldwork and for what purpose. But this approach also points to opportunities for researchers to have dialogues with people in the field about what they are "finding."

Abductive analysis is fundamentally a dialogical methodology that can accommodate several social theories and that, within an iterative process of working back and forth between theories and findings, may be especially useful for intersectional theorizing (Tavory and Timmermans 2014). Within abductive analysis, theory is never finished, but is a provisional pause or stopping point within an ongoing loop of experimental inquiry. Theorizing occurs within the recursive relationship between the questions, the evidence, and how useful the explanations (theories) are for the task at hand. In essence, abductive analysis is how we think—building questions from what we sense to be true from our partial perspectives, pausing to develop a "theory" or explanation of the social world around us, then testing that explanation through lived experience or by seeking out alternative explanations that in turn change our initial partial perspectives.[20] Within abductive analysis, knowledge is always provisional, waiting to be tested by the same community encountering new evidence or new problems or other phenomena that are the effect of their theorizing. Alternately, knowledge can be taken up by new communities of inquiry, who use the knowledge they inherit (or acquire) from others as part of their analysis. Within standard abductive analysis, the relational loop lies in an experimental method of asking useful questions, gathering evidence, and evaluating results. In this sense, it resembles standard scientific inquiry of experimental design.

Intersectionality's idea of dialogical engagement and the premises of abductive analysis as a methodological framework resemble one another. But in which ways might abductive analysis inform intersectionality as a form of *critical* inquiry? Here sociologist Dana Takagi's (2015) discussion of the methodological needs of critical ethnic studies sheds light on the critical dimensions of dialogical engagement and processes of abductive analysis. Takagi points out that critical ethnic studies sees itself as a transformative intellectual field that speaks to multiple publics, is grounded in collaboration, and is oriented toward social change. Takagi suggests that ethnic studies draw upon participatory action research (PAR) as an important form of ethnographic research and as a source of ideas for its critical methodology: "PAR is well known as a technique for working with communities to solve problems. But less well known is the embedded critique and rearticulation of conventional methods, buried, so to speak in the rules and steps—namely, iteration, reflection, and collaboration" (2015, 6). In this sense, Takagi uses PAR as a framework for conceptualizing broader methodological concerns within critical ethnic studies. Takagi is not proposing that PAR is the best method for critical ethnic studies. She suggests that PAR's implied critique and rearticulation of conventional methods is more in alignment with the critical mandate of this field.

Takagi identifies collaboration, iteration, and reflexivity as three interdependent principles of PAR that she sees as buried in the rules, but that, when excavated, constitute important defining principles of PAR itself. Collaboration (working dialogically) is central to PAR as a research design. The success of PAR relies on the successful collaboration among people who commit to a particular research project. Within ethnographic, community-based work, collaboration softens the hard barriers between researchers and their subjects that define conventional research designs. Rather, collaboration requires respecting the varying areas of expertise or specialized knowledges that people bring to the research process. This aspect of PAR speaks to the need to broaden the context of discovery within a research project. "A fundamental feature of PAR/AR is its adherence to democratic participation by people who are likely to be affected by the research. Research questions are defined by practical, real-world problems rather than drawn principally from academic literatures, though this does not mean questions are a-theoretical or irrelevant to academic literature. Research questions are co-constructed with others and reflect a democratic process of inquiry" (Takagi 2015, 6).

Defining and redefining research questions emerges from the iterative process of collaboration. Not only do people bring ideas that are new to others into the research project, but their questions and concerns are changed by the iterative processes of collaboration. This iterative process also influences the legitimation phase of research. PAR rejects binaries of active researchers who produce the theories, and passive providers of data who become evidence for those theories. Because research findings are co-constructed across the traditional differences in power that divide researchers and research subjects, a wider array of people participate in deciding how well the findings explain the situation at hand. Participants all actively contribute to constructing knowledge.

Reflexivity is a crucial element of PAR, which requires self-reflexivity from individuals. Rethinking one's own position and learning from others is part of the iterative process. But reflexivity is also built into the research design. Research may originate from any location—someone has to propose an initial plan of action—but the process of doing the research itself is not confined to mechanistically applying that initial plan. As Takagi points out, "PAR/AR uses the language of reflection to describe assessment by researcher and participants. Reflection in PAR/AR entertains expansive notion[s] of consciousness, unconscious beliefs, intersubjectivity, and dialogic interaction . . . All elements of the research process are open for reflection—measures and instruments, samples, data collection, and analysis are subject to reflection, fine tuning, assessment, as many times as necessary. Reflection is closely related to the interpretative and collaborative practices" (Takagi 2015). In practice, PAR is difficult to do, primarily because power relations generate conflict. And much conflict is hardwired into the very rules themselves that regulate epistemology, theories, and methodologies. These interdependent ideas flesh out the methodological implications of abductive analysis in ways that make it especially useful for critical projects generally and intersectionality in particular. PAR's guiding ideas of collaboration, iteration, and reflexivity provide methodological guidelines for working dialogically. Dialogical engagement works in theory, but its meaning is developed through its practices. Building democratic communities across differences in power remains challenging. Collaboration, iteration, and reflexivity within any community of inquiry must grapple with the effects of differences in power and how social inequalities shape internal group processes. The practices of epistemic oppression—for example, testimonial quieting and testimonial smothering—can operate even within the most motivated and critical group. Moreover, it may be no accident that PAR fell out of favor in the academy during the same period when the kind of epistemic power leveled at identity politics and standpoint epistemology emerged. The pressures to eschew collaborative scholarship and social action in favor of individual scholarly achievement within prevailing research designs remains strong.

In this context of power differentials, an abstract commitment to working dialogically is not a panacea. As Stoetzler and Yuval-Davis caution, "It would be very naive to assume that the understanding of what is 'actually possible,' feasible, affordable or a 'reasonable demand' in any particular society at any particular point in history is determined by a socially organized argumentative debate" (Stoetzler and Yuval-Davis 2002, 326–27). Instead, trying to communicate across differences puts teeth into dialogical engagement. For example, PAR may express a stated commitment to democratic participation within its research design, but without some sense of what it means in practice to collaborate across differences in power, it may be participatory in name only. Recognizing multiple points of view, some of which are obscured by power relations, some of which defy expression within an interpretive community that embraces a narrow epistemological framework, begins the kind of dialogical engagement that sparks epistemic resistance in a different place.

Neither the elegance of a theoretical argument nor the robustness of the evidence that is marshaled in its defense is sufficient in shaping a critical social theory. As Linda Tuhiwai Smith points out, "From the vantage point of the colonized, a position from which I write, and choose to privilege, the term 'research' is inextricably linked to European imperialism and colonization. . . . The ways in which scientific research is implicated in the worst excesses of colonialism remains a powerful remembered history for many of the world's colonized peoples. It is a history that still offends the deepest sense of our humanity" (2012, 1). Rather, the strength of a critical social theory also rests on the terms of its participation in processes of knowledge production as well as how its ideas and practices criticize prevailing power relations. There are no inherently "intersectional" methodologies or methods. But there are ways in which intersectionality's core premises, especially its premise of relationality, can influence methodological choices within intersectional scholarship. Intersectionality's entanglements with diverse knowledge projects, the cognitive architecture that its practitioners use when doing intersectionality, and the significance of power relations within and among communities of inquiry on intersectionality's praxis all contribute to intersectionality's methodological contours.

Intersectional Theorizing and Critical Self-Reflexivity

In a David and Goliath world regulated by dominant Western epistemologies and their concomitant methodologies, intersectionality cannot simply assume that it is playing by the same set of rules as everyone else. Critical theoretical projects resist and criticize not just the intellectual and political arrangements that accompany specific forms of domination, but also how dominant epistemologies make these structures of knowledge notoriously difficult to upend. At the same time, recognizing that communities of inquiry are organized by the testimonial practices of its members means that these epistemic relations are not preordained. They can go in multiple directions. This places epistemic agency in the hands of people who belong to a given community.

Whether intentional or not, coining narratives perform a form of epistemological gatekeeping that erases and sanitizes the radical potential of intersectionality's more unruly dimensions. By installing a more orderly, recognizable, and disciplined intersectionality that can safely fit within prevailing rules of epistemic power, such narratives enhance intersectionality's academic respectability. Yet such recognition comes with the cost of enhancing the testimonial authority of some epistemic agents at the expense of others. Some scholars want to claim the legitimacy of intersectionality as a recognized scholarly perspective while leaving behind the Black people, women, colonized subjects, poor people, stateless people, and similarly subordinated people whose social action created it. In its place, they wish to install a new narrative of intersectionality that privileges academic norms of objectivity and universality over the seeming particularity of intersectionality's ties to resistance. These efforts may be well-meaning, but they are ultimately shortsighted. Intersectionality does not aspire solely to be integrated into the pantheon of academic social theories, critical or otherwise. Its ties to resistant knowledge projects raise specific issues for intersectionality concerning the substance of its criticism of dominant knowledge and how methodologically critical it is for decolonizing knowledge. In this context, intersectionality's ability to tell its own story is a contested site of intersectional theorizing.

When it comes to developing intersectionality as critical social theory, it may be time to supplement intersectionality's accomplishments as a tool for criticizing social relations with more emphasis on developing its internal critical cognitive architecture. In the same way that critical race theory, feminist studies, and decolonial resistant knowledge projects engaged in dual forms of critical analysis—namely, criticisms of practices that were external to their discourse as well as criticisms of their internal practices—intersectionality's critical analysis may need a similarly complex critical eye. For intersectionality to deepen its critical theoretical dimensions, it needs to criticize not just the content of colonial knowledge but also its own taken-for-granted methodological assumptions that shape its critical theorizing.

Cultivating a dialogical methodology that is inclusive and democratic may be an important and perhaps essential dimension of intersectionality's cognitive architecture. A dialogical methodology can be used for critical analysis among interpretive communities—the case, for example, of dialogues among critical theories and resistant knowledge projects. In this book, I place a variety of disparate knowledge projects in dialogue. Doing so enables me to identify a range of ideas that expand intersectionality's context of discovery. But a dialogical methodology can also spark critical analysis within a given knowledge project. The kind of critical debates within Francophone social theory, British cultural studies, critical race studies, feminism, and decolonial studies illustrate the need for internal dialogues. One purpose of this book is to cultivate such internal dialogues *within* intersectionality. In this sense, in this book I do not just advocate in favor of a dialogical methodology in the abstract; rather, through my own methodological praxis, I explore how using a dialogical methodology might inform intersectional theorizing.[21]

For intersectionality to deepen its critical theoretical dimensions, it needs to cast a self-reflexive, critical eye on its own constructs, premises, and practices. Parts I and II of this book position intersectionality within a broad conceptual landscape that comprises established critical social theories as well as a pantheon of resistant knowledge projects. In parts III and IV, I take up questions of the internal dimensions of intersectionality's critical inquiry. In the remaining chapters, I explore important avenues of investigation for dialogical engagement among those who wish to deepen intersectionality's theoretical development. I present select puzzles that inform intersectionality's prospects as a critical social theory. As a stimulus for self-reflexivity within intersectionality, the following chapters are not proscriptive but rather are diagnostic.

PART III Theorizing Intersectionality

Social Action as a Way of Knowing

5

Intersectionality, Experience,
and Community

Intersectionality's critical theorizing faces the challenge of defining how it understands and uses the ideas that underpin its own practice. Experience is one such idea, and specifying how it is defined and used within intersectional inquiry constitutes one important goal. Competing perspectives on whether experience should count within social theorizing and, if so, the differential value granted the experiences of women, Black people, Latinas/os, poor people, LGBTQ people, and differently-abled people inform intersectionality's epistemological and methodological debates. Tools of epistemic resistance used by subordinated people—namely, testimonial authority, identity politics, and standpoint epistemology—all rest on implicit assumptions about the utility of experience for producing knowledge. In this context, developing a more robust understanding of experience within intersectionality, especially one grounded in the interaction of actions and ideas, might inform intersectionality's critical inquiry as well as its critical praxis.

Specifying how social structure is defined and used within intersectional inquiry constitutes a second challenge for intersectionality's critical theorizing. Contemporary social theories increasingly focus on individuals and discourse, thereby moving away from structural analyses of collective behavior and group-based experiences. Here the concept of community provides an analytical framework for conceptualizing social structural contexts that inform group-based or collective social action.[1]

In this chapter, I investigate how developing more robust analyses of experience and community might shed light on social action as a way of knowing. I do so by examining how these ideas appear in two very different discourses. Placing Black feminist thought and American pragmatism in dialogue provides distinctive angles of vision on conceptions of experience and community. The ideas of experience and community have been fundamental to Black feminist praxis, and Black feminist thought provides an important perspective on how these ideas work within resistant knowledge projects. Because the ideas of social interaction, community, and democracy have been important within American pragmatism, this specialization within the field of philosophy also provides an important perspective on these concepts. Together, these discourses suggest some important avenues of investigation for theorizing intersectionality.[2]

Intersectionality is in a position to learn from both discourses. Black feminist thought and American pragmatism suggest that experience constitutes a way both of understanding the social world and of taking action within it. Both discourses also provide distinctive perspectives on the construct of community as a way of understanding social structures and collective behavior. Intersectional theorizing requires critical self-reflexivity concerning these connections among experience, community, and social action.

Black Feminist Thought in Social Context

Intellectual histories provide much-needed discussions of the ideas of African American women thinkers, yet those ideas need to be placed in social, political, and intellectual context.[3] Rather than viewing Black feminist thought as a static set of ideas that sprang from the minds of a few African

American women intellectual-activists, situating Black feminist thought within the social context of intersecting power relations better captures the meaning of experience and community for social action. African American feminist thinkers worked within specific social contexts that not only shaped what they could see and what they could do, but also what they could imagine. The changing contours of Black feminist thought over time reflect ongoing efforts to solve the specific problems that African American women experienced within broader power relations of racism, heteropatriarchy, capitalism, and nationalism.

African American women have long advanced alternative explanations about the complex nature of oppression in the United States as well as American democracy's potential in fostering freedom (Bay et al. 2015). Because Black women experienced race/class domination in gender-specific ways, they were better positioned to see how gender and sexuality affected their lives within intersecting oppressions of racism and capitalism. In this context, racism, capitalism, and heteropatriarchy have long been salient forms of domination for African American women (Marable 1983a). Black women's deepening analysis of intersectionality was catalyzed by the specific configurations of these power relations both within U.S. society as well as within segregated African American communities.

As an intellectual arm of Black feminism, Black feminist thought constitutes an important case for studying how subordinated groups empower themselves within contexts of domination. African American women developed Black feminist thought as a resistant knowledge project that reflected Black women's political interests (Collins 2000). The ideas of intersectionality have been central to that knowledge project. Within Black feminism, understanding experiences with social injustices within U.S. society catalyzed intersectional analyses within Black feminism. Resistant knowledge projects also require social actions, both as sources of ideas and as ways of evaluating resistance itself. Experiences of trying to resist social injustices of race, class, gender, sexuality, and nation (citizenship) also stimulated ideas about how a flexible political solidarity was also important for resistance. Within Black feminist thought, ideas and actions are neither elevated one above the other, nor conflated into each other. Rather, intellectual production and political action are held as distinctive yet interdependent entities. The construct of intellectual activism captures this creative tension between thinking and doing (Collins 2013).[4]

Intersectionality and flexible solidarity constitute two interdependent dimensions of Black feminist thought that reflect this recursive relationship between ideas and action within intellectual activism. Intersectionality and flexible solidarity both draw meaning from and shape social action within a specific social context. In the case of Black feminist thought, Black women take action on behalf of and within African American communities. The contours of both also change in response to new political and intellectual realities. Each deepens over time in response to new constraints and opportunities of dominance and resistance.

Locating Intersectionality: Ida B. Wells-Barnett's Anti-Lynching Campaign

Ida B. Wells-Barnett's (1862–1931) anti-lynching crusade illustrates how African American women's intellectual activism reflects social action as a way of knowing. In this case, Wells-Barnett took informed social action in response to her experiences with the important social problem of lynching, and her actions in turn shaped her intersectional analysis of violence.[5] Ida Wells-Barnett has been remembered primarily as an activist, an irritant in the side of William E. B. Du Bois and other African American leaders. Without doubt, Wells-Barnett was an activist, and an extremely effective one for her times. During her adult life, she participated in an impressive constellation of antiracism and women's rights initiatives. Wells-Barnett also used her journalistic career, her speeches, her leadership in political organizations, her position papers, and her pamphlets to advance innovative analyses concerning the connections between African American disempowerment and the need for social justice. Because her activism and her intellectual work were so interconnected, she offers a window into the workings of Black women's intellectual activism.[6]

Wells-Barnett is best known for her decades long anti-lynching crusade that began in 1892 after three successful managers of a grocery business were lynched in an African American neighborhood just outside Memphis. Wells knew all three men, and she suspected that white citizens of Memphis resented these Black businessmen because their store successfully competed with a white-owned store in the same neighborhood. This painful personal experience with lynching was a turning point in her life. Expressing outrage that "the city of Memphis has demonstrated that neither character nor standing avails the Negro if he dares to protect himself against the white man or become his rival," Wells urged the African American citizens of Memphis to "save our money and leave a town that will neither protect our lives and property, nor give us a fair trial in the courts, when accused by white persons" (Duster 1970).

In response to the lynching of her neighbors, Wells-Barnett wrote a hard-hitting editorial that criticized the prevailing wisdom about lynching. Wells-Barnett claimed that not only were African American men often falsely accused of rape, but that because some white women were attracted to Black men, some sexual relations that did occur between African American men and white women were consensual. Fortunately, Wells-Barnett was out of town when this inflammatory editorial appeared, or she too might have been lynched. Instead, the white people of Memphis burned down the building housing the African American newspaper that published Wells-Barnett's editorial and threatened her life if she ever returned to Memphis. These specific events marked the beginning of Ida Wells-Barnett's impressive over twenty-year crusade against lynching that took the form of touring to speaking events, publishing editorials, preparing pamphlets, organizing community services, and participating in women's and civil rights groups.

In her writings, Wells-Barnett provides names, dates, and graphic details of the horrible violence inflicted upon African Americans through lynching. She also details the pain of both those who are lynched and the loved ones left behind. Her pamphlet "Mob Rule in New Orleans" provides an especially chilling example of Wells-Barnett's journalistic skills; in it she describes three days of violence that highlights its effects on African American victims (Wells-Barnett 2002, 153–203). Significantly, the precipitating incident concerned police officers who approached two African American men sitting on a doorstep engaged in conversation. The police, for no apparent reason, decided to arrest them. The men resisted, an altercation ensued, and one of the police officers was hurt. Rather than recounting the incident from the point of view of the police, Wells-Barnett instead envisions how this event looked to Charles, one of the Black men profiled by the New Orleans police:

> In any law-abiding community Charles would have been justified in delivering himself up immediately to the properly constituted authorities and asking [for] a trial by a jury of his peers. He could have been certain that in resisting an unwarranted arrest he had a right to defend his life, even to the point of taking one in that defense, but Charles knew that his arrest in New Orleans, even for defending his life, meant nothing short of a long term in the penitentiary, and still more probable death by lynching at the hands of a cowardly mob. (Wells-Barnett 2002, 158)

In this context, Charles not only ran from the police, he did the unthink-able of fighting back. Charles's resistance to what he perceived as police ha-rassment incensed the white residents of New Orleans such that, "unable to vent its vindictiveness and bloodthirsty vengeance upon Charles, the mob turned its attention to other colored men who happened to get in the path of its fury. Even colored women, as has happened many times before, were assaulted and beaten and killed by the brutal hoodlums who thronged the streets" (164). Wells-Barnett tells story after story of unsuspecting African Americans who were pulled from trolley cars, chased down streets, and murdered while they slept in their homes. Their only crime was being Afri-can American and having the misfortune of getting in the path of mob fury. "Mob Rule in New Orleans" is especially eye-opening because it refuses to depict African Americans as passively awaiting their fate as victims of mob rule, praying for salvation. Instead, it records the range of African American reactions to mob violence. Most Black people ran, hid, and tried to get away. Others, like Charles, fought back. Charles was eventually killed in a hail of bullets, but even in reporting on his death, Wells-Barnett refuses to portray Charles solely as a victim.

Wells-Barnett's analysis of lynching illustrates the power of testimonial authority to highlight the point of view of subordinated people. But it also lays a foundation for intersectionality's guiding premises of using race, sexu-ality, class, and gender as intersecting systems of power to solve social prob-lems (see figure 1.1 in chapter 1). In this regard, her work foreshadows Black feminist intersectional analyses that emphasize how social structures inter-lock to shape particular social outcomes (Combahee River Collective 1995). Wells-Barnett suggests that the crime of lynching grew less from the indi-vidual psyches of individuals in lynch mobs and more from structural power relations of race, class, nation, gender, and sexuality that legitimated the col-lective behavior of the lynch mob. Through her intellectual activism, Wells-Barnett lays a foundation for an intersectional analysis of state-sanctioned violence that Angela Y. Davis (1978; see also Crenshaw 1991; Richie 2012), Kimberlé Crenshaw (1991; see also Davis 1978; Richie 2012), Beth Ritchie (2012), and others take up much later.

Wells-Barnett's work on lynching lays the foundation for subsequent in-tersectional analyses of gendered violence. As many authors within modern Black feminism point out, the struggle to control African American women's bodies and sexuality has been a major part of intersecting power relations throughout the African Diaspora (Collins 2004). Wells-Barnett's work on lynching advances our understanding of Black sexual politics, but not through a focus on African American women. Instead, Wells-Barnett analyzes how the combination of racism, heteropatriarchy, and class produced controlling images of Black masculinity that were essential to controlling Black men's bodies and sexuality. Wells-Barnett produced a Black feminist analysis of Black masculinity, one that juxtaposed white masculinity as the source of lynching against the humanity of Black men as the victims of this crime. Wells-Barnett does not advance an intersectional analysis of the connections among Black masculinity and Black femininity, but she does lay a foundation for a Black sexual politics that draws upon an intersectional sensibility.

Wells-Barnett's work on lynching also posits a provocative intersectional analysis that incorporated sexuality. What is unique about Wells-Barnett's analysis is that she not only introduced a much-needed gender analysis into analyses of violence, she incorporated the controversial theme of interracial sexuality. Wells-Barnett's ideas generated considerable controversy when she dared to claim that many of the sexual liaisons between white women and Black men were in fact consensual, and most certainly were not rape. Moreover, she indicted white men as the actual perpetrators of crimes of sexual violence against African American men via lynching and African American women via rape. Consider how her comments in "Southern Horrors" concerning the contradictions of laws forbidding interracial marriage place blame on White male behavior and power: "The miscegenation laws of the South only operate against the legitimate union of the races: they leave the white man free to seduce all the colored girls he can, but is [sic] death to the colored man who yields to the force and advances of a similar attraction in white women. White men lynch the offending Afro-American, not because he is a despoiler of virtue, but because he succumbs to the smiles of white women" (Wells-Barnett 2002, 31).

In this controversial analysis, she reveals how ideas about gender difference—the seeming passivity of women and the aggressiveness of men—are in fact deeply racialized constructs. Gender had a racial face, whereby African American women, African American men, white women, and white men occupied distinct race/gender categories within an overarching social structure of prescribed places. Interracial sexual liaisons violated that space. In this regard, Wells-Barnett foreshadowed contemporary work on the connections between William E. B. Du Bois's famous "color line" and ideas about sexuality and its role in the construction of gender during this same period (Somerville 2000).

In explaining lynching, Wells-Barnett also incorporates an implicit critique of capitalism and the social class politics it engenders. Mob rule went on for several days, but as Wells-Barnett points out, it began to wind down when the "better element of white citizens" realized its financial costs to New Orleans. Wells-Barnett offers a biting criticism of the relation between affluent white citizens who benefitted financially from Black poverty, and poor and working-class white citizens who comprised the mob. As she points out, "the killing of a few Negroes" by mobs is not especially important in Louisiana. But when the "reign of mob law exerts a depressing influence upon the stock market and city securities begin to show unsteady standing in money centers, then the strong arm of the good white people of the South asserts itself and order is quickly brought out of chaos" (Wells-Barnett 2002, 168). That was the case for New Orleans: the "better elements of white citizens" became involved in suppressing the riot "for the purpose of saving the city's credit" (168).

Wells-Barnett was aware of the hegemonic politics of social class among the "good white people of the South" whereby affluent white people benefitted from the disadvantage of poor white people. She also experienced how the color line that separated "white citizens" across social classes from their impoverished and disenfranchised Black counterparts sustained social inequality. But she was also aware of how these broader politics of social class in the U.S. influenced class relations within African American communities. Wells-Barnett's experiences of growing up in the South in the aftermath of slavery showed her the trials of African American poverty and working-class life. Wells-Barnett was not born into the fledgling Black middle class, but rather moved into it through education. Her experiences with upward social class mobility provided economic experiences that differed dramatically from those of many of her counterparts. Wells-Barnett's participation in established African American and women's organizations, as well as her newfound middle-class lifestyle, often generated friction, compromise, and considerable insight. Wells-Barnett may have spent much of her adult life *in* the Black middle class, but she was not *of* the Black middle class.

Ida Wells-Barnett's anti-lynching crusade recognizes how knowledge itself can constitute a form of epistemic oppression (Dotson 2014). Wells-Barnett's nascent intersectional analyses challenged the taken-for-granted representations of African Americans that make lynching intelligible for the "good white people" of the South and the North. Before Wells-Barnett's intervention, the historical record on lynching advanced the thesis that African American men deserved to be lynched, primarily because their allegedly animal-like nature compelled them to lust after white women. The end of slavery, which ended white supervision, seemingly loosened these natural violent tendencies among Black men. In essence, slavery had been good for Black men because it suppressed their seemingly natural violent nature. Wells-Barnett directly refuted controlling images that pathologized African American men as being lazy, unintelligent, sexually wanton, and violent. The pressing need to address lynching meant that she focused on men, yet Wells-Barnett's approach suggests a similar set of controlling images for African American women. Such images were not simply benign representations but pivotal in sustaining power relations (Collins 2000, 2018).

Moreover, Wells-Barnett did not simply criticize this dominant story of white supremacy and black inferiority; she developed an alternative narrative. Using her own experiences, she used race, gender, sexuality, and class to explain the same set of social conditions. Because Wells-Barnett's parents were enslaved and she herself was born into slavery, she could draw upon the experiences of her family and community to refute derogatory, controlling images of African Americans. Wells-Barnett is quite clear that African Americans needed to reject this dominant narrative. In the preface to her pamphlet "Southern Horrors," she notes: "The Afro-American is not a bestial race. If this work can contribute in any way toward proving this, and at the same time arouse the conscience of the American people to a demand for justice to every citizen, and punishment by law for the lawless, I shall feel I have done my race a service. Other considerations are of minor importance" (Wells-Barnett 2002, 26). Wells-Barnett took a huge risk in challenging this conventional racial wisdom of Black male bestiality lurking just below the surface of normality—she was, after all, threatened with death if she ever returned to Memphis. Thus, her caveat that "other considerations are of minor importance" should be read against the context of late nineteenth-century politics in the U.S. South, where speaking out could be extremely dangerous.

Methodologically, *how* Wells-Barnett constructed her refutation of the historical record on lynching is just as important as the content of her arguments criticizing the dominant discourse. Wells-Barnett's brilliance lay in her decision to use the data collected by white journalists to challenge the prevailing wisdom on lynching. Wells-Barnett assembled an array of newspaper articles on lynching that had been published within the mainstream white press. Analyzing the themes in these articles, she argued that what seemed to be isolated events were in fact part of a larger pattern of lawlessness. Her data were difficult to refute because she used the very same data that were reported in the mainstream press, yet recontextualized it in response to the concerns of African Americans. In a reversal of traditional ethnography, in which academics rely on native informants for data to fit their theories, Wells-Barnett turned the white press into her "native informants." They provided the data for her theory of lynching as a form of state-sanctioned violence that included ideas about race, gender, sexuality, class, and citizenship. In this sense, Wells-Barnett claimed significant testimonial authority within the constraints of epistemic power that rested on unquestioned assumptions concerning race, gender, sexuality, and class (Dotson 2011). In the context of her times, her methodology constituted epistemic resistance (Kidd, Medina, and Pohlhaus 2017).

Wells-Barnett's work on lynching illustrates how Black feminist epistemology conceptualizes and values experience as part of epistemic resistance (Collins 2000, 251–271). Whether testifying on one's own behalf or, as the case of Wells-Barnett suggested, believing the testimony of others, lived experience is valued in analyzing the meaning of events. Such theorizing argues that, for African Americans and similarly oppressed people, looking to one's own experiences and those of similarly situated others is of value in resisting oppression. During Wells-Barnett's era, the harm done to the individual African American men, women, and children who were lynched and the harm done to African Americans as a collectivity who lived with the threat of violence served as daily reminders that victims of lynching needed to be believed and that the interpretations of African Americans about their own experiences were of special value. Valorizing lived experiences requires centering on the needs of a particular group harmed by social injustice and finding a prominent place for analyses advanced by victims within the narratives or stories that are told about or by that group.

This understanding of experience informs Black feminist theoretical analysis generally and the idea of intersectionality in particular. Wells-Barnett generated intersectional analyses about lynching because her intellectual activism remained grounded in the experiences of African American men and women. She disbelieved abstract theories about lynching that evaluated lynching as an appropriate punishment for Black male rapists, which were advanced by the "white citizens." The necessity of trying to solve the important social problem of violence brought an urgency and commitment to intellectual activism that she maintained over two decades. The corpus of Wells-Barnett's intellectual and activist endeavors demonstrates a synergistic relationship between her ideas and activism, specifically, her analysis of lynching as a form of state-sanctioned violence and her experiences as an African American woman facing the vulnerabilities of living with this threat of terrorism. Her activism was informed by ideas, and these same facts and new interpretations of old realities enabled her to chart an activist course for herself.

Necessity need not be just for oneself. Within contemporary Western feminist sensibilities that stress personal advocacy on one's own behalf as a hallmark of feminism, Wells-Barnett's support for women's suffrage ostensibly qualifies her as a "feminist." In contrast, because it is overly focused on men, Wells-Barnett's anti-lynching crusade seems more appropriate for African American social and political thought. Wells-Barnett recognized that, under the conditions of harsh racial segregation that she faced, the fate of African Americans remained just as closely tied—if not more so—to the interests of African American men as to those of white women. Because her work on lynching examines a form of sexual violence that fell more heavily on African American men than women, her advocacy can be seen as supporting a male-defined ethos of political struggle wherein the concerns of African American men take precedent over those of African American women. Yet this would be a misreading of Wells-Barnett's activism.

Wells-Barnett's anti-lynching campaign illustrates how the impetus for African American women's political activism often reflects a response to a social problem that affects African Americans as a community, for example, the concern for one's children, a loved one, and neighbors in a geographic community. But this same concern can also be generalized to African Americans as an imagined community, one that experiences a shared fate, even though its members may never meet face-to-face (Anderson 1983). The intellectual activism of Ida Wells-Barnett encompasses both dimensions of community.

Ida B. Wells-Barnett's intellectual activism also points toward the significance of Black women's community work within Black feminist thought (Collins 2006, 123–160). Community work constitutes a form of reproductive labor that was designed to (1) ensure the physical survival of African American children and youth; (2) build Black identities that would protect African Americans from the attacks of white supremacy; (3) uphold viable African American families, organizations, and other institutions of Black civil society; and (4) transform schools, job settings, government agencies, and other important social institutions. In the case of Wells-Barnett's anti-lynching campaign, community work involved strategies that opposed state-sanctioned murders of African Americans as a people or imagined community.

Locating Flexible Solidarity: Black Women's Community Work

The changing contours of community work within African American communities informs Black women's politics and Black feminist thought (Collins 2006, 123–160). Prior to mid-twentieth-century social movements, community work occurred primarily within racially segregated communities and encompassed both protest and survival politics, with survival taking the lion's share of resources.[7] For African American men and women, working for social change constituted an important path to personal dignity and individual freedom. African Americans confronted a long list of social problems that, while originating with enslavement, have had deeply entrenched, intergenerational effects. For example, mass incarceration may seem to be a new social problem, but locking up Black youth was a mechanism of control under slavery, under Jim Crow, and is codified into the thirteenth amendment of the U.S. Constitution (M. Alexander 2010). Yet in the face of assaults on Black men, the burden of community work has fallen more heavily on Black women.

Within Black civil society or the Black community, many women exerted leadership that was designed to help individuals within their communities survive, grow, and reject the practices of anti-Black racism.[8] Black women's motherwork, an important site of Black women's community work, illustrates the multilayered texture of Black women's politics (James 1993; Story 2014). Although motherwork resembles care work, especially understandings of care work as a set of principles for democratic participation (see, e.g., Tronto 2013), because motherwork is deeply embedded within the survival politics of African American communities, it has been infused with broader political intent. Whether they had biological children or not, the work that Black women did in caring for their communities constituted an important site that simultaneously *politicized* African American women and served for many as an expression of political activism.

In a world that devalues Black lives, to defend the lives of Black youth and aim to give those lives hope is an act of radical resistance. In this sense, contemporary expressions of motherwork that invoke these deep cultural roots bring a more politicized notion of care to political projects. Then and now, motherwork takes diverse forms. Ella Baker had no children of her own, but her work with youth during the Civil Rights movement in the 1950s and 1960s underpins her radical democratic vision (Ransby 2003). In the 1960s and 1970s, the young Black women of the Black Panther Party for Self-Defense engaged in a variety of projects that supported Black youth as a way of developing their communities (Farmer 2017). Currently, local grassroots activists who struggle for clean water, better schools, job training, and more responsive police and social services for their neighborhoods take action because they care for and care about their communities. Certainly, Black men have performed this kind of reproductive labor, but in the face of public policies of mass incarceration that remove so many men from African

American communities, motherwork continues to fall disproportionately on Black women.

In this sense, Black civil society provided an important arena for Black women's political activism as well as their consciousness concerning the political. Whether a moral, ethical tradition that encouraged African American women to relinquish the so-called special interests of issues as women for the greater good of the overarching community, or a survival politics that meant that if Black women didn't do it, it simply didn't get done, Black women's reproductive labor was placed in service to Black communities. Within this interpretive framework, fighting on behalf of freedom and social justice for the entire Black community and for a more inclusive society based on social justice was, in effect, fighting for one's own personal freedom. The two could not be easily separated.

Working within Black organizations both sensitized African American women to inequalities of gender and sexuality within Black communities and provided a venue for political action in response to gendered inequalities. For example, using their power as women, many African American women advocated for women's issues within their churches (Gilkes 2001; Higginbotham 1993). Others questioned interpretations of Christian scripture on the rightful place of women, offering alternative analyses of how Black women might use scripture to empower themselves (Grant 1989), of womanist ethics (Cannon 1988), and of the role of sexuality within Black churches (Douglas 1999). Many African American women developed a feminist consciousness in the context of working for African American civil rights (Anderson-Bricker 1999; Murray 1970b; Scanlon 2016). As the case of Ida Wells-Barnett suggests, gendered analyses were inherently tied to racial analyses.

Under conditions of racial segregation, Black women certainly encountered gender discrimination in their jobs as domestic workers as well as unwelcome sexual harassment in public places. Many experienced sexual assault, making public white space a space of danger. Under these conditions of second-class citizenship, Black communities provided places of respite from the advances of white men and the surveillance of white women. Yet Black women who lived in racially segregated neighborhoods also experienced so-called women's issues via daily interactions within organizations that formed the public sphere of African American communities. But there, as members of African American communities, they not only had obligations to uphold rigid views of Black solidarity but also opportunities to shape its meaning. Despite the need for Black solidarity in the face of an ongoing racial threat, African American women within African American civil society often questioned solidarity politics that demanded their loyalty without offering support for the specific issues that they encountered.

Working within the strictures of Black women's community work generated skills of flexible solidarity that simultaneously accepted and challenged male-defined understandings of Black solidarity. In racially segregated settings where the threat of violence was omnipresent, Black women's community work required a commitment to Black solidarity as a core feature of political engagement. Such solidarity occurred both *within* and *on behalf of* African American communities. Without solidarity among African Americans, political struggles to upend racial domination were doomed. Yet for Black women, an unquestioned solidarity could be neither inherently desirable nor effective when it rested on a male-dominated, intergenerational gender hierarchy. Such solidarity was rigid, and often backed up by religious theology or tradition, and it created roadblocks for effective political action. Black women saw the need for Black solidarity, yet they calibrated their specific ideas and actions in flexible ways that better suited actual political projects. Solidarity was not an essentialist category, a bundle of rules that was blindly applied across time and space.

Despite the united front presented to the public, within African American communities, Black women often questioned a solidarity politics that demanded their loyalty to Black men who not only failed to understand the social problems that Black women encountered, but also were often implicated in creating them. Rather than rejecting solidarity politics outright, they chose to massage that solidarity, sometimes working with Black men and other times opposing them.[9] This flexible understanding of political solidarity enabled Black women to work to mold social action to the challenges at hand. Flexibility that was tethered to principled social action did not mean that such women were uncritically obedient, but rather that Black women made strategic choices about what made most sense in response to the social problems they faced.

The reemergence of a vibrant Black feminism in the early twenty-first century, and its growing transnational ties with Black diasporic feminism, human rights initiatives, and similar social justice initiatives, points to the continuities and changes concerning intersectionality and flexible solidarity within Black feminism. Contemporary Black feminism explicitly self-defines in intersectional terms and increasingly draws upon flexible solidarity as a political strategy within its organizational practices. These concepts of intersectionality and flexible solidarity appear in both physical and digital space. For example, essays in *The Intersectional Internet: Race, Sex, Class, and Culture Online* (Noble and Tynes 2016) detail the varying ways that new communications technologies have enabled the conversations that formerly occurred in geographic communities to go online. Some Black women intellectual-activists have managed to find a way to straddle community building within academic venues and online, using digital space for blogs that catalyze discussions among African American women within the imagined communities of the blogosphere. Catherine Knight Steele's (2016) research on Black women and resistance discourse online and the Crunk Feminist Collective's blogs (Steele 2016; Cooper, Morris, and Boylorn 2017) are exemplary in this regard. In other cases, a new generation of Black feminists has not only embraced but has deepened understandings of intersectionality and flexible solidarity in its political projects (Carruthers 2018).

These ideas of flexible solidarity and intersectionality continue to challenge understandings of solidarity within African American communities and to inform broader social justice initiatives. In her aptly titled book *Making All Black Lives Matter: Reimagining Freedom in the 21st Century*, historian Barbara Ransby (2018) examines the intellectual and political meaning of the Black Lives Matter (BLM) movement. Significantly, Ransby identifies Black feminist politics as the "ideological bedrock of the movement" (2). The movement addresses the racism and violence experienced by LGBTQ communities. The BLM movement has grown into an international Movement for Black Lives initiative. Building on the foundation provided by the BLM movement, this broader Movement for Black Lives also rests on the heterogeneous particularity of local projects and bundles the concerns of many different local projects under one broad umbrella. Both movements illustrate the challenges of both using flexible solidarity *within* a particular political community and fostering solidarity among/across political communities. The initial BLM movement illustrates continuity with historical expressions of intersectionality and flexible solidarity of Black women's community work. Yet it simultaneously aimed to deepen both constructs by widening the circle of Black lives to incorporate Black trans* people and others who face discrimination both within and outside Black communities. The experiences of people were no longer to be excluded from, as Cathy Cohen (1999) describes it, "the boundaries of blackness," but rather were central to Black politics itself. In essence, by using an intersectional analysis, this approach expanded the meaning of Black community. Via these activities, the BLM movement emphasized the synergy of ideas and action both within its counternarrative concerning intersectional power relations and through its counter-politics grounded in collective action. Stated differently, its approach to solving social problems drew upon intersectionality as an analytical tool for analyzing intersecting power relations, and flexible solidarity as a necessary strategy for political action.

American Pragmatism and Creative Social Action

In discussing the significance of pragmatism for contemporary social theory, German social theorist Hans Joas identifies the ideas that lie at the heart of American pragmatism: "It is my contention that American pragmatism is characterized by its understanding of human action as *creative* action. The understanding of creativity contained in pragmatism is specific in the sense that pragmatism focuses on the fact that creativity is always embedded in a *situation*, i.e., on the human being's 'situated freedom'" (Joas 1993, 4).[10] Joas's description taps two important dimensions of pragmatism—namely, its belief in human creativity making sense of human experiences and actions through critical thinking, and the premise that such creativity and critical engagement always occurs within a social context.[11]

The notion of the social self is fundamental within both dimensions of pragmatist discourse. This social self is a human being who is situated within a network of transactional processes with other people. The experiences that a human being has within the social world through transactions with others constitute the substance that a person uses to make sense of the social and natural worlds. Social meanings are negotiated in the space of transaction.

The notion of experience is foundational for understanding this idea of the social self. Take, for example, philosopher John Stuhr's description of the centrality of experience for intersubjective understandings, or the meanings that people create by interacting with one another:

> They [James & Dewey] insist that experience is an active, ongoing affair in which experiencing subject and experienced object constitute a primal, integral, relational unity. Experience is not an interaction of separate subject and object, a point of connection between a subjective realm of the experiencer and the objective order of nature. Instead, *experience is existentially inclusive, continuous, unified: it is that interaction of subject and object which constitutes subject and object*—as partial features of this active, yet unanalyzed totality. Experience, then, is not an "interaction" but a "transaction" in which the whole constitutes its interrelated aspects. (Stuhr 2000, 4–5; emphasis added)

Within this expansive understanding of experience as existentially inclusive, continuous, and unified, individuals are not passive recipients of a finished social world; rather, through their relationships with one another, with social institutions, and with the environment ("the objective order of nature"), they actively construct their social world. Experiencing is a process of living in the social world versus experiences as artifacts of past interactions.[12]

In this sense, pragmatism's conception of human experiences and their connection to the social self differ from commonsense understandings of individual identity whereby an individual remains who he or she is regardless of the social context in which he or she is located. Individuals travel from place to place, collecting experiences as they go, taking their accumulated experiences into each new setting. Commonsense understandings of identity see a person as basically carrying one essential identity from one social setting to the next. Once so categorized, the experiences of individual women and men become reduced to each individual's perspective, bias, or mere opinion. Experiences become entities that an individual collects that shape her or his individual identity.

Pragmatism's understanding of experiences in social context rejects this understanding of identity. Because experiencing the social world is always subject to interpretation and reinterpretation, identities are social phenomena and as such are never finished. Rather, experiences and the identities they engender are always in the making; that is, people shape their social worlds through the actions they take as well as the experiences that their actions engender. In this sense, experience has a dual meaning: it is both the outcome of transactions in the social world (e.g., my biography, the meaning that I make of my own experiences), and it describes an active process of being in the social world (e.g., how I experience the world as an active participant by living in it from one moment to the next).

By situating individual experience in the center of the social world, pragmatism offers an analysis of experience that valorizes its contributions to intellectual inquiry. The pragmatic construct of creative social action stems from this understanding of experiencing the social world as one that stimulates critical thinking and imagination. In other words, people do not experience the world simply by observing it, much as one watches a movie. Rather, they actively work at making sense of the world through critical thinking and imagination, and, through their actions, they shape the social world. For example, Ida B. Wells-Barnett did not experience the lynching of her friends as a benign experience with little effect on her worldview. Instead, she critically analyzed the events so that she could make sense of them. And in doing so, she consulted with others, developing a provisional analysis of the causes of lynching based on her experiences. Taking action through experiences of speeches, writing, and travel not only deepened her analysis, it contributed to her commitment to imagine a world without lynching.

The pragmatist concept of experimentalism in everyday life puts teeth into this more amorphous category of creative social action. People experiment all the time, trying new things and learning from the differences between what they thought would happen and what actually happened. Experimentalism is not taught; rather, it's something that people do. For example, to the dismay of their parents, toddlers go through a phase where they put everything in their mouths. Is the baby teething or hungry, or is this a way of experimenting to learn what should go in one's mouth and what definitely does not belong there? The pragmatist concept of experimentalism in everyday life resembles the kind of critical thinking that has been formalized as the scientific method. Within pragmatism, *experimentalism* refers to a way of thinking that makes provisional assumptions, tests hypotheses through experiences by determining how they adhere to the provisional assumptions, and then forms new provisional assumptions based on what occurs. This is exactly what the toddler does. Toddler truth is never certain but is always provisional and subject to change. Within pragmatist frameworks, social truths are always provisional and are always subject to reinterpretation.

This concept of experimentalism suggests that the meaning of an idea comes from its pragmatic use in social context, and not exclusively from its internal logic or from some predetermined definition. The more an idea circulates among people who use it, the clearer it becomes because it has been tested in the crucible of experience. Within a pragmatist methodology, knowledge or "truths" are not absolute; they are continually reevaluated and reinterpreted by how well they function (their pragmatic value). Within this experimentalist framework, important social ideas such as freedom, social justice, equality, and democracy are never finished—they gain meaning through use. Social problems are also amenable to continual revision, reinterpretation, and renewed social action.

As a dimension of creative social action, experimentalism is especially useful for critical social theory.[13] For example, John Dewey avoided analyses of democracy whereby intellectuals developed theories and then applied abstract analyses to the topic of democracy. Dewey's approach was more abductive, examining how the meaning of democracy would deepen over time by how people experienced and used it. Rather than developing a grand theory of democracy as a political system and the ethics of trying to make it happen, Dewey's philosophy implied a more dialogical approach. In essence, the meaning of democracy in the U.S. would emerge from how the American public participated in democratic institutions. Dewey's commitment to public education stemmed from this sense that participatory democracy required an educated public. *The Public and Its Problems* (1954) illustrates Dewey's commitment to critical analysis as a way of diagnosing and solving social problems. Dewey (1954) aimed to cultivate individuals whose "intelligent thought" brings the best ideas to the table for participatory democracy. Dewey's work illustrates how experimentalism and developing meaning through social action might work.

At the same time, Dewey's approach to democracy as well as the general approach of the pragmatists sidestepped a conundrum within U.S. society. On the one hand, pragmatism does provide important conceptual tools for rethinking the construct of community as a site where the subjective worlds of people and the objective, durable social structures they create come together. American pragmatism espoused a desire to foster human creativity within democratic communities. On the other hand, the imagined communities of pragmatism were far more democratic than actual communities. Pragmatism had far less to say about how power relations influenced experience itself and the organization of communities. By this omission, pragmatism avoided for many decades the difficult question of how creative social action might work in situations of social inequality where human freedom was so clearly curtailed.

Writing Social Inequality into Pragmatism: Gender, Race, Indigeneity, and Nation

Classical pragmatist thinkers could neither understand how intersecting systems of power shaped their experiences within particular communities of inquiry, nor did they incorporate alternative understandings of pragmatism into their primary intellectual projects. Charles Peirce, William James, and other members of the initial pragmatist Metaphysical Club who met regularly to hash out the ideas of pragmatism constituted a very small community of inquiry (Menand 2001). Moreover, the homogeneity of their experiences within families, communities, and academic institutions that valorized whiteness, wealth, masculinity, and heterosexuality meant that they lacked exposure to people and ideas that lay outside their experiences.

Classical pragmatists certainly knew that social inequality existed— how could they miss it?—yet as privileged intellectuals, they treated it as unimportant. In this regard, they could neither draw upon experiences that they didn't have, nor could they consult others whose experiences were too far outside their daily experiences. During this same period of classical pragmatism, Black feminist thinkers faced a different social context that made it virtually impossible for them to ignore the workings of power in their lives. The members of the Metaphysical Club and Ida B. Wells-Barnett inhabited completely different social contexts, which had corresponding effects on their social theory. Had a broader range of people participated in pragmatist communities of inquiry, perhaps American pragmatism might have unfolded differently.

A resurgence of interest in pragmatism has catalyzed internal criticism within pragmatism concerning a host of themes. By the early twenty-first century, a number of philosophers criticized the pragmatist canon by questioning its taken-for-granted truths.[14] This resurgence of interest in pragmatism made it possible to bring questions of social inequality to bear on pragmatism as well as to ask how pragmatism might contribute to understandings of social inequality.

Reforming existing fields of study, especially those with the longevity and cachet of American pragmatism, takes time. Reforming existing disciplines requires criticizing a field's prevailing ideas and practices, ideally offering convincing arguments that a field itself will benefit if its existing practitioners embrace change. Lasting reform is best carried out by disciplinary insiders—critique may emanate from outside a field of inquiry, but people who already have a vested interest in the field are uniquely positioned to reform their discourse. This is especially the case for philosophy, a discipline with stringent requirements for entry.

A renewed attention to social inequality within American pragmatism by philosophical insiders has paralleled the resurgence of interest in American pragmatism itself. Three interrelated activities characterize this revitalization—namely, efforts to (1) remedy exclusions within pragmatism's discourse, primarily by including neglected thinkers whose ideas speak to pragmatism's main concerns; (2) revise pragmatism's narrative to correct for existing bias, explicate existing themes, or both; and (3) when warranted, imagine alternative framings of pragmatism itself that are recognizable as pragmatism but that cannot be comfortably incorporated within pragmatism's current self-narrative. Pragmatist philosophers have used gender, race, ethnicity, nation, and similar categories to criticize the pragmatist canon.

Within philosophy, analyzing the absence of gender from the pragmatist canon constitutes an important dimension of reform. Analyzing how the absence of work by individual women philosophers affected pragmatism constituted an important starting point for reform. In "Reclaiming a Heritage: Women Pragmatists," Charlene Seigfried (1996, 40–66) examines the work of women philosophers who drew upon pragmatist ideas, thus providing an important introduction to how feminism and pragmatism have and might inform one another.[15] Claiming Jane Addams as an important pragmatist thinker illustrates this strategy of inclusion as an important one for reform. Addams (2002) was a philosopher in her own regard, and recasting women thinkers such as Jane Addams, who worked outside philosophy, as philosophers and then including them within revisionist genealogies of philosophy itself challenges the boundaries of what counts as pragmatism. By taking gender into account, much of this work on individual women philosophers aims to revise the narrative to correct for existing bias. Incorporating women philosophers is a promising first step that opens the door to asking how gendered analyses, typically but not exclusively advanced by women, might provide new insights about the substance of pragmatism itself.[16]

Scholars of race and ethnicity have engaged in a similar process of reclaiming intellectuals, again with an eye toward reforming the pragmatist canon. William E. B. Du Bois is an obvious choice here, primarily because Du Bois's intellectual production remains so widely recognized across many fields (see, e.g., Lewis 1995). Du Bois's interdisciplinary intellectual work draws upon history, sociology, and philosophy, thereby demonstrating a theoretical breadth that makes it amenable to recontextualization within philosophy. Du Bois initially pursued his intellectual affiliations with sociology by seeking a job at the University of Pennsylvania; failing that, he spent a decade at Atlanta University spearheading research on aspects of race. A prodigious writer, Du Bois eventually relinquished his academic aspirations and turned his attention to other venues. Despite Du Bois's tenuous historical relationship to philosophy, part of pragmatism's revitalization has centered on investigating Du Bois's ties to philosophical concerns.[17] The persistence of social inequalities continues to push the envelope concerning pragmatism's relationship to the social issue of race and ethnicity (Lawson and Koch 2004), as well as its utility as a framework for understanding African American political action (Glaude 2007).

The focus on Du Bois is important, yet growing interest in the works of Alain Locke, an equally if not more significant figure for philosophy, illustrates the importance of incorporating neglected figures with an eye toward reforming the pragmatist canon (Fraser 1998; L. Harris 1999). As a philosopher who received his training at Harvard University under William James,

Locke was directly exposed to one of the key figures of classical American pragmatism. Yet unlike James, Dewey, Mead, and similar classical pragmatist philosophers, as an African American scholar, Locke followed a different career path. Locke's intellectual work illustrated a scope and depth of philosophical inquiry, among them literature, art, drama, music, aesthetics, and culture (Molesworth 2012). Locke's understanding of race prefigured contemporary analyses of race as a social construction, and his analysis of race and racism also introduces important questions of racial hierarchy and power (see, e.g., Locke's monograph *Race Contacts and Interracial Relations* [1992]).

Unlike Du Bois, Locke found an academic position as chair of the Philosophy Department at Howard University that enabled him to work as a professional philosopher. Just as the exclusion of Du Bois from the sociological canon shaped the development of sociology as a field (see, e.g., Morris 2015), Locke's scholarship within the discipline of philosophy may have enriched the contours of American pragmatism in ways that are only now receiving recognition. Nancy Fraser identifies Locke's work as expressing a "critical pragmatism" that not only advanced understandings of race and racism that foreshadow the contemporary period, but that also had significant implications for pragmatism's orientation to power and domination. As Fraser contends:

> Many commentators have noted the overly integrative and idealist character of the social thought of the classical pragmatists. Their many important insights notwithstanding, John Dewey, George Herbert Mead, Jane Addams, and W.I. Thomas are widely seen as having failed to give adequate weight to the "hard facts" of power and domination in social life. Assuming the inevitable unfolding of an increasingly integrated world civilization, and emphasizing culture at the expense of political economy, they tended at times to posit imaginary, holistic "solutions" to difficult, sometimes irreconcilable social conflicts. Yet Locke's 1916 lectures provide a glimpse of another pragmatism. Because he was theorizing about "race" and racism, he linked cultural issues directly to the problem of inequality; and he stressed the centrality of power to the regulation of group differences in the United States. Thus, in contrast to the mainstream pragmatists of the World War I period, Locke pioneered an approach to social theory that took domination seriously. (Fraser 1998, 158–159)

Fraser suggests that Locke advanced critical pragmatism that simultaneously criticized the classical canon and also developed alternatives to it.[18]

At some point, reform can either give way to transformation or catalyze a backlash. Reclaiming Jane Addams, Alain Locke, and other neglected figures and similar reformist projects is important, yet this strategy has its limits. As the cases of Du Bois and Locke suggest, reform through incremental steps is slow. Within Kuhn's framework of paradigm shifts, transformation would occur when pragmatism's narrative of its own origins and concerns cannot be simply fleshed out or revised within its traditional framing assumptions. Instead, alternative narratives emerge to replace it. Revitalizing contemporary American pragmatism may require casting a wider net for intellectuals whose ideas resemble those in the pragmatist canon but who are not typically included in it (see, e.g., McKenna and Pratt 2015). This broader context of discovery potentially provides alternative narratives for American pragmatism that take social inequalities and power relations into account. For example, in *Native Pragmatism: Rethinking the Roots of American Philosophy*, Scott Pratt (2002) identifies a novel point of origin for American pragmatism, one that enables him to build a genealogy on the interactions among indigenous peoples and major figures of American philosophy. Pratt's volume carefully develops three main premises: (1) the central commitments that characterize the classical pragmatism of Charles S. Peirce, William James, and John Dewey are apparent much earlier in Native American thought; (2) cases exist throughout the seventeenth, eighteenth, and into the nineteenth centuries that suggest how Native American thought influenced European American thinkers; and (3) this more robust social, intellectual, and political context out of which classical pragmatism emerged suggests that pragmatism was not simply a further development of modern European thought faced with the conditions of a "wilderness." Instead, American pragmatism constituted a philosophy of resistance that aimed to challenge the European perspective (Pratt 2002, xii).

Identifying selected core ideas of American pragmatism as originating with interactions among indigenous and European peoples not only undermines pragmatism's conventional narrative, but it stimulates new questions about democracy and American national identity. Drawing from patterns of indigenous/settler contact, this revised narrative associates the American origins of pragmatism with the quintessentially American social problem of how transactions among heterogeneous groups has shaped the meaning of American national identity. The interactions among indigenous people and their contact with European explorers and settlers are foundational to subsequent endeavors to build democratic communities among people who bring distinctive worldviews to this process. Pratt contextualizes American pragmatism within its specific geographic social context and also fosters a temporal shift identifying pragmatism's origins, not in the late nineteenth-century minds of its canonical thinkers, but rather in social interactions that occurred much earlier.

Because they criticize pragmatism's standard assumptions concerning power relations and social inequality, these strategies are crucial for reform. Scholars of gender, race, and indigeneity may be at the forefront of efforts to revitalize American pragmatism, yet the challenge of transforming American pragmatism goes beyond these particular contestations. In the opening pages of *Pragmatism and Feminism,* Charlene Seigfried (1996) issues a clarion call to move beyond pragmatism's legitimated genealogy: "I . . . begin by defining as pragmatism the positions developed by the members of the historically recognized movement of American pragmatism. But this is only a beginning meant to be left behind. One problem that immediately arises is that many writers defining the movement have focused almost exclusively on the pragmatic method and pragmatic theories of meaning and truth and have drawn their inferences from articles and books specifically addressed to this cluster of issues" (Seigfried 1996, 5). Themes raised by critics concerning pragmatism's treatment of gender, race, and indigeneity might have been more centrally located within the pragmatist canon had the work by "members of the historically recognized movement of American pragmatism" not been defined as coterminous with pragmatism itself. Had Alain Locke's "critical pragmatism" been incorporated earlier, American pragmatism itself might have been quite different.

Gender, race, and indigeneity constitute separate reformist strategies. By bundling these ideas together, intersectionality can build on and potentially extend these initiatives. Intersectionality's guiding premises potentially offer new directions for existing pragmatist questions and concerns. Because their scholarship draws from the intellectual production of women of color within feminism, the work of women of color philosophers is especially instructive here in bringing intersectionality to philosophy generally and pragmatism in particular. Edited volumes such as *Convergences: Black Feminism and Continental Philosophy* (Davidson, Gines, and Marcano 2010) break new ground because they draw from multiple theoretical traditions, placing Black feminism as an intellectual tradition in dialogue with poststructuralism, existentialism, standpoint epistemology, phenomenology, and similar areas within continental philosophy. Broadening this philosophical landscape creates space for more specific dialogues between Black feminist thought and American pragmatism (see e.g., V. James 2009).

How different American pragmatism might have been had the intellectual production of women of color been central to its ideas and practices since its inception. Social inequality and questions of power were at the center of Black feminist theorizing, not its margins. Black feminist theorizing posited that racism, classism, sexism and heterosexism, and similar systems of oppression required new analyses of social relations as well as new social practices to bring them about. Conversely, how differently Black feminist thought might have unfolded had African American women been able to work as philosophers. American pragmatism and Black feminist thought might have both benefited from the dialogical engagement that put the ideas of each discourse into contact with the other.

Community and Power Relations

Pragmatism potentially demystifies social structure, seeing it not as preordained or handed down through time immemorial, but rather as a result of human agency. Individual experiences are foundational to the social world, but the social world itself cannot be understood simply by aggregating individual experiences. It makes no sense for individuals to have creative and critical relationships that are then inserted into a social world characterized by such durability that it does not and cannot change. If people's experiences reflect their active engagement in their social worlds, experience becomes the key that joins the individual and the social, or the subjective and the objective worlds.

In this sense, pragmatism offers a framework for theorizing how communities are socially constructed by human agency and how communities are sites of social action. Significantly, communities have lives of their own that often predate the appearance of any one individual member and that live on regardless of when an individual leaves. The construct of community holds varied and often contradictory meanings that reflect diverse and conflicting social practices. People can share the same cultural symbols yet understand and deploy them differently, a situation that catalyzes varying meanings and practices. In this sense, the concept of community is not simply a cognitive, abstract construct; it is infused with emotions and value-laden meanings. Significantly, communities are vehicles for collective behavior.

Because theorizing occurs in specific social contexts, the construct of community provides an analytical framework for conceptualizing social contexts as places where group-based or collective action occurs (Collins 2010). Pragmatism provides some important conceptual tools for theorizing multiple types of communities. Community is an important construct for theorizing collective behavior as a process—namely, the interactions among people within a given community. But the construct of community also invokes the idea of a social structure that results from the collective decision making of social actors. Stated differently, community is simultaneously a process and a structure. Bringing a power analytic to this key idea of pragmatism provides a language for seeing how power relations operate within and among communities. At its core, people learn about social hierarchy in the context of community practices. They also learn resistance from within these same settings.

But does pragmatism's conception of community go far enough? In contexts of social inequalities, the malleable meanings of community itself can both catalyze contradictory definitions and facilitate their coexistence. Communities are characterized by power hierarchies both within a given community, such as the pecking order of epistemic agency within interpretive communities, as well as among communities—namely, the hierarchical ranking of communities within intersecting power relations, for example, the hierarchies of communities of color. Ignoring these power relations, specifically those of class, race, gender, ethnicity, and immigrant status that were especially prominent during pragmatism's formative years, limits its theory of social action.

Despite its provocative thesis of creative social action, pragmatism remains limited as a theory of social action primarily because it underemphasizes the influence of power relations both on the specific relationships between individuals and on how political and epistemic power structure the internal dynamics of interpretive communities. This means that pragmatism often has turned a blind eye to how power relations shape the practices within its own interpretive community. Action is not guided simply by rationality, by considering all the options, acting, and then folding new knowledge back into a feedback loop of recursive understanding. American pragmatism remains inherently reactive to social conditions because it fails to commit to a political or ethical agenda that says what it wants to do. Individual pragmatist thinkers have certainly been at the forefront of such endeavors, but pragmatism itself remains muted. Pragmatism's versatility enhances its capacity for action, yet its failure to embrace any guiding principles as central to the symbolic contours of its discourse means that its tools can be used for a variety of ends. This stance makes American pragmatism not fatally flawed, but rather incomplete.

The absence of a power analysis has consequences. Despite pragmatism's potential, its actual approach to social structure has tilted more toward understanding social order than toward understanding social change. Hans Joas explains this connection between pragmatism's approach to action and its corresponding emphasis on social order: "Pragmatism is a philosophy of action . . . It does not, however, attack utilitarianism over the problem of action and social order, but over the problem of action and consciousness. Pragmatism developed the concept of action in order to overcome the Cartesian dualisms . . . Pragmatism's theory of social order, then, is guided by a conception of social control in the sense of collective self-regulation and problem-solving" (1993, 18). Ironically, as a theory of action, social change within pragmatism is incremental, deliberative, and ultimately reformist. This approach to action and social order enables pragmatism to imagine that the structure of communication within communities of scientists—in other words, the "intelligent thought" required to participate in informed dialogue—should serve as the model for communities and democratic institutions. Dialogical engagement that is not tethered to power relations can quickly turn into idle conversation. Without some sort of guiding principles to help people place value on ideas, dialogues can continue on in infinite loops of communicative misunderstandings that erode possibilities for social change.

When informed by an analysis of social inequality, several characteristics of the construct of community make it a promising candidate for understanding how people's experiences and actions in collective contexts might inform intersectional theorizing (Collins 2010). First, communities constitute major vehicles that link individuals to the social institutions that organize complex social inequalities. Social inequalities of race, class, gender, age, ethnicity, religion, sexuality, and ability take form through social structures such as neighborhoods, schools, jobs, religious institutions, recreational facilities, and physical and cyberspace marketplaces. Typically hierarchical, these structures offer unequal opportunities and rewards. Whether intentional or not, people use the construct of community to make sense of and organize all aspects of social structure, including their political responses to their situations. Similarly, social institutions use the symbols and organizational principles of community to organize social inequalities.

Second, ideas about community often move people to action, often by catalyzing strong, deep feelings. Community is not simply a cognitive construct; it is infused with emotions and value-laden meanings. Whether an imagined community is a place-based neighborhood; a way of life associated with a group of people; or a shared cultural ethos of a racial, national, or ethnic group, or a religious collectivity, people routinely feel the need to celebrate, protect, defend, and replicate their own communities and ignore, disregard, avoid, and upon occasion destroy those of others (Anderson 1983). This ability to harness emotions means that the construct of community is versatile and easy to use. Yet these same characteristics foster unexamined and taken-for-granted assumptions about how communities are and should be (Cohen 1985). In everyday life and within much academic discourse, the term *community* is used descriptively, with minimal analysis or explanation. As a result, community can be imagined in many ways, from the micro-level of analysis so prominent within social psychology to the macro-level analysis of nations as imagined communities. One can imagine community through the lens both of multicultural inclusion and of racism, sexism, and similar categories of belonging and exclusion (Yuval-Davis 2011).

In this way, because people exercise power in their everyday lives as individuals within communities, they use the construct of community to think and do politics. Stated differently, the construct of community provides a template for describing actual power relations as people live them and conceptualize them. People use the idea of community to organize and make sense of both individual and collective experiences they have within hierarchical power arrangements. A community is more than a random collection of individuals. Rather, communities constitute important sites for reproducing intersecting power relations as well as contesting them. Within a given nation-state, social inequalities organize its national identity or sense of national community, with individuals embedded in actual communities as a way of thinking about their placement in intersecting power relations. Thus, community constitutes a core political construct because it serves as a template for political behavior.

Third, looking to community as a framework for the political constitutes one important factor in understanding the political behavior of subordinated groups. Individuals from oppressed groups often find little space for their individuality both within wider society and their religious and ethnic communities. Liberal democracies point to individual citizenship rights as the bedrock of democratic politics, presenting promises of personal freedom by leaving the strictures of the group behind. Yet social inequality means not only that individuals from oppressed groups cannot exercise these rights, but also that they are unlikely to gain such rights without sustained collective action. Oppressed groups need durable collective units that map onto durable social institutions. In essence, community as a template for power relations emphasizes collective politics over the valorization of the individual as the primary recipient of citizenship.

Finally, in a context of intersecting power relations, community is never a finished thing but is always in the making. A more dynamic, future-oriented understanding of community creates space for imagining something different than the present and a worldview that critically analyzes existing social arrangements. In this sense, participating in building a community is simultaneously political (negotiating differences of power within a group), dynamic (negotiating practices that balance individual and collective goals), and aspirational. The challenge of sustaining this dynamic conception of community, however, lies in finding ways to negotiate contradictions.[19]

Intersectionality and Social Action

This chapter places intersectionality in dialogue with Black feminist thought and American pragmatism, two knowledge projects whose approaches to experience and community are relevant for intersectionality's critical content and methodology. Because intersectionality draws from multiple critical discourses, it navigates an array of competing and complementary knowledge projects. Unlike both Black feminist thought and American pragmatism, intersectionality is not tightly wedded to particular social groups and interpretive communities—African American women for Black feminist thought or professional philosophers for pragmatism—but instead has a much broader constituency. Unlike American pragmatism and, to a lesser extent, Black feminist thought, intersectionality has not yet crystallized into a canon with founding figures, a coherent narrative of its points of origin, and a list of its core tenets. Rather, narratives of intersectionality within academic settings remain contested concerning which perspectives on intersectionality will prevail. I see three implications of intersectionality's dialogical engagement with Black feminist thought and American pragmatism.

First, Black feminist thought and American pragmatism make important albeit different contributions to thinking about experience in ways that facilitate intersectionality as a critical social theory. Black feminist thought demonstrates the epistemological and political significance of theorizing from individual experience in the context of a community with shared experiences, identities, and standpoints (Collins 2000, 251–271). Experience constitutes a source of wisdom, a way of knowing that is democratic precisely because it does not depend on formal education. Using experiences to theorize is not a privileged way of knowing; rather, it is one way of knowing that may be better suited to specific questions than the content of formal social theories.

In this sense, the substance of experience matters in relation to diagnosing social problems and in figuring out ways to address them. Relying on experience as a way of knowing can bring wisdom to critical inquiry, but only if that wisdom itself remains under construction. Black feminist thought demonstrates this use of wisdom that informs social action in struggling with an important social problem. Historically, this broader project of Black feminist thought as resistant knowledge drew from and influenced the everyday political behavior of African American women in the social context of families, jobs, communities, and civic participation. It also shaped how African American women as leaders, intellectuals, and activists understood power and politics. This is important because Black women bring a distinctive sense of political action both to intersectionality and, potentially, to democratic political institutions, a sensibility that reflects how those at the bottom of social hierarchies theorize power and take political action in response to domination.

Such knowledge emphasized complex understandings of how domination is organized and operates (intersecting oppressions), as well as complex perspectives on political possibilities within such contexts (flexible solidarity). African American women were able to conceptualize intersectionality in conjunction with, and not in opposition to, their experiences of social action. The richness of Black feminist thought, and its ability to influence so many other resistant knowledge projects, points to the benefits of broadening intersectionality's context of discovery to include similar theorizing traditions whose creative social action rests on experience. Black feminist thought may be so central to intersectionality because many other groups recognize the value of theorizing from experiences. Such groups have had to think through their experiences with oppression. In this sense, these connections between Black feminist thought, intersectionality, and flexible solidarity point to how social context matters in theorizing (experience and community) (Blea 1992; Collins and Bilge 2016, 63–87; Fischer and Seidman 2016).

American pragmatism's theoretical analysis of experience resonates with these Black feminist sensibilities. Within American pragmatism, experience informs social action within the social world that in turn influences thinking about the social world. Pragmatism's notion that ideas gain meaning through use taps this recursive relationship between ideas and action. This theme of ideas-in-action or action-in-ideas is an important one for critical analysis. Analysis bridges this seeming gap between thinking and doing, or knowledge and power, with analysis assigned to theory and action, to power. And if experience is a window into a critical analysis of ideas-in-actions and actions-through-ideas, intersectionality's critical theorizing might be similarly recursive. In essence, Black feminist thought and American pragmatism arrive at a similar destination regarding experience, with neither discourse having much direct contact with the other. Both bring a dynamic conception of experience as ideas-in-action or actions-through-ideas, and both situate this understanding of experience within a notion of community.

Second, by highlighting different aspects of dimensions of community, Black feminist thought and American pragmatism both illuminate how a more robust conception of community might inform intersectionality's critical inquiry. In essence, American pragmatism provides an interpretive framework that valorizes Black women's community work as a way of knowing. And Black feminist thought's dual focus on intersectionality and flexible solidarity within community work brings an analysis of power to American pragmatism. Together they suggest how a more sophisticated construct of community might influence intersectionality's interpretive communities and how such communities might facilitate intersectionality's creative social action. For example, by focusing on individual experiences within small groups, American pragmatism illuminates how epistemic power and epistemic resistance inform intersectional theorizing within a particular interpretive community. Yet pragmatist ideas about the processes of group participation need not be confined to small communities. Its principles can also inform imagined communities. But pragmatism remains limited by the long-standing absence of a critical awareness concerning how social inequality and intersecting power relations inform its own practice. Efforts to reform pragmatism from within by incorporating into the pragmatist canon critical analyses of gender, race, and indigeneity, as well as the critical interventions of women of color philosophers, are important reforms.

Black feminist thought's approach to community constitutes a template for understanding how power relations are organized and operate. For African American women, social action constituted a way both of understanding the social world and of taking action within it. The idea of community provided an essential connection between ideas and social structures. Black women's experiences occurred in communities whereby individual experiences were meaningless without some sort of collective analytical frame through which to interpret them. Black feminist thought drew upon the idea of community as an analytical tool to describe social inequality. But the idea of community was also a construct of hope. Black women's community work and the Black feminist thought that it engendered contain a strand of visionary pragmatism that points to the collective nature of experience, both geographically and over time, as well as to its political nature (V. James 2009; James and Busia 1993; Willett 2001).

Finally, by bringing more comprehensive understandings of experience and community to intersectionality's critical inquiry, Black feminist thought and American pragmatism suggest new ways to think about how social action might inform critical theorizing. Together they suggest that intersectionality's ideas come from people's self-reflexive experiences within the intersecting power relations of their social worlds. Intersectionality's core ideas and guiding premises may seem to be the insights of individual creativity. Ideas are certainly that, but they are also deeply social. And cultivating a broader interpretive community that draws on experiences as ways of knowing should foster rich and more complex ideas within intersectionality's critical inquiry. Ida Wells-Barnett and the members of the Metaphysical Club may seem to be unlikely intellectual partners, but intersectionality must make room for them both and others. Building such a diverse intellectual community for intersectionality makes it far less likely that intersectionality's ideas will remain just ideas. This dual focus on experience and community highlights the significance of building organizational structures that can house and advance intersectionality itself.

One important point of this chapter is that intersectionality that aims to remain critical *cannot* be accommodated within Black feminist thought, American pragmatism, or any existing discourse. Nor can it make it on its own, rejecting the ideas of other discourses as less relevant because they reflect the ideas of "dead white males" or because they seem insufficiently intersectional. Rather, to grow, intersectionality must become an intellectual leader. It is compelled to build something anew, drawing from knowledge projects such as Black feminist thought and American pragmatism without defining itself in opposition to them. Nor should intersectionality be categorized within any existing discourse, no matter how critical it may seem to be. Instead, intersectionality would do better to commit to an open-ended process of creative social action, incorporating the ideas and actions of these and other knowledge projects into its own praxis.

6

Intersectionality and the
Question of Freedom

Critical social theories often turn their attention to the question of human freedom. In the aftermath of the destruction wrought by World War II, Jean-Paul Sartre, Hannah Arendt, Zygmunt Bauman, and other European intellectuals faced the daunting task of explaining how fascism had so severely curtailed the freedom of so many. When it came to the question of freedom, William E. B. Du Bois, Ida Wells-Barnett, Frantz Fanon, and Stuart Hall, among others, expressed different concerns. If people of African descent were not seen as being fully human, what guidance might critical social theories provide for Black freedom struggles? Feminists also came to see freedom as vital for movements for women's emancipation and liberation, asking how feminism might conceptualize freedom in ways that spoke to the heterogeneous concerns of women. LGBTQ people asked a simple but profound question: Why are we not free to love whom we want? Because critical social theories have a vested interest in opposing political domination, the question of freedom has been central to many resistant knowledge projects.[1]

Given the centrality of freedom for so many resistant knowledge projects, I ask in what ways the idea of freedom might inform intersectionality as a critical theory in the making. To dig into this question, I compare two perspectives on freedom by French philosopher Simone de Beauvoir (1908–1986) and African American intellectual-activist Pauli Murray (1910–1985). Both thinkers offer analyses of oppression and the meaning of freedom, and significantly for intersectionality, both conceptualize the relationships among race, class, gender, sexuality as part of their analysis. Yet because they rely on different ways of theorizing, the substance of their arguments differs dramatically. Beauvoir relies on a traditional, philosophical use of analogical reasoning that assumes certain relationships among gender, race, class, sexuality, and age. In contrast, Murray offers a provocative glimpse of social action as a way of knowing, one that suggests that intersectional theorizing about gender, race, class, sexuality, and age more closely resembles a metaphorical journey of analyzing experiences in social context.

The lives of Beauvoir and Murray lend themselves to this kind of comparative analysis. Born two years apart and dying within one year of each other, Beauvoir and Murray were generational contemporaries. Both did significant intellectual work during the turbulent decades of the 1920s, 1930s, and 1940s, a pivotal period of social change. Yet their generational similarity means more than chronology, relating to, as Stuart Hall describes it, a "shared experience, a common vision, or thinking within the same 'problem space' as it does to a mere date of birth" (2017, 44). Although they shared generational sensibilities, the different national and class-specific social contexts in which they worked influenced their distinctive visions of freedom. Beauvoir was a highly educated member of the French intellectual elite whose social networks within French and continental European intellectual circles facilitated her philosophical career. In contrast, despite holding degrees from prestigious institutions, Murray was an attorney who was perpetually unemployed and underemployed throughout her life. Her social networks consisted of highly educated African Americans like herself who worked in activist settings for civil rights as well as broader networks of women's rights and labor activists. These different locations within intersecting systems of power help explain their distinctive standpoints on freedom.

Beauvoir and Murray both advanced important analyses of women's oppression and the possibilities for freedom, albeit through different means and with various outcomes. Beauvoir has long occupied a prominent position within the pantheon of feminist theorists, a place mapped out by the initial publication of her groundbreaking work *The Second Sex* (Beauvoir 2011 [1949]). Contemporary efforts to reinterpret her legacy abound, for example, a new translation of her core text that restores its initial meaning (Thurman 2011 [1949]), an analysis of her student diary that traces how her intellectual trajectory was independent of yet intertwined with that of Jean-Paul Sartre (see, e.g., Klaw 2006; Simons 2006), and an edited volume with new analyses of Beauvoir's scholarship (Hengehold and Bauer 2017). Beauvoir is receiving much-deserved recognition and reinterpretation as a feminist and existentialist philosopher.

In contrast, Murray has only recently been studied as an important Black feminist intellectual activist (Azaransky 2011; Bell-Scott 2016; Rosenberg 2017). In the context of her sustained involvement with civil rights and women's rights struggles, Murray was exposed not only to a wide range of ideas that opposed oppression, but also to the ways in which people used those ideas to advocate for freedom. Murray deepened her analyses of freedom less through disciplinary training and more by anchoring her unfolding analysis within specific freedom struggles. Murray critically engaged the explanations of oppression and freedom offered by African American social and political thought, socialism, law as an instrument for social change, mainstream feminist thought, and Christian theology, trying to put their ideas into practice.

Despite their similarities and differences, both intellectuals expressed strong commitments to feminism. Beauvoir and Murray both were critical of the treatment of women's oppression within their immediate social settings and within their respective societies. Each brought different understandings of race, class, gender, sexuality, nation, and age to their understandings of women's oppression. When coupled with their experiences within different interpretive communities, these distinctive understandings of oppression shaped their perspectives on freedom.

Simone de Beauvoir, Women's Oppression, and Existential Freedom

As a major existentialist philosopher, Simone de Beauvoir illustrates in her work a particular relationship linking oppression and freedom.[2] Beauvoir leaves a clear written record on freedom, one that I excavate via reading two core texts that were published almost simultaneously. *The Ethics of Ambiguity* (1976 [1948]) and *The Second Sex* (2011 [1949]), two of Beauvoir's most significant works, both engage questions of oppression and freedom. *The Second Sex* constitutes an extended treatise on the absence of freedom for women.[3] In contrast, *The Ethics of Ambiguity*, Beauvoir's theoretical analysis of existential freedom, engages core ideas within existentialist philosophy. Both texts illuminate different aspects of Beauvoir's philosophy of oppression and freedom.

Beauvoir's arguments about freedom in *The Ethics of Ambiguity* can be read by filling in one's own examples from one's own experiences. Abstract analyses such as hers often seem plausible because, when the author and readers of a text share the same worldview, they typically draw upon similar cultural material and therefore cannot see how their shared assumptions shape the truth they mutually construct. But because in this case *The Second Sex* provides the cultural material that is invoked yet unstated in *The Ethics of Ambiguity*, reading these two books together leaves far less to the reader's imagination. Beauvoir's masterwork, *The Second Sex*, deals less overtly with the question of freedom, yet the lengthy discussion of women's oppression in *The Second Sex* does suggest another dimension of Beauvoir's analysis of freedom. Together the books constitute companion pieces, one developing Beauvoir's theoretical arguments and the other detailing empirical evidence for claims about oppression and freedom.[4]

The Ethics of Ambiguity soars in places in spelling out the possibilities for human freedom—the sense of making one's own destiny and claiming one's freedom. Beauvoir's analysis of existential freedom seems clear-cut. Her foundational claim is that all humans are born free (with natural freedom) and humans can achieve ethical freedom by taking responsibility for their lives via social action. Yet each person seeks freedom in a context of ambiguity. There are no easy answers, no social scripts to follow for human freedom, no certainty, only ambiguity. Rejecting grand theories that seemingly have all the answers, she argues that "morality resides in the painfulness of an indefinite questioning" (Beauvoir 1976 [1948], 133). This is the space of ambiguity, of not knowing all the answers or even whether one's efforts will produce answers at all. Yet claiming this space of ambiguity constitutes a core principle of existential freedom.

Beauvoir sees this space of ambiguity as a space of possibility. The personal choices of humans shape the experiences that we have and our understanding of our own experiences. Freedom is always a state of becoming, of making choices whereby people experience the world. Ambiguity shapes both human choices—of never knowing with certainty in the moment of choice whether one choice is better than another—and the ambiguity of the situations in which humans make choices. Via this commitment to human experience, Beauvoir conceptualizes freedom as taking shape via creative social action and not through passive contemplative reflection. Beauvoir is clear that moving toward ethical freedom is not something that occurs as "indefinite questioning" in one's head, but is linked to actions in the world. Take, for example, her description of artists: "In order for the artist to have a world to express he must first be situated in this world, oppressed or oppressing, resigned or rebellious, a man among men" (Beauvoir 1976 [1948], 78). In other words, each human being must stake a place in the world through action in order to move toward freedom itself.[5]

The perpetual striving of creating oneself via experience underpins Beauvoir's notion of creative freedom. Beauvoir notes:

> To will is to engage myself to persevere in my will. This does not mean that I ought not aim at any limited end. I may desire absolutely and forever a revelation of a moment. This means that the value of this provisional end will be confirmed indefinitely. But this living confirmation cannot be merely contemplative and verbal. It is carried out in an act. The goal toward which I surpass myself must appear to me as a point of departure toward a new act of surpassing. Thus, creative freedom develops happily without ever congealing into unjustified facticity. The creator leans upon anterior creations in order to create the possibility of new creations. His present project embraces the past and places confidence in the freedom to come, a confidence which is never disappointed. (1976 [1948], 27–28)

Social action within such ambiguity is fundamentally an ethical commitment that sees one's own creative freedom as tied to that of others. Individual striving underpins Beauvoir's notion of existential freedom, yet such freedom is actualized within the social world. Ethics matter, not as rules, but rather as aspirational touchstones for creative action within the social world. "Ethics does not furnish recipes any more than do science and art," Beauvoir contends. "One can merely propose methods" (Beauvoir 1976 [1948], 134).

The Ethics of Ambiguity suggests that a commitment to existential freedom for oneself and for others is an ethical ideal in its own right. Beauvoir recognizes the tensions between aspiring toward the ideal of existential freedom (transcendence) and the reality of oppression. Defending herself against the claim that existentialists were gloomy and nihilistic, she argues, "We believe in freedom. Is it true that this belief must lead us to despair? . . . it appears to us that by turning toward this freedom we are going to discover a principle of action whose range will be universal" (23).

The Race/Gender Analogy and Women's Oppression

In both *Second Sex* and *Ethics of Ambiguity*, Beauvoir relies on analogies of gender and race to structure her arguments, making repeated comparisons between the status of women and Black people.[6] Criticizing this approach, Margaret Simons observes that Beauvoir's comparison of slavery and women's oppression remains limited both by her characterization of slavery and by an ethnocentric description of women's lives that generalizes from her own cultural viewpoint (1999, 26–28). Kathryn Gines offers a related criticism in her essay "Sartre, Beauvoir, and the Race/Gender Analogy: A Case for Black Feminist Philosophy" (2010, 36), contending that the race/gender analogy limits philosophy's understanding of intersectionality. Because Beauvoir uses the categories of race, gender, class, ethnicity, and age to construct her arguments about freedom and women's oppression, her work seems to be intersectional because these familiar categories of analysis are present. Yet *how* Beauvoir uses these categories speaks to the kind of intersectional analysis she presents, or whether it is intersectional analysis at all. This issue is especially significant because Beauvoir is a well-known philosopher working within an interpretive community with substantial epistemic power. How she builds her case about women's oppression is just as if not more significant than the substantive contours of her arguments.

The race/gender analogy appears repeatedly in both *The Ethics of Ambiguity* and *The Second Sex*. Beauvoir returns frequently to the metaphor of women as slaves to explain women's oppression, an idea that makes sense within Beauvoir's assumptions about Black people.[7] The theme of Black people as slaves also appears frequently, providing an important conceptual metaphor that travels uncritically via related metaphors of prison, enslavement, and entrapment. Beauvoir uses stereotypes of Black people as incarcerated, ignorant, unaware of their own lack of freedom, and happy with their predicament. Via this metaphoric shortcut, Beauvoir uncritically accepts scientific discourse and popular culture that recasts African American culture as carefree and already strangely "free." Via the race/gender analogy, Beauvoir uses Black people as an already known entity to invoke slavery as a touchstone for her claims about women's oppression.

Beauvoir quite rightly contends that ideological justifications for varying forms of oppression resemble one another. Take, for example, the following passage where Beauvoir draws upon analogies to point out the ideological similarities of oppressions of Black people, women, and Jews. Beauvoir has the makings of an intersectional analysis here that might have explored the interconnected experiences of these groups. Instead, she holds fast to the basic race/gender analogy and moves to exclude Jews from it:

> This convergence is in no way pure chance: whether it is race, caste, class, or sex reduced to an inferior condition, the justification process is the same. "The eternal feminine" corresponds to "the black soul" or "the Jewish character." However, the Jewish problem on the whole is very different from the two others: for the anti-Semite, the Jew is more an enemy than an inferior, and no place on this earth is recognized as his own; it would be preferable to see him annihilated. But there are deep analogies between the situations of women and blacks: both are liberated today from the same paternalism, and the former master caste wants to keep them "in their place," that is, the place chosen for them. (Beauvoir 2011 [1949], 12)

The early part of this passage makes the case that the ideological justifications for the oppression of women, Black people, and Jews (gender, race, and ethnicity) resemble one another. By the end, however, Beauvoir classifies Jews in a distinctive category based on the nature of the perceived threat. Jews constitute enemies that can be killed. In contrast, women and Black people share a common inferiority and should be dominated.

Beauvoir cannot seem to extract herself from analogies, substituting other categories that highlight the centrality of the race/gender analogy. Compare, for example, the logical chain of women, Black people, and Jews in the passage above with the analogical reasoning of women, Black people, and children in *The Ethics of Ambiguity* that follows:

> . . . To the extent that woman or the happy or resigned slave lives in the infantile world of ready-made values, calling them "an eternal child" or "a grown-up child" has some meaning, but the analogy is only partial. Childhood is a particular sort of situation: it is a natural situation whose limits are not created by other men and which is thereby not comparable

to a situation of oppression . . . the child is ignorant because he has not yet had the time to acquire knowledge, not because this time has been refused to him. To treat him as a child is not to bar him from the future but to open it to him. (Beauvoir 1976 [1948], 141)

In this passage, the idea of the child performs a different function than that of the Jew. The Jew is an enemy whose strength constitutes a threat. In contrast, the child resembles the inferiority of woman and Blacks. Yet the child can escape this inferiority of dependency by simply growing up. In this sense, the child becomes the trope for natural freedom, a baseline for evaluating the unfreedom or oppression of women and Black people. The child can escape subordination. They cannot.

Because age as a category of analysis is underemphasized within intersectionality, it is interesting to see how prominently it figures in Beauvoir's analysis of women's oppression. Beauvoir's analogical thinking casts Black people as slaves, and children as beings without history. The following passage from *The Ethics of Ambiguity* illustrates how analogies of race and age that rest on this premise enable Beauvoir to replicate stereotypes of non-Western women as underdeveloped:

There are beings whose life slips by in an infantile world because, having been kept in a state of servitude and ignorance, they have no means of breaking the ceiling which is stretched over their heads. Like the child, they can exercise their freedom, but only within this universe which has been set up before them, without them. This is the case, for example, of slaves who have not raised themselves to the consciousness of their slavery. The southern planters were not altogether in the wrong in considering the negroes who docilely submitted to their paternalism as "grown-up children." To the extent that they respected the world of the whites the situation of the black slaves was exactly an infantile situation. This is also the situation of women in many civilizations; they can only submit to the laws, the gods, the customs, and the truths created by the males. Even today in western countries, among women who have not had in their work an apprenticeship of freedom, there are still many who take shelter in the shadow of men. (Beauvoir 1976 [1948], 37)

Three categories of people lack fully human, adult consciousness—children, for whom infantilization is a natural and temporary state; Black people, whose infantilization results from the trauma of being slaves; and non-Western women, whose submissiveness to men enslaves them.

Beauvoir's treatment of class also falls victim to the analogical thinking of her race/gender analogy. Because Black people are so closely associated with slavery, they become a class like no other, one without internal distinctions of economic status, gender, or citizenship. Their race signifies their class. Bracketing Black people from the very category of class, defines class by default as white, Western, and focused on working-class men. Beauvoir's depiction of the proletariat is brief and seems designed to strengthen her theoretical analysis of women's oppression: "Proletarians are not a numerical minority either, and yet they have never formed a separate group. However not *one* event but a whole historical development explains their existence as a class and accounts for the distribution of these individuals in this class. There have not always been proletarians: there have always been women" (Beauvoir 2011 [1949], 8). With the white proletariat granted history and therefore situated within class relations, Beauvoir turns her attention to Western, white, bourgeois women, again through use of analogy:

They have no past, no history, no religion of their own, and unlike the proletariat, they have no solidarity of labor or interests; they even lack their own space that makes communities of American blacks, the Jews in ghettos, or the workers in . . . factories. They live dispersed among men, tied by homes, work, economic interests, and social conditions to certain men—fathers or husbands—more closely than to other women. As bourgeois women, they are in solidarity with bourgeois men and not with women proletarians; as white women, they are in solidarity with white men and not with black women. (8)

Beauvoir's analogical reasoning puts her on a slippery slope. One would think that with women's oppression defined via analogies with Black people, Jews, children, non-Western women, and white male proletariats, no space remained for women's freedom. Yet Beauvoir does identify a category of the free woman by the end of *The Second Sex*. In an especially troubling passage Beauvoir argues: "It is understood that the male has integrated the forces of the species into his individuality, whereas the woman is the slave of the species . . . it is out of the question to think of her as simply free. In France, especially, the free woman and the easy woman are stubbornly confused, as the idea of easy implies an absence of resistance and control, a lack, the very negation of freedom" (Beauvoir 2011 [1949], 730). Women's oppression is so complete that they are the "slave of the species." This construct makes sense as a plausible hypothesis that emerges from Beauvoir's analogical reasoning.

Interestingly, Beauvoir's analogical reasoning positions Western white women as being worse off than children, Jews, Black people, and white working-class men because (1) children have natural albeit not unfettered freedom; (2) Jews possess history that provides evidence both of their oppression as well as traditions that resist it; (3) Black people are so resigned to their downtrodden state that they no longer feel the pain of slavery; and (4) proletarian white men possess a union history of solidarity for resisting class oppression. These groups all have something that women lack. Women's oppression rests on premises established by Beauvoir's treatment of these other groups: women are denied adult status and treated like children; women have no history of themselves like Jews do; women's subordination resembles that of enslaved Black people; and unlike Western white working-class men, women lack visible traditions of effective political protest and organizing.

The effect of this method of theorizing through the use of analogies is a curious *privileging* of women's oppression. Beauvoir's claim that women's oppression is universal, fundamental, and unique is explicit. In the introduction to *The Second Sex*, she argues that the self/other relationship of man/woman is like no other:

> Women are not a minority like American blacks, or like Jews: there are as many women as men on earth. Often, the two opposing groups concerned were once independent of each other; either they were not aware of each other in the past, or they accepted each other's autonomy; and some historical event subordinated the weaker to the stronger: the Jewish Diaspora, slavery in America, and the colonial conquests are facts with dates. In these cases, for the oppressed there was a *before*: they share a past, a tradition, sometimes a religion, or a culture. (Beauvoir 2011 [1949], 7–8)

Comparing people without history (children) to those who have histories that they struggle to control (Jews, Black Americans, and the colonized) to those whose power and authority enable them to make history (men) leaves women curiously *within* history yet without one of their own.

Women's Oppression as a Test of Existential Freedom

Beauvoir's analysis of freedom in *The Ethics of Ambiguity* is highly useful as a tool for imagining political behavior. Yet placing the main arguments of *The Ethics of Ambiguity* in dialogue with those of *The Second Sex* reveals a fundamental irony—the *abstract* existentialist argument regarding freedom as the state of being for human beings falters on the shoals of *actual* unfreedom (gender oppression) of women. Stated differently, Beauvoir theorizes freedom in the abstract yet has a much harder time imagining her own arguments working in the concrete world of women's oppression. This inconsistency is not necessarily a contradiction or a conceptual slippage. Rather it represents the challenge of working within two distinct sets of assumptions: the former clearly framed within the epistemological and methodological frameworks of philosophy, and the latter more closely aligned with the empiricism of social science. Interestingly, Beauvoir's philosophy project and her social science project may have had different goals, yet Beauvoir relies on analogical thinking in both.

Beauvoir's approach to women's oppression in *The Second Sex* seemingly undercuts her own arguments. Via Beauvoir's analogical thinking, entire categories of humans are exempted from this struggle for ethical freedom, for acceptable and not so acceptable reasons. The child as archetype, for example, "escapes the anguish of freedom" (Beauvoir 1976 [1948], 36), as do slaves and submissive women who choose to remain childlike. Beauvoir's assumption that broad swaths of the population lack agency and political will enables her to narrow her search for free women to people very much like herself. Beauvoir casts a sharp eye on privileged women in the West, finding them complicit with gender oppression: "It is then that we discover the difference which distinguishes them from an actual child: the child's situation is imposed upon him, whereas the woman (I mean the western woman of today) chooses it or at least consents to it" (38).

The sole chapter in *Second Sex* that examines women's agency and social action comes late in the text. The section titled "Toward Liberation" contains one chapter titled "The Independent Woman." This chapter focuses exclusively on educated Western, white, and, given the examples, most likely French women. Viewing educated, white French women as standardbearers for women's freedom installs women very much like Beauvoir at the center of analysis. The main challenges that face the French independent woman (i.e., the emancipated, liberated, or free woman) resemble Beauvoir's own experiences. Drawing upon one's own experiences as an independent woman for insight is one thing. Installing one's own group experience at the center of the possibility for *all* women's freedom is entirely another. Beauvoir ignores the agency of non-Western and working-class women just as thoroughly as she perceives men as ignoring women.

Social action for women also becomes stymied within Beauvoir's framework. She dismisses the arguments of some feminists as polemical because they frame their demands for women in terms of women's relation to men. Feminists try to prove women equal to, superior to, or inferior to men. For Beauvoir, framing political demands as women's issues is passé. In contrast, impartial women like herself (her use of the "we" is telling in this passage) stand at the front line of liberation:

> I think certain women are still best suited to elucidate the situation of women . . . it is not a mysterious essence that dictates good or bad faith to men and women; it is their situation that disposes them to seek truth to a greater or lesser extent. Many women today, fortunate to have had all the privileges of the human being restored to them, can afford the luxury of impartiality: we even feel the necessity of it. We are no longer like our militant predecessors: we have more or less won the game . . . many other problems seem more essential than those that concern us uniquely: this very detachment makes it possible to hope our attitude will be objective. Yet we know the feminine world more intimately than men do because our roots are in it. (Beauvoir 2011 [1949], 15)

Not only are women who are not like Beauvoir complicit in their own domination—the case of "militant" feminists getting it wrong because they lack objectivity and impartiality—Beauvoir finds it difficult to consider that women other than those in her own circles have agency or analysis. This is a major contradiction that seems to undercut her foundational claim that all humans are born with natural freedom and humans can achieve ethical freedom by taking responsibility and social action.

Beauvoir's analysis in the chapter "The Independent Woman" comes closest to specifying how she approaches the question of freedom. Yet here, too, the argument is so bent on bending data to fit into a women's oppression framework that even the achievements of women who might approach freedom are rendered inadequate. Economic independence is not enough: "One must not think that the simple juxtaposition of the right to vote and a job amounts to total liberation; work today is not freedom" (Beauvoir 2011 [1949], 721). Achieving a profession comes with its own set of special challenges: "Even the woman who has emancipated herself economically from man is still not in a moral, social, or psychological situation identical to his. Her commitment to and focus on her profession depend on the context of her life as a whole" (723). Beauvoir also presents the dilemma of the "emancipated woman": "She refused to confine herself to her role as female because she does not want to mutilate herself; but it would also be a mutilation to repudiate her sex" (Beauvoir 2011 [1949], 723). Moreover, for women, no matter what their accomplishments, appearances still matter: "The woman . . . knows that when people look at her, they do not distinguish her from her appearance: she is judged, respected, or desired in relation to how she looks" (724). Sexuality provides special challenges: "It is in the area of sex that the most difficult problems will arise" (725).

In an especially telling passage, Beauvoir takes pains to plead the case of the intellectual as a special category of independent woman: "The independent woman—and especially the intellectual who thinks through her situation—will suffer from an inferiority complex as a female" (Beauvoir 2011 [1949], 725). She then goes on to describe the burdens on independent women, their inability to keep up with beauty rituals, their lack of elegance, how they try to act like the other women but fail. Her realization: "If she has trouble pleasing men, it is because she is not like her *little slave sisters*, a pure will to please" (726; emphasis added). The demeaning "little slave sisters" constitutes the logical end point of recurring analogies.

Simone de Beauvoir's core existentialist premise is that people who were free at birth spend the rest of their lives in search of the freedom that was lost when they were thrust into the world. Yet, even though men and women may both be born free, it seems that women will have a much harder time becoming free again, if ever, because male domination has so profoundly rigged the deck. The world that she paints in *The Second Sex* is indeed grim, and one wonders how women could gain freedom when the weight of the world was so heavily stacked against them. Women exist in a space of perpetual domination, a state of immanence, never reaching male transcendence. If Beauvoir herself, with so many advantages, could not reach freedom, then what hope was there for all the other women? Beauvoir's masterful rendition of women's oppression seemingly squeezes the life out of existential freedom.

Pauli Murray, Intellectual Activism, and Social Justice

Beauvoir arrived at her analysis of women's oppression and freedom by working *within* the boundaries of conventional scholarly practice, in this case, analogical reasoning as a convention of philosophy and Western social theory. Beauvoir is often held up as a feminist icon, but this close read of her philosophy of women's oppression and existential freedom raises questions about the substance of her feminist theory. Similarly, Beauvoir's analysis of women's oppression is clearly critical of oppression, yet her methodology of analogical reasoning undercuts her main ideas. In brief, neither her theory of women's oppression and existential freedom nor her method of theorizing through the use of analogies is intersectional. The categories of race, gender, ethnicity, age, and class are all there, but are defined and used in ways that are not intersectional.

I was able to use Beauvoir's own words in generating this analysis. By comparing the treatment of the ideas in two signature texts that were authored by Beauvoir, I examine how her use of analogical reasoning made connections among categories of race, gender, class, age, and ethnicity. I could not use the same strategy with Pauli Murray, and this too is part of the story of women's oppression. Like Beauvoir, Murray did author her own ideas, yet unlike Beauvoir, Murray was also an activist. Because Pauli Murray and similar African American women are typically categorized as activists and not intellectuals, studying Murray's theoretical work raises special challenges that do not occur in studying Simone de Beauvoir and similar feminist philosophers.[8] Murray was an intellectual activist whose critical analysis was informed by a lifelong commitment to African American freedom struggle but not confined by it. Murray would more appropriately describe herself as struggling for social justice. Freedom and social justice were not replacements for one another. Rather, social justice was a broader framework that encompassed the particulars of freedom struggles.

Studying Murray's ties to intersectionality requires a different strategy that sees social action as a form of theorizing and informed political action as central to critical social theory. The trajectory of Murray's journey throughout her life course, where she moved among categories of race, class, gender, sexuality, and nation, constitutes a metaphor for intersectional theorizing.[9] This approach requires interpreting biographical information and experiences as central to the process of intellectual production. The ideas themselves constitute the tip of the iceberg, visible signs of far broader intellectual engagement. Because Murray was both a writer and an activist, I am interested both in what Murray thought as well as what she did. Moreover, Murray's life course was guided by a search for social justice that took her into and through different interpretive communities of race, class, gender, sexuality, and nation. Murray was a renegade, always living in a borderlands space and expressing a *mestiza* consciousness long before Gloria Anzaldúa (1987) provided the language to name this space. Stated differently, Murray's journey was one that tested and continually reframed Beauvoir's notion of existential freedom via experience and social action. Significantly, Murray's embrace of existential freedom potentially informs understandings of intersectionality.

During different phases of Murray's life, race, gender, class, sexuality, nation, and age as systems of power, either singularly or in combination, were differentially salient in shaping her experiences and social action. Because Murray did not have access to an intersectional framework (she contributed to building one), she theorized about the social problems that she encountered, using the categories that made the most sense in a given social context. It is important to point out that Murray's deepening intersectional framework does not map neatly onto a particular stage or event in her life. While it's tempting to argue that Murray had a "race" phase in the 1920s and 1930s and a phase of emerging gender consciousness in the 1960s, the extant scholarship on Murray does not yet support these claims.

Rather, a better interpretation suggests that systems of power may be theoretically intersectional, yet in practice, some forms of oppression will be especially salient during particular periods of time and in particular social contexts. In Murray's case, some aspects of social inequality were more apparent to her as forms of oppression in large part because of her social location. Murray had access to African American social and political thought that conceptualized political action as an ongoing freedom struggle. This discourse was well known within Black civil society, organized through established community institutions, involved women and men, and had intergenerational components. Murray's individuality was honed within the context of this ongoing freedom struggle that examined how racism, class exploitation, and the denial of citizenship framed social inequality. These were public concerns that shaped the contours of African American communities.[10] Yet Murray simultaneously experienced other aspects of social inequality as private concerns. When it came to gender and sexuality, there was no readily available community for her that provided language for her personal struggles. Gender and sexuality were always there, but they became publically salient as categories of analysis later in her life when she was able to find and contribute to building women's communities.[11]

The metaphor of a journey animates this process of discovery as a lifelong learning process of recognizing and using the distinctive categories of intersectionality.[12] This metaphor of a journey also grounds the idea of creative social action in political action. In this sense, the importance of Murray's journey lies in how it fleshes out abductive analysis as a methodology—namely, how her critical posture toward social injustices, her dialogical engagement with multiple interpretive communities, her ongoing self-reflexivity and willingness to reconsider her position, and her consistent commitment to social justice serves as a rubric for intersectional theorizing. The significance of Murray's contributions to intersectionality lies not only in the content of her intellectual production, but also in her praxis.

The Journey as a Metaphor for Creative Social Action

The metaphor of the journey encapsulates how Murray experienced systems of race, class, gender, sexuality, and nation during her life course. Black communities emphasized freedom as a fundamental goal of a formerly enslaved population.[13] American leaders and intellectuals engaged in ongoing debates about the "race" question. Within the confines of Black communities, they debated the best course of action to oppose racial segregation both in the U.S. and worldwide.

During her lifetime, Murray was exposed to a broad spectrum of African American social and political thought concerning the best way to defeat racism. This rich intellectual tradition for civil rights and racial equality exerted an important influence on Murray's commitment to social justice. Murray was twenty-one years old in 1931 when the infamous Scottsboro Boys case of unfounded interracial rape preoccupied Black intellectual and political circles. Murray was twenty-four years old in 1935 when the Spanish Civil War erupted and African American intellectuals debated the merits of Black Internationalism, with many choosing to travel to Europe in support of democracy. She was in her early thirties in 1945 when, in the aftermath of World War II, African American troops who fought for democracy abroad were denied democracy at home via racially discriminatory policies in housing, education, and employment, effectively a racial segregation that belied American democratic postures in a global context. Murray came of age as an intellectual during a period in which communism, Black Internationalism, civil rights, and Black nationalisms (the remnants of the Garvey movement and the rise of the Nation of Islam) were all debated within African American social and political thought. Gandhi's effective strategic use of nonviolence and a long-standing civil rights struggle that took new inspiration from his ideas were not abstractions for her. She was exposed to radical Black political and social thought of the 1930s and 1940s (before the McCarthyism of the 1950s), to the political philosophy of a staunch nonviolence campaign as a way of toppling racism, as well as to radical Black nationalism of the 1960s and 1970s (Adi 2009; Kelley 1994; Putnam 2009).

Despite racism's predominance within U.S. society as well as within African American social and political thought, Murray refused to reduce everything to race.[14] Murray learned firsthand how class inequalities and the social problems they engendered also affected large numbers of white Americans. Poor whites' experiences of being evicted and struggling to find work resembled those of Black people. Foundational to her political development was her own economic situation and how much racism did or did not explain about it. Murray graduated from college in 1933, the worst possible time to finish school and try to start a career. Because she was an African American woman, even if times had been good, no one would hire her. Murray was poor in New York City, with barely enough money to pay rent. At the height of the Depression, with no job prospects in sight, she hitched rides on freight trains across America. As she reminisced, "the national toll caused by unemployment, which I glimpsed in the faces of the hordes of men and boys who haunted freight yards and lived in hobo jungles, and the struggle for survival I had experienced briefly on the road, made my own problems seem comparatively mild" (Azaransky 2011, 10–11). After some time, she was able to find work with the Worker's Education Project (WEP), a program of the Works Project Administration under the New Deal. The social conditions that Murray witnessed while travelling around the U.S., her experiences working with WEP, and her own economic precariousness offered a perspective on poverty and class that affected her intellectual work.

The 1930s and 1940s constituted a significant period for Murray, a time characterized by her political education as a "young radical" (Azaransky 2011, 9–35). Murray's attentiveness to the interconnections of racial oppression and class exploitation deepened during this period. In 1940, she was offered the position of travelling secretary at the Workers' Defense League (WDL) to raise money on behalf of Odell Waller, a Black sharecropper who had been convicted of killing his white landlord. Her travels in a broader national context deepened Murray's analyses of the issues facing African American communities. As Murray travelled the country arguing Waller's case, her impassioned speeches about the need for equal protection under the law provided a platform for her increasingly sophisticated views on racism and nation-state power. Murray worked tirelessly to save sharecropper Odell Waller from execution, not by a mob, but by the very government that should have protected his rights. Murray came to see the significance of democracy, citizenship, and the need to engage the federal government for African American empowerment. The WDL and Murray were no match for state power. The state of Virginia executed Waller. The failure of their direct action campaign left Murray and others with unanswered questions. What difference did it make to have abstract freedoms (rights) on paper if one could not exercise them (Azaransky 2011)? Murray decided to attend law school.

Murray's formal affiliation with feminism occurred in the aftermath of these multilayered experiences with racism, capitalism, and the differential use of nation-state power. In the 1940s and 1950s, Murray's analysis of women's oppression became more visible, most likely in response to a series of events that caused Murray to modify her individualistic understandings of gender to one of seeing women as a collectivity whose oppression resembled but was not the same as African American oppression. One incident stands out as a catalyst. Despite a stellar career at Howard Law School, and expecting to be offered entry to Harvard University that was reserved for the top graduate from Howard, Harvard refused to admit her because she was a woman. Murray had been violating gender norms her entire life, but events like this showed her how gender was individually experienced but was at root a collective, structural concern. Murray's individualized rebellion concerning norms of gender and sexuality became public when she became involved in feminism. Murray's understanding of the intersections of racism and sexism became more nuanced as she moved through her life. By the time Murray advanced her analyses of gender in her signature writings, during the same period as Beauvoir, Murray's work increasingly expressed an intersectional sensibility about racism and sexism (Murray 1970b; Murray and Eastwood 1965).

By contemporary standards, Murray would most likely be seen as transgendered. Murray's experiences with sexuality remained a private theme throughout her life, taking form in her letters to friends and within her poetry. She did not write about her sexuality, nor did she use the theme of her individual identity as the catalyst for broader discussions of sexuality. It is clear, though, that sexual identity was an important theme in Murray's life, as an adolescent and young woman. Murray often dressed in men's clothes and was mistaken for a boy. As a young woman, she consulted a physician to see whether her gender could be changed. Then-prevailing views on sexuality and on sexual identity explained Murray's belief that she was in the wrong body as an individual aberration, the chance event of bad luck or some sort of moral failing. Had Murray come to see sexuality itself as a system of oppression, she might have found meaning in Beauvoir's philosophy of existential freedom. For most of her life, there was no social movement to queer gender or sexuality.

This brief biography introduces the complexities of Murray's experiences with race, class, nation, gender, and sexuality. These systems of power were theoretically all there, all of the time, yet they became differentially salient to Murray in response to specific experiences during her lifetime. Because the life and ideas of Pauli Murray have only recently garnered academic attention, I can only sketch out a provisional analysis of Murray's contributions to intersectionality. Murray did understand the importance of authoring her ideas, and through her writings she exerts testimonial authority over the meaning of her own life. But there is so much that we don't know and may never know.

However, the corpus of Murray's written work does provide promising evidence for developing this metaphor of the journey as a frame for intersectional theorizing. During different phases of her life, she wrote two autobiographies that map her changing political analyses (Murray 1978 [1956], 1987). Murray's autobiographies were written in first-person prose, yet by contemporary standards, they reveal far less about her intimate life than contemporary memoirs. Murray's legal writings also were directly tied to various aspects of the civil rights movement. While teaching law in newly free Ghana, she co-authored a textbook on the constitution of Ghana (Murray and Rubin 1961). Murray's political writings on feminism have yet to be published in a volume of collected works, but they do provide access to her ever-developing analyses of gender (see, e.g., "The Liberation of Black Women" (1970, 87–102). Murray became an Episcopal priest late in life, and her sermons offer another lens on her lifelong commitment to social justice (Murray 2006). A resurgence of interest in Murray within religious studies shows the breadth, growth, and substance of her ideas (Pinn 2008).

Murray's public writings dealt with race and gender, yet her private writings showed far more self-reflexivity and self-doubt than her public persona. Murray's poetry provides insight to her innermost thoughts. Published in 1970, her book *Dark Testament and Other Poems* contains selections of her poetry, some of which she copyrighted as early as 1939. Her poetry expresses her private, intimate voice, one that could not be conveyed as freely in the 1930s as today. Murray's letters to her teacher and mentor Caroline Ware, a correspondence that began in 1943 and ended with Murray's death in 1985, constitute yet another piece of a published record of Murray's intellectual development in her own words (Scott 2006). Pauli Murray wrote constantly across different genres; the forms her writing took demonstrate a breadth that remains underappreciated within contemporary scholarly emphases on specialization. For example, Murray's work was situated within debates about the meaning of poetry for democracy (Peppard 2013). Unfortunately, Murray's lifelong precarious economic situation of being chronically unemployed and underemployed meant that she neither got "a room of her own" in which to write, nor saw her work published as she would have wished.

Reconstructing Pauli Murray's Intersectional Theorizing

Thus far, I have suggested that Pauli Murray's intellectual activism reflected her ongoing struggles to understand how race, class, nation, gender, and sexuality shaped both her individual experiences as well as the social organization of the society around her. In essence, Murray's creative social action reconfigured Beauvoir's abstract analysis of existential freedom, not as a birth pang of throwing oneself into the unknown, leaving all that is known behind, but rather as a more pragmatic, ongoing journey of freeing oneself from the constraints of social injustices and taking what is worth knowing with you. Because she never fit comfortably anywhere, Murray did not retreat into herself. Instead, Murray chose to throw herself into a future that she struggled to craft, thereby creating herself anew. Moreover, because she did so in the context of intersecting power relations of race, class, gender, and sexuality in the U.S. context, her journey toward freedom foreshadowed not only the content of intersectionality as a form of critical inquiry, but also an important mechanism for intersectional theorizing itself.

But where is the evidence for this argument? Because Pauli Murray was an intellectual activist, even though she believed in authoring her own ideas, she often lacked the time or resources to do so. Developing a comprehensive analysis of how her work informs intersectional theorizing means working with what she left us. That said, in order to examine whether and how Murray's experiences deepened her intersectional perspective, we need more secondary analysis of Murray's life and works that analyzes how her books, published work, speeches, and journalistic work form a holistic, ongoing critical theoretical project.

No two books authored *by* Murray lend themselves to the same reading strategies that I deployed in analyzing the two philosophical works authored by Beauvoir. Fortunately, two biographies *about* Murray's life detail her experiences and provide a window into her thinking. Because they were published at the same time, they also lend themselves to a comparative reading strategy. Rosalind Rosenberg's *Jane Crow: The Life of Pauli Murray* (2017) and Patricia Bell-Scott's *The Firebrand and the First Lady: Portrait of a Friendship* (2016) fill an important gap in scholarship on Pauli Murray. Both biographies not only lay a scholarly foundation for studying Pauli Murray's journey toward freedom, but also point toward a more complex analysis of intersectionality itself. By taking different perspectives on the same material, both books illustrate that the story of Pauli Murray's connections to intersectionality will be written and rewritten for some time.

When it comes to intersectionality, each biography relies on a different interpretive framework. Bell-Scott frames Murray's commitment to the struggle for social justice as the core analytical framework for her volume, one that originates in Murray's long-standing involvement with civil rights and racial justice projects, and that deepened and expanded over the course of her life. The years of the 1930s through the 1960s are central to Bell-Scott's biography, a time period when Murray developed increasingly sophisticated analyses of racism, poverty, sexism, and the centrality of nation-state institutions in remedying social injustices. These years laid a foundation for Murray's participation in and analysis of different aspects of the struggle for social justice that unfolded in subsequent decades. Bell-Scott also makes the surprising editorial decision to highlight Pauli Murray's friendship with First Lady Eleanor Roosevelt as a core organizational tool for *The Firebrand and the First Lady*. Characterized by mutual respect, their friendship occurred during this important historical era when norms of race and gender were changing. Within their friendship, Pauli Murray was a "firebrand," a term of endearment coined by Eleanor Roosevelt, who saw Murray as an irritant. Murray respectfully thanked Mrs. Roosevelt for her support for progressive causes, but also consistently encouraged her to do even more.

In contrast to Bell-Scott's framework, Rosenberg's *Jane Crow* presents a panoramic view of the long arc of Pauli Murray's entire life that highlights Murray's gendered sensibilities in relation to race. Murray understood the concept of Jane Crow not just as a metaphor for intersections of race and gender inequalities that took concentrated form for African American women, but also as a solid legal doctrine that might influence law as an instrument of social change. The term *Jane Crow* challenged the male bias within the civil rights movement, arguing in essence that an intersectional analysis of race and gender would be needed to address the economic inequalities that were particular to African American women. Rosenberg titles her volume *Jane Crow* as a way of acknowledging these interconnections.

By examining Murray's ideas and experiences, *The Firebrand and the First Lady* and *Jane Crow* shed light on different aspects of intersectional theorizing. First, in their renderings of Murray's biography, both books draw upon race, class, gender, and sexuality as categories of analysis, yet they place different analytical weight on these concepts. Whereas Bell-Scott focuses on Murray's antiracist political struggles against economic exploitation and state-sanctioned violence, Rosenberg takes pains to trace how sexuality and gender shaped Murray's life choices and actions. In a sense, the books read as complementary narratives, one placing race and class front stage and the other, gender and sexuality. This kind of analytical emphasis is possible with the life of any historical figure, yet because Murray's intellectual and political work engaged all of these categories, it lends itself especially well to this treatment.

When synthesizing Murray's life using works from such disparate genres, as well as across different periods of time, it is important not to impose contemporary sensibilities on the life of a historical figure as a way to speak to contemporary audiences. In this regard, because Bell-Scott focuses on Murray's public life, she has an easier task than Rosenberg. Murray's public record on race, class, and gender exists across many archives, including Murray's own. Emphasizing Murray's friendship with Eleanor Roosevelt, a recognizable public figure, further narrows Bell-Scott's frame to social justice actions, primarily in the public sphere. While warm, the letters between Murray and Roosevelt avoid the kinds of personal disclosures often shared by close friends. Bell-Scott's analysis is also in keeping with conventions within Murray's own autobiographies as well as with historical strategies of Black women's narrative traditions of deliberately protecting their privacy via cultures of dissemblance (Hine 1989).

During the years of her friendship with Eleanor Roosevelt, Murray held a series of jobs that never paid her what she was worth or allowed her to gain financial security. Yet she stayed involved in progressive political causes, predominantly antiracism endeavors. During this period, Murray wrote repeatedly to Eleanor Roosevelt, often asking the first lady to get the president's ear about something that Murray found to be especially egregious. Eleanor Roosevelt could have simply walked away from this "firebrand" who was never satisfied with Roosevelt's well-meaning albeit cautious responses to the race problem. Murray could have given up as well, abandoning the kind of incremental change that "ladies" like Roosevelt endorsed. Yet neither did.

Murray's friendship with Roosevelt was one of Murray's many friendships with white and African American women that she held dear. Yet the significance of Murray's particular friendship with Eleanor Roosevelt lies in what Bell-Scott is able to say about Pauli Murray's understanding of social justice work. From different generations, Pauli Murray and Eleanor Roosevelt bridged historical eras when race and gender relations were dramatically changing. Roosevelt served as a quasi-mentor to Murray, yet the ways in which they influenced one another illustrate the significance of dialogue across differences of power that characterize race, class, and generation. Murray was on a short list of people who challenged Roosevelt's beliefs and actions. And Roosevelt appreciated her honesty. Conversely, Roosevelt offered Murray the wisdom of a broad perspective on social issues and the wisdom of experience. As a lone wolf carving her own path, Murray appreciated Roosevelt's support, but as a firebrand, she came to her own conclusions. One strength of Bell-Scott's volume is that she doesn't try to resolve the tensions within this ongoing relationship, organized via a friendship. Rather, by leaving this shared commitment to social justice open-ended, Bell-Scott suggests that the struggle for social justice was larger than either Murray or Roosevelt and would have been impoverished if either woman had abandoned the other.

In contrast, Rosenberg develops a provocative argument about how Murray's personal experiences with her identity catalyzed her critical perspectives on race and gender. Focusing on Murray as an individual enabled Rosenberg to highlight Murray's racial and gendered identities as paramount, thus supporting her exploration of how Murray resisted the seemingly fixed boundaries of race and gender. Murray's multiracial and multiethnic identities constituted an important theme in her life, providing evidence for Rosenberg's thesis that Murray consistently challenged the fixed boundaries of race. Murray's writings certainly provide ample evidence for this thesis. For example, Murray named her first autobiography *Proud Shoes: The Story of an American Family* (1978 [1956]). Written during the 1950s, a period when the U.S. government aggressively questioned the patriotism of progressive artists, intellectuals, and activists, Murray aimed to expand the meaning of what it meant to be American. Murray's volume eschewed understandings of racial identity that rendered a person a Negro who had "one drop" of Negro blood. Instead, Murray saw herself as fully American, claiming all aspects of her multiracial heritage. Murray did not want to assimilate into a preconceived notion of race; rather, she wanted to change its meaning such that American national identity would include as equals persons like herself and her family. In this sense, Rosenberg situates Murray's political action, and the specific actions that Murray took in the context of her times, in support of a vision of racial equality that prefigured contemporary color blindness.

Rosenberg also places far more emphasis than Terborg-Penn on the significance of gender and sexuality throughout Murray's life. *Jane Crow* examines

Murray's growing analytical awareness of gender, beginning with the conundrum that her sexuality and gender presented for her in her childhood. *Jane Crow* sheds light on how Murray rebelled against the conventional categories of sexuality and gender to which she was assigned. Her refusal to accept these categories stimulated lifelong questions concerning gender as a fixed category of analysis. Murray struggled with her gender identity in childhood and adolescence, believing that she was really a male in a female body. Sexuality was also a catalyst for Murray's gender identity. She was attracted to straight women, not as a lesbian, but rather as if she were a man. Initially, Murray thought the explanation for the mismatch of her gender and sexuality with prevailing conventions lay within biology itself. This conviction propelled her to consult medical personnel in search of scientific reasons why she felt so strongly that she was in the wrong body. Murray was clearly decades ahead of political, medical, and theoretical research that underpins contemporary analyses of the socially constructed nature of gender and sexuality.

In this sense, neither Murray's racial identity that defied binary categorizations of black and white, nor her gender identity that rejected binary categorizations of masculinity and femininity, could be accommodated within prevailing understandings of race, gender, and sexuality. Rather than capitulate to social norms concerning race, gender, and sexuality, Murray rejected such norms because they limited her personal freedom. Murray was armed with experiences, yet the theoretical tools that she had at hand throughout her lifetime could only yield limited results. Murray's actions as a "firebrand" and her refusal to go willingly to her assigned intellectual and political places give credence to Rosenberg's understanding of Murray's life as animated by racial and gender identifications. But Murray was also a "firebrand" in the context of structural oppressions of race and gender that animated her critical analysis of social justice.

Second, when it comes to conceptualizing Murray's journey as a metaphor for intersectional theorizing, identifying what both books underemphasize also merits review. Significantly, neither book presents capitalism as a core *analytical* category within their narratives or within Pauli Murray's life. Class is certainly there, but it doesn't explain much of anything beyond Murray's economic status at given points in her life. By highlighting gender and race, respectively, *Jane Crow* and *The Firebrand and the First Lady* both treat class as a descriptive, structural background factor, and by doing so, work within taken-for-granted assumptions of capitalism. Yet depictions of Murray's economic insecurity and vulnerability, let alone her poverty at various points in her life, are no substitutes for a class analysis that might explain both the trajectory of Murray's economic life as well as how that trajectory influenced her critical inquiry. If economic insecurity was such a factor in her life, one that she shared publically with so many other people, why didn't Murray herself analyze the obvious? Was class so taken for granted within existing racial analyses that she, like others, assumed that conquering racism would level the class playing field? Was Murray reticent on the issue of class because it became increasingly dangerous for her to be so by the 1950s? Because Rosenberg seems to be more attuned with responding to the mantra of race, class, gender, and sexuality, she is careful to include all four categories of analysis. For example, Rosenberg relies on current debates concerning how the norms of Black middle-class respectability with an assumed Black patriarchy constrained Murray. Because Murray worked closely throughout her entire life with African American men, she certainly was positioned to see patriarchy in action within African American communities. Yet what are the effects of a more distant but potentially more powerful patriarchy by white men on Murray's choices and analyses?

Reflecting a similar trend within intersectionality itself, the absence of a class analysis is a missed opportunity within both books. The 1930s Great Depression elevated questions of capitalism and socialist and communist responses to it in a global context. Pauli Murray was living in New York during this period, a time of heightened political awareness among African American activists and intellectuals who increasingly examined how capitalism and racism were intertwined. With friends and colleagues who were part of this intellectual community, Murray was familiar with these questions, understanding how racism in the U.S. was tied to capitalist development. Like others during this period, Murray developed a critical perspective on capitalism, yet seemingly did not tie it to her increasingly critical analysis of racism. In the 1940s and 1950s, Murray may have felt pressured to play down any radical class analysis of either racism or sexism, recognizing the chilling effects of the Cold War on U.S. domestic politics. By emphasizing race and gender/sexuality, respectively, neither book treats class as an analytical category, and in doing so, both position capitalism and its class relations as a backdrop for racial and gender analyses. In this regard, both books write to the sensibilities of contemporary U.S. audiences wherein class analyses remain secondary to other theoretical frameworks.

Similarly, resembling their treatment of class, both biographies also have less to say about nation as a category of analysis. This is an interesting editorial choice because, as an attorney, Murray was well aware of how the U.S.

nation-state facilitated racial oppression. Despite the tireless efforts of Ida Wells-Barnett's anti-lynching campaign, lynching persisted with little government intervention or censure. Achieving social justice was not just a matter of personal politics, but was a collective project that required analyses and action concerning national belonging, nationalism as an ideology, and national identity.

Murray's sustained attention to making American democracy work provided an important venue for her analyses of social justice. Murray's autobiographies are preoccupied with questions of citizenship, national belonging, and race. Murray recalls that when she graduated from college in 1933, she wanted to write her family history as part of her aspiration to become a writer. Yet her pathway to being a published author was repeatedly blocked. In *Proud Shoes*, published two decades later, Murray invokes her family as metaphor for a broader struggle for an inclusive, socially just American national identity. Murray aimed to unsettle the dominant American narrative that relegated African Americans to second-class citizenship. In the introduction to the 1978 edition of *Proud Shoes*, Murray reflects on her own journey: "The writing of *Proud Shoes* became for me the resolution of a search for identity and the exorcism of the ghosts of the past. No longer constrained by suppressed memories, I began to see myself in a new light—the product of a slowly evolving process of biological and cultural integration, a process containing the character of many cultures and many peoples, a New World experiment, fragile, yet tenuous, a possible hint of a stronger and freer America of the future, no longer stunted in its growth by an insidious ethnocentrism" (xvi).

Terborg-Penn and Rosenberg provide substantive descriptive material on American politics, but discourses of citizenship that are so central to nationalism and nation-state policies are not major analytical themes in either volume. Fortunately, Sarah Azaransky's book, *The Dream Is Freedom: Pauli Murray and American Democratic Faith* (2011), fills this void. Azaransky examines how Murray looked to broader discourses of citizenship, being aware from a young age of the gaps in the dominant narrative about American identity and the discriminatory behavior that faced its African American citizens. This is the tension between the promise of U.S. democracy and the reality of unequal citizenship. Murray didn't just want to be included into American democracy as it currently existed—she wanted American democracy to have a more accurate accounting of its own principles and actions. Murray advanced an alternative argument of what it might mean to be an American, one that rests on equality and social justice.

Finally, *The Firebrand and the First Lady* and *Jane Crow* both offer provocative evidence that Murray's understandings of race, class, gender, and sexuality within a framework of social justice constituted a precursor for intersectionality as a form of critical inquiry and praxis (Collins and Bilge 2016). Reading these two volumes together provides different puzzle pieces for understanding Murray's actual and potential contributions to contemporary understandings of intersectionality. At varying points in her life, not only did Murray emphasize race, class, gender, sexuality, and, with Azaransky's contribution, nation as categories of analysis; because she took creative social action across and within multiple interpretive communities, Murray was positioned to see race, gender, sexuality, class, and nation as intersecting phenomena.

Because Murray lived such a long life that reaches out in so many different directions, contemporary scholars often emphasize the part of Murray's biography that most appeals to them. For example, queer scholars and activists find inspiration in Murray's courage as a trans person and acknowledge her accomplishments within queer theory. Similarly, religious activists are attracted to Murray's late-in-life embrace of religion, bringing newfound recognition to the centrality of ethics to Black women's intellectual work and politics (Pinn 2008). This piecemeal approach can make important additions to ongoing debates in a given field. Yet no matter how well intended, the fact that many distinctive and seemingly unconnected interpretive communities increasingly claim Murray as an icon for their respective projects can flatten the complex, intersectional nature of her life and work. Prematurely assembling pieces of Murray's life—neatly categorized into gender, or sexuality, or race, or class—into one synthetic narrative that seemingly demonstrates her growing awareness of intersectionality is tempting. This approach may advance intersectionality yet inadvertently presents a narrative about Murray's life that she herself might not recognize. Mapping Murray's deepening intersectional framework onto a simple linear model that assigns consciousness of racism, or heterosexism, or gender oppression, or capitalism to a particular stage or series of events in her life course is not only premature; it may also be incorrect. There is simply not enough scholarly evidence for this perspective.

The metaphor of the journey seemingly provides a more useful orienting strategy for understanding Murray's search for social justice, her subsequent understandings of freedom, as well as the methodological implications of this journey for intersectional theorizing. Murray's life work illustrates a critical praxis model of moving within and through different systems of power, specifically race, class, sexuality, nation, and gender. Murray's angle of vision on the interrelationships among these forms of inequality did not emerge full blown. Instead, Murray engaged categories that seemed most salient for advancing social justice in a specific social context, then drew insight from other categories that were salient in other social contexts.

Murray grappled with varying types of inequality, some more prominent during some phases of her life than others. The arc of her biography suggests that she refused to settle on one system of power—namely, race, class, gender, sexuality, nation, or age—as more fundamental than others. Instead, she attended to the system or systems that were most salient to her experiences during different phases of her life, putting her earlier knowledge in dialogue with that gained later on in life. Rather, because she was engaged in a broader struggle for social justice, she kept multiple systems at play with increasing complexity as her life progressed. Murray used her experiences with social action and with intellectual production as touchstones for analysis, yet her individual experiences and the standpoints they engendered did not determine her analysis. Murray was a critical thinker, and her patterns of critical engagement looked both ways: to the social relations of the communities of which she was most closely aligned (for most of her life, this was the African American community), as well as to broader communities that seemingly lay outside her immediate concerns, for example, the labor movement, the women's movement, the social justice actions of religious organizations, and broader initiatives in support of American democracy writ large. Via this analysis, Murray was also open to multiple alliances, with white feminists, with African colleagues who challenged her understandings of what it meant to be American, with poor African Americans whose desperate economic situations were so central to her views of social justice, and even with Eleanor Roosevelt.

Pauli Murray's work resonates with the idea of visionary pragmatism within Black feminist thought, but it carries such thought into different arenas (James and Busia 1993). Informed by Black women's community work, Black women had a distinctive, intersectional angle of vision on the notion of freedom that was associated with African American social and political thought. They also had a more expansive experiential understanding of the kind of political solidarity that would be needed in moving toward freedom. This visionary pragmatism that embraced social action as a way of knowing the social world and of theorizing social inequality fostered a pragmatic understanding of how change occurs in the social world. The struggle for freedom required a concomitant commitment to social justice, and moving toward social justice required flexibility and persistence. Pauli Murray may never have used the phrase "visionary pragmatism" to describe her journey, yet her actions speak just as loudly as her words.

Implications for Intersectionality

Simone de Beauvoir and Pauli Murray followed different paths to engage the question of freedom, each achieving partial perspectives on its meaning. Beauvoir was able to live as, in her words, an "independent woman" within French society. As a well-known philosopher and prominent member of French intellectual circles, Beauvoir enjoyed the time and material resources that she needed to write and to practice her craft. Her status as a philosopher in a privileged interpretive community enabled her to develop a groundbreaking analysis of women's oppression that remains a signature text of feminism. Yet Beauvoir also had difficulty looking beyond her own experiences in ways that granted all women the agency that she possessed. Her thesis of existential freedom was compromised by her reliance on the race/sex analogy to make the case for women's oppression. Beauvoir's partial perspective on freedom reflected these experiences.[15]

Murray made her way through life as a different kind of independent woman, never achieving economic security and political protection. Murray neither had the refuge of belonging within any one community, including Black communities, nor did she express a desire to do so. Her travels among multiple, diverse communities fostered a distinctive perspective on what it would take for a person like herself to be free. Murray could not focus on freedom as an abstraction, but rather engaged ideas of freedom as a state of becoming, a process of moving toward freedom that affected her own life. For Murray, the meaning of freedom was grounded in its achievement, one that was calibrated through pragmatic action. Her legal writings, autobiographies, and poetry reflected a hope that achieving social justice and fairness would facilitate freedom. Despite its scope, Murray's perspective on freedom was also partial and unfinished, leaving us a historical record that has yet to be fully examined.

Neither Beauvoir nor Murray developed a coherent narrative that explained how their analysis of the meaning of freedom went beyond their own circumstances. The partial perspective on freedom that each provides has two implications for intersectionality, one substantive and the other methodological.

First, this chapter cautions that the mere appearance of categories such as race, class, gender, and sexuality, among others, within a critical analysis does not mean that an argument is necessarily intersectional. Beauvoir and Murray both attended to similar categories, and for many scholars, Beauvoir seemingly offers the most comprehensive intersectional analysis because she incorporates more than one category in her analysis. She could have made the decision to write about "women's oppression," leaving readers to imagine which women she had in mind. Instead, she develops her analysis of freedom by relying on a race/gender analogy that incorporates other categories of analysis. Her argument contains categories of gender, race, ethnicity, class, and age, using her assumptions about how they are related to build her case. Her categories are related, but is her argument intersectional?

In contrast, Murray ostensibly takes on fewer categories, examining race and gender in her analysis of Jane Crow (Murray and Eastwood 1965) not by comparing them, but by examining their interconnections. In this work, Murray explains women's oppression not through analogy, but by arguing how race and gender are related. Focusing on the particularities of African American women's experiences in a context of race and gender discrimination informed her intersectional analysis. Beauvoir and Murray both see connections between gender and race but advance different arguments. How is intersectionality served by these two approaches?

The answer may lie in how each thinker handles the idea of difference wherein the relationships of categories can be understood in oppositional or relational terms. Frameworks of oppositional difference stress comparing entities as being *either* same *or* different. Such binary thinking assumes that entities are separate, distinct, nonoverlapping, and opposite (e.g., men are from Mars and women are from Venus). In contrast, frameworks of relational difference recognize distinctions, yet seek patterns of connection among entities that are understood as different. For relational difference, the challenge lies in uncovering points of connection, overlap, or intersection (e.g., men and women may be different but their gender experiences are interconnected). Comparing race and gender within assumptions of oppositional difference would ask, How are racism and sexism alike and unlike one another? In contrast, comparing race and gender within assumptions of relational difference would ask, What does the relationship between racism and sexism reveal about these entities as separate systems of power as well as how they shape one another?[16]

This distinction between oppositional difference and relational difference sheds light on how Beauvoir and Murray approached the relationship of categories of race and gender. Beauvoir's comparative use of race and gender seems more closely aligned with frameworks of oppositional difference, with important consequences for her critical theoretical analysis of women's oppression. In this regard, Beauvoir's analogical thinking that seeks similarities and differences between women's oppression and that of Black people reflects traditional ideologies of Western science and philosophy. Ideologically, analogical thinking rests on a logical circuit that assumes that children are like animals (naturally free), that blacks are like animals, that women are trapped by their biology (animals being more embodied), and that women are childlike (Stepan 1990). Beauvoir is certainly aware of the power of ideology—in *The Second Sex* she details the pernicious effects of gendered ideology. Yet uncritically relying upon a framework of oppositional difference that equates Black people, children, poor people, animals, and women limits her analysis. Ironically, Beauvoir provides the tools to make an argument about the interconnected oppressions of Black people and women but fails to do so.

Murray's social theorizing seems more wedded to ideas of relational difference, perhaps because her experiences as an activist inform her critical theorizing. Murray's activism put her in dialogue with many different kinds of people, where the success or failure of a particular project rested on finding common ground. Building coalitions among distinctive projects required identifying points of similarity and difference among them. African American women's experiences with flexible solidarity illuminate how relational difference works within the context of Black women's community work. This framework of relational difference might underpin the idea of flexible solidarity. And this idea of flexible solidarity, and by implication, relational difference, speaks to important issues of intersectional praxis. As an African American intellectual-activist whose critical praxis moved among multiple political projects, and had multiple forms of expression, Murray's understanding of both oppression and freedom became increasingly sophisticated because she was constantly looking for connections between ideas and action.

Beauvoir and Murray both relied on comparative thinking, but as this distinction between oppositional difference and relational difference suggests, not in the same way. Beauvoir's analysis of women's oppression was compromised in large part by how her use of analogical reasoning compared women with other similarly oppressed groups, an approach that *suppressed* intersectional analysis. She used the familiar terminology of gender, race, class, and age as categories of analysis, yet the way that she did so provided a partial perspective on oppression and freedom. In contrast, Murray relied on comparative analysis by bringing what had been learned in one project to the next, changing the meaning of both in the process. The trajectory of her intellectual work resembles American pragmatism's theme of experimentalism. Murray's critical analysis of oppression deepened via social action as a way of knowing, with experiences informing the meaning of oppression and freedom. Neither Beauvoir nor Murray had a comprehensive perspective on the meaning of freedom. In this context, superficial comparisons that elevate Beauvoir as a theorist who provides theoretical analysis for Murray, who tests those ideas through social action, are especially shortsighted.

Second, this comparative discussion of Beauvoir and Murray raises questions of how dialogical engagement might inform intersectionality's critical theorizing. Murray and Beauvoir were contemporaries; how interesting it would have been had they been able to meet and share ideas. Yet how might such a dialogue proceed without some criteria for managing the differences between two women who lived such different lives? And their lives weren't just different, they were unequal. In this regard, Murray's friendship with Eleanor Roosevelt models dialogical engagement across a substantial difference in power. Both women learned to listen to one another and both calibrated their ideas for their particular conversations. This theme of dialogues across differences of power is important for intersectionality's interpretive communities, primarily because such dialogues illuminate partial perspectives. Without dialogical engagement, whose partial perspective on freedom should be believed? And if we pick Murray over Beauvoir, or vice versa, what criteria are we using in making such a choice?

When it comes to freedom, placing the ideas of Beauvoir and Murray in dialogue illuminates the complementary nature of abstract analyses of existential freedom and theorizing that emerges from creative social action in working for freedom. Existential freedom is meaningless without critical praxis, yet critical praxis needs theoretical ideas such as existential freedom. This suggests that the respective contributions and limitations of these different ways of theorizing intersectionality itself may be compromised when it emphasizes one over the other. This case suggests that conceptions of existential freedom not only emerge from critical praxis, but also are tested by the ability to influence it. This view incorporates experience as important in shaping knowledge. But more importantly, it also points to the significance of intentional social action. Similarly, critical praxis without a community and a goal is aimless and ineffective.

Murray's intellectual activism not only prefigures the core ideas of intersectionality's content, but also informs the kind of dialogical engagement that might ground intersectionality's methodology. Murray's strategies of drawing upon experience and social action over time, framed by an ethical commitment to social justice, suggest that the metaphor of a journey is an apt description of her intellectual activism. Murray's journey is less one a "success story of grasping toward freedom" and more "an alternative route to what could not be transcended. There is something dialectical about this process: the imperatives of identification are perpetually paradoxical" (Hall 2017, 22). Murray's identifications of race, class, gender, sexuality, age, and nation were differently salient, either singularly or in combination, during different phases of her life and, as a result, remained "perpetually paradoxical." Theoretically, they were all there all the time, but critical praxis required seeing them and using them when they were the best fit for the situation at hand. In this regard, Murray's journey fostered a deepening intersectional analysis.

Owning the power of a language, a culture, a style of communication can be the mark of power for individuals and for interpretive communities. Yet without established interpretive communities that cultivate communication, individuals remain scattered and this communicative power remains unrealized. Dialogues are essential because no one individual or interpretive community can wrap its arms about the magnitude of intersectionality itself, nor can the arguments of a small number of intellectuals or the practices of one resistant knowledge project become the template for intersectional theorizing. Just as Beauvoir and Murray had partial perspectives on freedom, many others have similarly partial understandings of a host of themes. When it comes to freedom or any other topic, the challenge for intersectionality lies in theorizing the relationships among them.

PART IV Sharpening Intersectionality's Critical Edge

7

Relationality within Intersectionality

The idea that race, gender, class, and similar phenomena are maintained through relational processes now functions as such a taken-for-granted truism that intersectionality's insight of recognizing these categories of analysis as interconnected is no longer novel (Phoenix and Pattynama 2006, 187). Intersectionality has not been alone in its embrace of relationality.[1] Within academia, the idea of relationality is widespread, reappearing across social science projects as diverse as relational sociology (Powell and Depelteau 2013), network analysis (Castells 2000), and conversational analysis, as well as projects that aim for greater citizen participation in democratic processes (see, e.g., Sirianni 2009). Relationality lies at the heart of theoretical analyses of social inequality, the case with class relations within Marxist social theory. Within a global context, terms such as *international* and *transnational* signal new understandings of how political phenomena are interconnected. Given the significance of relationality to the very construct of intersectionality, as well as the growing attention to relationality within academia, intersectionality has much at stake in distinguishing itself within the multiple and cross-cutting uses of the term *relationality* that now exist. Relationality constitutes a core theme of intersectionality's paradigmatic thinking (see table 1.1 in chapter 1). If relationality is so central to intersectionality, developing a more comprehensive analysis of this core theme is an essential task for intersectionality's theory-building project.[2] But how is relationality currently understood and used within intersectionality? Moreover, how might these understandings of relationality inform intersectionality's critical theorizing? These questions are important for clarifying how relationality has and might be used for intersectionality as critical social theory.

In this chapter, I examine relational thinking *within* intersectionality by exploring the relational logic that informs intersectionality's scholarship and activism. I sketch out three modes of relational thinking—namely, relationality through addition, articulation, and co-formation. These modes of relational thinking constitute focal points for how I see intersectionality's practitioners conceptualizing and using relationality. Because they inform intersectionality's critical inquiry, these three focal points of addition, articulation, and co-formation map how relationality is used within intersectionality.[3] Within my discussion of addition, articulation, and co-formation, I also include a preliminary analysis of how each form of relational thinking potentially informs the question of how to theorize intersecting power relations. Gaining a better grasp on relationality is especially important for sharpening intersectionality's analysis of intersecting power relations. The relational nature of power relations has been an important guiding premise of intersectionality since its inception. But what is the evidence for this claim?

Because addition, articulation, and co-formation constitute starting points for relational thinking, not end points for analyzing relationality, they offer one way of organizing the thinking tools that people take into varying intersectional projects. My argument in this chapter concerning relationality within intersectionality is speculative and provisional. It is meant to spark dialogue about intersectionality's paradigmatic thinking—namely, how relationality might be developed as a core theme and the ways in which intersecting power relations inform intersectionality's guiding premises (see table 1.1). Sharpening intersectionality's critical edge requires developing agreed-upon understandings, however provisional, of its core constructs and guiding principles.

Additive Frameworks

For many of intersectionality's practitioners, relational thinking through addition is a malleable thinking tool that lends itself to different uses. Additive approaches often signal what's missing, revealing how the absence of race, gender, sexuality, and similar categories compromises a particular study, theory, or set of practices. The heuristic use of intersectionality often relies on additive frameworks, the case, for example, of adding race and gender to studies of work.

Additive frameworks may seem to be simple, yet their strategies fundamentally disrupt taken-for-granted knowledge. Individual researchers, activists, and practitioners have found additive strategies to be quite useful for particular studies. Yet when it comes to applying additive strategies to bodies of knowledge created by communities of inquiry, additive strategies take on a different meaning. For example, adding intersectionality into a well-established field can generate debate about taken-for-granted frameworks. Depending on the case, the field can undergo a paradigm shift. A more daunting task lies in trying to *add together* fields of inquiry that have developed independently. When a field of inquiry has undergone additive changes—the case, for example, of women's and gender studies being receptive to analyses of sexuality, and conversely, sexuality studies being attentive to the gendered nature of material—a new framework may emerge that draws from the separate parts. New terms such as *heteropatriarchy* seemingly combine these separations. Intersectionality itself emerged as a field of inquiry that initially added together what had been separate. Before intersectionality emerged, class, race, and gender each functioned as dominant or master categories in their own right, with their own communities of inquiry and concerns. Yet because each of these categories has a distinctive genealogy, the process of adding them together illuminates various aspects of the additive process.

Despite their seeming simplicity, additive strategies fundamentally challenge the logic of segregation that underlies social relations and their knowledge projects. Relationality through addition disrupts the logic of segregation that underlies Western knowledge. This core logic of segregation has several distinguishing features. First, within the logic of segregation, everything has *one* place, a place has meaning only in relation to other places, and every place has its rank. This logic of segregation underpins racism, sexism, heterosexism, nationalism, colonialism, and similar structures of power. In this context, relational thinking of any kind is not just a small task but rather challenges the categorical logic that underpins Western epistemology. Second, knowledge projects generate ideologies that classify ideas, people, and social practices within legitimated segregated space.[4] The workings of this logic of segregation for colonialism, nationalism, racism, sexism, and similar systems of power has been criticized, but it is important to point out that this same logic underpins practices that do not seem to be implicated in power relations. For example, practices such as dividing knowledge into specialized fields of study, or even distinguishing between the sciences and the humanities, is part of this categorical logic that underlies Western social thought. In essence, the norms of the logic of segregation are remarkably similar to the norms of normal science—namely, a belief in classification, objectivity, linearity, and empiricism (Harding 1986; Collins 1998a, 95–123). Finally, maintaining segregated spaces requires maintaining boundaries. To distribute social goods, one needs to know who truly belongs to the category at hand and who is an interloper. Citizenship debates are very much about this issue of belonging (Davis 2011). Boundary maintenance as part of a logic of separation also informs how epistemic power is exercised in deciding who gets to do intellectual work in the first place.[5]

During the initial excitement accompanying intersectionality's discovery, addition seemed to be one step that might move intersectionality closer to more complex forms of relational thinking. Yet transcending the logic of segregation via additive strategies is more daunting. Categories of race, class, gender, sexuality, ethnicity, age, and ability, as well as critical discourses that have grown up around them, are not free-floating ideas unmoored within social relations. Instead, interpretive communities disagree on the meaning of each category of analysis just as staunchly as political communities disagree on the politics of these terms. Trying to add two ideas together within intersecting power relations highlights the challenges of dialogical engagement across differences in power. Moreover, because unequal power relations do not simply disappear within intersectional spaces, but rather can reorganize themselves within those spaces, intellectual vigilance is needed, even for what seems to be simple addition.

One danger with simple addition lies in privileging one's own favored category as the so-called master category of analysis and accommodating lesser categories by adding them into the master category. Simone de Beauvoir's analysis of women's oppression treats gender as a master category; she added the categories of race, ethnicity, class, and age *into* her gendered analysis.

Beauvoir views gender both as her object of investigation and as her primary analytical category. In contrast, she sees race, age, and class as descriptive, self-evident entities, many of which did not need analysis at all. If the ideas of "Black people" and "slave" become interchangeable, with the slave experience used as the archetype of race itself, adding them together really becomes less "adding into" than "adding onto" what is already assumed to be true. In this case, incorporating ideas about race, age, ethnicity, and class did not result in a better explanation of how intersecting oppressions shape gender oppression. Rather, Beauvoir's analogical reasoning simply added in other categories of analysis that upheld her hypothesis of the fundamental nature of gender oppression (Beauvoir 2011 [1949]).

Relationality through addition may be better approached by adding together categories over time rather than all at once at one point in time. This shift suggests that the temporal sequence by which things are added together elevates relationality through addition as a theoretical tool for intersectionality. Theoretically, one can add together gender, race, and class in any order. But practically, the sequence in which one adds a particular category to others matters (V. Smith 1998). The meaning of one category is changed when it is added to another. Processes of dialogical engagement within intersectional inquiry resemble a journey, where the starting point of one's journey provides a point of origin and shapes subsequent knowledge. One starts in gender and "adds in" additional categories by incorporating class, or starts in ethnicity and moves toward sexuality, or stands on a prior intersection of race and class to move toward ability. Engaging the social world, even a critical engagement of the social world, from such different points of origin provides different outcomes. For example, Pauli Murray's journey toward intersectionality reflected the particulars of her life. Another individual who engaged in a similar intersectional journey might draw upon different experiences, thereby adding categories in a different sequence. Mechanistic understandings of relationality through addition that draw on simple mathematical addition to understand this dimension of intersectional inquiry overlook the richness of possibilities of additive approaches.

The Challenge of Adding Class

The treatment of social class within intersectionality illustrates some of the challenges of adding together distinctive knowledge projects. Class has been a curious master category within the triad of race/class/gender. Some critics quite rightly point out that class has been neglected within intersectionality (Acker 1999). Yet class reappears within intersectionality, sometimes as a hypervisible category that is mentioned so often that it loses meaning (chapter 4's discussion of the repetition of Crenshaw's "coining" narrative comes to mind); as a descriptive, nonanalytical category referencing class identities within a system of social stratification; and as an analytical category within Marxist social thought that analyzes capitalism and the social relations it engenders (see chapter 2). Given the differences among markedly different versions of class, which class is being invoked when it is added together with race and gender?

The shorthand term *class* often does too much heavy lifting within intersectional scholarship, precisely because prior questions of which types of class analysis are being added into intersectional projects remain unexplored. For example, West and Fenstermaker's influential article "Doing Difference," published as part of a symposium in *Gender and Society*, ignores the structural contours of class and capitalism in favor of imagining how class is performed (West and Fenstermaker 1995). This extension of the poststructuralist idea of performativity to class was criticized for its erasure of structuralist analyses of class (Collins 1995). By itself, examining how people perform class identities is not a problem. The broader issue concerns the significance of ignoring structural class analyses that offer analyses of political economy, capitalism, ideology, and class relations in favor of understanding class fundamentally as a performance.

Apparently alarmed by the treatment of class within intersectionality, some scholars of social class have resisted intersectionality's additive strategies, arguing that Marxist social theory *already* provides an adequate explanation for social inequality. And because it does, little need exists to add class into intersectionality. Rather, intersectionality would be better served if it were, in fact, added into Marxist class analysis. The value added by intersectionality lies in strengthening a preexisting class analysis by adding into it race, gender, or both. From this perspective, class is a master category that can be reformed by intersectional criticism, but is not itself in need of transformation.

The significance of Marxist social theory's analysis of class cannot be ignored, primarily because Marxist social theory has had such a strong influence on Western critical social theory itself. And as part of that Western critical theoretical tradition, intersectionality draws from this stock of Western knowledge. One can trace a significant albeit unacknowledged influence of selected ideas from Marxist social theory on the critical social theories and resistant knowledge projects described in chapters 2 and 3. The Critical Theory of the Frankfurt school, Fanon's liberation theory, critical race theory, some strands of feminism, and British cultural studies have taken up varying ideas from Marxist social theory for their own projects. This does not mean that these projects are derivative of Marxist analysis, or that they would self-define as influenced by Marxist social theory. Rather, many critical social theories have been engaged in dialogues with the ideas of Marxist social theories without attribution.[6]

Rather than trying to add class into intersectionality, working with examples of class analysis that are already within intersectionality may be sufficient. It's less that no class analysis exists within intersectionality than that class is conceptualized using uneven patterns within intersectional analysis. The intellectual production of Angela Y. Davis is instructive here. Davis's early scholarship has a robust analysis of capitalism at its core that prefigures intersectional analyses. Take, for example, her signature article "Rape, Racism and the Capitalist Setting" (1978), published a decade before Kimberlé Crenshaw's groundbreaking article on intersectionality and violence against women of color. Tellingly, Davis's analysis of rape as a tool of violence parallels Ida Wells-Barnett's analysis of lynching offered decades earlier. In this sense, Davis invokes these analyses of violence against women. But in Davis's argument, capitalism is a significant analytical category. It doesn't determine violence against women of color but rather is an essential dimension of explaining its contours. Davis provides an argument that combines rape (sexual violence toward women), racism (slavery as a police state), and slavery as a particular instance of a capitalist setting within one synthetic argument. Because this article precedes the naming of intersectionality as a framework of analysis, Davis does not add race, gender, and sexuality into capitalism, nor does she add class as proxy for capitalism into prevailing views on race, gender, and sexuality. Rather, her early work shows how an innovative critical analysis can emerge from an initial strategy of adding together entities that seemingly do not go together. The trajectory of Davis's work writ large suggests that beginning with relationality through addition may seem straightforward, but the process of working dialogically through addition reveals new questions and connections that may not have been available before.[7]

These debates about social class within intersectionality identify an important challenge for intersectionality's theory building. The ongoing process of incorporating additional categories of analysis seemingly destabilizes understandings of intersectionality that are already in place. How many categories can be added in before intersectionality itself becomes meaningless? Feminist philosopher Judith Butler seems to suggest as much with her summary dismissal of intersectionality as something that deteriorates into ever-smaller categories into a meaningless "etc." Butler identifies an important challenge to an intersectionality that simply continues to add new categories of analysis without self-reflection about how each category changes all the others. Yet uncritically assuming that intersectionality is a simple assemblage of seemingly similar entities that when added together produce intersectionality trivializes this discourse.

Grappling with these challenges of relational thinking through addition involves carefully assessing how intersectionality is changed by ever-expanding categorical growth. These debates concerning the treatment of class within intersectionality suggest that simply adding categories into one another is insufficient. Taking seriously the argument that class itself rests on different ontological foundations as intersectionality's other categories, Floya Anthias and Nira Yuval-Davis observe that "class, gender and race may be dependent on different existential locations, but they are not manifestations of different types of social relations with distinct causal bases within distinct systems of domination" (1992, 109). In other words, there's no such thing as an independent race, class, or gender effect—no such thing as "purely gender." Rather, the knowledges developed within a logic of segregation can take intersectionality only so far. At this point, additive conceptions of relationality foreshadow articulation as another aspect of relational thinking, one that brings different insight to intersectional analysis.

Relational Thinking through Articulation

Stuart Hall's (2017, 91) conception of articulation provides a solid analytical starting point for exploring how relationality through articulation informs intersectionality.[8] For Hall, the term *articulation* has a "nice double meaning" that invokes social relations and ideas. In its first meaning sense, the term *articulation* refers to a joint or juncture, such as among bones, a movable joint. Using a metaphor of the coupling and uncoupling of the front and rear sections of a truck, Hall posits that to work as a truck, the two parts become connected or articulated to one another through a specific linkage. The distinctive parts of the truck remain intact, yet the focus shifts from the parts of the truck to the varying ways that trucks can be created using different configurations of parts. With tangible objects, neither part is changed in the process of articulation, but rather the articulation creates a new, complete truck. An articulation is thus "the form of the connection that can make a unity of two different elements, under certain conditions. It is a linkage which is not necessary, determined, absolute and essential for all time" (Grossberg 1996, 141).

This use of articulation suggests that society is not an organic totality, but rather constitutes a series of moving parts with an overall structure that reflects the dynamic patterns of those parts. When it comes to the organization of intersecting power relations, this dimension of articulation provides a framework for the changing relationships among multiple systems of power. In essence, racism, sexism, capitalism, nationalism, homophobia, and xenophobia, among others, are articulated differently in and across varying social contexts. Relationships among systems of power are contingent and not fixed. And because society is not organized via rules that can predict structural outcomes, intersecting power relations reflect struggles concerning how the elements of society will be articulated (Mercer 2017, 9).

Hall's second meaning of articulation focuses on the interconnection of ideas with each other as well as how ideas and society interrelate. Hall suggests that a theory of articulation is both a "way of understanding how ideological elements come, under certain conditions, to cohere together within a discourse, and a way of asking how they do or do not become articulated, at specific conjunctures, to certain political subjects" (Grossberg 1996, 141–142). This second meaning refers to how language "articulates" or brings new ideas by combining existing ideas into new patterns, by attaching new connotations to them, or both. Within this use, sets of ideas can be coupled and uncoupled, yet both the new entity as well as the separate parts are changed by these transactions. Because language and communication always occur in social context, this understanding of articulation invokes the ideas-in-action and action-in-ideas of American pragmatism.

This dimension of articulation raises some important questions for intersectionality as a form of critical inquiry. For example, what are intersectionality's core ideas and how did they come to "cohere" the way that they did? How would intersectional analysis be changed if different elements were articulated, for example, examining how ability and religion informed public policies? Moreover, what are the connections between intersectionality's ideas and "political subjects," or people who either advance those ideas or are represented by them?

Both meanings of articulation are important for intersectional theorizing. For example, when it comes to theorizing social inequality, articulation posits that arguments are always provisional. Rather than trying to prove the truth of any one perspective, this approach looks for multiple articulations of race, class, and gender, among others, in explaining social inequality, wondering why some interpretations prevail over others in specific social contexts. Articulation posits contingent, non-necessary connections between different practices, for example, between ideology and social forces, between different elements within ideology, between different social groups within a social movement, and between different knowledge projects. Articulation focuses on the significance of ideas in structuring relations of domination and resistance. Within the logic of articulation, one important task of intersectional theorizing is to examine how varying relationships, both unintended as well as actively cultivated, foster or retard particular intersections. Stated differently, intersectional theorizing should try to explain social phenomena using provisional analyses that can be perpetually recast.

Because the notion of *conjunctures* is informed by both uses of articulation, it constitutes an especially rich construct for examining how knowledge shapes and is shaped by intersecting power relations.[9] Conjunctures are places that connect various parts. In some cases, a seeming crisis at the conjunctures of factors—for example, the combination of circumstances and events that propelled right-wing governments to power in 2016—catalyzes a crisis that lends itself to intersectional analysis. New understandings of social problems can also emerge from such crisis situations, for example, the outpouring of intersectional scholarship after Hurricane Katrina and similar seemingly natural disasters.

The notion of *conjunctures* raises questions about new knowledge that is produced via processes of articulation in the space of conjuncture. Often, the appearance of a new term signals a new articulation of existing ideas and practices. Pauli Murray's creation of the term *Jane Crow* to describe how racism and sexism took particular form in the experiences of African American women also illustrates the use of articulation as a strategy of critical theorizing. Murray recognized that no term existed that could explain how racism and sexism together shaped the experiences of African American women. Murray was familiar with both racism and sexism, studying both and living both. She created the term *Jane Crow* as a way of naming this conjuncture in actual relations (Murray and Eastwood 1965).

French feminist Colette Guillaumin's term *sexage* illustrates how relationality through articulation might draw upon the idea of a conjuncture among discourses to explain a particular intersection. In *Racism, Sexism, Power and Ideology*, Guillaumin (1995) develops a feminist materialist analysis of sexage as a conjuncture among capitalism, racism, and sexism as articulating systems of power. Expanding Marxist social theory's materialist analysis of how capitalism appropriates the labor power of people, Guillaumin argues that capitalism appropriates not just the labor but also the very bodies of people. Seeing this bodily appropriation as an important similarity between racism and sexism, Guillaumin uses analogies to foreground similarities in the processes of producing the categories "race" and "sex," neither of which exists as a biological entity or as a natural social group. Guillaumin's subsequent analysis of sexage is informed by her analysis of racism as a system of appropriation of black bodies and sexism as an appropriation of women's bodies. Guillaumin initially approached racism and sexism as analogous, but used their resemblance to one another to develop her social theory of sexage. By examining racism and sexism as articulating systems of power, Guillaumin's creation of sexage is situated in the historical and analytical conjunction between racism, sexism, and capitalism.[10]

Articulation and conjunctures may be more visible in times of crisis, but conjunctures that seem ordinary may be invisible because they are so taken for granted. The premise that systems of power mutually construct one another is fine at face value, but certain ideas and practices must be more important than others in their ability to do so. Saturated sites of power or conjunctures where systems of power meet provide a starting place and a lingua franca for analyzing power itself that are simultaneously grounded in actual social processes and include space for theoretical analysis. Saturated sites of intersectionality constitute hypervisible sites of intersecting power relations and have this feel of an important conjuncture. They are places where intersecting systems of oppression converge, yet they are not static. They change as the systems to which they are attached change.

Saturated sites are theoretical tools for analyzing the conjunctures of intersecting power relations. Take, for example, how reconceptualizing the construct of the family as a saturated site of power invites new insight on relationality through articulation. Each of the major systems of power that currently fall under intersectionality's framework—gender, class, sexuality, nation, race, ethnicity, ability, and age—often rely on varying claims about family. We know a fair amount about how distinctive scholarly traditions discuss social inequality generally, and family in particular, *within* a given system of power. For example, Western feminists were one of the first groups to question taken-for-granted, naturalized ideas of family within gender as a system of power (Collier, Rosaldo, and Yanagisako 1992; Thorne 1992). Using the relationships that women had with their families—as daughters, sisters, wives, mothers, and grandmothers—feminists raised important questions about gender inequality. During this period of formation, Western gender scholars and activists made important contributions in analyzing how the Western, middle-class family ideal differentially benefitted women, harmed them, or both (Coontz 1992). Similarly, unlike gender scholars, and perhaps in partial response to sustained attacks on feminism as being antifamily, scholars of race and ethnicity have defended family as an important protection against the worst assaults of racism and xenophobia. African American scholarship has struggled with a dominant discourse that uses frameworks of Black family dysfunction to explain everything from school achievement to poverty. These different uses of family within mono-categorical analyses of social inequality—for example, from *either* gender as a system of power *or* race as a system of power—use different conceptions of family to explain gender and racial inequality, respectively. Using articulation to analyze rhetoric and organization of family shows how, despite wide variability across social contexts, the social institution of family serves a similar function across intersecting systems of power. Ideas about family form the bedrock of all societies. Families may be organized differently from one society to the next, yet families underpin important social functions of gaining citizenship rights, regulating sexualities, and intergenerationally transferring wealth and debt. Family rhetoric and practices organize social inequalities of gender, sexuality, race, ethnicity, religion, class, and citizenship, yet they normalize social inequalities by naturalizing social processes (Collins 1998a, 2001).[11]

Sometimes particular conjunctures among multiple systems of power produce recurring social problems that cannot be ignored. For example, intersectionality has generated a solid research tradition on violence (Collins 1998c, 2017b); violence also constitutes a saturated site of power relations. Because violence has long been a topic of concern for feminists, antiracist organizers, scholars, community organizers, and practitioners, a rich body of knowledge about violence that is informed by intersectionality exists across multiple fields of study and forms of political praxis. Within intersectionality, violence has long been accepted as an important social problem. Gender violence of domestic abuse, incest, and sexual harassment in the workplace is far more visible than in the past. Repeated waves of refugee populations and the growth of numbers of stateless people often reflect the catalyst of state-sanctioned violence and warfare in home countries. Armed with awareness of the scope and dynamics of violence as a social problem, scholars and activists involved in antiviolence projects have elevated awareness of violence as a social problem. Understandings of gender violence, racial violence, and sexual violence, among others, have been greatly informed by intersectional frameworks. In this sense, relationality through articulation seems especially well suited to the critical problem-solving focus of intersectionality.

Violence provides a window into the connections among multiple systems of power. Much of this literature has drawn upon intersectionality's guiding assumption that systems of power mutually construct one another in shaping social problems and social phenomena writ large.[12] Here, drawing upon the knowledge base on violence that has been catalyzed by intersectionality might shed light on one core theoretical premise of intersectionality. Violence might serve as a navigational tool for investigating intersectionality's core theoretical premise that systems of power mutually construct one another. Stated differently, focusing on violence may provide a window into the workings of capitalism, colonialism, racism, and heteropatriarchy as distinctive systems of power as well as how violence constitutes a common thread that binds them together. If violence is organized at the conjuncture of multiple systems of power, what does this mean?

Violence as a Saturated Site of Intersecting Power Relations

This growing understanding of violence as a social problem potentially illuminates how violence may be essential to the organization and operation of intersecting power relations. Stated differently, violence is not just an "add-on" to power relations, one of many strategies for enforcing domination. That it most certainly is, but violence and power relations may also be closely intertwined. Across varying social contexts, the use or threat of violence has been central to power relations that produce social inequalities, for example, rape and domestic violence within sexism, lynching within racism, and hate crimes against LGBTQ people.

Violence may be essential to capitalism, colonialism, racism, and sexism, yet the characteristic forms that it takes within these systems of power vary considerably. Across distinctive systems of power, some forms of violence are more visible than others, the case, for example, of the interpersonal violence of domestic abuse that women experience (sexism); the hate speech targeted toward Muslims, Jews, and religious minorities within multicultural democracies (religious intolerance); the routinized violence of extrajudicial policing of racial and ethnic minorities (racism); and militarism as the state-sanctioned violence of warfare (nationalism). This does not mean that other expressions of violence do not exist. Rather, some expressions will be more visible than others, leaving the impression that other expressions of violence are less important.

Despite the ubiquity of violence, theoretical analyses of how violence and intersecting power relations are interconnected remain elusive, precisely because the characteristic forms that violence takes within racism, colonialism, and heteropatriarchy vary tremendously. Treating violence as a *saturated site of power relations* wherein the workings of power within and across capitalism, colonialism, racism, and heteropatriarchy are especially visible provides an entry point into theorizing intersecting systems of power. Saturated sites bundle together practices, social institutions, representations, and patterns of everyday social interaction that appear and reappear across seemingly separate systems of oppression. Saturated sites are important because their hypervisibility and ubiquity makes the points of convergence or transactions of intersecting power relations more visible.

I see several reasons why focusing on violence as a saturated site of intersecting power relations is important for intersectionality's theoretical development. First, violence and similar saturated sites are important nodes within power relations that organize and facilitate interconnected or interlocking systems of power. Stated differently, violence constitutes a form of *conceptual glue* that binds intersecting systems of power together (see, e.g., Collins 1998c). Yet violence is more than the conceptual glue that theoretically joins multiple systems of power; as a constellation of practices, violence is also essential to organizing and managing power as domination. People do not go willingly to their assigned places. Here the connections between hate speech and violent acts, the routinized and normalized nature of violence, and the mechanisms that legitimize this entire endeavor from within distinctive systems of power become more visible within frameworks that see violence as one node of the connective tissue of systems of power.

Second, conceptualizing violence as a saturated site of intersecting power relations opens up new pathways for conceptualizing domination. Violence is clearly an important dimension of capitalism, colonialism, racism, and heteropatriarchy as distinctive forms of political domination. The expansive literature on political domination, which has largely developed uninformed by intersectional frameworks, does provide important clues concerning intersecting power relations. For example, by distinguishing racisms of extermination or elimination (exclusive racisms, such as Nazi genocide) from racisms of oppression or exploitation (internal racisms, such as racial segregation in the U.S., racial apartheid in South Africa, and colonial racisms), Etienne Balibar (1991) provides a crucial intervention in critical racial theory. Balibar argues that these ideal types are rarely found in isolation, and that connections among these types are more common. Zygmunt Bauman's classic book *Modernity and the Holocaust* (1989) develops this thesis of a racism of extermination, extending Balibar's argument beyond nationalism to link racisms of extermination to modernity itself. Political theorist Hannah Arendt had little theoretical interest in racism, yet her parallel histories of domination within the magisterial *The Origins of Totalitarianism* (1968) resonate both with Balibar's thesis of internal and external racisms and Bauman's analysis of racism and modernity. Because intersectional analysis of violence reframes violence not as a matter of human nature or circumstance, but as fundamental to power as domination, conceptualizing violence as a saturated site of intersecting power relations provides a potentially important perspective on political domination.

Heteropatriarchy, neocolonialism, capitalism, racism, and imperialism constitute forms of oppression that characterize global geopolitics, take different forms across nation-states, and catalyze social inequality. Intersectionality's emphasis on intersecting systems of power suggests that distinctive forms of oppression will each have its own power grid, a distinctive "matrix" of intersecting power dynamics (Collins 2000, 274–276). For example, intersections of racism, capitalism, and sexism within the U.S. will differ from those in Brazil, producing a distinctive matrix of domination within each nation-state as well as in relations between the two nation-states. Both nation-states may share general histories of domination, for example, how their extensive engagement with the African slave trade, as colonies and as free, democratic nation-states, was integral to their incorporation in global capitalism. Yet the distinctive patterns that domination has assumed within each nation-state differ dramatically; racial, class, and gender domination in the U.S. and Brazil can neither be reduced to one another nor to some general principles of domination absent the specifics of their histories.

Finally, conceptualizing violence as a saturated site of intersecting power relations also sheds light on resistant knowledge projects of antiviolence initiatives.[13] Viewing violence as hegemonic and omnipotent can frame small actions to resist it as ineffectual and doomed to failure. But conceptualizing antiviolence initiatives as also being saturated sites of intersecting power relations invites entirely new questions concerning the types of ideas and actions that oppose violence. When violence becomes naturalized and normalized to the point where it becomes invisible, political domination seems hegemonic. Yet when political actors peel back this hegemonic veneer and resist hate speech, violent acts, and routinized and normalized institutional-ized violence, their political actions can have far-reaching effects.

Allowing violence to remain uncontested reifies oppression as natural, normal, and hegemonic. Alternately, political activism and resistance that investigate how violence binds together seemingly disparate systems of power can have impact far beyond simple political opposition. Such contes-tation shows how expressions of violence are not discrete events but rather form part of an interconnected whole that refutes political domination as hegemonic. One act of intellectual or political resistance, when joined with many other such ideas and actions across multiple systems of power, can have considerable cumulative effect. Unmasking violence as illegitimate within one specific location can have repercussions that reach far beyond the case at hand. Such reframing of antiviolence within intersectional frameworks can foster understanding of power as empowerment, the op-posite of domination.

Violence as a saturated site of intersecting power relations lies at the heart of domination, and pressure applied to nodes where power relations interconnect potentially resists domination across multiple, interconnected systems of power. In this sense, conceptualizing violence as a saturated site of intersecting power relations highlights the significance of seemingly indi-vidual and disconnected acts of resistance, because it shows how antiviolence ideas and actions are themselves interconnected. Whether racism or sexism, resistance is always present, even if it seems to be invisible. Just as violence is routinized within social institutions, immanent and tangible political re-sistance also persists. Because the possibility for resistance and protest exists within political domination, targeting saturated sites of intersecting power relations as venues for political resistance matters. An intersectional analysis that attends to political domination captures the complexities and instabili-ties that characterize how oppression and resistance coexist.

Keeping an eye on violence as a touchstone for such analysis is a pre-scient reminder of what's at stake for getting it right. Because violence is so deeply embedded in the fabric of many societies, it is unlikely to yield to the efforts of any one theory or group of social actors. Yet, just as intersecting oppressions are far from static, forms of political resistance that are simi-larly flexible are well positioned for such sustained intellectual and politi-cal struggle. In this endeavor, developing a more sophisticated theoretical analysis of forms of relationality within intersectionality should illuminate new connections between intersecting systems of power and new possibili-ties for political resistance.

Relational Thinking through Co-formation

Relational thinking through co-formation adds another layer of complexity to intersectionality's critical theorizing. While theoretically compelling, how would one go about pragmatically theorizing co-formed phenomena of any kind, let alone something as daunting as intersecting systems of power? How does one move beyond co-formation as an abstract, theoretical argument? Comparing relationality through articulation and relationality through co-formation may clarify what's at stake. Articulation comes closest to describing what people actually do when they engage in intersectionality's critical theorizing. And, as the discussion of violence as a saturated site of intersecting power relations suggests in the previous section, relational thinking through articulation can retain the distinctiveness of various parts that need not be assembled in the same way. Because articulation is contingent and produces varying conjunctures, whether expressions of violence or systems of power, the various parts can separate and re-form. Articulation is inherently flexible, open-ended, and resists closure.

In contrast, co-formation seemingly dissolves the categories themselves, aiming for a universal argument or theory of intersecting power relations. It's meaningless to argue that race and gender co-form one another without assuming that they are separate entities. In this sense, co-formation more often lies in the imagination of an individual thinker or theorist than is hammered out in actual social relations. As a result, co-formation is far easier to imagine intellectually than it is to achieve methodologically or to "find" in the social world using standard tools of social science research.

I've approached relationality through addition and articulation as forms of relational thinking that might inform intersectional theorizing. These modes inform processes of theorizing and provide a methodology for doing intersectionality (e.g., dialogical engagement and analysis of saturated sites of power at the conjunctures of power relations). In contrast, co-formation posits holistic analysis of a seamless process of mutual construction of race, class, and gender as phenomena. It seems to describe a reality that it can neither observe nor study empirically. As a result, the idea of relationality through co-formation either becomes purely a philosophical view from the humanities that is off limits to social scientific theorizing, or it faces the daunting task of proving itself by methodologies that were developed for other purposes. Intersectionality can offer guiding premises that race, class, and gender are interdependent and mutually construct one another (see figure 1.1). But is it possible to use co-formation as a methodological strategy to build a critical theory about mutually constructing systems of oppressions? Would that theory provide sufficient evidence for the utility of co-formation itself? The challenges of theorizing co-formation and its possible methodology are daunting.

When it comes to intersectional theorizing that relies on co-formation, the fundamental differences in how various disciplines and fields of study conceptualize social theory as well as the processes used to generate it influence the different approaches that people take. This harkens back to my discussion in chapter 1 of the differences between how social theory is understood and practiced within the social sciences and the humanities. Western social sciences rest on a specific view of social theory that has a particular, recursive relationship to empirical data. Within sociology, political science, economics, geography, and anthropology, theorizing emerges in explaining the truths of the social world. The social world itself is not simply a holistic, self-evident entity that can be understood solely by thinking about it. Rather, the social world has structures that can be uncovered via scientific processes. Social theories emerge from empirical data, but the truth of social theories lies in whether they can be tested.

Despite the daunting challenge of theorizing co-formation, social theorists working within the social science conventions have laid a foundation for examining co-formation as an object of analysis.[14] Efforts to examine complexity as an important dimension of intersectionality are especially promising in theorizing co-formation. In a widely cited article, "The Complexity of Intersectionality," Leslie McCall (2005) provides a provisional template for thinking through the relationship between complexity and intersectionality. McCall identifies three methodological approaches that scholars of intersectionality use when making sense of analytic "categories" (such as race, class, gender, and so on); each approach treats the complexity of such categories differently. McCall provides a useful taxonomy of categorical thinking that aligns with broad philosophical trends of Western knowledge.[15] British sociologist Sylvia Walby (2007) also sets about the difficult work of examining the connections between social inequality, complexity, and intersectionality.[16] Walby shows the challenges of operationalizing the idea of co-formation within the social sciences, especially for research that wishes to develop a theory of co-formation that is adequate for intersectionality, or that aims to incorporate co-formation within its methodological approaches to social phenomena. These are promising directions for the social sciences, yet theorizing relationality through co-formation may benefit from additional ways of working beyond those suggested by the traditional approaches of McCall and Walby, among others.

The humanities' different approach to social theory fosters a correspondingly distinctive approach to theorizing co-formation. Philosophy, literary criticism, history, and the humanities theorize about important questions. Theorizing about broad philosophical topics such as democracy, inequality, freedom, social justice, and power stem from efforts to make sense of the human condition. There are no right or wrong arguments, no absolute truths, only better or worse arguments. Thus, the humanities more often offer reading strategies for interpreting the social world. Discourse analysis and textual analysis examine less the "truth" of co-formation as an entity and more the ways in which co-formation may work. For example, in *Not Just Race, Not Just Gender: Black Feminist Readings*, literary critic Valerie Smith (1998) uses Black feminism to explore what it means to use intersectionality as a mode of cultural or textual analysis. Via a series of chapters that focus on a topic that seemingly engages only one category of experience— race, class, sex, or gender—over and above the others, Smith examines how the "ostensible dominance of one category masks both the operation of the others and the interconnections among them" (1998, xiv–xv). Smith artfully shows how race was already in a text that ostensibly was about gender, and how gender permeated racial analysis. Because the worldviews of separate areas are so distinct, there is a tendency to claim the area with which one is most familiar and try to add the rest in. Yet her simultaneous reading strategy suggests that the chapters can be read in any order because the category that is assumed to be missing is already there. Smith's analysis resonates with the theme of saliency invoked in Pauli Murray's intellectual journey toward an intersectional analysis—race, class, gender, and sexuality were theoretically there all along, but intersectionality, the act of discovering what is already there, marks coming to the recognition of co-formation.

Because intersectionality encompasses both social sciences and humanities, it can be conceptualized alternately as a social theory that guides the search for truth and as a social theory that guides the search for social meaning. Each of these approaches has implications within intersectionality for relational thinking through co-formation. When it comes to co-formation, the challenge for intersectionality lies less with the distinctions between the social sciences and the humanities and more with how the social sciences and the humanities both adhere to the assumptions of Western epistemology. Fundamentally, co-formation is a holistic concept. In essence, analyzing co-formation within the premises of Western logic basically tries to put back together holistic views of the social world that Western logic itself aimed to destroy. Regardless of whether one works in the social sciences or the humanities, Western epistemological and methodological tools were designed to destroy holistic entities in order to make sense of them. This is the idea of dissecting something to see how it works, or breaking down text to see how it makes meaning.[17]

Relationality through co-formation lies at the heart of intersectionality itself, and I have taken pains in this book not to begin with existing scholarship on co-formation within intersectionality, but rather to uncover the layers of analysis that are required to deepen relational thinking through co-formation. In this volume I make a distinction between top-down and bottom-up theorizing that informs my arguments. I have not started with the work that explores co-formation itself, identifying core constructs and then applying those ideas to intersectionality on the ground in order to ascertain intersectionality's theoretical contours. Instead, I have focused on identifying the methodological tools that would be needed to ground an argument about co-formation in intersectionality's social context as it is actually unfolding. In meeting the challenges of theorizing relationality through co-formation, metaphors provide an important methodological tool for such theorizing.

Metaphors of Co-formation

Metaphoric thinking that actively resists Western colonial knowledge and epistemic practices may be especially useful for envisioning co-formation and intersectionality. By broadening intersectionality's context of discovery, I see three metaphors that emerge from the knowledge projects of subordinated people that stimulate alternative ways of thinking about co-formation. Each emphasizes different aspects of the social world as holistic and each is grounded in specific social relations.

Chicana feminist Gloria Anzaldúa's metaphor of borderland theorizing, with its components of borderland space, border crossing, and *mestiza* identity, provides one such metaphor. Anzaldúa's classic text *Borderlands/La Frontera* (1987) invokes relationality through co-formation as a way to theorize the space of intersectionality's crossroads. Resting on concepts of the new mestiza and mestiza consciousness, Anzaldúa's borderland theorizing invokes the ethos of co-formation. As Patrick Grzanka points out:

Her "borderlands" . . . signify a geographic, affective, cultural, and political landscape that cannot be explained by binary logic (black/white, gay/ straight, Mexican/American, etc.) or even the notion of liminality, that is, *the space between.* Anzaldúa's borderlands are a very *real* space of cutting, overlap, collision, violence, resistance, blending and complexity; simultaneously, the borderlands are nearly unrepresentable insomuch as no singular scientific, geometric, or cartographic framework can adequately capture the dynamic, co-constitutive processes that characterize life in the borderlands. In this sense, Anzaldúa's work exemplifies the concept of intersectionality . . . because Anzaldúa denies any logic that presumes there were ever discreet dimensions of difference that collided at some particular point: in the borderlands, mixing, hybridity, unfinished synthesis, and unpredictable amalgamation were always already happening, and are forever ongoing. (2014, 106–107)

The construct of borderlands is a spatial metaphor of co-formation. Anzaldúa's borderland theorizing highlights the political nature of borders of all sorts and the challenges of navigating them. By pointing out how movement across spatial and symbolic borders is rarely smooth, and how borders themselves are always contested in some way, Anzaldúa's borderland space resembles intersectionality's impetus toward co-formation. This is a powerful metaphor that illustrates the interdependence of entities that are articulated not as finished projects, but rather as necessarily connected and perpetually co-forming. These borders cannot be uncoupled and reassembled at will because they take symbolic form, existing in memory, and as tangible material borders of nations, racial categorization, and gender binaries. Because borders are walls that have symbolic and material meanings, they are perpetually unstable. They cannot be theorized out of existence as pure discourse, yet they are amenable to analysis via postmodern social theory's deconstructive tools.

In claiming mestiza identity, Anzaldúa valorizes borderland spaces as sites of intellectual and political engagement. She uses her own experiences as a way of knowing to theorize the dynamic, changing, and unstable nature of borderland identifications. Such identifications are always under construction, as are borderland spaces as spaces of possibility. The borderland metaphor signals an epistemic shift for intersectional theorizing. Western frameworks of centers and margins within a logic of segregation fade into a construct of the borderlands as a space of heterogeneity, multiplicity, and transgression that constitutes a touchstone for critical theorizing. Intersectionality's spatial metaphor of the crossroads is not a dead space where durable roads converge and then continue on, unaffected by crossing the intersection. Instead, for intersectionality's critical theorizing, intersectional spaces are better conceptualized as borderland places where ideas co-form via dialogical engagement. In this sense, this metaphor references border-land space as a dynamic yet structured set of interactions that, because they constantly form and re-form over time and within space, encapsulate co-formation. Intersectionality is a space of co-formation.

Live jazz provides yet another metaphor for imagining co-formation, both the process of creating the music as well as the music itself as a holistic outcome of co-formation. The holistic experience of the live performance is real—the people who play the music and those who experience the music and are moved by the experience do not exist in virtual space, but rather are real to one another in context of community. One can still trace the varying parts—the score, the instruments, the feel of the room—yet the music itself is entirely new and, because it is live, always unique. Because live jazz assem-bles a particular constellation of people where improvisation holds sway, no two creative events are ever the same. But improvisation does not signal an absence of structure. In order to be recognized as jazz, live events may re-semble one another and share certain structural similarities. The elements of the metaphor of jazz—call and response, a leader of the group, and involve-ment of the listeners—provide a framework for performance, but something new is created that cannot be repeated. A complex co-formation occurs at each event that illustrates the collective nature of creative social action. Live jazz can also be transcendent, offering its participants an invitation to enter a space of universal experience where the everyday world falls away, and the new world of co-creation via experiencing jazz takes its place. Jazz as live performance speaks to the fleeting yet durable nature of co-formation, something that ceases to exist once its musicians stop playing, yet that its co-creators take with them through emotions and memories.

Jazz provides a distinctive epistemological basis for co-formation, one that reflects the influence of indigenous African worldviews and their cultural reinterpretation throughout the African diaspora. Moving from metaphors of sight that are so central to Western social theory (seeing the coupling or uncoupling of trucks) to metaphors of sound that carry value within non-Western cultures (storytelling, poetry, music, and dance as creative collec-tive endeavors) suggests new avenues of investigation for intersectionality. Because jazz is a synthetic soundscape, drawing from and borrowing from various aspects of Western and non-Western sounds, jazz constitutes a con-juncture among multiple cultures. Jazz works within yet changes the rules of

Western music itself. It is simultaneously part of material relations of articulating systems and a site for imagining articulation. Jazz may be the metaphor of co-formation, with the actions of creating jazz illuminating aspects of articulation.[18] When it comes to actual social relations, the complexity of melodic lines, moving singularly or in combination, suggests a kind of articulation that resembles social dynamics. Rather than envisioning a social group as a constellation of people, one might envision a social group as having its own rhythm, sound, feel, or "vibe." Music becomes a universal language for dialogical engagement.[19] Jazz as a metaphor for co-formation provides an alternative pathway for conceptualizing intersectionality as a site of co-formation.

Within Western societies, spaces of live co-creation such as jazz, dance parties, and spoken word poetry carve out alternative ways of experiencing and interpreting the social world. Yet because intersectionality is such a Western concept, honed within a Western epistemology, this question of alternative conceptions of co-formation within existing Western epistemological frameworks remains open. In his article "The Spider's Web: Creativity and Survival in Dynamic Balance," Bill Cohen (2001) uses the metaphor of a spider web as an entry point into an alternative way of imaging social structure and our experiences with it. By offering a pathway for understanding the complexities of indigenous worldviews, Cohen's rich use of the metaphor suggests the holistic thinking of co-formation.[20] Cohen eschews the academic tendency to create a generalized indigenous worldview that erases the particularities of indigenous peoples. Rather, Cohen remains focused on the particular—namely, taking responsibility for his narrative by situating himself in his story as an Okanagan educator, whose narrative is devoted to problem-solving for Native youth. Cohen opens his article with a provocative question: "What is your vision for positive change for First Nations people?" (2001, 140). His metaphoric use of a spider's web is not designed to be seen as part of an essentialized indigenous worldview. Rather, his use of that metaphor seems more closely aligned with traditions of teaching through storytelling. Cohen's notion of the web draws upon the world view of Okanagan people concerning the interconnectedness of life itself: "A central element of Okanagan world view—and, I venture, Indigenous world view generally—is the belief that humans are not the supreme beings on the planet; and that although humans are pretty special, our health and vitality are directly related to the health and vitality of the natural world of which we are a part" (142). Cohen provides a detailed discussion of the world or web of interconnections, not to present the "truth" of an indigenous worldview, but to revisit how core ideas of the Okanagan people might form a foundation for educating youth. He presents a complex cosmology, one grounded in a spiral of creativity. As Cohen notes, "the spider's web reflects awareness, creativity, structure, and symbolizes the interplay between creativity and survival" (144).

The web is an organic entity, not just the remnants of past creativity left as evidence of the spider's actions. Instead, the weaving of the spider's web becomes central to Cohen's metaphoric use of this story. Weaving stories together in a web invokes the narrative dimensions of doing social theory. Cohen notes that "the vision I share is a weave or synthesis of story, history, theory, poetry, epistemology and creativity—a web. This weaver is a 21st-century Okanagan learner and teacher, artist, poet, and lately critical theorist and philosopher. I present my ideas as a contribution to a continuing dialogue" (2001, 140). Cohen avoids romanticizing indigenous ways of knowing as somehow having ready-made answers to modern problems. Rejecting nostalgia, Cohen offers a restorative vision that looks to the past to envision "positive change for First Nations people."

Through this interpretation of the ideas of one indigenous people, the metaphor of the spider's web provides a provocative glimpse into the implications that alternative, indigenous, non-Western worldviews have for intersectionality. Within Cohen's discussion of the worldview of the Okanagan people, the need to theorize co-formation seems nonsensical because it is based on a logic that entities that have been separated need to be put back together. Rather, this view of co-formation aims to step outside of colonial logic to reimagine a holistic world of connectedness and interdependence for the future. We as human beings may be "pretty special," but our "health and vitality are directly related to that of the natural world of which we are a part." In this sense, the metaphor of the spider's web sparks insight and offers a different way of envisioning the social world and human social interaction as already co-forming. It signals a different politics and a different ethics.

By stepping outside the epistemological conventions of Western theorizing, each of these metaphors offers alternative starting points for relational thinking through co-formation and for rethinking the metaphor of intersectionality itself. The first metaphor from Latina feminist thought suggests that co-formation was part of the emergence of intersectionality itself; the second metaphor reflects how oral aesthetics of a Black diasporic soundscape moves beyond the limitations of Western epistemologies of sight and seeing; and the third metaphor draws from the knowledge traditions of indigenous peoples to reimagine the connectedness of all living creatures.

Metaphors matters for epistemic resistance because they do not simply criticize what is; rather, they imagine what is possible. In this case, these three metaphors of borderlands, jazz, and the web are not unknown within Western epistemologies. But when Western knowledge projects discover and often appropriate these terms, the social context that animates these distinctive ways of viewing the world, as well as the women and people of color who authored these ideas, often drops from sight. Decontextualization and abstraction are the hallmarks of how Western epistemologies exercise epistemic power. Terms such as *borderlands, jazz,* and *the web* may continue to circulate, but they become redefined when they are annexed for different purposes. For example, the complexities of Anzaldúa's borderlands theorizing is supplanted by its overuse. Jazz is now a subject in some college conservatories of music, ensuring that it receives institutional recognition. But where are jazz and related forms of African American music being created in live venues? Similarly, the fields of network analysis, information sciences, complexity studies, and globalization studies, among others, have all been influenced by the construct of the web (see, e.g., Castells 2000; Urry 2005), yet with very different questions and perspectives than those suggested by the metaphor for the spider's web. The metaphor of the spider's web is not the internet, with its core contribution one of providing a superficial term for a new paradigm.

The examples in this chapter and throughout this book, such as metaphors of the borderlands, jazz, and the spider's web, all provide partial perspectives on and potentially promising approaches to co-formation as relationality. Together they highlight both the possibilities for a broader context of discovery and the difficulties of dialogical engagement for theoretical work. The epistemological boundaries that circumscribe theory routinely exclude many ways of theorizing. Such boundaries are drawn such that certain forms of theorizing—for example, theorizing through social action, or creation through the arts—fall outside the boundaries of theorizing itself, if, in fact, such work is recognized as theoretical at all. While significant, the work of scholars such as Gloria Anzaldúa, the spider's web that lacks a designated author, and jazz as a collective endeavor can remain marginalized or appropriated within the social theories of Western epistemologies.

Relationality and Intersectionality

My analysis of relational thinking through addition, articulation, and co-formation presents a provisional framework for describing relationality within intersectionality. Each conception highlights how a particular understanding of relational thinking has or might be used within intersectionality itself. Because these modes of relational thinking aim to solve specific social problems, they gain meaning through use. They are not pristine, static, mutually exclusive entities; rather, they distill the essence of ideas in action.

Because this is a provisional framework, I close this chapter with several implications of my argument thus far. First, when it comes to intersectional inquiry, I present addition, articulation, and co-formation as equally useful forms of relational thinking; one does not signify a better approach to intersectionality than the others. Here I reject the assumption that underlies much Western social theory: a linear narrative of progress from seemingly simple to ever-higher forms of achievement. Within this assumption, co-formation represents a more advanced form of relational thinking than its additive and articulatory counterparts, supplanting them with its greater complexity. As examined here, relationality through addition, through articulation, and through co-formation are equivalent strategies, each with its own characteristic complexities. In doing the work of intersectionality, some forms of relational thinking may be better than others for the task at hand. Scholars and activists take up different forms of relational thinking within the communities of practice to which they owe allegiance that are applicable to the social problems they aim to solve. Collectively, they provide navigational tools for thinking through how varying understandings of relationality stimulate distinctive analyses of intersecting power relations.

Second, these categories of relationality through addition, articulation, and co-formation are abstractions that, when read together, provide a provisional map of relationality within intersectionality. In this sense, they contribute to intersectionality's cognitive architecture (see figure 1.1). They also speak to why methodology matters for intersectionality. Because understanding relationality through addition, articulation, and co-formation stresses the processes of doing intersectional work, having a specific project in mind grounds intersectional analysis.[21] My analysis of violence as a saturated site of power provides one such project that has been central to intersectionality itself. Yet there is much theoretical work to be done in analyzing relationality and power. The question of theorizing intersecting power relations, especially those that are visible through the lens of violence, means asking what conceptions of relationality inform our understandings of intersectionality in general and of intersecting power relations in particular. Examining how violence and similar saturated sites of intersecting power relations are organized and operate constitutes a provocative direction for theorizing intersecting power relations. If systems of power are interconnected and mutually constructive in shaping violence and similar phenomena, what does this mean? Relationality is a core construct of intersectionality, and intersectionality alludes to the relational nature of power.

Finally, it may be time to build on the body of knowledge and praxis produced by intersectionality's metaphoric, heuristic, and paradigmatic use in order to take a closer look at relationality itself. While I present relational thinking through addition, through articulation, and through co-formation as analytically discrete, in practice they are interconnected, recursive, and inform one another.

Additive approaches catalyze new questions and perspectives that emerge from the process of trying to combine what was formerly seen as distinctive. One important contribution of additive approaches lies in how they sustain the analytical and political integrity of distinctive entities; for example, race is not the same as gender, and class is not the same as race. This focus suggests that these entities, which carry different histories, different interpretive communities, and different areas of emphasis, cannot be substituted for one another. They resemble one another, but they are not equivalent. Additive conceptions constitute useful ways of checking the boundaries of a given discourse; for example, the process of adding class and sexuality together may reveal patterns of overemphasis or underemphasis in each.

In contrast, articulation suggests ways that the process of putting into dialogue race, class, and gender, for example, might work. Articulation theorizes how different discourses might be connected, making sure to emphasize the contingent and provisional nature of connections. Moreover, articulation retains a focus on social context as an important dimension of the saliency of connections. Its construct of conjunctures provides an analytical framework for exploring how systems of power intersect. Together, addition and articulation provide important methodological tools for intersectional theorizing.

The construct of co-formation references an in-between space—not just between disciplinary knowledges of the social sciences and the humanities, but more importantly, between Western and non-Western epistemologies. Intersectionality names this in-between, dynamic, liminal space on the borders of entities that are ostensibly separate and different. Intersectionality faces the challenge of taking a closer look at articulations that occur in inter-sectionality's crossroads or border space. Yet at what point does articulation flow smoothly into co-formation, primarily by dissolving the old categories, and perhaps generating new ones? Perhaps the space of intersectionality is inherently a space of co-formation, awaiting a new language that better describes what happens there.

8

Intersectionality without Social Justice?

Intersectionality is often perceived as fundamentally critical of unjust societies because social justice seems to be so central to many of its projects. It
certainly seems that intersectionality is on the side of social justice. Social
movements for worker's rights, women's equality, reparations for Black and
indigenous peoples, antidiscrimination protections for LGBTQ people, immigrants' rights movements, and similar political projects draw upon intersectionality as a frame for their social justice work. Overviews of intersectionality
routinely depict it as a form of resistant knowledge that is inherently dedicated
to social justice (Collins and Bilge 2016; Dill and Kohlman 2012; Granza 2014;
May 2015). Yet despite this widespread assumption, is intersectionality *inherently* committed to social justice? Is social justice a defining feature of intersectionality itself, or might its commonsense association with progressive causes
mean that intersectionality's advocates simply assume that it is?

One way of exploring these questions is to examine a discourse that is generally recognized as explicitly *not* grounded in social justice principles but that also makes relational thinking central to its logic and practices.[1] When it comes to social justice, eugenics projects seem to be as far from intersectionality as one can get, serving, for many, as a poster child for social *in*justice. Societies that embrace eugenic philosophies typically aim to transform social problems such as unemployment, increasing crime rates, childbearing by unmarried adolescents, and poverty into technical concerns that are amenable to social engineering by the nation-state. Eugenics projects combine a "philosophy of biological determinism with a belief that science might provide a technical fix for social problems" (Proctor 1988, 286).

Placing intersectionality in dialogue with eugenics, a discourse that is not committed to social justice, illuminates the significance of ethical criteria within intersectionality as a critical social theory. Eugenics achieved prominence as normal science in the absence of self-regulatory ethical practices within its own discourse. How else could its practitioners produce knowledge that upheld racism, heteropatriarchy, colonialism, and nationalism without some forms of scholarly collusion that ignored the ethical implications of their scholarship? As discussed throughout this book, assumptions that research is inherently objective because epistemologies mandate that it be so fall short. When interpretive communities claim that social justice or similar normative principles are the responsibilities of individuals and not of their own communities of inquiry, they overlook how neglecting their own ethics has very real effects on the questions, methods, and social consequences of scholarship. Hence, the question of ethics is especially important for intersectionality's prospects as a critical social theory.

The Relational Logic of Eugenics

Despite its popular association with Nazi Germany, eugenics, as a scientific discourse, has been far more ubiquitous than this highly visible and troubling case (Goering 2014).[2] Before World War II, eugenics projects enjoyed a long and storied history within both Western science and the public policies of many modern nation-states, influencing public health experts, welfare reformers, and policy-makers (Barrett and Kurzman 2004; Weindling 1999, 180). Originating in the United States and Great Britain, eugenics movements proliferated in Europe, North and South America, and the Soviet Union in the 1920s. Many other nation-states, among them China,

India, South Africa, and Australia, also supported public policies that were informed by eugenics projects. Historically, such projects can be divided into three periods: the pre–World War I period, when eugenics emerged in tandem with the founding of Western sciences, social sciences, and humanities; the interwar period, during which the science of eugenics more directly informed public policies; and the post–World War II period, when eugenics projects seemingly disappeared. Throughout this history, eugenics projects were a site of intellectual and political contestation; scholars, politicians, and ordinary citizens lobbied both for and against eugenics.[3]

The use of eugenics in the German nation-state (1933–1945) remains the archetypal example of eugenics primarily because the German government implemented the ideological tenets of eugenics to their logical conclusion within public policy. Armed with a scientific rationale provided by the science of eugenics, the Nazi state systematically killed, imprisoned, or engaged in medical experimentation on millions of people. In this sense, the use of eugenics as a scientific discourse guided and legitimated extreme state-sanctioned violence. Genocides had happened in prior eras between groups. But the science of eugenics was associated with the political emergence of the modern nation-state. This modern state went beyond turning a blind eye to its citizens' lawlessness (the case of lynching) or killing citizens via state-sanctioned capital punishment. In this case, the state was an active agent in organizing and administering state-sanctioned violence on a massive scale.

The name may have changed, but the logic that underlies eugenics persists. By the 1950s, the term *eugenics* was so maligned that it vanished from scholarly and public policy arenas. Despite the disappearance of the term, the ideas of this once dominant framework persist within contemporary science and public policy (Barrett and Kurzman 2004). As Troy Duster (2003, 2015) points out, the visibility granted eugenics within past scientific and national practices, coupled with the departure of formal eugenics projects, fails to account for the potential albeit invisible effects of eugenics within contemporary science. Following Duster, scholars have studied how the *term* eugenics may have been abandoned after World War II, yet the logic of eugenics may have ongoing effects on both science and public policy.[4]

Eugenics projects provide a compelling and instructive case of how a scientific discourse, *absent* an ethical commitment to social justice, helped reproduce social inequality. In constructing their overall argument, eugenics projects assembled scientific and commonsense beliefs about bodies, fitness, evolution, reproduction, science, and the state, as well as about ability, race, ethnicity, gender, sexuality, age, and nation. Eugenics was not an explicitly racial project (Omi and Winant 1994). Race, or ethnicity, or ability, or similar categories of analysis were not its main object of investigation. Rather, eugenics drew upon these categories of analysis within a relational framework that was implicitly intersectional. In essence, eugenics was a coded discourse about ability, race, ethnicity, gender, sexuality, and nation that, by bundling together ideas from these distinctive categories, had an effect that was broader than any one strand of its analysis. Significantly, eugenics relied on a relational logic whereby ideas of ability, race, gender, and ethnicity reappear throughout its discourse. Eugenics was not an *intentionally* intersectional project, but rather a project whose overarching goals relied on relational thinking that resembles intersectionality's own.

Eugenics has been studied within scholarship on Western science, typically in conjunction with analyses that emphasize the organization of eugenics within a particular academic discipline or the significance of eugenics within public policy. Eugenics projects used ideas about race, gender, class, sexuality, ethnicity, age, and citizenship from biology, anthropology, history, sociology, and similar academic disciplines. Conversely, the ideas of eugenics influenced many of the core concepts of academic disciplines that seemingly were unrelated to these categories of analysis. Existing scholarship on eugenics also indicates that eugenics was certainly connected, in varying ways, to categories of ability, race, ethnicity, religion, gender, sexuality, age, and nationality (citizenship status). For example, scholarship on scientific racism that characterized various academic disciplines examines how such fields provided the interpretive frameworks and empirical evidence for eugenics projects (Tucker 1994). Other literature focuses on eugenics itself, exploring how biology, sociology, anthropology, history, and medicine contributed different sets of ideas to eugenics (T. Duster 2003, 2015).

Some of this literature moves beyond the race-only or gender-only frameworks to investigate how eugenics was involved in how systems of power themselves are interrelated. In this regard, feminist scholarship on nationalism and eugenics provides an especially rich source of intersectional analysis of eugenics. For example, Nancy Stepan's monograph *"The Hour of Eugenics": Race, Gender, and Nation in Latin America* (1991) uses an intersectional framework to examine the history of eugenics in Latin America. Drawing upon queer theory, Nancy Ordover's volume *American Eugenics: Race, Queer Anatomy, and the Science of Nationalism* (2003) brings an important queer analysis to standard approaches to eugenics. Wendy Kline's book *Building a Better Race: Gender, Sexuality, and Eugenics from the Turn of the Century to the Baby Boom* (2001) traces how approaches to reproduction and female sexuality articulate with eugenics in the United States. While this literature provides a solid foundation for seeing eugenics as an intersectional knowledge project, this literature does not focus on *how* eugenics operated to connect multiple systems of power. Here I sketch out such an argument, suggesting that part of the success of eugenics laid in its ability to bundle together ideas from the treatment of race, ethnicity, religion, gender, sexuality, class, age, and ability within scientific disciplines as well as commonsense understandings of these same categories.

Eugenics projects illustrate a chain of relational reasoning whereby race, gender, and similar categories of analysis gain meaning from one another (Stepan 1990).[5] Scientific understandings of intelligence, violence, emotion, motivation, rationality, and similar constructs seemingly reflect universal categories that apply to all humans, yet stereotypical ideas about ability, race, ethnicity, gender, sexuality, and nationality are often embedded in the meanings of the terms (Collins 2018). Through the use of metaphors and analogical reasoning, a less familiar concept is explained in terms of one that is more known. Take, for example, how understandings of intelligence reflect commonplace stereotypes of women, men, blacks, and children that assume that women are childlike and less intelligent than men, blacks are childlike and less intelligent than whites, and thus because both women and blacks are childlike and less intelligent than white men, women and blacks are *both* inferior. In this way, race, gender, and age become bundled together in a chain of meaning. These same stereotypes underlie conceptions of rationality and emotion, constructed as essentially different: blacks are less rational and more emotional than whites, blacks are less rational and more violent than whites, and women are more emotional and less rational than men; thus because blacks and women are less rational and more emotional than white men, blacks and women are *both* inferior to white men. These conceptions of intelligence, rationality, and emotion contribute to understandings of constructs of violence and sexuality that become comprehensible within this chain of analogical reasoning. Another strand of analogical reasoning underpins constructs of normality and abnormality. In this chain, blacks are sexually deviant because they engage in non-normative (excessive) heterosexual sexuality, white homosexuals are sexually deviant because they engage in non-normative (insufficient) heterosexual sexuality, and because blacks and white homosexuals both engage in non-normative sexual practices, they are *both* inferior to straight white people (Stepan 1990, 1991, 9–14). Via a chain of reasoning that accommodates flexible combinations of race, gender, sexuality, class, religion, ability, ethnicity, and national identity, scientific ideas can be explained and seem plausible because they seemingly reflect "what everybody knows."

These ideas of intellectual inferiority, the distinctions between rationality and emotions, and phenomena such as violence and sexuality become mapped on the social groups that carry stereotypes. When joined with the framework of evolution, these ideas and the racialized and gendered ideas that make them comprehensible take on added meaning. Evolution explains social change in the natural world as a gradual, natural process of survival of the fittest. When applied to social relations, the theory of evolution or social Darwinism provides an overarching framework explaining ostensibly naturalized hierarchy among individuals and, more importantly, among social groups. Within evolution as an explanatory framework, universal, seemingly benign concepts of intelligence, rationality, emotions, violence, and sexuality begin to explain group differences. Drawing on this relational logic about group difference, eugenics projects provide a rationale for social hierarchy and its consequences for unequal citizenship. Treating people differently is a reasonable outcome when people themselves are inherently different.

Eugenics projects positioned the problem of social inequality within this overall explanatory framework of evolution and social Darwinism. The relational logic that is described here both explains social inequality and offers a remedy for fixing it. In this sense, eugenics itself offers a familiar approach to problem solving within Western epistemologies. Three unifying principles within eugenics discourse draw upon this relational logic—namely, (1) a body politics of immutable difference; (2) family as a mechanism for naturalizing and normalizing hierarchy; and (3) the importance of social engineering for national well-being. Using these principles, eugenics projects explain the links between the seemingly natural world (body politics), the social world (families as a template for naturalized hierarchy), and the political world (nation-state solutions for eliminating inequality). Significantly, eugenics projects also offer policy options for bettering society through science.

Body Politics and Immutable Difference

Eugenics projects conceptualized bodies as sites of immutable difference and used this basic assumption to explain social phenomena. Classifying bodies into categories of immutable differences that were permanent and not subject to change was foundational to eugenics arguments (Collins 2004, 87–116)—in other words, a unique essential nature as being either a woman or a man, or black or white, or heterosexual or homosexual. Immutable difference and oppositional difference worked together. Once the different bodies were categorized, eugenics projects routinely ranked them and assigned them social value. This sorting and ranking of bodies seemingly transformed the immutable differences of bodies into social conditions that were unresponsive to change.[6]

Intersectionality's categories of race, gender, sexuality, and ability were important in laying a foundation for eugenics's approach to body politics. Concepts of ability/disability draw from these fundamental assumptions of essential and immutable differences. Within medical models, societies view ability and disability as rooted in the body; these models conceptualized ability and disability as overriding characteristics of each body. Physical disabilities may be more visible because they can be seen on bodies, but mental disabilities that ostensibly reside inside the body seemingly have a similar essence. Eugenics discourse used an evaluative language of fit and unfit, a binary that meshed with scientific discourses about normality and abnormality with moral discourses of normal and deviant.

Arguing that disability is socially constructed, contemporary scholarship in critical disability studies rejects these views of Western science (Wasserman et al. 2016). Critical disability studies suggest that the social meanings attached to *all* bodies is socially determined and is not inherent in bodies themselves. The discourse on disabled bodies highlights this process of social construction, one that views discourse on ability and actual bodies as recursively linked. In this way, a body politics of essential and immutable difference rests on notions of normal and abnormal bodies that underlay discourses of normality and abnormality, of fitness and unfitness, as well as the meaning of socially determined categories of ability and disability.[7]

Because eugenics projects drew heavily on frameworks of immutable difference that invoke a core metaphor of normality/abnormality, this idea of immutable difference shapes categories of human/nonhuman (e.g., who counts as a fully human being); categories of personhood (e.g., individuals may all be human in some sense, but they may not be the same kind of human); and how understandings of racial, ethnic, gender, and religious groups reflect this logic. The conceptual progression from a biological human to a person or human being moves from the purely biological (the natural world); to the social world (humans as social animals that require domestication, containment, or extinction); and to groups (natural social units that structure the social world).

Setting boundaries between humans and animals on the basis of their oppositional differences was central to this project. By comparing the bodies and behaviors of humans and animals, biology, anthropology, sociology, history, and similar academic disciplines have spent considerable time researching what it means to be human. Theoretically, these comparisons may seem clear-cut, but practically, the nature of the relationship of humans and animals has been and continues to be a matter of political and scientific debate. The Great Chain of Being privileges some groups over others on the basis of their resemblance to animals. The same binary categories of rationality/ emotion, intelligence/instinct, controlled/violent, and domesticated/wild that emerge in the chain of reasoning from stereotypes become applied to the bodies of humans and animals. Within an anthropology that grew in conjunction with colonialism, people of African descent and indigenous peoples became classified as primitives whose bodies were more natural, sexual, emotional, and violent than people who enjoyed the civilizing influences of European culture (Torgovnick 1990).

Neither fully human nor fully animal, indigenous people and people of African descent have occupied a borderlands space in this body politics of immutable difference. Such peoples were deemed to be closer to animals than other categories of humans. Moreover, the emergence of a racial biology that linked inferiority with immutable, biological differences meant that the stigma of race was seen as intergenerational and permanent. As primitives, people of African descent and indigenous people carried the stigma of immutable difference with them wherever they went. Across different national contexts, this classification and ranking of bodies has shaped discourse about people who became described as "primitive" (Torgovnick 1990).

In the United States, neither indigenous peoples nor Black people, America's so-called primitives, were seen as being able to assimilate into American society.[8] The worldviews of both groups incorporated a distinctive relationship with the natural world, yet within colonial frameworks, both groups were seen as people from the "wild" whose humanity was in question. Taming the wild animal in each group required removing them from the "wilderness" through conquest, enslavement, or both. For indigenous peoples, enslavement failed, thereby fostering a reliance on conquest and mass incarceration in reservations. For people of African descent, enslavement was more successful in its ability to appropriate bodies for labor and reproduction. Viewing both groups as primitives required strategies of domestication, discipline, and control.

Modern understandings of race and practices of racism in a global context rest on these body politics. Shifting down from the more generalized human race to the level of the races that, when added together, comprise the human race enables the body politics that classify individuals to be applied to group behavior. By segmenting the human "race" into smaller racial units, this type of thinking allows different groups to be racialized or constructed as racial opposites, depending on the needs of the specific political and economic context. The metaphors applied to Black people and other groups racially constructed as inferior are often similar to those applied to weak groups. Seen in this context, the jump from seeing individuals with putatively weak characteristics—the "imbeciles, the maimed, and the sick" as categories of disability, for example—to viewing entire *groups* or "races" as inherently weak (e.g., women as emotionally and physically weaker than men and Black people as intellectually inferior to whites) becomes easier to fathom. The bodies carry the stigma of ability or disability that informs a more generalized notion of ability for groups.

Family and Naturalized Hierarchy

A second unifying principle of eugenics projects relied upon family rhetoric and practices to explain social hierarchy. As Anne McClintock observes, "the family image came to figure *hierarchy within unity* as an organic element of historical progress, and thus became indispensable for legitimating exclusion and hierarchy within nonfamilial social forms such as nationalism, liberal individualism and imperialism" (1995, 45). So-called normal families are expected to socialize their members into an appropriate set of societal norms. Hierarchical relations of gender, age, and ability within families articulate with the placement of the family unit within hierarchical social relations of race, class, and citizenship. Family thus becomes a site of reproducing social hierarchy or resisting it. While individuals typically learn their assigned place within hierarchies of race, gender, ethnicity, sexuality, nationality, and social class within their families of origin, they simultaneously learn to view such hierarchies as natural social arrangements rather than socially constructed ones. Social hierarchy and social inequalities become naturalized and normalized because they are associated with seemingly natural processes of the family.

Naturalized hierarchy within families lays the foundation for understanding systems of hierarchy outside family boundaries. For one, hierarchies of families as normal and abnormal install one family type, and by implication, the social relations within it, as normal and natural. In Western societies, the nuclear family long held sway as the ideal family type, studied in science, celebrated in popular culture, and enjoying public policy benefits.

For another, hierarchies of gender, wealth, age, and sexuality within actual family units correlate with comparable hierarchies within society. Other social institutions, for example, the media or the workplace, often understand and organize their own practices through the rhetoric of family. For example, familial relationships among fathers and sons or mothers and daughters can influence how faculty and students understand mentoring relationships within academic departments and programs.

Eugenics projects explicitly drew upon what families symbolize and on actual practices as a template for explaining social hierarchy. The ubiquity and universality of family fostered the basic idea that family is the building block of society. According to Western logic, the Great Chain of Being that categorized life itself into a social hierarchy that privileged the West as the highest form of civilization drew meaning from differential understandings of some families as superior to others. Such projects understood family as an ostensibly natural entity because it was ubiquitous, universal, and seemingly part of the natural order of living beings. Within this logic, the non-normative families and cultures of indigenous peoples, as well as those of non-Western groups formed within slavery, colonialism, and imperialism, contributed to their backwardness. Significantly, non-normative families within sovereign nation-states also were suspect as sites for backwardness and the deterioration of civilization.

In contrast to idealized versions of family that mask these relations, actual families remain organized around varying patterns of hierarchy.[9] Families teach entitlement and responsibility via how they are organized and how they function. Most families have a specific authority structure that articulates with family ideals of their given religion, community, ethnic group, or national culture. For example, parents demand obedience from their children (age); firstborn sons are granted authority over their younger siblings (age); firstborn sons, and increasingly firstborn daughters, inherit family wealth or debt (class); mothers and daughters submit to their fathers, husbands, and brothers (gender); and children are expected to carry on the family itself through heterosexual marriage (sexuality). Families are expected to remain racially, ethnically, and religiously pure by passing on culture to their offspring. Individuals may negotiate these family ideals as separate entities, yet collectively they foster hegemonic understandings of family that are more often performed than analyzed.

This internal hierarchy *within* families informs institutional norms of entitlement and responsibility (Williams 1995). The significance of kinship systems is especially important for the idea of *nation* as the distribution of citizenship rights. Nation is often conceptualized as synonymous with one's "people" and all that goes into that imagined category. A working definition sees the construct of *nation* as equivalent to "people" or population. The term *nation* can reference the physicality of population or social group, and has close affiliation with "tribe," ethnic group, and in many societies "race." In this sense, the construct of *nation* gains meaning from related constructs of *ethnicity* and *race*. Ethnicity comes closest to this idea of peoplehood, one of a group that has a distinctive history and culture, and that is often seen as premodern and dating before the modern nation-state. In contrast, race as claimed as a sense of peoplehood is typically assumed to be a modern invention. The term *race* carries multiple meanings, yet it routinely refers to a group of people, for example, the generic use of the term *race* to mean the human race, or *race* as synonymous with ethnic groups, such as at turn of the twentieth century with reference to the Irish as a race, the Italian race. Modern definitions of race and ethnicity have changed over time. For example, European ethnic groups became Americans by using their ethnicity to get jobs. They then erased their ethnicity by assimilating into a white, American identity. Becoming American meant becoming white.

Constructing ideas about nation on the foundation of body politics of immutable difference conjoined with family rhetoric and practices illustrates how the relational logics of ability, race, gender, sexuality, and age all inform one another in constructing the ideas of nation, nation-state, and nationalism. For example, the understandings of naturalized hierarchies that are associated with families inform understandings of first- and second-class citizenship within a nation-state as well as immigration policies (e.g., which people belong to the nation or national family at all). Hierarchy may be determined by order of arrival: either birth order or immigration order. In the United States, claims that early-migrating white, Anglo-Saxon Protestants are entitled to more benefits than more recent immigrants of color reflect this notion. Or hierarchy accompanies gender. In many families, girls and boys are treated differently regarding economic autonomy and freedom to move in public space. This differential treatment serves as a foundation for sex-typing occupations in the paid labor market. As is the case with all situations of hierarchy, actual or implicit use of force, sanctions, and violence may be needed to maintain unequal power relations. The question is how all this provides a link from eugenics projects to the modern nation-state.

A third unifying principle of eugenics projects concerns their emphasis on social engineering as a legitimate function of the nation-state. Social engineering rests on the belief that the nation-state has a justifiable interest in encouraging and discouraging specific behaviors within its citizenry. For example, tax policies do not simply collect money to support government functions. They also encourage certain behaviors; in the U.S., for example, single people are taxed at a higher rate than married couples, thereby penalizing those who remain single. This logic of rewarding good people and punishing bad ones constitutes a taken-for-granted dimension of public policy.

Eugenics tied social engineering to issues of biological and social reproduction. For eugenics projects, regulating the reproductive capacities of social groups constituted public policy for the public good. So-called positive eugenics policies should encourage "fit" persons and population groups to reproduce, whereas negative policies should discourage "unfit" ones from doing so. Public policies to regulate reproduction had an ethical mandate to better society. In practice, punitive population policies regulated the biological reproduction of women, men, able-bodied people, members of different racial and ethnic groups, and young people. Not everyone had a right to reproduce. On the basis of people's classification as desirable or undesirable citizens, or whether they were seen as citizens at all, social engineering policies aimed to produce more or less of seemingly desirable people.

Social engineering rests on a conception of the modern nation-state as an "imagined community" of people with shared interests (Anderson 1983). As imagined communities, modern nation-states can define their national identities and national self-interests through democratic institutions of equality of citizenship that reject views of naturalized hierarchy. Theoretically, participatory democracies as imagined communities can accommodate heterogeneity, multiculturalism, and difference within national identity. Such states have a self-interest in cultivating the talents of all citizens so that they can contribute to the state's well-being. Alternately, nation-states can define their national identity and self-interests via government policies that see the nation-state as facing ongoing threats. Such states perceive some of their citizens as internal threats to the nation-state's well-being and neighboring external nation-states as threats to their national identity. Eugenics policies can be annexed to both understandings of the nation-state as an imagined community; many eugenics policies have been implemented by democratically elected governments.

Sociologist Zygmunt Bauman (1989) argues that eugenics as science exemplifies an "activist, engineering attitude toward nature and toward itself" that characterized the modern world from the Enlightenment on. Within this scientific logic of the modern world, "science was not to be conducted for its own sake; it was seen as, first and foremost, an instrument of awesome power allowing its holder to improve on reality, to re-shape it according to human plans and designs, and to assist it in its drive to self-perfection" (70).[10] Social engineering by the state thus reflected the impetus toward human betterment, drawing upon eugenics as normal science to assist with these national projects.

Social engineering projects that are implemented by state bureaucracies require a more uniform understanding of social groups. When state apparatuses embrace a logic of eugenics, they typically implement public policies that differentially target what they see as different populations within the same nation-state. In this regard, demography as a scientific discourse provides planning tools that help the nation-state categorize and manage populations (Zuberi 2001; Zuberi and Bonilla-Silva 2008). As a signature discourse of modern social science, demography offers a series of tools and perspectives that assist the state in classifying bodies as male and female, as well as categorizing families and racial and ethnic groups. As a field that studies patterns of birth, death, marriage, and immigration, demography has been central to the creation and manipulation of population groups. In this endeavor, demography both legitimates the categories that underpin eugenics arguments about desirable and undesirable populations and also contributes to the managerial functioning of the state by collecting data on such categories (Zuberi 2001). As scientific constructions, populations ideally describe the families, ethnic and religious groups, and genders in a given society, but the concept of population refers to a discreet analytical category created by researchers and policy analysts.

Take for example, how the category "unwed teen mothers" creates a population group that can be studied as a social problem in ways that allow researchers to examine patterns of race, age, class, and ethnicity within this statistical category. Within eugenics thinking, the emphasis is not on the social problems that unwed teen mothers might experience but rather on unwed teen mothers *as a social problem* for the nation-state (Gordon 1994). Interest in this population seems to wax and wane in relation to costs to the nation-state. But in what ways are unwed teen mothers a social group?

Is there a homeland for this group? Are they a "people" or a "nation" in the traditional sense of race and ethnicity? Would they recognize themselves as part of a bigger tribe of "mothers"? Seeing the social world through the demographic lens of populations enables certain kinds of scientific questions to be pursued and forecloses others. Because such groups are used for comparisons, definitions of population groups should remain fixed from one project to the next. The existence of the field of critical demography suggests that demography itself is not the problem. Rather, because specifying the contours of populations and designing appropriate population policies on the basis of that classification has been an important dimension of eugenics, eugenics projects have drawn upon demography as a modern framework for classifying people.

Social engineering lies at the heart of the ideology and public policies of eugenics projects (Bauman 1979). Such projects uphold the legitimacy of controlling populations in the national interest. Public policies of nation-states aim to manage the size and composition of the national population, ostensibly for the public good, through, for example, jobs, housing, schooling, health, and the fair distribution of resources. In doing so, they rely on categories of unequal citizenship that draw from ideas of naturalized hierarchy. Moreover, in their efforts to shape the reproductive capacities of populations within a given nation-state, eugenics projects advance a form of social engineering that draws on the body politics of fit and unfit bodies. State-sanctioned policies that encourage or discourage childbearing and childrearing by desirable or undesirable populations constitute forms of population control that fall disproportionately on women. State-sanctioned policies of immigration that shift in relation to the perceived needs of the nation constitute another form of population control that falls more heavily on racial/ethnic groups.

German nation-state policies during the Nazi era of 1933–1945 bring transparency to the logic of eugenics. More importantly, they illustrate the implications of social engineering carried to its logical extreme within a modern nation-state. One sees in this example how the logic of eugenics influences both the causes and the consequences of unequal citizenship. Politically, the Nazi nation-state implemented eugenics in three main ways. First, they divided humanity into categories of immutable difference—for the German population, these were Aryans and Jews, Germans and foreigners, heterosexuals and homosexuals, men and women, and able-bodied and disabled people. These categories were ranked using binaries of oppositional difference (e.g., deserving and undeserving, fit and unfit) and assigned value in relation to national interests. Second, using ideas about social evolution and degeneracy, the Nazi state used these categorical differences to explain national identity, prosperity, and decline. It blamed Jews, the Roma people, homosexuals, and political dissidents for failed economic and political policies, and it labeled these groups outsiders in the homeland of the German national family. Such groups not only were blamed for Germany's past failures; their continued presence hindered its future progress. Finally, the state designed population policies for their unequal citizens, controlling birth through policies that encouraged and discouraged childbearing among different categories of women, and policies targeted to the already born through favorable treatment for desirable people and genocidal policies for others (Zuberi 2001).

Public policies need not be explicitly about race or gender or ability, and the relational logic of eugenics that makes these policies intelligible need not name intersectionality's familiar categories of analysis. The public discourse of eugenics did not present itself as a theory of ability, race, gender, sexuality, or class. Rather, these ideas made eugenics comprehensible. When it comes to public policy, eugenics projects link the body politics of naturalizing and normalizing hierarchy (often through the rhetoric of family) with national agendas that imagine nation-states as imagined communities. They explain the links between the seemingly natural world (body politics, now comprehensible through categorization and ranking), the social world (families as a template for naturalized hierarchy), and the imagined national community (nation-state policies). Not only do they provide an explanation for a hierarchy of unequal citizenship, they offer an analysis of social change. Evolution constituted the overarching model for explaining this naturalized hierarchy as well as social change, with related ideas concerning degeneracy tapping a series of fears. Evolution of the ideas fit and unfit mapped onto actual people who became associated with societal success or failure. A given society or nation can improve by increasing its share of the right kind of people, and can stave off its decline by containing or removing the wrong kind of people. Stated differently, more desirable populations need to increase their numbers while less desirable populations not only need to be discouraged from increasing their numbers but removed from society altogether.

Despite the decline of eugenics as a legitimate scientific discourse, its unifying principles persist. Core concepts within Western science and the social practices that it upholds and that were central to eugenics projects—for example, social engineering for common good, evolution as the survival of the fittest, and measuring the value of life on the basis of the ability to contribute to social good—continue to hold sway. The important idea here is that projects with disparate political perspectives can draw upon a common set of principles concerning bodies, families, and national interests. Such projects may no longer be called "eugenic," yet these unifying principles can continue to influence public opinion and public policy.

As is the case with eugenics, knowledge projects need not intentionally focus on race, class, gender, sexuality, and nation, yet such projects can rely on a similar relational logic. In the U.S., for example, the strident language of immigration debates draws upon representations of Latino migrants as unworthy human beings who are undeserving of legal protections. Similarly, as the case of marriage equality initiatives suggests, family remains a contested site of public debates. Policies that result in unequal citizenship—whether punitive policies of mass incarceration, fiscal policy that gives homeowners lucrative tax advantages, or immigration policies that aim to manage access to citizenship—rest on implicit assumptions of social engineering that is targeted to specific categories of citizens. State intervention in reproductive issues remains a contentious issue, shaping debates on abortion, reproductive rights, family leave, and access to contraception by minors. The assumption that the state should intervene is largely taken for granted, even among political groups that seemingly oppose such intervention.

Eugenics and Intersectionality

The post–World War II era represents an important conjuncture when visible support for eugenics ideologies diminished and vocal support for social justice increased. Human rights projects and social movements increasingly took a stand against the kind of social injustices that eugenics typified. Collectively, these distinct initiatives for gender, racial, class, and sexual equality pointed toward intersectionality as a reasonable next step for a growing global commitment to social justice. The difference between eugenics and intersectionality seemingly marks a mid-twentieth-century break whereby intersectionality as a discourse committed to social justice displaced the earlier logic of eugenics. In some ways, intersectionality and eugenics can be seen as mirror images of one another that pivot on their relationships to social justice.

As discourses, eugenics and intersectionality do not share the same objectives, the same practitioners, the same time period, or the same political goals. Yet eugenics offers significant insight for intersectionality's challenge of evaluating the criteria that inform its critical theorizing.

First, eugenics provides insight into how relational logic can help reproduce and legitimate social inequality. Eugenics projects and intersectionality
both rely on a similar relational logic in constructing their respective core
constructs and guiding premises. The relational logic of eugenics has several
characteristics: (1) it constructed its arguments about social inequality by
situating ideas about race, class, gender, ability, sexuality, ethnicity, and age
drawn from distinctive disciplines into a new overarching scientific logic; (2)
it provided a compelling explanation for social inequality; and (3) it enabled
eugenics projects to advance an activist agenda regarding social inequality
that demonstrated the pragmatic use of eugenics for public policy.[11] Once
installed as normal science, eugenics projects were not content to explain
the world and instead aggressively set out to change it. Eugenics projects
make power relations especially visible because they simultaneously link
multiple systems of power and influence the organization of power relations.
This case of eugenics suggests that other projects that do not call themselves
intersectional may rely upon a similar relational logic with a comparable
effect. Conversely, it also suggests that projects that self-identify as intersectionality may be far more variable than assumed, with some more dedicated
to social justice than others. Specifying how the relational logic within eugenics was tied to specific political outcomes suggests that relational logic in
and of itself may be necessary but not sufficient for intersectionality.

Second, eugenics can be seen as a saturated site of intersecting power
relations that make the interconnections among systems of power especially
visible.[12] Saturated sites bundle together practices, social institutions, representations, and patterns of everyday social interaction that appear and reappear across seemingly separate systems of oppression. Conceptualizing
eugenics as a saturated site of power relations not only enables us to see how
the practices of eugenics—for example, public politics of nation-states—
constitute mechanisms of power, but also illuminates how narratives shape
power relations. Eugenics had clear ties to state and economic power, had
an identifiable discourse that reflected and shaped multiple communities
of practitioners, and was complex and unstable, with the contingency that
outcomes were not deterministic but rather might have many possible outcomes. Although organized differently, eugenics does the same intellectual
work as violence and family at the conjuncture of multiple systems of power.
Eugenics may serve a similar function in contributing to the articulation of
systems of power.

In this sense, eugenics projects provide insight into the nature of relationality itself. My sense is that eugenics projects demonstrate relationality

through articulation. Eugenics is situated in the conjuncture among multiple knowledge projects and, as a discourse, articulates them in new ways. Here, *articulation* refers to Stuart Hall's description of how language "articulates" or brings forth a set of ideas by combining existing elements into new patterns or by attaching new connotations to them (Grossberg 1996, 141; Hall 2017, 91). Within this use, sets of ideas can be coupled and uncoupled, yet both the new entity and the separate parts are changed by these transactions. In this case, articulation is both a way of understanding how the ideological elements of race, class, gender, sexuality, ethnicity, and nation came, under different political conditions, to cohere within eugenics as a discourse. Eugenics demonstrates articulation in action. Such projects could be taken up by many communities of inquiry, primarily because they could make the conceptual leap of explaining less familiar aspects of social reality by relying on what they knew to be true. They themselves had contributed the material on race or gender. Articulation also investigates how these ideas become attached to particular political projects (Grossberg 1996, 141–142). In this case, eugenics was able to influence public policy. Eugenics projects also point toward articulation over time that catalyzes a new overarching scientific logic that rests on relational thinking of co-formation. Within Western science, the categories of race, class, gender, age, sexuality, age, and nation have become so interdependent that they are taken for granted and indistinguishable within scientific discourse.

A third insight from eugenics concerns the differential salience of race, gender, sexuality, and age as categories of analysis in crafting specific eugenics projects from one social context to the next. In essence, eugenics theoretically drew upon race, class, gender, age, sexuality, ability, and nation—these categories were all there all the time. Yet practically, some were more prominent and visible, even while others seemed to be benign background factors. There was no fixed frame of race/class/gender that could be easily transported from one setting to the next. Instead, categories of analysis were differentially salient within different eugenics projects. The strength of eugenics lay in its malleability and elasticity; its universal logic could be tailored to the particulars of local contexts.

This issue of saliency is significant for seeing how the combination of categories is what matters, not that particular categories must always be present in order for an analysis to be intersectional. Take, for example, how categories of ability and nation were especially salient ideological axes or anchor points for eugenics projects. Eugenics could not have functioned without ideas about normality and abnormality that rested on interpretations of able and disabled bodies as well as political projects of social engineering. For eugenics projects, the concept of disability was fundamental. Ability was not a marginal category to be added into eugenics as an afterthought. Rather, incorporating (dis)ability mandates rethinking intersectional analyses of eugenics itself. Much of eugenics discourse becomes comprehensible in terms of the saliency of disability as a category of analysis. Nationalism, for example, draws heavily upon ideas of ability and disability in understanding national identity and public policy. The notion of able and disabled bodies appears in literature on nationalism and masculinity, for example, the duty of able-bodied men to protect women, children, their property, and their homeland (nation). The related question of a person's fitness or unfitness to serve the nation also draws from understandings of ability/disability. Women are seen as being less fit for combat and similar service responsibilities of able-bodied men, but they are especially fit for reproduction; women's bodies are valued for their abilities in sexual pleasure, childbearing, and childrearing. Debates about the suitability or fitness of nonwhite peoples for access to education, jobs, housing, and citizenship also links a body politics of normality/abnormality and fitness/unfitness to social agendas of deserving and undeserving. The saliency of categories of ability and nation within eugenics discourse points to the necessity of attending to particular social contexts.

Finally, eugenics projects illustrate how social theories have political outcomes, especially when the interpretive communities that advance them aim to shape public policy. Ironically, taking inspiration from one premise of Marxist social thought, eugenics as science set out not only to explain but also to change the world. Ideas matter, often long after the particular conditions that shaped them fade away. This seems to be the case with eugenics: the resilience of its ideas has been its most significant feature. The idea that nation-states should engage in some forms of social engineering for the public good is a taken-for-granted truism of modern democratic states. Arguments advanced by conservative and progressive politicians alike may disagree on the content of specific state intervention—for example, whether abstinence or sex education constitute the better way of addressing unplanned teenage pregnancies—or even the scope of social engineering by expanding or shrinking the state itself, but they share a commitment to social engineering broadly defined as a legitimate responsibility of the state.

The resilience of the ideas of eugenics raises an important question: How do knowledge projects, especially critical social theories, sustain themselves over time? Eugenics persisted because its advocates continued to embrace its principles and fight for them in political arenas. Even after its practitioners stopped using the term *eugenics*, eugenics's influence continued, not because eugenics ideas were inherently superior to other explanations of social inequality, but rather because these ideas exercised epistemic power and that had built up over time. Bundling together ideas about ability, race, class, gender, sexuality, age, ethnicity, and nation as categories within eugenics projects became so taken for granted as normal science that they were unremarkable. Normal science itself then relied on its taken-for-granted premises that ostensibly did not contain these categories to help reproduce the material conditions of racism, sexism, and similar systems of power. This particular discourse illustrates the workings of epistemic power and why it is so difficult to upend. Relying on institutional roots in science and government, the logic of eugenics persisted because the norms of normal science made certain questions possible while precluding others. Eugenics practitioners had no need to defend their questions, methodologies, and findings because they worked within epistemological frameworks that they themselves created and protected.

Ideas matter, but they are unlikely to matter much without advocates who aim to institutionalize those ideas within the institutional structures of any given society. Having the power to set the rules of what will count as truth (e.g., epistemic power) has greater impact than criticizing knowledge created within those rules. Epistemic resistance to the rules themselves is far more formidable than simple criticism or dissent. Do intersectionality's proponents express a similar commitment to the "truth" of their own ideas and practice? In many ways, this kind of certainty is anathema to prevailing academic norms that eschew absolute truths. Paying attention to the terms under which intersectionality is developed and finds institutional support shifts attention from theories of power to the political realities of institutional practices. Within academia, the shrinking institutional support for transformative scholarship is maintained through strategies of epistemic dominance. Practices of testimonial smothering and quieting can be effective strategies for suppressing epistemic resistance (see chapter 4). The signs of past critical projects can remain on university doors, masking the shells that remain. In this context, intersectionality faces the challenge of building sustainable communities of inquiry that see the development of intersectionality as a critical social theory as a political necessity.

When it comes to institutionalizing intersectionality, what will the long arc of intersectionality be? Eugenics drew upon a relational logic to advance a politically successful knowledge project that lacked a commitment to social justice. Significantly, eugenics projects provide a clear sight line for intersectional analyses of contemporary power relations, precisely because ideas drawn from past eugenics projects persist, albeit differently organized, within contemporary social relations. What kind of sight line will intersectionality provide for intersectional projects in the future? Eugenics projects shaped science and the state during a period when both were undergoing substantial social change. When armed with the same relational logic as well as a commitment to social justice, what might intersectionality accomplish during a contemporary period of social change?

Intersectionality and Social Justice

Because intersectionality has traditionally been closely associated with social justice projects, a commitment to social justice is often assumed to be one of its signature dimensions. Yet moving into academic settings that did not prioritize social justice raised a new question: Was intersectionality's commitment to social justice sustainable? Intersectionality has been changed by its institutional incorporation, but in what direction and to what effect?[13]

No longer taken for granted, intersectionality's relation to social justice is increasingly a matter of debate. Some academics interpret intersectionality's weakening ties to social justice projects as a good thing, arguing that bringing social justice and similar politically contentious issues into intersectional research erodes intersectionality's academic stature. Social justice may be an appropriate topic for intersectional analysis, but incorporating a commitment to social justice into the normative structures of intersectional inquiry is epistemologically inappropriate and methodologically suspect. Using social justice as a principle to guide intersectionality's critical inquiry allegedly clouds the kind of objectivity needed for strong theoretical analysis. Moreover, because social justice has been so heavily implicated in political action, intersectionality's scholarly rigor and objectivity would be compromised by committing to particular political ends (e.g., reducing social inequality) and claiming particular ethical principles (e.g., social justice).

Intersectionality's shift away from the assumed particularities of race, class, and gender and toward seemingly more universal Western social theory indicates, for many, a maturing of the discourse. Some counsel that intersectionality will benefit from jettisoning its ties to African American women, Latinas, and similarly subordinated social actors who were pivotal to intersectionality's formation (Nash 2008). Because they seem to be mired in a particularistic, self-serving identity politics that ostensibly undermines universalistic criteria, they are ill-equipped to contribute to intersectionality. In an epistemological context that preaches the value of decontextualized objectivity, projects that seem unduly political or politicized (unless they represent the interests of those in power) are typically devalued. From this perspective, in order to ensure its survival, intersectionality should aspire to fit into academia's existing epistemological and methodological standards. This would mean bringing intersectionality's theorizing into alignment with the standards of traditional social theory. Given the corporate university's embrace of neoliberalism, this advice seems prudent (Nash and Owens 2015). Assimilating and claiming disciplinary respectability are attractive survival strategies, yet they may ultimately be failing strategies both for intersectionality as a critical discourse as well as for the intellectuals who follow this advice.

Yet, while well-intentioned, striving to be just another traditional social theory within academia may not be enough to shield intersectionality from the tough ethical and political questions raised by social injustice. Fundamentally, social justice projects not only criticize social inequalities as being unjust, they routinely and explicitly work to dismantle them. And such projects need not be positioned outside academia within grassroots projects or broad-based social movements. Critical social theories with a social justice ethos have carved out space within academia as well. Much academic inquiry has been implicitly, if not explicitly, informed by some sort of commitment to social justice. Max Horkheimer's analysis of Critical Theory identified a commitment to social change and, by implication, to social justice as a core premise of critical social theory itself. Frantz Fanon's liberation theory had direct ties to anticolonial social movements that wanted social justice. British cultural studies was animated by the social injustices of class, ethnicity, and citizenship within British society, creating a new field in which to theorize those relations. Within intersectionality's genealogy, as well as that of these and other critical theories within the academy that inform it, critical analysis has been placed in service to this overarching ethical objective.

This commitment to social justice is especially apparent within resistant knowledge projects. For example, critical race studies, feminist studies, and postcolonial studies all express an explicit commitment to making the world more just. The significance of Frantz Fanon's liberation theory transcended its ties to existentialism; Fanon's ideas also contributed to a broader project of philosophies of struggle within the African diaspora (Outlaw 2017). His work, along with that of others, provided intellectual resistance within actual liberation struggles. Moreover, the search for social justice has constituted a necessary and defining feature of Black feminist thought, one that shapes intersectionality and flexible solidarity as important dimensions of this knowledge project (Collins 1998). It is no accident that Ida Wells-Barnett's autobiography is titled *Crusade for Justice* (A. Duster 1970). Her antilynching campaign and her long career as an intellectual activist were explicitly devoted to social justice.

Uncoupling intersectionality from its commitment to social justice might garner academic legitimation for intersectionality, but it also might undermine the integrity of intersectionality's *critical* inquiry. The meaning of critical social theory is far from settled, and as I explore in chapter 2, intersectionality needs to tread carefully in analyzing the contributions and limitations of critical social theory in the academy. Postmodern social theory, for example, provides a powerful set of analytical tools for criticizing society; these tools can be used in service to social justice. But such tools need not be used for this purpose. Moreover, poststructuralism's rejection of the grand narratives of the Enlightenment makes it impossible to reconcile a commitment to social justice within poststructuralism's epistemological framework. Moving too far away from its intellectual and political roots in grassroots social justice initiatives as the cost of academic respectability may strip intersectionality of its critical vision. Eschewing a commitment to social justice and its political implications may irreparably change intersectionality, and not for the better. How effective a critique can intersectionality launch against social injustices when it seems to benefit from and is complicit with social inequalities within its own academic backyard?

Rather than assuming that social justice is implicitly part of intersectionality, the question of intersectionality's ties to social justice constitutes an important and ongoing question for theorizing intersectionality itself. Social justice has been a core construct of intersectionality, but what are the benefits and risks of taking an ethical position in favor of social justice as part of intersectionality's guiding premises (table 1.1)? During times of political upheaval, when social inequalities and social injustices intensify, this is not a theoretical question. Because academic and activist communities both claim intersectionality, the answers to this question have important consequences. Social justice is one of intersectionality's core constructs that reappears across heterogeneous intersectional projects. Relationality, social inequality, and social context all constitute themes that describe the content of intersectionality as well as methodological choices that shape such projects. Power operates in a different register, providing a core construct that distinguishes intersectionality from other projects that do not take power into account. In contrast, social justice may seem to be more contingent. The detailed analysis of eugenics presented in this chapter illustrates how a knowledge project can cognitively resemble intersectionality but also lack a commitment to social justice. The case of eugenics raises an important question about the necessity of thinking through how a commitment to social justice as one of intersectionality's core constructs might inform its guiding premises.

An explicit or even implicit commitment to social justice need not be a guiding premise of intersectionality. Some forms of intersectional scholarship do quite well and make important contributions without explicitly referencing social justice as essential to their projects. For example, ongoing debates about how intersectionality might inform existing paradigms for health policy; disparities in health outcomes; and the clinical practices of doctors, nurses, and patients have stimulated new questions and scholarship. These scholars and practitioners certainly are sensitive to issues of social inequality and social injustice, but these are not their main concerns. They may not see their scholarship as part of a social justice project. In this sense, using intersectionality as a heuristic device can contribute to much-needed paradigm shifts. Across research and practice, health researchers raise a wealth of new questions that deepen intersectionality. Does it really matter whether scholars who make important contributions to intersectionality explicitly claim a commitment to social justice?

The challenge that intersectionality now faces is to figure out how to accommodate the heterogeneity of the perspectives and practices of its current practitioners. Throughout this volume, I have cautioned against prematurely elevating one expression of intersectionality above others, calling instead for dialogical engagement across disciplines, methodologies, identifications, social theories, and political practices as essential for developing intersectionality as a critical social theory. I have also cautioned that differences within and among the interpretive communities that ground the knowledge projects that do and potentially can shape intersectionality are not simply differences in points of view. Instead, they signal real differences in power.

The challenge of this volume is to think through the implications of these actual and potential practices for intersectionality as a critical social theory. Intersectionality's visibility within and across a variety of knowledge projects is all well and good, but what characterizes the essence of intersectionality itself? What is essential to its very being? Relationality is a core construct for intersectionality that infuses intersectionality's guiding premises. Might social justice be a comparable unifying principle? Working dialogically across differences in power requires some sort of common goal, vision, or unifying framework, not to suppress differences, but rather to hold them together. Social justice (or a similar term that expresses a similar ethical sensibility) may provide that unifying framework. In this sense, social justice may not be tangential to intersectionality's epistemological frameworks, but rather may provide an important orienting strategy for intersectionality's critical inquiry, especially as the field continues to grow.

Yet even identifying social justice as a unifying principle raises additional issues. It's easy to say that you are for social justice. But what exactly does that mean? And what does it mean within intersectionality? *How* social justice appears within areas of intersectional inquiry and praxis is more significant than whether intersectionality writ large pays lip service to some amorphous idea of social justice. Because understandings of social justice vary across activist and academic communities, the meanings of social justice that are available to intersectionality are similarly heterogeneous (Sen 2009). The issue for intersectionality is less one of claiming an agreed-upon definition of social justice and more of acknowledging that varying understandings of social justice emerge from and inform diverse intersectional projects. Stated differently, depending on social context, distinctive and often competing views of social justice may align with different dimensions of intersectionality. I raise these questions to identify work that is yet to be done concerning social justice for intersectionality as critical social theory. It's impossible to analyze whether social justice should or should not be central to intersectionality's critical analysis without specifying what sense of social justice one has in mind. Intersectionality's multifaceted approaches to working for social justice resonate with core ideas within an expansive, interdisciplinary scholarly literature on social justice (Reisch 2016).[14] It also encounters the widespread use of the term *justice* within political activism. Just as the term *critical* has become a prefix for a range of projects, the term *justice* is used as a suffix for contemporary activist projects and movements as a way of signaling critical intent. The convention of referring to activist projects by referencing the word *justice* seems increasingly commonplace—the case, for example, of the environmental justice movement. The use of the term *justice* can also identify specific dimensions within an existing social movement, as in the case, for example, of the distinctions between reproductive rights and reproductive justice within feminism. Informed by this broader idea of social justice, the term *justice* seems to travel freely among activist projects. Sometimes it is aligned with traditional categories of race, class, and gender, but often it is not. These uses do not supplant social justice as a universal construct, but rather aim to further specify its contours.

If social justice is to be a unifying principle for intersectionality, intersectionality needs to develop a critical analysis of how it conceptualizes and uses social justice. Because this literature is so vast, the work of feminist theorists and philosophers in criticizing traditional scholarship approaches to social justice may be especially useful.[15] For example, Iris Young, in her classic work *Justice and the Politics of Difference* (1990) as well as throughout her scholarship (2011), provides an important critical analysis of how justice must take oppression into account. Similarly, feminist political philosopher Nancy Fraser (2009, 100–115) provides a comprehensive interpretive framework of social justice as parity or equality of participation—namely, that each individual has an equal right and an equal opportunity to be in a public or social group.[16]

Attending to the relationship between disability and social justice provides important directions for how intersectionality might develop a critical analysis of social justice (Mladenov 2016; Wasserman et al. 2015, 2016). Teodore Mladenov points out that criticizing how assumptions of interdependence and self-sufficiency articulate with conceptions of equity and social justice has been an important dimension of critical disability studies: "Critical disability studies emphasizes that all humans rely on infrastructures and relations of support . . . . We are just temporarily able-bodied, but even when able-bodied we are still interdependent—it is just that in such periods, the infrastructures of support and care that we depend on remain invisible or unrecognized, receding in the background of familiarity or hidden in the realm of power" (2016, 1235).

Mladenov's analysis of dependency, independence, and interdependence provides an important set of analytical tools for seeing how these ideas underpin ideas of social inequality and social injustice. He discusses the changing value of self-sufficiency as a social norm under industrial capitalism whereby independence gradually became the norm and dependence a deviation. The desirable subject or citizen is a rational, independent decision-maker who is free from external or internal constraints. The undesirable subject or citizen is one who relies on others, particularly the state, for assistance. These social relations can be reformed via more humane forms of assistance. As feminist theorists have pointed out, the very notion of dependency is fundamental to the architecture of the welfare state, fostering categories of deserving and undeserving citizens who are deserving and undeserving of care (Gordon 1994). Yet for Mladenov, a transformative strategy would seek to "deconstruct self-sufficiency—for example, by exposing self-sufficiency as rooted in relations of interdependence" (2016, 1232).

Replacing the independent/dependent binary with a notion of interdependence provides a radical challenge to the ideology of self-sufficiency that valorizes the independent individual and stigmatizes dependency. Drawing upon both feminist studies of the social welfare state and the insights of critical disability studies, Mladenov contends that "the perspective of the caregiver endorsed by feminists needs to be complemented by the perspective of the recipient of care highlighted by disability scholars—otherwise, the citizenship of the former could overpower the citizenship of the latter" (2016, 1234). In essence, the construct of interdependence brings yet another vocabulary to intersectionality's relational thinking. By stressing the interconnected, dynamic nature of intersecting power relations, of the communities that organize such relations, and of relationships among individuals, this construct of interdependence can inform debates within intersectionality about social justice.

A commitment to social justice has been such a common thread of feminism, decolonial projects, critical race studies, and similar resistant knowledge projects that, as is the case with critical disability studies, these projects may be important sites for critical analysis of social justice. Just as critical disability studies fosters a rethinking of interdependence, resistant knowledge projects potentially offer a rich tapestry of ideas about social justice that illustrate how social action as a way of knowing contributes to intersectionality. Because theorizing often emerges from and contributes to social action, resistant knowledge projects are attentive to how ideas are negotiated within unjust communities of inquiry. Within grassroots activism and broader social movements, this recursive relationship between ideas and creative social action informs critical analysis. The ideas-in-action and actions-through-ideas in activist settings constitute a distinctive form of theorizing that elevates the significance of social justice. Because these groups confront similar problems, they draw upon varying understandings of justice to craft specific political projects. In doing so, they bring multifaceted understandings of social justice, both implicit and explicit, to intersectionality as a critical social theory in the making.

In crafting multifaceted understandings of social justice, intersectionality draws upon both this legacy of social justice within social movements as well as the conceptual vocabulary provided by feminist theory, critical disability studies, and other resistant knowledge projects. Just as the term *intersectionality* facilitated new relationships among various social movements, so too might new understandings of *social justice* benefit from dialogical engagement among intersectionality's heterogeneous practitioners.

How Ethics Matter

Within much of academia, social justice has been the elephant in the room, one that has to be ignored in order to carry on with academic business as usual. Social justice is often a topic of scholarly inquiry, as in, for example, courses on philosophies of social justice or professional courses on business, law, or medical ethics. Substantial improvement has occurred in regulating the ethical practices of some forms of scholarship—the case, for example, of responding to medical experimentation on African Americans and vulnerable populations without their consent by installing institutional review boards (IRBs) that review medical and social science research projects.[17] This is a step in the right direction, yet few fields claim ethics as part of their own self-regulatory practices. One can find a code of ethics that scholars within a field are encouraged but not required to follow. Yet few formal mechanisms exist for censuring the substance of scholarship on ethical grounds, for example, as either pursuing unethical ends or knowingly producing dangerous knowledge. Instead, ethical concerns are relegated to informal mechanisms such as individual conscience or assuming that a community of scholars can self-regulate its own behavior regarding its epistemic practices.

In this book, I challenge this view. These institutional and informal strategies are a step in the right direction, but intersectionality may need a stronger ethical touchstone than this. Such a strategy would involve an ongoing commitment to a unifying ethical principle that would be revisited and reinterpreted as part of intersectionality's critical inquiry. It would also encompass mechanisms for evaluating such practices. In making this claim, I am arguing neither for nor against any particular ethical claim or way of bringing ethical concerns into intersectionality. Thus far, I have examined social justice as one such principle, in part because it has been central within intersectionality, and in part because social justice is a window into broader ethical concerns. The ways in which ethics generally, and the treatment of social justice in particular, remain circumscribed within academic venues are important considerations for intersectionality's critical inquiry.

Intersectionality may seem to be on the side of an ethics that embraces social justice, yet as I discuss in this chapter, this assumption cannot be taken for granted. Moreover, with so much attention granted social justice, it is important to point out that other terms have invoked similar ethical commitments. *Freedom, equality,* and *democracy* are also terms that invoke important Western ethical traditions that have been highly meaningful for Western societies and for the aspirations of subordinated people. Black and indigenous people resisted slavery, colonialism, and imperialism by aspiring toward *freedom.* Women also invoked the emancipatory language of freedom, as in the case of Beauvoir's conception of existential freedom as a form of resistance to women's oppression. Western democratic societies have expressed a commitment to fairness, equal treatment, and equal opportunity for all people and citizens. Grounded in classical liberalism, the term *equality* invokes certain ethical ideas concerning how human beings should treat one another. The idea of *democracy* that rests on equal opportunity and equal participation of citizens shares much with intersectionality (Collins 2017a).

Intersectionality's relationship to ethics has been an important albeit implicit theme in this book, precisely because Western social theories routinely position the ethical implications of their ideas and practices *outside* intellectual business-as-usual. If ethics are a personal matter, individual scholars are the ones who should take responsibility for them. Moreover, within Western epistemologies, political action also receives distinctive treatment. Here political action is seen as biased and nonobjective, and therefore should remain outside scholarship itself. When combined, these perspectives on ethics and politics as lying outside the collective responsibility of interpretive communities make it more difficult for intersectionality to take ethical stances within academic venues, especially if such stances seem overly politicized or biased.

Intersectionality has to grapple with the politics of how ethics are organized and conceptualized within academic venues. Ethical concerns are often treated as special topics within professional fields, for example, as courses in business ethics or medical ethics. The organization of disciplines through specializations also influences which fields have responsibility for studying and researching ethics. As a specialization of Western philosophy, the study of ethics reflects epistemological, secular frames of Western philosophy, which historically has advanced a critical analysis of religion. Similarly, positioning ethics as the specialized knowledge of religion effectively ghettoizes ethical concerns within divinity schools as the proper location for critical analysis of religion. Philosophy and religion both have important contributions to make to an analysis of how intersectionality might engage ethics. But it is difficult to have this conversation within the institutional and epistemological constraints of academia.

My sense is that academia does not lack a commitment to ethics. Rather, it has been more committed to a secular ethics that emphasizes the goal of protecting individual rights at the expense of protecting the rights of groups and communities. Secular ethics are vital for upholding freedom of speech for individuals, which underlies the free exchange of ideas. Such ethics are essential for critical analysis itself. I value the protections that free speech provides for my own intellectual work. Yet I also wonder whether a secular ethics that valorizes individual rights over the collective needs of communities can ever be enough. Within academia, for example, how can ethics be managed within a situation of hyper-individualism that turns students and faculty alike into entrepreneurs, salespersons, and consumers?

Intersectionality also has a complicated relationship with how ethics are organized and conceptualized in nonacademic settings. Ethics are central to organized religions, with the theologies and core texts of world religions open to many different interpretations. Varying interpretations of the same religious texts often have huge social consequences, many of them quite tragic. The issue is less with a religion, but rather with its interpretation. For example, within many religions, fundamentalism has harmed women, children, and other vulnerable people. In response, across a range of religions, women have organized against fundamentalism (Dhaliwal and Yuval Davis 2014).

Despite the important focus on fundamentalism and religion, here I focus on what the faith-based ethics of religious traditions often do for people that the secular ethics of academia cannot. Faith-based ethics provide principles for living daily life and in doing so, give meaning to everyday life. They also offer explanations for phenomena that are seemingly beyond human comprehension. Faith-based ethics take on issues of the meaning of life, birth, death, human suffering, evil, and beauty—themes that typically have not been central to secular ethics. Whether faith-based explanations can be empirically verified or true is not the point. Instead, faith-based traditions offer meaning to the difficulties of life itself, even if, ironically, the explanation is one of not knowing.[18]

Significantly, in bringing a worldview on the meaning of life to their adherents, faith-based traditions have the ability to harness emotions, passions, and commitments to ideas that are bigger than individual self-interest. Faith-based ethics are collective and communal, gaining strength from a community of believers. Body politics need not be wedded to the individualism and notions of immutable difference of eugenics projects. Body politics can be collective and tied to community constitutions, offering meaningful experiences that animate pragmatism's notion of creative social action. This sense of belonging to something bigger than oneself resonates with the collective aspirations of subordinated people. Social movements that have been able to invoke the power of faith-based traditions and place them in service to ethical ideas such as freedom and social justice can catalyze substantial social change. Martin Luther King Jr.'s ability to mobilize Americans to build a beloved community was informed by analysis, but would have been impossible without its adherents' faith that such a community was worthwhile and possible. Critical analysis can provide clarity, yet ethical commitment, especially if organized via faith-based understandings, catalyzes action. In this regard, when grounded in communities, faith-based ethics do considerable political work.

For intersectionality, the tensions between secular and faith-based ethics means that the spaces for critically examining the meaning of social justice and similar ethical ideals has been both circumscribed within the academy and positioned outside it. Because many of intersectionality's adherents who are not in the academy also claim religious or spiritual ways of knowing, these tensions create challenges for intersectionality. For example, within the secular ethics of the academy, the binary framing of reason and faith within assumptions of oppositional difference leaves little room for exploring the relational differences of these categories. Ironically, this binary depiction of secular knowledge and religion aligns with the very same binary categories that intersectionality has set out to dismantle. These binaries of reason/emotion, mind/body, male/female, white/black, and rationality/irrationality, for example, provide yet another epistemological constraint for people who are categorized as emotional, embodied, female, Black, and irrational. The relational logic of eugenics illustrates the significance of this binary thinking for structuring social inequality. At the same time, this same thinking presents a challenge within religious communities. Some replicate these ideas within their ranks, requiring unquestioning loyalty from their members. Others actively engage social hierarchies, trying to unpack their influence on their own practice. Even the most dedicated faith-based traditions continue to struggle with ideas of social hierarchy within their own theologies and practices that naturalize and normalize inequality. Faith itself can be empowering for some adherents while disempowering others.

These issues of the organizational politics of ethics as well as the substance of ethical ideas raise important issues for intersectionality as a critical social theory in the making. Secular ethics and faith-based ethics both speak directly to intersectionality's need to evaluate the meaning of its own praxis.

They both grapple with the power of ideas, pointing to how people use and interpret ideas as central to their practice. The combination of rationality and faith need not be oppositional; rather, they can inform one another. Both potentially contribute to intersectionality's broader project. Yet the kind of critical analysis and the kind of faith matters.

Consider, for example, how faith-based ethics are used within many religious traditions to encourage their adherents to understand how ethical principles provide guidance but not certainty in understanding the meaning of the social world, and how secular ethics are used within the academy to encourage intellectuals to critically examine all aspects of the social world, especially their own analyses and practices. In both cases, the meanings of ideas lie not in texts themselves but in their interpretation. The meaning of the ideas within the theology of religion or the theory of science lies not in the substance of the texts, but rather in how people interpret those texts. Critical analysis is central to both discourses. The content of these projects differs: one focuses on the wisdom gained by serious reflection on the meaning of their shared scripture, and the other focuses on inherited knowledge traditions. Moreover, because emotions and beliefs come into play for both the secular ethics of the academy and the religious ethics of organized religions, both can draw upon similar passions in their adherents in defense of their respective causes.

Within both venues, a commitment to social justice can carry a depth and sophistication that can move people to action. Yet as the rise of ultranationalism suggests, passionate commitments that remain untethered from informed critical analysis can be fraught with danger. Academic and religious communities alike face the danger of blind faith, whereby members simply believe and obediently follow, regardless of the content of discourse itself. Religious fundamentalism and fascism illustrate the pitfalls of blind faith in religious theologies and political ideologies. Social theories can fall victim to the same groupthink if their adherents are not equally vigilant in challenging their own cherished epistemological beliefs. Intersectionality as critical social theory must stand for something, yet it needs to remain critical and open-ended at the same time. Understanding any set of ideas exclusively through the lens of applying dogma (regardless of the ideas themselves) through blind faith rather than critical analysis of dogma (including one's own) constitutes an important ethical challenge for intersectionality. A dogmatic, rigid intersectionality that masquerades as critical social theory may be worse than no intersectionality at all.

I have been careful throughout this book to point out that the meaning of ideas is not intrinsic to the ideas themselves. Rather, it lies in how people use those ideas, not solely through intellectual prowess or political action, but also through how their ethical commitments inform their ideas and actions. Part of intersectionality's appeal may lie in its usefulness to individuals who are searching for meaning within their everyday lives; in its utility to mobilize individuals and communities in support of broader social and ethical goals (e.g., social justice); and in its versatility to have diverse meanings for segments of society distinguished by ability, social class, ethnicity, race, gender, sexuality, immigrant status, age, and religion. This malleability constitutes intersectionality's promise and its danger. To fulfill its promise, intersectionality must examine its own ethical position within the intersecting power relations that it analyzes, hopefully embracing its potential as critical social theory. This does not mean embracing the ideological perspectives of any established political party, religion, or set of customs, but rather taking a stand by defending the right to be critical. Both inside and outside academic venues, those of us who support visionary ideals of freedom, democracy, truth, equality, and social justice must come to terms with how our scholarship and activism facilitate or erode these ideals. Because intersectionality has been so closely associated with these ideals, those of us who work with intersectionality must critically assess how intersectionality's ethical commitments influence our inquiry and practice.

Epilogue

Intersectionality and Social Change

Intersectionality offers a window into thinking about the significance of ideas and social action in fostering social change. Although intersectionality has been consistently aligned with visionary ideals such as freedom, social justice, equality, democracy, and human rights, neither change itself nor intersectionality's connections to such change is preordained. The only thing that is truly certain about human existence is that it will change, but not necessarily in the evolutionary, linear fashion of Western notions of progress. Rather, social change is a cyclical process brought about by people, whereby what was once new has become old, and what once seemed old has become new again. This is the concept of the *changing same*: we sense that "we've been here before," but it all feels different. In this social context of the changing same, we are acutely aware that no one has experienced what we now face. New forms of telecommunications and transportation, and new social problems of environmental damage and militarization that characterize an interconnected, new world order are game changers for the twenty-first century. Nostalgia for an imagined past that never was may be seductive. Yet we cannot cling to scripts that have already been written for us and simply follow the rules. Our families, schools, religious institutions, and cultural beliefs signal the strong pull of tradition, but through critical analyses we can reinterpret those traditions and imagine new possibilities for ourselves and our societies. Our current ideas and actions become the new traditions.

During times of such visible and contentious change, it's reasonable to question the worth of intellectual work, especially when everyday social problems seem so pressing. Yet because we've been here before, we cannot search for certainty, but rather for critical analytical tools that will enable us to grapple with the ever-changing contours and durable effects of important social problems. In a time when weapons of mass destruction are real and not imaginary, critical inquiry that does not shy away from tough questions is essential. Critical social theory that refuses to look away from the hard questions that accompany oppression and social injustice is needed more now than ever. Change is not new, and critically analyzing a changing social world has been the special task of critical social theory.

When it comes to social change, the ideas that I examine in this book reflect only a small sample of the myriad ways that people try to change the world through the power of their ideas. Intersectionality is not the only knowledge project that engages in social problem solving, but it is one that speaks to the complexity of a changing social world. Moreover, intellectual work that falls under intersectionality's umbrella is far broader than I have examined here. I've focused on the theoretical dimensions of intersectionality, seeking ways to map what's there with an eye toward understanding intersectionality's critical theoretical possibilities. Yet in examining intersectionality, I've drawn inspiration from the questions, analyses, and actions of activist projects that have been vital to its creation and sustenance. Such projects bring distinctive worldviews to social problem solving as well as demonstrate a degree of commitment to social change. Those of us who come from those spaces have an obligation to recognize them and speak out. I've also relied heavily on social theory from different academic disciplines, in part because such theories bring important insights to intersectionality's theoretical work, and in part because such knowledge defines disciplines of power within the pantheon of academia's gatekeeping practices. By setting the epistemological terms of what counts as knowledge, these areas occupy the belly of the beast, as it were. Those of us who have been able to enter these spaces have an obligation to speak up and speak out.

In *Intersectionality as Critical Social Theory*, I approach intersectionality as a critical social theory in the making. This book is neither an uncritical celebration of intersectionality nor a premature rendering of its ultimate demise. This project does not aspire to move beyond intersectionality, leaving the present behind for some better, imagined future. Rather, by engaging in a self-reflexive look at intersectionality's current organization and practices, this volume is a pragmatic effort to make intersectionality work in the here-and-now and to prepare for the future. In this book, I provide a set of analytical tools for intersectionality's practitioners, current and future, who want to develop intersectionality's critical analyses with an eye toward social problem solving and social change. Strengthening intersectionality's theoretical core is essential for meeting this goal.

Throughout this book I've used the constructs of truth, power, and ethics as touchstones to guide my analysis. The search for truth constitutes an important—and in many ways the most contentious—dimension of my investigation into intersectionality as critical social theory. Truth is not an absolute. Instead, the rules that determine what counts as truth mean that some truths count more than others. My focus on epistemology in this volume stems from the need to specify the rules of theorizing as well as what counts as social theory. Epistemology is crucial for understanding why some truths are present in intersectionality's knowledge base while others remain neglected, as well as whose truths are believed and whose are dismissed. How we come to believe in what we see as true is just as important as the substance of the ideas that we take as true. Most of us synthesize truths that are produced by others and that we find believable. Despite the blurring of fact and fiction within political discourse, knowing that some provisional truths are substantially stronger than others is essential to critical analytical work. No one can definitely prove the truth of climate change. But the evidence for such truth is all around us. No one can definitely prove the truth of a sexual assault that has no witnesses. But the evidence for sexual assault as a social problem brought forward by those harmed by such practices well after the events themselves should be evidence enough. The truth of each survivor can be disputed, but the truth of the pattern itself can no longer be denied.

Developing a robust analysis of power is crucial for understanding intersectionality as a critical social theory in the making. Rather than positioning politics outside of social theory, I see power relations and the politics that they engender as central to critical theorizing. *Power* is an overused term in academic circles, signifying much but saying little that is theoretically new about the workings of domination and oppression, and, more importantly, about political resistance. I focus on the processes of theorizing in order to highlight the multifaceted workings of power relations, politics, and intellectual resistance within and for intersectionality. Because dominant social theory in the West is often poorly equipped to explain complex social inequalities and resistance to them, it can inadvertently stand in the way of social change. In contrast, for many of its practitioners, intersectionality is a knowledge project of resistance that aims to bring about change. Without political resistance there would be no intersectionality. Power relations are never so absolute that they eliminate all dissent. They are never so inviolable that all we can do is imagine a better yet unattainable world. This view belies all the hard work of so many people who contributed to building intersectionality. Intersectionality's survival and growth are a testament to intellectual and political resistance.

Ethics constitutes a third touchstone for analysis in this book. The treatment of social justice within activist and academic settings constitutes an important dimension of this volume. When different interpretive communities hold different ethical values, the knowledge they produce is similarly impacted. In this book, I challenge the simplistic binary of heroic activists outside academia who uphold the banner of social justice juxtaposed to the ethically bankrupt academics who look away from social injustices. I also reject the equivalent analysis that juxtaposes seemingly backward, everyday people, many of whom are mired in religion, to the enlightened intellectuals whose cosmopolitanism and secularism offers a way forward for everyone. Intersectionality as I understand it has no place within these narrow epistemic boxes. Instead, I present a self-reflexive critical analysis of intersectionality itself that raises more fundamental questions: What is the place of ethics within intersectionality as critical social theory? What role should ethics or normative principles play within intersectionality's methodology or way of arriving at truths? Can ethical issues such as social justice be so neatly cordoned off and ignored because they seemingly lie outside intersectionality's theoretical concerns?

These themes of truth, power, and ethics not only lie at the heart of how we might theorize intersectionality, they speak to what it means for intellectual work to become and remain critical during times of social change. Developing intersectionality's potential as a critical social theory rests on attending to questions of how we know what we know (the truths of epistemology), what social actions are possible within the complex social inequalities that organize our daily lives (the politics of power), as well as our agency and actions in response to the social injustices that confront us (the commitments of ethics). Together, these themes of truth, power, and ethics shape the contours of social change. They also constitute cutting-edge concerns for sustaining intersectionality's critical analysis.

When it comes to developing intersectionality as a critical social theory, in this book I focus on the ideas and actions of individuals and groups that aim to bring about social change. I've certainly read my fair share of social theories that explain social order—namely, how oppressions are organized and why they seem so invincible. Such theories offer significant insight on the durability of social inequities, but they typically have less to say about social change, save how difficult it will be. Yet I think it is important to highlight knowledge projects whose understandings of truth, power, and ethics point toward meaningful social change. The resistant knowledge projects that have had the most influence on intersectionality didn't just study how racism, or heteropatriarchy or class oppression, were pillars of the social order, hoping to mitigate the damage done by such systems by producing ever more eloquent analyses of oppression. Instead, their reason for existing was to change these systems of oppression. Some did so via their ideas and arguments, whereas others placed more emphasis on political action. Significantly, these resistant knowledge projects incorporate a normative commitment to social justice, equality, freedom, and human rights as central rather than peripheral to their critical projects.

Is some sort of commitment to social justice required for intersectionality's critical analysis? More importantly, should it be? This book raises these questions, yet the answers lie within us. As the rise and fall of eugenics suggests, the ways in which we take up particular sets of ideas, within specific social contexts and at certain points in time, may matter more than most of us realize. The methodologies that we choose to use to analyze our worlds shape the truths that we find. And the diverse paths that we follow to come to intersectionality's common ground frame the dialogues we can have when we get there. When it comes to intersectionality as a critical social theory, asking the wrong questions is a far bigger problem than offering eloquent answers to what seem to be the right questions. Intersectionality is well on its way to becoming a critical social theory that can exert intellectual leadership in bringing about much-needed social change. In this sense, intersectionality is not just ideas, but has an important role to play in the social world.

Appendix A

Detailed Table of Contents

Introduction

Part I. Framing the Issues: Intersectionality and Critical Social Theory

1. Intersectionality as Critical Inquiry

   Intersectionality as a Metaphor

   Why Metaphors Matter

   Intersectionality's Heuristic Thinking

   Intersectionality and Paradigm Shifts

   Core Constructs and Guiding Premises

   Intersectionality, Social Theory, and Theorizing

2. What's Critical about Critical Social Theory?

   The Critical Theory of the Frankfurt School
   Horkheimer's Definition of Critical Theory

   Critical Analysis and British Cultural Studies
   Stuart Hall and Articulation

   The Contested Terrain of Francophone Social Theory
   Frantz Fanon, Liberation Theory, and Existentialism

   Reform, Transformation, and Critical Social Theory

Part II. How Power Matters: Intersectionality and Intellectual Resistance

3. Intersectionality and Resistant Knowledge Projects

   Antiracism and Critical Race Theory

   Feminist Politics and Feminist Theory

   Decolonization and Postcolonial Theory

   Intersectionality and Resistant Knowledge

4. Intersectionality and Epistemic Resistance

   Who Gets to Tell Intersectionality's Story?
   Epistemic Power and Critical Theorizing
   Epistemic Resistance and Testimonial Authority
   Identity Politics and Standpoint Epistemology

   Why Methodology Matters for Intersectionality
   Working Dialogically Across Differences of Power
   The Case of Abductive Analysis

   Intersectional Theorizing and Critical Self-Reflexivity

Intersectionality and Social Justice

How Ethics Matter

Epilogue: Intersectionality and Social Change

Notes

References

Notes

Chapter 1. Intersectionality as Critical Inquiry

1 Several articles and books offer overviews of intersectionality's content (see, e.g., Carastathis 2016; Collins and Bilge 2016; Dill and Kohlman 2012; Hancock 2016; May 2015).

2 Michel Foucault's use of genealogy provides an important methodological framework for this book (Foucault 1980; Koopman 2011). Genealogy is a historical methodology that traces the emergence and descent of the technologies and practices used to produce discourses—in this case, discourses of intersectionality. Genealogy is also a form of political critique that diagnoses how such discourses, practices, and technologies are embedded in unequal power relationships—in this case, how shifting patterns of unequal power relations frame the emergence of intersectionality. A genealogical account of intersectionality would not assume nor seek to posit any so-called scientific hypotheses about intersectionality. Rather, a genealogical account would examine the social structures of power and knowledge that made it possible for thinkers to produce claims about intersectionality in the first instance. Genealogy constitutes an alternative to the linear narratives of history and causal analyses of social science.

3 Philosopher John Stuhr's (2000) description of American pragmatism also provides a useful way of thinking about intersectionality as a field: "It may be defined by its exponents' common attitudes, purposes, philosophical problems, procedures, terminology, and beliefs. It is in virtue of such a shared complex of features that we identify, understand, and differentiate philosophical developments, movements, and 'schools of thought.' Such a unity of character, we must recognize, is not a single and simple essence, some necessary and sufficient

feature of classical American philosophy, some property present always and only in classical American philosophy. Instead, it is an identifiable configuration, a characteristic shape, a resemblance, an overlapping and interweaving of features (present to differing degrees in the writings of the individual philosophers) that, as a relational whole, pervades and constitutes this philosophy and these philosophers" (2–3).

4 Conceptual metaphor theory provides a comprehensive analysis of how metaphors contribute to understanding and experiencing one kind of thing in terms of another (Lakoff and Johnson 2003, 4). Lakoff and Johnson offer a far more comprehensive analysis of conceptual metaphors than I can attempt here: "When we say that a concept is structured by a metaphor, we mean that it is partially structured and that it can be extended in some ways but not in others" (13). Cognitive processes of conceptual metaphors include structural metaphors, orientational metaphors, and ontological metaphors. The basic experiences of human use of space give rise to orientational metaphors. Most of our fundamental concepts are organized in terms of one or more spatialization metaphors, with the idea that these spatial metaphors are rooted in physical and cultural experience and explain social phenomena. People's experiences with physical objects, especially their own bodies, provide the basis for a wide variety of related metaphors that in turn shape ways of viewing events, activities, emotions, and ideas as entities and substances (Trout 2010, 25). The example of personification whereby physical object (or concept) is further specified as being a person, "Intersectionality tells us, or intersectionality did . . ." possibly explains why personal narrative is so prominent within intersectionality, both in the personal narratives of individuals and in the metaphor of telling intersectionality's story. "We conceptualize our visual field as a container and conceptualize what we see as being inside it. Even the term 'visual *field*' suggests this" (Trout 2010, 30).

5 Because conceptual metaphor theory examines how metaphors work within critical thinking about the social world, it sheds light on intersectionality's resilience. In a study of the use of metaphors in the Spanish press's treatment of corruption, Isabel Negro (2015, 213–216) provides an extensive bibliography of conceptual metaphor theory as well as a discussion of recent developments in the field.

6 Gloria Anzaldúa is increasingly recognized as a major feminist theorist. See, for example, Mariana Ortega's introduction to a cluster of articles in *Hypatia*, a journal of feminist philosophy, that examines how "recent Latino philosophers and theorists disrupt and, at the same time, enrich traditional philosophical understandings of knowledge, selfhood, liberation, and transformation" (2016, 313).

7 Judith Butler's work (1990, 1999) has greatly influenced this burgeoning approach to identity, especially through the workings of queer theory. Butler's important idea of performative subjectivities is often linked with intersectionality's framework of interconnected and co-forming phenomena. Yet, Butler has distanced herself from intersectionality. See, for example, Butler's dismissive comments about intersectionality in her classic work, *Gender Trouble* (1999, 182). Ironically,

many people draw upon both Butler's arguments concerning performativity and intersectionality's insights concerning co-formation to the point where intersectionality is often understood as a social theory of identity.

8 In chapter 3, I develop this theme of the relationship between particularity and universality by examining intersectionality's ties to resistant knowledge traditions with social action components. Critical race studies aims to resist racism, feminist studies resists heteropatriarchy, and decolonial studies resists neocolonialism. In this sense, each project reflects the particular social problems confronting Black people, women, and colonized people. Yet each project also sees beyond the particulars of any one group.

9 I use Kuhn's work here not as a theory to be tested, but rather as a heuristic or rubric for approaching intersectionality. Kuhn's framework for changes within science have been criticized from many directions. But because his basic framework has been extrapolated from the specific context of science, this approach to paradigms is itself useful as a heuristic (Kuhn 1970). In *Chaos of Disciplines*, Andrew Abbott (2001) offers a more complex and comprehensive analysis of how knowledge changes in the social sciences. His analysis of constructionism is especially significant for intersectionality.

10 Relationality is such an important core construct that I take it up in varying places throughout this volume. Subsequent chapters emphasize one or more of these paradigmatic constructs, presenting different configurations of them in relation to relationality; for example, critiques of Simone de Beauvoir's use of categories of race and gender as a feminist analysis of women's oppression that lacks an intersectional analysis (Gines 2010); Emirbayer's (1997) manifesto for a relational sociology that makes no mention of intersectionality; and analyses of globalization via lenses of complexity and network analysis that make scant mention of race, gender, sexuality, and similar categories of power (Torres 2012).

11 The idea of standpoint epistemology is grounded in the concept of social context. People who occupy multiple social locations within intersecting power relations catalyze varying standpoints, epistemologies, and knowledges (Stoetzler and Yuval-Davis 2002). This heterogeneity within social context can be a source of new ideas—again, the potential to contribute to an innovative intersectional analysis.

12 I have written extensively about these premises in "Intersectionality's Definitional Dilemmas" (2015) and in *Intersectionality: Key Concepts*, co-authored with Sirma Bilge (2016, 25–30). The version of intersectionality's guiding principles presented here builds on this prior work. Because I engage these premises throughout the volume, I list them in Table 1.1 and examine them more thoroughly in future chapters. I'm less interested in investigating the truth of these various premises (e.g., testing them empirically) than in interpreting how people use them within intersectional practice.

13 Social theorist Craig Calhoun further specifies these distinctions between social sciences and the humanities. Calhoun contends that theory constitutes the

"systematic examination and construction of knowledge—in the case of social theory, knowledge about social life" (1995, 4). When it comes to knowledge about the social world, Calhoun identifies a distinction between truth and meaning, which he describes as "causal" and "narrative," that invokes the distinctive approaches of the social sciences and the humanities: "[Social theory] may be causal or narrative in form, with each form suggesting different approaches to generalization and specification. While causal reasoning may be applied to discrete events, it is more commonly used in social science to refer to classes of phenomena, treated as internally equivalent, that influence other classes of similarly equivalent phenomena . . . . Narrative [reasoning], conversely, is often described as inherently particularizing but (1) the particularities may be global (as in narratives of world history), and (2) comparisons among narratives facilitate a form of general, cross-situational knowledge" (4).

Chapter 2. What's Critical about Critical Social Theory?

1   This use of the term *critical* resembles a similar use of the prefix *post* to signal a temporal sense of being after something to which one is connected but that is no longer central, for example, postcolonialism, postmodernism, poststructuralism, post-reality, and post-feminism. The use of both prefixes indicates the use of othering—namely, marking the boundaries of a project by appealing to what it is not. Upon occasion, a project invokes both meanings. For example, David Hoy's *Critical Resistance: From Poststructuralism to Post-Critique* (2004) combines both signifiers, aiming to tease out the *critical* dimensions of resistance implied within *post*structuralism and theoretical projects engaging in *post*-critique. This is a worthy cause, yet the chapters in the book follow a familiar logic. Chapters on the intellectual traditions of Nietzsche, Foucault, Bourdieu, Levinas, and Derrida invoke the figurehead of a school of critical thought, with a chapter on post-Marxism using the prefix *post* to signify the Marxism social theory in the aftermath of Marxism.

2   Many philosophical traditions and the theories that they engender also lend themselves to this kind of comparative analysis, for example, postmodernism, poststructuralism, positivism, Marxism, phenomenology, and critical realism. I am in no way suggesting that the three areas discussed here are the only or the best cases for my argument.

3   I've been using the term *discourse* as being equivalent to related commonsense terms such as *narrative* or *story*. Yet *discourse* has a specific meaning that has generated considerable attention to discourse analysis. In this text, *discourse* refers to the complex system of power relations in which ideas, actions, beliefs, and practices construct both subjectivity and social structures. Communities of inquiry matter because they point to a power analytic that potentially explains why we get certain expressions of critical social theory, when we get them, and their effects.

4   Standard renditions of social theory rely on intellectual histories of ideas, effec- tively treating the social context in which theories develop as a passive backdrop for the active process of theorizing. Here I've taken a different approach, claiming a broader understanding of discourse that sees critical inquiry as influenced by the recursive relation between power relations and knowledges that ensue and that, in turn, shape power relations (Foucault 1980). Critical discourse not only includes the knowledge (ideas, actions, and beliefs) developed in a given social setting, but also refers to how intellectuals are situated within social institutions, the opportunities and constraints they experience, as well as how their theoreti- cal and methodological choices are part of power relations.

5   The critical theory of the Frankfurt school has had a broad and important effect beyond the intellectuals discussed in this section. For example, the work of Jür- gen Habermas resonates with those of other philosophical traditions, such as the resemblance between the critical theory and American pragmatism (Joas 1993; Gross 2007).

6   Throughout this book, I use the more generic term *fascism* to allude to an ideol- ogy and set of practices that were associated with specific events within Germany or Italy but that go beyond these specific cases. Germany became a fascist nation- state when the Nazis assumed power within its government. This is the fascist threat that Frankfurt school scholars faced. The fall of the Nazi state did not eliminate fascism. I take up this theme of fascism throughout this volume, espe- cially in chapter 8. For accessible introductions to fascism, see Passmore (2002), Albright (2018), and Stanley (2018).

7   Here I focus on British cultural studies as the initial expression of cultural studies writ large. The field of cultural studies is simply too broad for me to do it justice here. *Cultural Studies*, a massive 730-page book that contains forty papers that were delivered at a 1990 conference in the United States, marks an important moment when the ideas of British cultural studies were taken up by thinkers from distinctive disciplinary backgrounds and concerns (Grossberg, Nelson, and Treichler 1992). This volume provides a map of the field as it was emerging, one that rejected disciplinary boundaries in favor of a methodology of drawing from "whatever fields are necessary to produce the knowledge required for a particular project" (Nelson, Treichler, and Grossberg 1992, 2). The editors point out that the field of cultural studies "in fact has no distinct methodology . . . It's methodology, ambiguous from the beginning, could best be seen as a bricolage. Its choice of practice . . . is pragmatic, strategic and self-reflective" (2). In this section, I rely on Lee's (2003) overview and analysis of the field.

8   Hall has written extensively on various aspects of the work issuing from the Cen- tre through the 1980s (Hall 2017; Mercer 2017b; Morley and Chen 1996).

9   Louis Althusser's (2001) thesis of the state ideological apparatus identified new avenues of investigation with increased emphasis on cultural analyses. Ironically, this was a dimension of French Marxism that travelled into the British context during a period when Marxism in France was grappling with its post–World War

II legacy. For a discussion of how the ideas of Althusser and other Marxist theorists laid a foundation for cultural studies, see Lee (2003, 86–89).

10 In this regard, this scholarship on how young people, Black people, women, and similarly subordinated groups used popular culture to empower themselves implicitly criticizes Horkheimer and his thesis of how mass culture cultivates political passivity. This approach to culture is also in stark contrast to scholarship that evaluated culture primarily through the lens of aesthetic criteria (form), for example, Pierre Bourdieu's *Distinction* (1984), a classic that argues that cultural differences distinguish the bourgeoisie from the working classes. British cultural studies explored how people from different social classes used culture for a variety of purposes.

11 The relationship between race and ethnicity informs both scholarship and public policy in Britain. This is a complex topic that I can only mention here. For an overview of some of the ideas and key figures in the multiculturalism in the 1990s, see the essays in Barnor Hesse's edited volume *Un/settled Multiculturalism: Diasporas, Entanglements, Transruptions* (2000). Stuart Hall provides a concluding essay on multiculturalism.

12 Because British cultural studies was grounded in critique, it was open to criticisms from within its own ranks. Race and gender made important interventions in the emerging intersectional framework of British cultural studies. For a discussion of these internal critiques, see Lee (2003, 124–137). The critical progression within British cultural studies seems to be an initial analysis of class and nation that shifts to make room for race and ethnicity and that is changed yet again through the lenses of gender and sexuality. For an example of Black feminist criticism that was influenced by British cultural studies, see Hazel Carby's (1992) essay on multiculturalism.

13 In chapter 8 I examine how eugenics constituted another quite different discourse that was intersectional but not recognized as such. Other discourses may be intersectional as well, a course for future empirical investigation.

14 This can be explained in part by the dismantling of the Centre itself, leaving the ideas of cultural studies scattered across multiple institutional locations. When the Frankfurt school's Institute was exiled, it found an important patron in Columbia University. In contrast, cccs could not replicate the energy of its initial years at the University of Birmingham by moving to another university. I cite these institutional histories because they speak to how academic institutions wield considerable power in legitimating entire fields of study as well as the careers of individual scholars.

15 Stuart Hall and Pierre Bourdieu both advance similar arguments about the interconnections of culture and structure, yet Hall and Bourdieu are not treated as theorists of similar stature. Bourdieu's vocabulary of habitus, field, position, various types of capital, and so on to develop reflexive sociology located in a third space that encompasses *both* structure and subjectivity/culture resonates with Hall's understanding of culture. *Habitus* can also be read as a theory of cul-

ture. Stuart Hall's work can arguably be positioned in the same space, engaging a similar project: linking structure and culture in ways that move beyond Marxist base/superstructure (ideology) arguments. Bourdieu's and Hall's work both have merit and have received substantial attention in their respective national settings. Yet Bourdieu receives greater recognition as a social theorist within American institutions, whereas Hall is only now being discovered.

16 In chapter 7, I take up this connection in greater detail in an analysis of additive, articulated, and co-forming conceptions of relationality within intersectionality.

17 A small group of French intellectuals who shared similar experiences laid the foundation for postmodern social theory and poststructuralism. They are Jean-Francois Lyotard (1924–1998), Michel Foucault (1926–1984), Jean Baudrillard (1929–2007), Pierre Bourdieu (1930–2002), and Jacques Derrida (1930–2004). Except for Derrida, who was born in Algeria into a Jewish family, the remaining theorists were born in France to Christian families. They attended many of the same schools during their formative years and had similar early career experiences. Except for Baudrillard, all studied philosophy and all spent some time in North Africa. Lyotard taught philosophy at a lycée in Algeria between 1952 and 1959, Derrida taught at another Algerian lycée between 1957 and 1959, and Bourdieu served in the French army, taught at a university, and conducted research in Algeria between 1956 and 1960. Foucault taught at the University of Tunisia between 1965 and 1968. These theorists all also had important ties to Marxism. Althusser's influence was significant in the academic and political development of Foucault, Bourdieu, and Derrida. Althusser was at the École Normale Supérieure when Foucault, Bourdieu, and Derrida studied there. Whereas Derrida was not affiliated with any Marxist organization, all the other theorists were involved in associations and activist groups to some extent. Lyotard was a member of Socialisme ou Barbarie between 1954 and 1963. Foucault was a member of the French Communist Party from 1950 to 1953. Baudrillard was involved in the formation of the Franco-Chinese People's Association in the 1960s. Whereas these three seemingly rejected Marxism in the late 1960s, Bourdieu was involved in the worker's movement until the end of his life. I do not discuss French Marxism in this chapter but include this information to suggest that the major figures of poststructuralism were all involved in rejecting Marxism in some fashion. They all also had exposure to the cultures and politics of North Africa.

18 Significantly, most tried to make sense of the altered social relations brought about by political demands for equality within France and freedom from French colonial rule. The thesis that massive social upheaval fosters parallel intellectual disruptions seems especially apt for understanding the theoretical changes within French intellectual circles during the decolonial era (Turner 2006).

19 I focus on Fanon, but examining the impact of Mahatma Gandhi on liberation struggles in India, the crown jewel of the British empire, provides another angle of vision on colonial relations during this same period.

20 As subsequent commentary on Fanon's legacy points out, Fanon did not get everything right. The work on Fanon is expansive and growing, including a revision of his biography (Cherki 2006); Fanon as an intellectual (Posnock 1997); his status as an Africana existentialist philosopher (Sithole 2016); and critical commentary on Fanon's intellectual influence (Bhabha 2004 [1963]; Hall 1996a). There has also been increased attention to specific themes within the corpus of his work. See, for example, papers presented at the Conference on "Fanon on the Fact of Blackness" (Read 1996). See also work on how Fanon has been recast for Western audiences. In his foreword to the 2004 edition of *The Wretched of the Earth*, Homi Bhabha recognizes the challenges of "Framing Fanon" for privileged audiences in Europe and North America. Broadening the French intellectual context, for example, points to Francophone theories advanced by intellectuals within decolonial political struggles as not only critical; they aimed to be liberatory or emancipatory.

21 Claiming a border space as a site of creativity is an important theme within the work of Latina and Third World feminists. See, for example, Gloria Anzaldúa's important discussion of the new *mestiza* in her classic work *Borderlands/La Frontera* (1987). I return to this theme in chapter 7.

22 For example, see works such as Amilcar Cabral's "National Liberation and Culture" (1973); Stokely Carmichael and Charles Hamilton's *Black Power: The Politics of Black Liberation in America* (1967); Pauli Murray's "The Liberation of Black Women" (1970b); Manning Marable's "Beyond Identity Politics: Towards A Liberation Theory for Multicultural Democracy" (1993). I develop these ideas of libration and freedom more fully in chapter 3's discussion of resistant knowledge projects and chapter 6's comparative analysis of the treatment of freedom in the work of Simone de Beauvoir and Pauli Murray.

23 Philosopher Eduardo Mendieta provides an alternative reading of the relationship of academic discourse and activist thinking. Mendieta identifies a "Philosophy of Liberation" as a philosophical movement and method of doing philosophy that emerged first in Argentina during the late 1960s and spread throughout Latin America in the early 1970s. Mendieta contextualizes liberation philosophy within Latin American philosophy, but he also sees it as a "chapter within the broader history of European philosophy" because "even as it defined itself as a critique of Eurocentrism and the hegemony of European philosophy, it has evolved out of and made use of its philosophical currents, movements, concepts and debates" (Mendieta 2016, 1).

24 This is a matter of some debate. Sartre's biography points to his critical engagement with anti-Semitism, anticolonialism, and antiracist projects, within his books of essays titled *Anti-Semite and Jew* (1995 [1948]) and *Colonialism and Neocolonialism* (2006 [1964]). At the same time, as we move beyond the solitary genius model of intellectual work to view it as more collaborative and collective, one wonders how much Sartre did on his own. The revisionist scholarship on Simone de Beauvoir, a feminist philosopher who worked closely with Sartre,

suggests that Beauvoir also contributed to existentialism's development. I take up this issue in chapter 6.

25 Poststructuralism is a movement in literary criticism and philosophy begun in France in the late 1960s. Drawing upon the linguistic theories of Ferdinand de Saussure, the structuralist anthropology of Claude Lévi-Strauss, and the deconstructionist theories of Jacques Derrida, it held that language is not a transparent medium that connects one directly with a "truth" or "reality" outside it. Rather, language is a structure or code whose parts derive their meaning from their contrast with one another and not from any connection with an outside world. Writers associated with the movement include Roland Barthes, Jacques Lacan, Julia Kristeva, and Michel Foucault. Other prominent poststructuralist thinkers are Jean Baudrillard, Judith Butler, Giles Deleuze, Luce Irigaray, and Jean-Francois Lyotard. Judith Butler's philosophy illustrates how poststructuralism has influenced her work (see, e.g., Butler 1990, 1993). The three main ideas of decentering, deconstruction, and difference that I use in this chapter are variations of the key characteristics of poststructuralism as applied to knowledge production (Collins 1998a).

26 Marxist social thought also influenced liberation struggles, and its ideas reappeared across specific projects. While liberation struggles were about capitalism, they were also antiracism struggles. Significantly, Marxism's traditional emphasis on capitalism and class analysis provided scant interpretive space for analyses of racism, colonialism, and similar systems of power. Then and now, Marxist intellectuals who prioritize capitalist class analysis as explaining everything have been ill-positioned to hear the demands of liberation movements that organize around categories of racism and colonialism. Individual intellectuals certainly have been able to see beyond this framing assumption that classical Marxist analysis explained everything. See, for example, Balibar (2007). Balibar's scholarship on race, class, and nationalism is significant in bringing the insights of class analysis to what can be seen as a precursor to intersectionality (Balibar 1991; Balibar and Wallerstein 1991).

27 Bourdieu has had an important influence on sociology. His signature work, *An Invitation to Reflexive Sociology*, has made an important contribution to interpretive sociology (Bourdieu and Waçquant 1992). His scholarship also has shaped social theory, for example, *The Logic of Practice* (1980) and *Distinction: A Social Critique of the Judgement of Taste* (1984). Bourdieu's ideas about habitus and forms of capital have been taken up within education. See, e.g., Bourdieu and Passeron (1977).

28 This perspective on Fanon and liberation theory was not marginal to Bourdieu's thinking but rather seemingly informed his later thinking on antiracist and anticolonial political activism. With Loïc Waçquant, Bourdieu published in 1999 an article titled "On the Cunning of Imperial Reason." The catalyst for the article was Michael Hanchard's volume *Orpheus and Power* (1994) on the Black consciousness movement in Brazil. Echoing Fanon's (1963) notion of the importance of national culture, Hanchard argues that constructing a Black consciousness was

part of Afro-Brazilian resistance to racism. A lively and contentious debate in *Theory, Culture and Society* ensued, with scholars of color criticizing Bourdieu and Waçquant's assumptions concerning the agency of subordinated groups. For a representative response within this debate, see Hanchard's (2003) response to Bourdieu and Waçquant's initial article.

29 I devote an entire chapter in *Fighting Words* to this theme (Collins 1998a). To clarify, the tools themselves can be powerful interventions for projects that aim to decolonize knowledge. In *Fighting Words*, I argue that the ideas of decentering, deconstruction, and difference were prefigured in Black feminism. My criticism lies not with poststructuralist tools but rather with how poststructuralist discourse implicitly upholds conservative political projects while seeming to do the opposite. Specifically, during the 1990s, poststructuralism provided little guidance concerning the growth of mass incarceration as public policy. It seemed to be a social theory that, by criticizing both the Enlightenment ideals that guided social movements and the group-based identities of social movements themselves, weakened social justice initiatives. This reflects less the ideas themselves than how individuals used poststructuralist ideas. It also speaks to the distinctions between social science and narrative understandings of critical theorizing. One form of theorizing may be unsuited for addressing the questions raised by the other. Because intersectionality encompasses both social science and narrative traditions, it must adjudicate these differences.

30 Imagining particular laypeople drives this point home. Black people, women, Latinas, and working-class white men can all be inserted into the category of laypeople who are in need of liberation. In essence, crafting narratives of liberation that such laypeople can neither understand nor confront because they are excluded from critical theory's tight-knit intellectual community undercuts the critical aspirations of the theory itself. This is a damning critique that goes beyond standard criticisms of the language of Habermas, Bourdieu, and other contemporary social theorists as being dense and difficult to understand. The failure goes far deeper than an inability to make ideas clear to a broader public. Rather, the use of dense, insider language constitutes a form of epistemic power. The form that discourse takes becomes part of relations of ruling, ironically itself a barrier that a "discourse on liberation" would have to overcome. Certainly, dense language can be translated for laypeople, yet this introduces the additional question of how to evaluate translations that speak to the needs of laypeople. Dense language can contain powerful ideas, but for whom and for what purpose?

Chapter 3. Intersectionality and Resistant Knowledge Projects

1 A word on how I am using the term *Global South* in this book. This term references a geographic location: Africa, Latin America, Asia, the Caribbean, and the Middle East. But the term *Global South* also refers to power relations of

formal colonialism and contemporary neocolonialism that sustain contemporary global social inequality. Within this power framework, it is possible to have colonial relations of domination and subordination within the "Global North," either as remnants of internal colonialism within colonial powers, as in the case of Ireland within the United Kingdom, and within white settler societies, as in the case of Black and indigenous peoples within the United States and Brazil. For work on internal colonialism, see (Blauner 1972) and (Hechter [1975] 2017).

2 Critical social theorizing within the nation-states of the Global North can demonstrate a similar critical ethos. Broader political struggles of resistance have always needed independent knowledge projects that were designed with the interests of women, people of color, the working poor, colonial subjects, and sexual and religious minorities in mind. Campaigns for women's suffrage, rebellions against dictatorships in the Americas, antislavery initiatives, or unionization of domestic workers seemingly exemplify resistance. When it comes to resistance, political projects of antiracism, feminism, unionization, and the liberation struggles of anticolonialism could not have gone forward without some sense of resistant knowledge at their core.

3 Like intersectionality, these gained considerable visibility within the academy in the late twentieth and the early twenty-first centuries. I selected these particular sites because their ideas are closely aligned with those of intersectionality. Many of the intellectuals working in intersectionality also work within one or more of these areas. Many of the people discussed in this volume may be associated with particular areas but have not been confined by them, for example, Gloria Anzaldúa, Stuart Hall, Frantz Fanon, and Kimberlé Crenshaw. To foreshadow, this chapter contains extensive discussions of William E. B. Du Bois and Edward Said, and future chapters include similar discussions of Pauli Murray. Many of these intellectuals are not well known within Western social theory. That's exactly my point and why I spend so much time on them here. Moreover, these fields influence each another, and their ideas also align with many of intersectionality's paradigmatic concepts. Because each resistant knowledge project is also connected to broader forms of political action, each provides a distinctive angle of vision on critical theorizing within the academy. Ideas themselves, especially critical ideas, know no strict boundaries.

4 I introduce critical theorizing through praxis here in relation to the needs of resistant knowledge projects. As discussed in this chapter, critical theorizing through praxis analyzes social action as a way of knowing for social justice projects. In chapters 5 and 6, I return to this theme through an extended discussion of social action as a way of knowing.

5 I recognize that some readers may see my focus on race in the United States as itself a strategy of American national dominance. This is a rhetorical choice made in order to make this argument manageable; it is not an intellectual oversight. Within the U.S. academy, race has often been treated as an ancillary issue that primarily concerns racial minorities, rather than as a major category of analysis

that explains social inequality. Yet, given the colonial history of genocide against indigenous peoples and the enslavement of African peoples in the U.S., race and racism have been fundamental to American national identity (Collins 2001).

Throughout the book, I signal how broader projects of decolonizing knowledge have influenced freedom struggles generally and projects for national liberation in particular, including those in the United States. Critical race theory writ large is fundamentally transnational. This discourse has been influenced by the liberation theories of Fanon and others who have raised concerns about the lack of freedom for people of African descent. It has also been influenced by broader projects of anticolonialism and anti-imperialism. Here I focus on critical theorizing that aims to resist anti-Black racism in the United States, one important response within academia to this broader narrative.

6 Up to a point, they are right. Ideas about race permeated Western knowledge projects, yet race was typically seen as derivative of other seemingly more fundamental theoretical concerns associated with a particular discipline or school of thought. Racial knowledge remained scattered across several academic disciplines, often as an unmarked signifier attached to some other concern. Biology, sociology, history, literature, political science, economics, medicine, and education have all had distinctive and often storied traditions of scholarship that produced knowledge about race, and that often used race as part of some other project. For example, biology ostensibly sought to understand human intelligence and capacity for morality, yet scientific findings grounded in racial logic provided evidence for white superiority. Yet these were not primarily theoretical discourses about race, even though ideas about race were central to their scholarly projects. Moreover, because racial scholarship focused on empirical questions and concerns, racial theory was an afterthought.

7 Emirbayer and Desmond's volume, *The Racial Order* (2015), provides a pristine example of these tendencies. In their opening pages, they mention in passing the scholarship by African American thinkers and broader insights from critical race theory. By mentioning scholars of color but not engaging their ideas, they dismiss William E. B. Du Bois and similar intellectuals as having good ideas but not producing scholarship that was sufficiently theoretical to be considered as racial theory. Safely bracketed away as providing empirical data for their argument, the authors proceed to develop a new racial theory for sociology that draws upon three core figures. Ironically, they select Pierre Bourdieu, described earlier in this chapter as expressing such a negative reaction to Frantz Fanon and the Algerian revolution, as one of three main theorists for their argument. This is a textbook case of how to build an argument by excluding or containing your critics—in this case, antiracist discourse, much of it raised by African American and African diasporic scholars. Emirbayer and Desmond identify the poor quality of racial theory within sociology as the main social problem within the field. They then set out to remedy this problem by using traditional social theory (which itself has been deeply implicated in reproducing racism) as a remedial template.

In essence, they reduce race to a neglected topic within social theory that can be remedied by drawing upon existing social theory. Yet because existing social theory itself is predicated on a century of racial exclusions, the result is a book that yet again leaves scholars of color outside the boundaries of social theory. The framing of critical race theory within this text illustrates many of the tenets of chapter 4's discussion of epistemic power.

8 In this book I provide examples of African Americans whose intellectual production was situated both inside and outside academia and that used different epistemological criteria. Fixing this problem goes beyond recruiting African Americans and similarly excluded intellectuals of color into academia. In this volume, I entertain the various strategies of resistance that Black intellectuals used to do intellectual work. Specifically, for strategic reasons, those who were able to attain tenuous academic jobs in mainstream institutions had to package their antiracist theorizing within academia's normative standards. Despite his credentials in history, philosophy, and sociology, Du Bois was denied an academic position at the University of Pennsylvania. Others gained jobs in historically Black colleges and universities, sites that provided more freedom for their intellectual production (e.g., Du Bois at Atlanta University and Alain Locke at Howard University; see chapter 5). Others never gained entry in the first place, or they left to work within other venues such as teaching and journalism (e.g., Ida Wells-Barnett [chapter 5] and Pauli Murray [chapter 6]).

9 Racial formation theory is not the progeny of African American social and political thought. It certainly demonstrates the influence of such thought, as well as analyses informed by Marxist analysis of class relations and a poststructuralist focus on discourse analysis. Conceptualizing race, racism, racial inequality, and racial injustices as situated within the recursive relationship between social structures and cultural representations, racial formation theory explains both racial order and racial change.

10 Racial formation theory retains the agency of individual human actors as well as the actions of groups. I return to this relationship between ideas and actions throughout this book. American pragmatism's notion of creative social action comes closest to describing how racial projects specifically, and knowledge projects more generally, work (see chapter 5). Racial formation theory's emphasis on human agency is reminiscent of existentialism's claims that people make their own reality (see chapter 2 as well as Beauvoir's thesis of existential freedom in chapter 6). Unlike existentialism's focus on the individual, racial formation theory emphasizes group knowledges and their roles in social change. Resistant knowledge projects are fundamentally collective, a position I explore in chapter 5's discussion of Black women's community work. See also chapter 4's discussion of epistemic resistance within groups. Critical social theory itself can be seen as a knowledge project.

11 The concept of racial projects is useful for critical theorizing of African Americans, Latinos, Asians, Muslims, indigenous peoples, and similarly subordinated

social groups, where racism works to suppress resistant knowledge projects and malign critical analyses that do enter public space. By providing a theoretical discourse that explains the group-based resistant knowledge projects produced by subordinated groups, racial formation theory articulates with standpoint epistemology (Collins 1998a, 201–228).

12   This statement and the identity politics it engendered constituted a form of epistemic resistance. I provide an analysis of this issue in chapter 4.

13   Butler herself makes mention of both Beauvoir and Sartre in the 1990 preface to *Gender Trouble* (xxvii) and to poststructuralism in the 1999 preface to the same volume. In this way, Butler's work takes different inspiration from French existentialism (Sartre and Beauvoir) and poststructuralism (chapter 2). My close reading of Beauvoir juxtaposed to the work of Pauli Murray brings a critical intersectional lens to Beauvoir's work (chapter 6).

14   The criticisms of queer theory were equally if not more telling as queer theory's criticisms of structuralism. In the 1999 preface to *Gender Trouble*, Judith Butler acknowledges the influence of poststructuralism on her work. Butler, describing her work as that of cultural translation, notes that "poststructuralist theory was brought to bear on U.S. theories of gender and the political predicaments of feminism" (Butler 1990, ix). By the 1990s, Butler was, as she puts it, well aware that the "critiques of poststructuralism within the cultural Left have expressed strong skepticism toward the claim that anything politically progressive can come of its premises" (ix).

15   For a survey of key issues within sexuality studies, an enormous, interdisciplinary endeavor that criticizes a host of framing assumptions of Western knowledge, see Fischer and Seidman (2016).

16   The emergence of *heteropatriarchy* as a term signaling the joining of theories of gender and sexuality raises important issues for intersectionality's understandings of relationality. In chapter 7, I introduce addition, articulation, and co-formation as three forms of relational thinking within intersectionality. The joining of gender and sexuality required a period of articulation—namely, forming provisional intellectual coalitions and alliances among the interpretive communities that advanced each discourse. At what point did the perceived need for a new term arise? My sense is that heteropatriarchy accommodates the distinctions of articulation but names a permanent co-forming relationship.

17   In this book, following Bettcher (2014), I use the term *trans* as one of a set of terms for describing the complex identifications of gender-nonconforming people. Bettcher provides an accessible yet substantive discussion of terminology as well as a genealogy of the emergence of trans discourse. The intellectual production of Pauli Murray, who in this book is treated as an important figure within intersectionality, demonstrates how the absence of the analyses that became central to trans politics affected her critical thinking (see chapter 6).

18   Intellectuals within the West do take up important themes, but to be credible, this work must adhere to the standards of Western epistemologies. Topics such

as how Western discourse imagines colonial spaces, the contours of anticolonial resistance, how the West looks from non-Western spaces, and doing intellectual work that falls both inside and outside the West reappear across postcolonial analyses (Gandhi 1998; Goldberg and Quayson 2002; Loomba 1998; Williams and Chrisman 1994).

19 The anthology *Colonial Discourse and Post-Colonial Theory: A Reader*, published in 1994, provides a provisional map of the contours of the field of postcolonial theory. Interestingly, postcolonial theory gained visibility in the academy in the 1990s, the same decade as intersectionality. Moreover, many of the figures included in the reader on postcolonial theory are also included in the 1992 anthology *Cultural Studies* (Grossberg, Nelson, and Treichler 1992). This suggests that more fluid boundaries among postcolonial studies, cultural studies, and intersectionality existed in the 1990s. Each of these fields followed a different trajectory as its ideas became more codified into academic canons. For narratives of postcolonial studies that mapped the fields as they appeared at the time, see (Gandhi 1998; Loomba 1998). For retrospective narratives published after these seminal works, see the anthology *Relocating Postcolonialism* (Goldberg and Quayson 2002).

20 For example, Toni Morrison's *Playing in the Dark* (1992) examines how an unmarked whiteness characterizes American literature.

21 A number of intellectuals identify how their social location shapes their intellectual production; for example, Gloria Anzaldúa in *Borderlands/La Frontera*. Themes of forced migration, exile, and statelessness reappear in the work of many other contemporary intellectuals.

22 There is a substantial body of literature of feminist engagement with postcolonial studies. For a summary of these debates, see (Gandhi 1998, 81–101).

23 The very term *postcolonial* invokes specific notions of space and time that reify Western categorical notions of sovereign space and linear time. Terms such as *premodern, modern,* and *postmodern* invoke colonial discourses that relegated natives to premodern colonial space that existed outside of time (anthropology); to modern space of a relationship between modern sovereign nation-states with dominion over their colonies and empires; and to postmodern space that signals the fragmentation of this social order and, with the emergence of sovereign nation-states, a postcolonial period. As used within social theory, the term *postcolonial* seems undercut by the new realities that challenge these linear assumptions, and by new social actors who seem far less vested in criticizing Western theoretical debates (reform) than in creating new knowledge and practices.

24 In *Racial Oppression in America*, Bob Blauner (1972) develops the thesis that African Americans are an internal colony within the United States and as such are exploited through American capitalism. Originally published in 1975, Michael Hechter's *Internal Colonialism* (2017) investigates a similar thesis. Presenting the Irish as the Celtic fringe of British national identity, Hechter contends that their treatment constitutes a colonial relationship. British national identity thus rests on its ties to both its internal colonies, such as Ireland, and its external colonies.

25 Interest in critical race theory in the academy seems to wax and wane in response to changes in broader racial politics. When Black social movements are active, as in the case of the civil rights movement in the 1950s, the Black Power movement in the 1960s and 1970s, and the contemporary Black Lives Matter movement, academic interest in questions of race and racism, but not necessarily antiracism, is more prominent. When seeming quiescence sets in, scholarly interest often wanes.

Chapter 4. Intersectionality and Epistemic Resistance

1 The coining narrative is ubiquitous and does not need extensive citations. My concern is not with the substance of the scholarship that uses the coining framework. My point concerns the cavalier use of this narrative, in the same way that researchers label intersectionality as a theory. Being critical, however, requires being self-reflexive about all aspects of one's own practices. It is in this spirit that I offer the following criticism of the coining narrative.

2 Here I draw upon Albert Memmi's (1965) discussion of colonialism as a relationship between three main categories of social actors—namely, colonizers who accept colonialism, the colonized who refuse, and an interim category of colonizers who refuse. This third category of colonizers who refuse occupy a liminal space between the other two, expressing varying patterns of collaboration and contestation.

3 In this regard, there are parallels here between Kimberlé Crenshaw and Pauli Murray in how both saw law as an instrument for social change. Crenshaw was positioned at the intersection of antiracism and feminism and used law to analyze both the contradictions that she found there as well as possible solutions to them. Murray expressed a similar sensibility several decades earlier (see chapter 6).

4 In this chapter, I rely on feminist philosopher of science Sandra Harding's categorization of epistemology, methodology, and methods as a useful rubric for thinking through the interconnections of theory and praxis for intersectional research (Fonow and Cook 2005). Within Harding's (1987) schema, epistemology constitutes an overarching theory of knowledge that shapes research. For example, structuralism and poststructuralism provide epistemological frameworks, whereas methodology encompasses the broad principles of how to conduct research within the epistemological assumptions (e.g., qualitative and quantitative social science research methodologies). Methods are the particular techniques used in the course of scientific research that address where and how best to utilize specific methods (e.g., interviewing and survey analysis).

5 Specific interpretive communities gain or lose authority by how they are placed within academia itself. Practices such as patterns of citation, themes of journal articles, articles selected for student readers, invitations to deliver keynote addresses, and the composition of panels at academic conferences collectively shape who gets to speak about and for intersectionality, and how credible and believable their testimony is.

6 This case provides a provocative example of how a male-defined narrative that presented Black male suffering as synonymous with the racial oppression of Black people exercised epistemic power over a Black woman's challenge to that narrative. This case highlights the often contentious gender politics within African American communities. In an essay titled "Whose Story Is It Anyway? Feminist and Antiracist Appropriations of Anita Hill," Kimberlé Crenshaw (1992) weighed in on these dynamics. Crenshaw analyzed how narratives of subordinated groups can be appropriated by more powerful groups and annexed to their causes. In this case, Anita Hill's testimonial authority to speak from the intersectional location of being a Black woman did not fit within either antiracist or feminist narratives at that time.

7 The televised 2018 congressional hearings of now Supreme Court justice Brett Kavanaugh demonstrated an eerie resemblance to the Thomas hearings. Like Thomas, Kavanaugh was also accused of sexual harassment, and like the earlier hearings, the testimony of Kavanaugh's accuser was also disbelieved.

8 For example, the phrase "the master's tools will never dismantle the master's house" is the title of a signature essay in Audre Lorde's classic volume *Sister Outsider* (1984). Lorde's writings were fundamental to the foundations of modern Black feminism, modern feminism, and intersectionality. In this particular essay, Lorde takes white feminists to task for their exclusionary practices at a literary conference, basically accusing them of using the "master's tools" in organizing the conference. Lorde criticized the terms under which she was included in the conference, exercising epistemic resistance through this essay by criticizing not just the substance of the conference but how it had been organized. The sophistication of Lorde's analysis disappears in the uncritical circulation of the phrase. How many people who use this phrase know its origins, or have even heard of Audre Lorde?

9 For example, Michel Foucault's *Power/Knowledge* (1980), Pierre Bourdieu's *Distinction* (1984), and Judith Butler's *Gender Trouble* (1990) are all important books. Yet neglecting their intellectual trajectory by reading them as decontextualized social theories does not do justice to them.

10 This testimonial tradition reappears in the critical intellectual production of women, taking form in autobiographies, speeches, and first-person narratives as a format for fiction. See, for example, testimonial autobiographies such as *I, Rigoberta Menchu*, testifying about how militarism in Guatemala affected Indian people (Menchu 2010); *Child of the Dark: The Diary of Carolina Maria de Jesus,* a memoir that details her experiences as mother in a Brazilian favela (de Jesus 2003 [1960]); and *Woman at Point Zero*, a novel by Egyptian feminist Nawal El Saadawi's (2015) that uses the format of a first-person testimonial of a woman convicted of murder as critical commentary on gender politics.

11 The resistant knowledge projects of liberation theory, existentialism, British cultural studies, critical race theory, feminism, and decolonial studies all attend to identity as a site of political analysis, albeit differently. Projects such as these reflect

the integrity of a group to organize in relation to common interests and to identify with critical analyses advanced by a particular interpretive community. Similarly, American pragmatism and Black feminist thought both contain analyses of experience and creative social action that suggest that identity politics and standpoint epistemology, broadly defined, can be important if not essential elements of democratic communities. This does not mean that these ideas are beyond criticism, but rather that they should be critically examined on their own terms.

12 To foreshadow, in chapter 5, I examine Black feminist thought's critical theorizing as a resistant knowledge project. I argue that Black feminist thought's core ideas of intersectionality as a theoretical perspective on the social world and flexible solidarity as a form of political praxis that is grounded in communities highlight the significance of experience and social action within critical theorizing. Both of these ideas inform Black feminist thought and intersectionality. The criticisms of identity politics and standpoint epistemology that are assumed to be associated with intersectionality constitute one way to weaken the epistemic resistance of such projects.

13 Identity politics within academic discourse may have waned in popularity, but the use of identity politics has persisted in other venues. A comparative analysis of identity politics within hip hop and within academia illustrates the significance of how different interpretive communities understand and use identity politics (Collins and Bilge 2016, 114–135).

14 In a testament to testimonial smothering, few scholars are sufficiently diligent in searching for and citing the scholarship of women of color and similarly subordinated intellectuals. Because intersectionality is so vast, a thorough analysis of practices of coerced silencing within it is an important empirical question. Tactics of testimonial smothering within intersectionality can best be traced by the thematic mapping of scholarly publications that claim intersectionality in some fashion since its naming. This mapping would embed a thematic analysis within the testimonial community of intersectionality as evidenced by how this idea unfolded within journals, textbooks, conference proceedings, edited volumes, and solo-authored monographs. This analysis would take note of certain stylistic practices, for example, the "mentioning" of Crenshaw's work as an agreed-upon proxy. It would also identify emerging themes within intersectionality (e.g., sexuality) as categories of analysis or the contemporary shift to materialist and structural analyses.

15 See, for example, my analysis of how Black women's knowledge and Black feminist thought navigated the processes that I describe here (Collins 1998a, 11–43).

16 I use a methodology of dialogical engagement to structure this book. For example, this chapter introduces how working dialogically across differences of power is an important methodological premise for intersectionality. Many of the other chapters here rely on a strategy of reading that is informed by dialogical engagement. For example, the dialogical reading of Black feminist thought and American pragmatism in chapter 5 compares the two discourses for insight about

experience and social action. Similarly, the analysis in chapter 6 of how Simone de Beauvoir and Pauli Murray conceptualized freedom presents dialogical engagement, not between discourses but between individual intellectuals. I've also placed chapters next to each other so that they can be read dialogically, showing, for example, how the critical social theories in chapter 2 and the resistant knowledge projects in chapter 3 collectively shed light on the meaning of being critical. Through this organization, I aim to ground my theoretical analysis of intersectionality in a methodology that upholds my theoretical claims.

17 Understandings of relationality shape research projects; it matters what concept of relationality a particular researcher has in mind when she or he claims to be engaged in intersectional inquiry. Varying conceptions of relationality also map directly onto actual social relations of social inequality. There too it matters how social actors both envision their relationships to others as well as act on those beliefs. Relationality is an important core construct both within contemporary social relations and in the epistemological concerns of intersectionality, yet the question remains—What conceptions of relationality do people have in mind when they engage in intersectional inquiry and praxis? How do scholars and activists conceptualize the *relationships* among race, class, gender, sexuality, age, ability, nation, and age as systems of power and as social formations, and the social practices that ensue?

18 The construct of abduction, drawn from pragmatist philosophy's concept of experimentalism (see chapter 5), provides a useful methodological framework for intersectionality. Pragmatism itself had no political aims, yet drawing upon pragmatism's abductive framework to develop intersectionality's critical methodology is especially promising. Throughout this book, I take the position that placing intersectional theorizing in dialogue with pragmatism is highly productive in developing intersectionality as a critical social theory. Pragmatism constitutes a social theory that provides orienting concepts for addressing existing social problems. Yet, as explored here, pragmatism also contains important methodological implications. Together they suggest a framework for a critical methodology whereby pragmatism fleshes out the processes of doing critical theoretical work, whereas the tenets of critical social theory provide a more expansive list of qualities that characterize that process. Philosopher Lara Trout's (2010) analysis of the work of Charles Peirce provides an important philosophical foundation for analyzing this work. See also Igor Douven's (2017) treatment of abduction as a philosophical construct.

19 Ethnography has a storied history within qualitative social science research traditions (Denzin and Lincoln 1994). My treatment here examines a small segment of a very broad methodological area. Resistant knowledge projects of gender, race, ethnicity, and similar categories of analysis have investigated the possibilities and limitations of ethnographic research for their respective areas. For feminist analyses of social science research with an emphasis on ethnography, see Craven and Davis (2013) and DeVault (1999). For an important discussion of

how intersectionality might inform sociological research, see Choo and Ferree (2010).

20 I conceptualize the methodology that I use in this book as one of textual ethnography. It involves the abductive framework of putting theories in dialogue with one another. But instead of examining the social world via fieldwork with people, a range of texts constitute my data. My approach resembles but differs from discourse analysis.

21 For example, in this volume, I rely on abductive analysis to investigate the meaning of being critical. My discussion of intersectionality and its related critical knowledge projects in academia (namely, broader critical theories of the Frankfurt school; British cultural studies; and liberation theory, existentialism, and poststructuralism within Francophone social theory) is supplemented with select resistant knowledge projects (namely, critical race theory, feminism, and decolonial studies). Together, these projects provide a provisional map of how knowledge projects make different contributions to the same goal—namely, being critical. This use of abductive analysis requires comfort with ambiguity versus certainty.

Chapter 5. Intersectionality, Experience, and Community

1 Communities are alternatively romanticized as places where individuals find a comfortable home or demonized as obstacles to individual fulfillment. Yet communities constitute important sites that organize power relations (Collins 2010). The discussion of interpretive communities in chapter 4 points to how epistemic power works within and among communities.

2 These two discourses have different histories within the academy. Black feminist thought examines the contours of Black women's intellectual production within U.S. and African diasporic spaces (Collins 2000). Because African American women have been highly visible in cultivating intersectionality, Black feminist thought has been pivotal in shaping intersectionality's cognitive architecture. American pragmatism is a subdiscipline within philosophy, itself a relatively small discipline whose centrality to Western knowledge grants it influence beyond the small number of professional philosophers. The ideas of American pragmatism have influenced fields such as education and sociology (Gross 2007). Because scholars across several disciplines and national contexts have applied pragmatism's core ideas to a variety of questions, pragmatism has recently enjoyed a scholarly revitalization (Bernstein 1992). Significantly, pragmatism's longstanding academic record points to intertwining genealogies both of pragmatism and academic disciplines, and of Black feminist thought and similar resistant knowledge projects.

3 Note that social context is a core construct within intersectionality (see table 1.1 in chapter 1). It is a broad category that is invoked but not specified. Here I focus

on two aspects of social context: First, I discuss the external social context that influences the content of Black feminist thought. This external social context is organized via intersecting power relations that produce the complex social inequalities that characterize Black women's experiences. I also focus on the internal social context of life within African American communities. Here I also use intersectionality's guiding premises to analyze Black feminist thought within social context (see figure 1.1 in chapter 1).

4   Black women's historiography emphasizes these kinds of connections between ideas and action (see, e.g., Thomsen 2015). Black women's history provides a foundation for Black feminist thought. Important scholarship that framed the field of Black women's historiography includes that by Giddings (1984) and Hine, Brown, and Terborg-Penn (1993). Significantly, the combination of intellectualism and activist involvement differs from one African American woman to the next—differences of personal choice, circumstances, opportunities, and coercion.

5   Black feminism as a social justice project and Black feminist thought as its intellectual center have been inextricably linked, taking different forms over time in response to challenges facing African American women (Collins 2000). The persistence of violence constitutes one deep-seated challenge. As such, within Black feminist thought, violence constitutes one catalyst for developing an intersectional analysis of both violence itself and the intersecting power relations that engender it (see Collins 1998b). In this case, as a form of state-sanctioned violence, lynching was the visible tip of the iceberg of a constellation of practices that devalued Black life. Figuring out ways to survive within and to contest the forms of violence that touched their lives constitutes an important thread that runs through African American women's intellectual activism. I return to this question of violence as a social problem that requires intersectional analysis at various points in this book.

6   Black feminist scholarship has recently investigated the scope of Wells-Barnett's intellectual work (see, e.g., Collins 2002; Giddings 2008). Until the emergence of the modern Black feminist movement in the 1970s, Wells-Barnett remained a neglected figure within African American historiography, largely because African American women's history was neglected. The resurgence of work in African American women's history created a new context for reclaiming neglected figures such as Wells-Barnett. Angela Davis's 1981 edited volume *Women, Race, and Class* positioned Wells-Barnett within the burgeoning interest in race, class, and gender studies largely catalyzed by Black feminism, and it contextualized Wells-Barnett's analysis of lynching within this emerging interpretive framework. In a similar vein, the essays on African American women in Bettina Aptheker's *Woman's Legacy: Essays on Race, Sex, and Class in American History* (1982) also explored the significance of Wells-Barnett's anti-lynching campaign to Black women's political activism for women's suffrage.

7   Within democratic societies, *institutional politics* examine the mechanisms of governance, viewing elected officials, bureaucrats, voters, and citizens as bona fide political actors. Lacking citizenship rights, at one time being defined as less

than human, Black women have historically been denied positions of power and authority within U.S. social institutions. *Protest politics* in the public sphere complements liberal definitions of institutional politics, typically framed through a focus on social movement activism. In contrast, *survival politics*, the hard work needed to ensure that a group of people is prepared to enter public institutions and is capable of protest, constitutes the bedrock of community politics because it is associated with the private sphere and is black, female and poor. Mid-twentieth-century social movements created opportunities for many Black women to enter institutional politics.

8 I am using the terms *Black civil society*, *Black community*, and *Black public sphere* interchangeably to refer to the constellation of organizations that stand between African American families and broader civil society. In this sense, African Americans are not just individuals within white society.

9 African American women were not of like mind in sharpening their understandings of intersectionality and solidarity. For example, many African American women who worked in the Student Nonviolent Coordinating Committee during the civil rights movement experienced a growth in feminist consciousness as a result of the organization's gender politics (Anderson-Bricker 1999). In contrast, others failed to challenge hierarchies of gender and sexuality, arguing that focusing on issues that seemingly lay outside civil rights agendas would dilute antiracist action. Similarly, African American women have long held multiple perspectives on and taken an array of actions within Black religious organizations. Many African American women used the theology of a male-run church to advocate for gender equity, whereas others questioned their ministers' interpretations of Christian scripture on the rightful place of women (Higginbotham 1993). Some left churches altogether, finding other faith traditions more suitable to their political perspectives. Black women were more likely to encounter women's issues via daily interactions within organizations that formed the public sphere of African American communities than within formal feminist organizations.

10 Joas also points out that this dimension of American pragmatism has garnered criticism: "It is precisely this emphasis on the interconnection of creativity and situation that has given rise to the repeated charge that pragmatists merely possess a theory that is a philosophy of adaptation to given circumstances. This accusation fails to perceive the antideterministic thrust of the pragmatists. In their view the actors confront problems whether they want to or not; the solution to these problems, however, is not clearly prescribed beforehand by reality, but calls for creativity and brings something objectively new into the world" (1993, 4).

11 Standard accounts of American pragmatism approach it as a subfield of philosophy, whose classic version emerged in the U.S. context from the late 1880s to the 1940s. Charles Peirce, William James, John Dewey, and George Herbert Mead are routinely mentioned as seminal figures in the classical pragmatist canon. A series of anthologies of the works of key figures in the field provide a generally agreed-upon history of American pragmatism (late nineteenth-century origins to con-

temporary expressions as a uniquely American philosophy) that is explained by the following provisional chronology: (1) the founding of the field, primarily through seminal essays and actions of participants in the "Metaphysical Club"; (2) the maturing of the field through the copious works of philosopher John Dewey; (3) a period of decline during the 1940s and 1950s, when Dewey's ideas went out of favor; and (4) a period of resurgence and revitalization, marked by new social movements in the 1960s and 1970s and the increased scholarly attention to the ideas themselves in the 1980s to the present.

According to the stock story, by the 1980s and 1990s, American pragmatism became revitalized in the academy, especially within philosophy. Two philosophers are identified as spearheading this movement. Richard Rorty (1999) approached it as a neopragmatist. German philosopher Jürgen Habermas also turned to American pragmatism for its utility in shaping his theories of communicative action and democracy, a move that further gave legitimacy to the field. It also reappeared within other disciplines that had drawn upon pragmatism but had not recognized it as such. Given the period of quiescence, the revitalization of American pragmatism has been significant.

I am presenting a very general depiction of pragmatism. For useful introductions, Cornelis De Waal's *On Pragmatism* (2005) provides a solid summary of the main ideas and history for philosophy students. Hans Joas's *Pragmatism and Social Theory* (1993) emphasizes expressions of pragmatism in the U.S. and Europe. Not all histories of pragmatism are uniformly favorable. Cornel West's volume *The American Evasion of Philosophy: A Genealogy of Pragmatism* (1989) aims to broaden the pragmatist canon to include themes and thinkers that routinely did not appear in histories. Focusing on pragmatism as a subfield of philosophy, West aimed to show pragmatism's potential utility for a more democratic agenda. Scott L. Pratt (2002) engages in a similar project. Pratt also examines the connections between pragmatism and philosophy, yet casts a much wider net than West and others by incorporating the encounter between native peoples and settlers as core. Still within this tradition of linking pragmatism within the confines of philosophy specifically and social theory in general, Larry A. Hickman's *Pragmatism as Post-Postmodernism: Lessons from John Dewey* (2007) examines the provocative thesis that pragmatism may constitute the next step after poststructuralism.

12 In this regard, pragmatism and phenomenology share important framing assumptions about the socially situated nature of human consciousness (Gross 2007).

13 This construct of experimentalism highlights the significance of critical analysis for creative social action as a way of knowing. In this book, my analysis of critical thinking within intersectionality is informed by a pragmatist understanding of experimentalism (see figure 1.1 in chapter 1). For example, within intersectionality, when individuals identify and use metaphors in new ways, use heuristics for solving problems, and foster paradigm shifts in what has been taken to be true, these actions are basically experimental. The distinctive aspects of intersectionality's

cognitive architecture draw upon basic ideas of critical thinking as tools for creative social action. Similarly, dialogical engagement is fundamentally a pragmatist approach to experience, the case, for example, of abductive analysis as a way of theorizing (see chapter 4). When sufficient creative and critical work has been done, processes of creative social action may catalyze critical social theories.

14 Some critics returned to figures whose associations with pragmatism had been neglected, for example, Ralph Waldo Emerson (West 1989, 9–41). Other work explored thinkers who had been neglected within the pragmatist canon, most notably, William E. B. Du Bois (Posnock 1998; West 1989) and Jane Addams (Seigfried 1996). In other cases, figures who were routinely associated with other fields were analyzed for their ties to pragmatism, the case, for example, of seeing Jürgen Habermas as carrying on the ideas of the Frankfurt school's Critical Theory (Joas 1993, 125–153). Casting a wider net also sheds light on how historical figures who were foundational to American democracy potentially influenced contemporary understandings of pragmatism, the case, for example, of Benjamin Franklin (Campbell 1999; Pratt 2002).

15 Reclaiming the work of prominent feminist philosophers who are not associated with pragmatism has also been promising. For example, the corpus of Simone de Beauvoir's scholarship has received considerable and long overdue attention (see, e.g., Hengehold and Bauer 2017). I make a similar argument in chapter 6 regarding the treatment of the work of Simone de Beauvoir within existentialism. Discussions of canonical existentialism routinely point to Sartre, Camus, Fanon, and other male figures, often aligning Beauvoir with existentialism based on her association with this group. More recently, Beauvoir has been treated as an existentialist philosopher in her own right, with some critics asking how her ideas might have shaped the existentialist ideas that are routinely attributed to Sartre.

16 Several works stand out in this endeavor, among them, Charlotte Seigfried's "Shared Communities of Interest: Feminism and Pragmatism" (1993, 1996); and Shannon Sullivan's (2000) reading of John Dewey's pragmatism with an eye toward reconfiguring gender, as well as her analysis of the intersections of pragmatist and continental feminisms (Sullivan 2015). These efforts to examine the relationship between gendered analyses, which may or may not be feminist, and pragmatism can open up new avenues of investigation.

17 See, for example, Cornel West's analysis of Du Bois as a "Jamesian Organic Intellectual" (1989, 138–149), or Ross Posnock's (1998) analysis of Du Bois's pragmatism and its lineage. Sociology has also engaged in a similar project of identifying and incorporating the intellectual work of individual African American thinkers, many of whom were excluded from the field. Aldon Morris's (2015) analysis of how Du Bois's exclusion from sociology shaped its subsequent trajectory advances a similar argument.

18 The authors in Leonard Harris's edited volume *The Critical Pragmatism of Alain Locke* (1999) take up this thesis, offering essays discussing Locke's treatment of value theory, aesthetics, community, culture, race, and education.

19 In this regard, the symbolism associated with community is key, with the elasticity of the symbol serving as a measure of its effectiveness. Symbols are often most useful when they are imprecise: the specific content of a given political project is less significant than how the construct of community enables people to imagine new forms of community, even as they retrieve and rework symbols from the past (Cohen 1985).

Chapter 6. Intersectionality and the Question of Freedom

1 The ideas of freedom and social justice are often used interchangeably within intersectionality, but they have different histories and mean different things. The thinkers cited in this paragraph and throughout this book draw on different understandings of each term.

2 Beauvoir's status as a major existentialist philosopher in her own right provided access to people, places, and ideas that were unavailable to people of a different class, race, or citizenship. As a privileged intellectual, Beauvoir travelled in rarefied circles where ideas were debated by a relatively small number of people. Beauvoir experienced gender discrimination, but few dared to question her legitimate participation in existentialism; the fact that she was a bona fide philosophical insider is taken for granted and constitutes the starting point for analysis. For example, the important archeological work done concerning the degrees of influence that Sartre and Beauvoir had on one another's work aims to correct the historical record that routinely takes the intellectual production of women and attributes it to men (see, e.g., Simons 1999, 2006). Beauvoir's relationship with Sartre may have reflected both of these responses. Contemporary revisionist scholarship on Beauvoir's relationship with Sartre suggests that they were intellectual co-partners to a much greater degree than existing scholarly records suggest (Klaw 2006; Simons 2006). Despite the significance of this excavation of Beauvoir's original contributions to existentialism, the fact of her inclusion can be taken for granted.

3 In *The Second Sex*, Beauvoir does a masterful job of unpacking the sexism of dominant discourse. For English-speaking audiences, the eight-hundred-page translation by Borde and Malovany-Chevallier provides a more accurate rendition of Beauvoir's arguments than were previously available (Beauvoir 2011 [1949]). Correcting errors in the original translation, and restoring substantial sections of original text, the 2011 translation provides ample evidence for both Beauvoir's diligence as a scholar as well as her analysis of male domination and women's oppression. I remain astounded that Beauvoir was able to use the extant scholarship that was available to her in the late 1940s at such an early point in her career (she was thirty-eight) to produce a work of such scope, insight, and lasting value.

4 I also consulted *America Day by Day* (1999 [1954]), Beauvoir's memoir of her four-month sojourn in the United States in early 1947, for additional evidence

concerning the experiences that shaped Beauvoir's analysis. This memoir documents Beauvoir's reflections in 1947, the year prior to the publication of *The Ethics of Ambiguity* and *The Second Sex*. I present this material more fully elsewhere (Collins 2017c).

5 Pragmatism's experimentalism offers a view of human rationality and choice that might inform existentialist perceptions of humans as choosing freedom because they cannot rely on tradition. When it comes to freedom, these connections among American pragmatism and existentialism might spark important avenues of investigation for intersectionality as critical social theory.

6 Beauvoir's analogical reasoning has roots in Western epistemology. Abbot identifies the use of analogy as a core search strategy for the heuristic use of intersectionality. As a thinking tool, variations of analogy can be sources of insight for one's own puzzles and problems. Analogies provide new angles of vision on the familiar: "The origins of analogies are generally well concealed by those who use them. And analogy often provides only the starting point for an argument, which must then be carefully elaborated and critically worked out on its own" (Abbott 2004, 118).

7 I discuss the significance of metaphors for critical thinking in chapter 1. Beauvoir's analogical reasoning relies on a chain of metaphors that each give meaning to the others.

8 Scholarly analysis of African American feminist-activist Pauli Murray's intellectual production remains in its infancy. Yet Murray is receiving long overdue accolades for her lifelong contributions to social justice projects for race, gender, and class equity. In a 2017 article titled "The Many Lives of Pauli Murray" in the *New Yorker*, Kathryn Schulz heralded Murray as an architect of the civil rights struggle and the woman's movement and asked readers a provocative question: "Why haven't you heard of her?" That same year, Yale University renamed one of its colleges after her, making her the first African American woman so honored. The publication of two book-length biographies of Murray's life within a year of one another—Rosalind Rosenberg's *Jane Crow: The Life of Pauli Murray* (2017) and Patricia Bell-Scott's *The Firebrand and the First Lady: Portrait of a Friendship* (2016)—speak to Murray's growing importance within women's history and Black feminist thought. Moreover, many of the fields of critical analysis that are most closely associated with intersectionality have shown varying degrees of interest in different aspects of Murray's life.

9 Cognitive strategies of using metaphors and analogies are fundamental to how humans make sense of the world. We build on what we think we know, often root metaphors that seemingly need no explanation, in order to extrapolate from the familiar to the unfamiliar or unknown. Regardless of content, because metaphors are pervasive in everyday life, they form the bedrock of thought and action (Lakoff and Johnson 2003 [1980]; Trout 2010). Root metaphors serve as touchstones that make unfamiliar phenomena comprehensible. Comparative or analogical thinking (e.g., how entities do or do not resemble one another) build on metaphors to enable people to make sense of the world.

10 Murray most likely was familiar with the works of William E. B. Du Bois, Oliver Cox, Alain Locke, and others who advanced antiracist analyses, often in conjunction with other categories, for example, Du Bois's *The Souls of Black Folk*, Oliver Cox's *Race and Class*, and the works of major figures of the Harlem Renaissance. Anna Julia Cooper's work on the Haitian Revolution may also have been of interest.

11 During this period, Murray wrote publicly about her multiracial identity and privately about her sexual identity. In both cases, she "struggled to negotiate the construction of her own experience at the same time that she resisted normative accounts of who she was, either as a multiracial person or as a woman who loved other women sexually" (Azaransky 2011, 9). This early self-consciousness about identity seemingly informed Murray's later claims that imagining new identifications can inspire greater democratic possibilities for all Americans.

12 This metaphor of the journey resonates with abductive analysis in American pragmatism. Murray's biography grounds these ideas in her specific project of working for social justice.

13 Resembling the existential freedom of existentialism's focus on individual consciousness, the collective freedom of an African American community also required creating itself anew in response to changing racial conditions. In his book *Freedom Dreams* (2002), historian Robin D. J. Kelley presents an idea of a "Black radical imagination" that underpins various periods of social activism, as well as the themes that were particularly prominent during those periods. Notably, Kelley identifies Black women generally, and Murray as a figure whose long involvement in civil rights and feminist activism was part of a collective Black freedom struggle (2002, 138).

14 It is important to point out that race and class have not always been seen as discrete within African American social and political thought. Contemporary intersectionality overlooks critical traditions of antiracism that incorporate critiques of capitalism. Similarly, African American intellectual-activists who incorporated gender into Black intellectual production grappled within an unequal analytical relationship between race and class. For example, in her analysis of slavery and reproduction, Angela Davis's (1978) critique of capitalism incorporates a gendered analysis into a class-based understanding of slavery. Manning Marable's (1983a) gendered analysis of racism and capitalism demonstrates a similar sensibility. These seeming additions to the literature on colonialism, capitalism and racism constitute important revitalizations of the fields.

15 This idea of partial perspectives articulates the open-endedness of metaphors within theorizing. As conceptual spatial metaphors, neither intersectionality nor the idea of the borderlands provide coherence, consistency, or closure. Both travel, sometimes working in tandem for some projects and apart in others. Yet when a concept is structured by a metaphor, it is only partially structured and can be extended in some ways but not in others (Trout 2010, 13). The puzzle of intersectionality lies in exploring the characteristic ways of thinking within intersectionality's

contributing discourses. Discourses of race, class, gender, sexuality, age, ability, and nation all rely on metaphoric thinking; as partial perspectives, their metaphoric thinking is similarly partial.

16 Dialogical engagement involves comparative thinking. Comparative analysis is an important dimension of critical thinking, typically in search of sameness or difference. Here I compare the ideas of Beauvoir and Murray on the topic of freedom in order to highlight similarities and differences in how they understood this idea.

Chapter 7. Relationality within Intersectionality

1 Quantitative and qualitative research methodologies also draw on different assumptions about how one studies the social world; the objectivity of the scientific method as a way of approaching truth differs dramatically from interpretive traditions that account for the social location of the researcher. The idea of relationality also reappears across distinctive Western philosophical traditions; pragmatism, phenomenology, and critical realism each take different positions on how central relationality is within their analyses of the social world. By claiming the interconnectedness of peoples, generations, and the natural environment, relationality also invokes alternative epistemologies of indigenous peoples. Collectively, these projects signal a conceptual shift that rests on "a tradition of relational thinking about the social world . . . [that] conceives of social life as consisting in processes not substances, in dynamic, unfolding relations rather than in static, unchanging, things" (Emirbayer and Desmond 2015, 79).

2 Throughout this book, I aim to lay a foundation for such an analysis by using relationality as a fundamental premise to guide my argument. For example, in chapter 4 I discuss how working dialogically across differences of power is an important methodological premise for intersectionality, and I present abductive analysis as one methodological tool for doing so. I also rely on dialogical engagement by pairing discourses that do not typically go together, for example, a dialogical reading of Black feminist thought and American pragmatism in chapter 5, and a discussion of relational thinking within the work of Beauvoir and Murray in chapter 6. I've also placed chapters next to each other that can be read dialogically, for example, how the critical social theories in chapter 2 and the resistant knowledge projects in chapter 3 shed light on the meaning of being critical. Aiming for an analysis of relational difference, I present these projects as different from one another yet interconnected in how their approach to being critical might inform intersectionality.

3 Here I take a similar approach to conceptualizing relationality as I did in analyzing intersectionality's cognitive architecture. To identify these focal points, I surveyed a range of documents in order to see how researchers and theorists conceptualized relationality within their projects. This involved reading empiri-

cal works, especially in the social sciences, to identify how the varying definitions of intersectionality reflected certain understandings of relationality. Ideas about dialogical engagement within the work of critical theorists who are not typically associated with intersectionality—for example, Stuart Hall, Zygmunt Bauman, and Michael Burawoy—has also been useful for mapping these focal points. Scholars within intersectionality itself have also cast a self-reflexive eye on this topic, albeit not consistently and not in the same way.

4 Simone de Beauvoir provides an exhaustive analysis describing how gender ideology facilitates women's oppression by using the category of woman to structure women's assigned places. Working-class men, women, LGBTQ people, and African Americans may seem to go willingly to their assigned places, especially when confronted by hegemonic ideologies that naturalize social inequality. On a societal level, however, individuals inherit specific social positions and must grapple with the positive and negative attributes associated with their assigned places. Controlling images can be part of relations of rule when people accept social relations, but they also can be part of relations of resistance when people refuse to stay in their assigned places (Collins 2018).

5 The concept of essentialism, a set of ideas that assumes that people who share assigned social classifications also share basic biological or cultural attributes, is one way of justifying what are basically socially constructed boundaries. Pauli Murray railed against such essentialism, rejecting prevailing norms of masculinity and femininity because she believed that she was a man in a woman's body; she also rejected prevailing categories of racial identity as either Black or white, pointing out that her family of mixed-race individuals was also an American family. Segregation of all sorts highlights practices of disciplinary power needed to sustain relations of inclusion and exclusion, but for many individuals, such segregation merits resistance (Foucault 1979).

6 When it comes to relationality as a topic of intersectional investigation, Marxist social theory contributes the important construct of class *relations* for explaining social inequality and social injustice. Because Marxist social theory has had such a long and storied history within Western knowledge projects, especially in Europe, one sees many efforts to incorporate race, gender, ethnicity, and sexuality as formerly missing systems of power into an overarching class model.

7 It may not be that it is too complicated to incorporate class, or that class already explains everything, but rather that there may be other sources of resistance to intersectionality among Marxist social theorists. The critics of intersectionality are right. Critical analyses of capitalism that are either added into or added together with similar categories are neglected within intersectionality.

8 I ground this discussion in British cultural studies. But the ideas of articulation reappear in other settings. Relationality through articulation also can be found in the work of African American sociologist Oliver Cromwell Cox (1945, 1948). Cox's declarations that "race relations can be studied as a form of class exploitation" (Cox 1945) and "we can understand the Negro problem only in so far as we

understand their position as workers" (Cox 1948) seem antithetical to intersectionality. Yet, despite its tendency of giving primacy to class analysis, discarding it would be misguided, as it overlooks the fact that the type of analysis Cox offers is part of the same effort of establishing linkages and relations between systems of domination.

9 Within historical materialism, a conjuncture signals a rupture that is associated with social change. "In setting his sights on crisis moments 'where cultural processes anticipate social change,' Hall directs our attention to surfaces of emergence that give us analytical access to the potential for transformation latent in each historical conjuncture" (Mercer 2017, 10).

10 Collette Guillaumin and Simone de Beauvoir both rely on analogical reasoning to theorize women's oppression. Beauvoir launched a highly effective critique of deterministic systems of thought, marshaling copious evidence of women's oppression to show that women were a group, that they were an oppressed group, and that they were unfree. Yet by comparing women's situation to that of others who also were oppressed, Beauvoir developed her analysis of women's oppression by relying upon a troubling use of analogical reasoning whereby "women are like children" or "blacks are like animals." Beauvoir focused on the master category of women's oppression and added in, via analogy, race, ethnicity, age, and class as descriptive and often stereotypical categories.

11 Family is a universal social institution. The construct of community fulfills a similar function, serving as a taken-for-granted framework for how people think and do politics, as well as an ideological template for imagining political groups (Collins 2010). Violence, family, and community are essential for reproducing and resisting political domination *within* racism, sexism, class exploitation, and homophobia. Yet because these core constructs also operate as saturated sites of intersecting power relations, they offer possibilities for resistance that transcend any one system.

12 For example, the ways in which violence as a social problem has catalyzed intersectional analyses has been a recurring theme within Black feminist thought. Violence has constituted the visible tip of a very large iceberg: Black feminist intellectuals and activists quickly found out that the specific expression of violence that most concerned them could not be remedied exclusively within the confines of any one system of power. For example, Ida Wells-Barnett's crusade against the lynching of African Americans constitutes one such case (chapter 5); Pauli Murray's reactions to witnessing the execution of sharecropper Odell Waller (chapter 6) another; and Angela Davis's analysis of rape as a form of state sanctioned violence yet another (this chapter). U.S. Black feminism's impetus toward intersectionality has been informed by the need to respond to expressions of violence across time and space. These ideas may be essential to Black feminism, but this perspective is in no way peculiar to Black feminism.

13 Articulation and rearticulation can contribute to analyses of political action and social change. Hall makes an important contrast between a provisional mode of temporary closure that is receptive to revision, thereby staying open-ended, and an approach that aims for finality. In his interpretation of Hall, Kobena Mercer argues that "the arbitrary closure . . . is not the end but . . . makes both politics and identity possible" (2017, 19).

14 A small but significant scholarly literature examines co-formation. The idea of mutual construction is often a taken-for-granted truism that reappears across intersectionality. The methodological conventions within interpretive fields such as philosophy and literary criticism facilitate theorizing complex entities such as intersectionality. Philosophical areas of ethics, epistemology, and aesthetics theorize about the meaning of the social world, offering interpretations that are validated and refuted through dialogical engagement with other comparable discourses. Literary criticism offers another interpretive tradition wherein co-formation is more compatible with using or theorizing co-formation. Within these interpretive traditions, texts are typically used as data for analysis. Ironically, such traditions use inductive approaches to theorizing, selecting a text and then explaining its meaning. Yet the epistemic power of this way of proceeding often remains invisible. Co-formation, for example, may be completely plausible when one text is used as the exemplar but nonsensical if another is selected. Here I focus on social science theorizing that might be useful in developing co-formation.

15 Anticategorical analyses deconstruct categorical boundaries by exposing their socially constructed nature; intercategorical complexity strategically assumes the reality of such categories in an effort to document social inequalities between different categorical groups. The third approach, intracategorical complexity, adopts analytic features of anticategorical and intercategorical complexity by deconstructing categories while strategically accepting their existence in an effort to document social inequalities within a "master" category. McCall (2005, 1779) points to the work of Crenshaw (1991) and other feminists of color as working within this intracategorical register of analysis. Notably, McCall recognizes that varying types of methodological approaches shape different intersectional knowledge projects (1774).

16 There are some methodological distinctions here. The idea of co-causality comes closest to relationality through co-formation. But whereas co-formation assumes equal theoretical weight for each dimension of the relationship—for example, race, gender, and class are theoretically all conforming in any situation—co-causality resembles intersectionality's theme of salience to determine which entities are more important than others.

17 As a colleague of mine once described it, Western philosophy often seeks knowledge about life through death. The classic case lies in killing and then dissecting an animal in order to see its component parts. These parts may reveal the

categories that made the animal whole, but they cannot explain life itself, nor can putting the animal back together make it whole or bring it back to life.

18 The idea of contrapuntal motion in music theory seems apt here. Contrapuntal motion, the general movement of two melodic lines with respect to one another, resembles articulations by bringing together formerly distinct entities into a new sound of some sort. Yet contrapuntal motion offers several ways in which sounds or melodies can be coupled together. It is important that each melodic line maintains its independence within the collective melody (jazz provides a rhythmic and melodic example of these general principles). Melodies accomplish this through four types of motion: (1) contrary motion, or the same direction with the interval between them changing; (2) similar motion, or melodies moving in the same direction with the interval between them changing; (3) parallel motion, which refers to melodies in the same direction and at the same interval; and (4) oblique motion, whereby one moves while the other remains at the same pitch.

19 There are simply some places that Pierre Bourdieu cannot go, let alone imagine (see the chapter on working class culture in Bourdieu's *Distinction* [1979]).

20 There is no "indigenous worldview" implied by my use of the spider's web. The debates within and about indigenous studies as a field of study are wide-ranging, and I do not attempt to summarize them here. Using the framework of this book, the ideas of what I would call indigenous knowledge projects are intellectually heterogeneous, localized, and global. They represent the many different indigenous peoples. Organizationally, the concept of "indigenous studies" has arisen out of preestablished local departments such as Maori studies in New Zealand, Aboriginal studies in Australia, and Native studies in Canada and the United States. Brendan Hokowhitu describes the theorizing that comes for this history: "It is extremely important that the universalising and reductive concept of indigeneity does not pretend to have the capabilities to underpin local Indigenous studies departments, lest we follow the universalising footsteps of European modernism . . . Indigenous peoples will continue to theorise their existence through the sharing and comparison of localised knowledges, for it is the complexity of the 'glocal' Indigenous positioning that demands and will determine the development of a more coherent multi-layered Indigenous studies discipline" (2009, 103). For discussions of these issues, see Hokowhitu et al. (2010); L. Smith (2012).

21 I encourage readers to bring a specific project to the reading of this material. One reading strategy might be asking oneself which mode(s) of relational thinking best describes the idea of relationality one has in mind in one's own work. The use of these modes of thinking unfolds and shifts over time, with some modes more appropriate than others for specific social problems or components of research projects. Just as intersectionality remains a dynamic knowledge project, these concepts of relationality provide malleable conceptual tools for a variety of intersectional projects.

Chapter 8. Intersectionality without Social Justice?

1 This distinction harkens back to the discussion of traditional and critical social theory in chapter 2. In essence, social justice marks the difference between these two theoretical projects. Chapter 2's discussion of the meaning of *critical* also lays a foundation for the arguments presented here.

2 Sociology illustrates how implicated eugenics was within Western disciplines. In the early twentieth century, sociologists grappled with varying aspects of emerging eugenics discourse. Issues of race, gender, class, nation, and eugenics were openly debated within *The American Journal of Sociology*, a foundational journal for the field. Several articles on eugenics preoccupied early sociologists, among them pieces by Francis Galton in 1904 and 1905, and one by Lester F. Ward in 1912–13. A 1907 article by Edward A. Ross entitled "Western Civilization and the Birth Rate" engendered a lively discussion in the journal. Venues such as this illustrate the working through of a range of ideas concerning race, ethnicity, class, gender, sexuality, nation, age, and ability across national settings and during an important formative period for both imperialism and the knowledge projects that it engendered.

3 Eugenics had never gone unopposed (Barrett and Kurzman 2004; Weingart 1999).

4 A burgeoning literature examines the contemporary aspects of eugenics (T. Duster 2003, 2015). See, e.g., the essays in Wailoo, Nelson, and Lee (2012).

5 For a detailed analysis of how this chain of reasoning works, see my discussion of Beauvoir's analysis of women's oppression (chapter 6).

6 Body politics is based on selecting some aspects of bodies as being more salient than others (color, genitalia) and categorizing and valuing bodies accordingly, then categorizing existing groups or constructing new ones based on those criteria. Associated with the impetus for classification of Western science, the categorization of body politics can create new social groups, sui generis, or build on existing social groups. The issue is how the logic of essential and immutable difference that rests on ideas of normality and abnormality contribute to a hierarchy among groups. Here eugenics drew upon preexisting groups as understood under colonial relations of slavery and imperialism and slavery for ranking social groups.

7 Theoretically, because ability is so fundamental to and yet so often invisible within ideologies and practices of multiple forms of oppression, it may be an important construct for developing relationality through co-formation. If so, the invisibility of ability within intersectional discourse may stem more from the centrality of ideas about ability and able-bodiedness to power itself. Ideas about ability naturalize and normalize social inequality to the point where they become invisible. By highlighting the interconnections of core ideas within one discourse, the body politics and use of biology to explain social processes within eugenics projects become prominent.

8 Largely provided by European anthropological discourses emerging with imperialism, the notion of Blacks as primitive framed understandings of Africa and peoples of African descent (Bash 1979; Torgovnick 1990). As McKee points out, "because they [Blacks] had lived in rural isolation in the South, they were regarded as the nation's most backward people, and that was how they appeared in the sociological literature" (1993, 8).

9 At the turn of the twentieth century, colonialism, imperialism, the growth of wage labor, and the aftermath of slavery all shaped understandings of family. In this political and interpretive context, elites identified the nuclear family ideal as the template for evaluating families of all sorts. This particular family form is useful in that it constituted the ideal toward which all families should strive, yet it was and remains virtually impossible to achieve for the majority of the world's population.

10 Bauman continues: "Gardening and medicine supplied the archetypes of constructive stance, while normality, health, or sanitation offered the arch metaphors for human tasks and strategies in the management of human affairs . . . . Gardening and medicine are functionally distinct forms of the same activity of *separating and setting apart useful elements destined to live and thrive, from harmful and morbid ones, which ought to be exterminated*" (1989, 70). Bauman's overarching point is that eugenics projects follow a logic of social engineering that sees the state as *actively* involved in shaping its national interests through population policies. This seems to be the belief that all share, with disagreements about which areas the state should manage and which areas it should leave alone.

11 In chapter 7, I examined relational thinking through addition, articulation, and co-formation within intersectionality as a way to analyze the *processes* of relational thinking within intersectionality. Here I focus on the *content* of a particular relational argument. The question of how eugenics projects actually constructed this argument is an empirical one. Stated differently, different strategies of relational thinking many have been more closely associated with aspects of eugenics. How might relational thinking through addition, articulation, and co-formation drawn from race, gender, and similar categories shape the new overarching scientific logic?

12 Theoretically, conceptualizing eugenics as a saturated site of power relations enables intersectionality to drill down into the knowledge/power nexus to flesh out Foucault's genealogical approach to knowledge/power relations. Because eugenics projects are local and specific, yet global in scope, they provide a brake on the rush toward ungrounded abstraction.

Such sites also illuminate resistance, precisely because they are so important to reproducing social hierarchy. In this sense, saturated sites are important nodes within political and intellectual fields that provide vital interconnections among political, intellectual, and moral fields. Saturated sites of power relations provide the language for political contestation as well as the practices that make power relations visible. Identifying sites that have been effective in explaining social inequalities of race, gender, sexuality, class, nation, and age, especially if the workings of such sites remain invisible, constitutes an important tool for intersectional theorizing.

13 Many knowledge projects that predate intersectionality and that border it have encountered similar challenges of institutional incorporation. Participants in mid-twentieth-century social justice projects routinely took their commitment to social justice for granted. Their intellectual activism existed to oppose oppression and to facilitate social justice. Such projects drew upon ethical frameworks that spoke not primarily to the substance of their political projects, but to *why* their projects were necessary. Moving into the academy changed everything when taken-for-granted assumptions concerning social justice came under epistemic scrutiny. Black feminism and similar social justice projects found an increasingly inhospitable environment within colleges and universities that continuously remade themselves in the image of the neoliberal marketplace. Many fields of study that were organized during this period of academic incorporation grapple with this question of how social justice informs their praxis. For example, the edited volume *Interdisciplinary and Social Justice* (Parker, Samantrai, and Romero 2010) surveys many such fields, documenting their progression from criticizing academic disciplines, to criticizing the interdisciplinary fields that emerged from that critique, to investigating interdisciplinary claims for social justice. Collectively, the essays in that volume raise important questions about the need for interdisciplinary fields to look beyond their own particular concerns and toward something that binds them together. Work such as this raises important questions concerning the compatibility of resistant knowledge projects with academic norms that resist social justice initiatives.

14 In searching for a more nuanced understanding of social justice for intersectionality, the vast scholarly literature on justice that specifies, for example, distributive, restorative, and reparative types of justice provides an important vocabulary for conceptualizing social justice. Focusing on themes of equality of opportunity and treatment, distributive justice emphasizes equal treatment and equal opportunity within major social institutions. Actualizing distributive justice remains central to many activist projects. Yet, by recognizing the harm that has been done by unjust systems of race, class, gender, and sexuality, activist projects have also advanced claims for restorative or reparative justice. While recognizing the significance of distributive justice, social movement actors are far more likely to see the need for social action to grant restitution to victims of harm and to repair society itself. Distributive justice does not challenge the individualism of neoliberalism. In contrast, claims for reparative and restorative justice are especially compatible with the collective ethos of subordinated groups whose political sensibilities encompass a politics of community. Depending on social context, these distinctive and often competing views of social justice—for example, the distributive justice claims of the capitalist marketplace versus the restorative and reparative justice claims of subordinated people—can align with varying expressions of intersectionality.

15 The work of philosophers has been especially helpful here in providing analyses of justice that have important implications for aspects of intersectionality (see, e.g., Dieleman, Rondel, and Voparil 2017; Fraser 2009; Willett 2001; Young 1990).

16 According to Fraser, achieving parity of participation rests on three sets of social justice strategies—namely, those of economic redistribution, cultural recognition, and political representation. For intersectionality in search of a unifying principle, a tripartite emphasis on redistribution, recognition, and representation as dimensions of social justice has important implications for intersectionality's existing achievements and its plotting of future directions. For Fraser, redistribution is associated with deep structural economic changes of socialism. A strategy of redistribution could foster reform or transformation. It could "promote surface reallocations of economic inputs without touching the underlying structures that generate economic inequality, or it could attempt deep level economic restructuring" (Mladenov 2016, 1229). Fraser discusses recognition as similarly broad. In her words, it "is not limited to the sort of valorization of group differences that is associated with mainstream multiculturalism. Rather, it also encompasses the sort of deep restructuring of the symbolic order that is associated with deconstruction" (Mladenov 2016, 1229). "A strategy of recognition could seek to affirm, on the surface level, previously devalued differences or commonalities that transcend differences; or, alternatively, could attempt to transform culture in-depth by deconstructing the underlying frameworks that produce differences in the first place" (1229). Representation follows a similar path of reform or transformation. Representation "encompasses both ordinary-political democratic processes such as . . . voting in national elections, and meta-political processes that determine who is entitled to participate in ordinary-political processes" (1229). Such strategies either affirm the existing system by trying to reform it, or try to transform the existing system. Economic redistribution, cultural recognition, and political representation can each accommodate social reform or social transformation, but only transformation can achieve real change" (1237).

17 Specific cases of this phenomenon include the infamous Tuskegee syphilis experiment and the harvesting of the genetic material of Henrietta Lacks. Pharmaceutical companies' appropriation of indigenous knowledges and ecological materials also illustrate this process.

18 To clarify, my discussion of faith-based traditions is not meant to celebrate organized religions. Rather, I aim here to point to the power of faith itself. I recognize that organized religions come with their own set of challenges. This is a huge topic that is beyond the scope of this book. I will say that ranking religions according to predetermined criteria such as tolerance and backwardness is part of the colonial legacy. The meaning of the religious scripture lies in the interpretation of its sacred "texts" and in how people take up those interpretations within social action. The same premises that I use in studying intersectionality can also be used to study religions.

References

Abbott, Andrew. 2001. *Chaos of Disciplines*. Chicago: University of Chicago Press.

Abbott, Andrew. 2004. *Methods of Discovery: Heuristics for the Social Sciences*. New York: W. W. Norton.

Acker, Joan. 1999. "Rewriting Class, Race, and Gender: Problems in Feminist Rethinking." In *Revisioning Gender*, edited by Myra Marx Ferree, Judith Lorber, and Beth B. Hess, 44–69. Thousand Oaks, CA: Sage.

Addams, Jane. 2002. *Democracy and Social Ethics*. Urbana: University of Illinois Press.

Adi, Hakim. 2009. "The Negro Question: The Communist International and Black Liberation in the Interwar Years." In *From Toussaint to Tupac: The Black International Since the Age of Revolution*, edited by Michael O. West, William G. Martin, and Fanon Che Wilkins, 155–178. Chapel Hill: University of North Carolina Press.

Agger, Ben. 2013. *Critical Social Theories*. 3rd ed. New York: Oxford University Press.

Alarcón, Norma. 1999. "Chicana Feminism: In the Tracks of 'The' Native Woman." In *Between Woman and Nation: Nationalisms, Transnational Feminisms, and the State*, edited by Caren Kaplan, Norma Alarcón, and Minoo Moallem, 63–71. Durham, NC: Duke University Press.

Albright, Madeleine. 2018. *Fascism: A Warning*. New York: HarperCollins.

Alexander, M. Jacqui. 1997. "Erotic Autonomy as a Politics of Decolonization: An Anatomy of Feminist and State Practice in the Bahamas Tourist Industry." In *Feminist Genealogies, Colonial Legacies, Democratic Futures*, edited by M. Jacqui Alexander and Chandra Talpade Mohanty, 63–100. New York: Routledge.

Alexander, M. Jacqui. 2005a. "Imperial Desire/Sexual Utopias: White Gay Capital and Transnational Tourism." In *Pedagogies of Crossing: Meditations on Feminism,*

Sexual Politics, Memory, and the Sacred, edited by M. Jacqui Alexander, 66–88. Durham, N.C.: Duke University Press.

Alexander, M. Jacqui. 2005b. *Pedagogies of Crossing: Meditations on Feminism, Sexual Politics, Memory, and the Sacred*. Durham, NC: Duke University Press.

Alexander, M. Jacqui, and Chandra Talpade Mohanty, eds. 1997. *Feminist Genealogies, Colonial Legacies, Democratic Futures*. New York: Routledge.

Alexander, Michelle. 2010. *The New Jim Crow: Mass Incerceration in the Age of Colorblindness*. New York: New Press.

Althusser, Louis. 2001. *Lenin and Philosophy and Other Essays*. New York: Monthly Review Press.

Amott, Teresa L., and Julie Matthaei. 1991. *Race, Gender, and Work: A Multicultural Economic History of Women in the United States*. Boston: South End Press.

Andersen, Margaret L., and Patricia Hill Collins. 2016. *Race, Class, and Gender: An Anthology*. 9th ed. Belmont, CA: Wadsworth.

Anderson, Benedict. 1983. *Imagined Communities: Reflections on the Origin and Spread of Nationalism*. London: Verso.

Anderson-Bricker, Kristin. 1999. "'Triple Jeopardy': Black Women and the Growth of Feminist Consciousness in SNCC, 1964–1975." In *Still Lifting, Still Climbing: African American Women's Contemporary Activism*, edited by Kimberly Springer, 49–69. New York: New York University Press.

Anthias, Floya, and Nira Yuval-Davis. 1992. *Racialized Boundaries: Race, Nation, Gender, Colour and Class and the Anti-Racist Struggle*. New York: Routledge.

Anzaldúa, Gloria. 1987. *Borderlands/La Frontera: The New Mestiza*. San Francisco: Spinsters/Aunt Lute Press.

Aptheker, Bettina. 1982. *Woman's Legacy: Essays on Race, Sex, and Class in American History*. Amherst: University of Massachusetts Press.

Arendt, Hannah. 1968. *The Origins of Totalitarianism*. New York: Harcourt.

Arredondo, Gabriela F., Aida Hurtado, Norma Klahn, Olga Nájera-Ramírez, and Patricia Zavella, eds. 2003. *Chicana Feminisms: A Critical Reader*. Durham, NC: Duke University Press.

Azaransky, Sarah. 2011. *The Dream Is Freedom: Pauli Murray and American Democratic Faith*. New York: Oxford University Press.

Balibar, Etienne. 1991. "Racism and Nationalism." In *Race, Nation, Class: Ambiguous Identities*, edited by Etienne Balibar and Immanuel Wallerstein, 37–67. New York: Verso.

Balibar, Etienne. 2007. *The Philosophy of Marx*. New York: Verso.

Balibar, Etienne, and Immanuel Wallerstein. 1991. *Race, Nation, Class: Ambiguous Identities*. New York: Verso.

Barrett, Deborah, and Charles Kurzman. 2004. "Globalizing Social Movement Theory: The Case of Eugenics." *Theory and Society* 33 (5): 487–527.

Bash, Harry. 1979. *Sociology, Race, and Ethnicity: A Critique of Ideological Intrusions upon Sociological Theory*. New York: Gordon & Breach.

Battle, Juan, Cathy J. Cohen, Dorian Warren, Gerard Fergerson, and Suzette Audam. 2002. *Say It Loud, I'm Black and I'm Proud: Black Pride Survey 2000.* New York: Policy Institute of the National Gay and Lesbian Task Force.

Bauman, Zygmunt. 1989. *Modernity and the Holocaust.* Ithaca, NY: Cornell University Press.

Bay, Mia, Farah J. Griffin, Martha S. Jones, and Barbara D. Savage, eds. 2015. *Toward an Intellectual History of Black Women.* Chapel Hill: University of North Carolina.

Beauvoir, Simone de. 1976 [1948]. *The Ethics of Ambiguity.* New York: Citadel Press.

Beauvoir, Simone de. 1999 [1954]. *America Day By Day.* Translated by C. Cosman. Berkeley: University of California Press.

Beauvoir, Simone de. 2011 [1949]. *The Second Sex.* Translated by Constance Borde and Sheila Malovany-Chevallier. New York: Vintage.

Bell-Scott, Patricia. 2016. *The Firebrand and the First Lady: Portrait of a Friendship.* New York: Vintage.

Bell, Derrick. 1992. *Faces at the Bottom of the Well: The Permanence of Racism.* New York: Basic Books.

Berger, Michele, and Kathleen Guidroz, eds. 2009. *The Intersectional Approach: Transforming the Academy through Race, Class, & Gender.* Chapel Hill: University of North Carolina Press.

Bernstein, Richard J. 1992. "The Resurgence of Pragmatism." *Social Research* 59 (4): 813–840.

Bettcher, Talia. 2014. "Feminist Perspectives on Trans Issues." In *The Stanford Encyclopedia of Philosophy,* spring 2014 ed., edited by Edward N. Zalta. https://plato.stanford.edu/archives/spr2014/entries/feminism-trans/.

Bhabha, Homi K. 2004 [1963]. "Foreword: Framing Fanon." In *The Wretched of the Earth,* Frantz Fanon, vii–xli. New York: Grove Press.

Blackwell, Maylei. 2011. *Chicana Power! Contested Histories of Feminism in the Chicano Movement.* Austin: University of Texas Press.

Blauner, Bob. 1972. *Racial Oppression in America.* New York: Harper and Row.

Blea, Irena I. 1992. *La Chicana and the Intersection of Race, Class, and Gender.* New York: Praeger.

Bohman, James. 2016. "Critical Theory." In *The Stanford Encyclopedia of Philosophy,* edited by Edward N. Zalta. Palo Alto, CA: Stanford University.

Bonilla-Silva, Eduardo. 2003. *Racism without Racists: Color-Blind Racism and the Persistence of Racial Inequality in the United States.* Lantham, MD: Rowman and Littlefield.

Bourdieu, Pierre. 1980. *The Logic of Practice.* Stanford, CA: Stanford University Press.

Bourdieu, Pierre. 1984. *Distinction: A Social Critique of the Judgement of Taste.* Cambridge, MA: Harvard University Press.

Bourdieu, Pierre, and Jean-Claude Passeron. 1977. *Reproduction in Education, Society, and Culture.* Beverly Hills, CA: Sage.

Bourdieu, Pierre, and Loic J. D. Waçquant. 1992. *An Invitation to Reflexive Sociology.* Chicago: University of Chicago Press.

Bourdieu, Pierre, and Loïc Wacquant. 1999. "On the Cunning of Imperialist Reason." *Theory, Culture and Society* 16 (1): 41–58.

Brown, Michael I., Martin Carnoy, Elliott Currie, Troy Duster, David B. Oppenheimer, Marjorie M. Schultz, and David Wellman. 2003. *Whitewashing Race: The Myth of a Color-Blind Society.* Berkeley: University of California Press.

Browne, Irene, and Joya Misra. 2003. "The Intersection of Gender and Race in the Labor Market." *Annual Review of Sociology* 29: 487–513.

Buss, Doris. 2009. "Sexual Violence, Ethnicity, and Intersectionality in International Criminal Law." In *Intersectionality and Beyond: Law, Power and the Politics of Location,* edited by Davina Cooper, 105–123. New York: Routledge.

Butler, Judith. 1990. *Gender Trouble: Feminism and the Subversion of Identity.* New York: Routledge.

Butler, Judith. 1993. *Bodies That Matter: On the Discursive Limits of "Sex."* New York: Routledge.

Cabral, Amilcar. 1973. "National Liberation and Culture." In *Return to the Source: Selected Speeches of Amilcar Cabral,* edited by Africa Information Service, 39–56. New York: Monthly Review Press.

Calhoun, Craig. 1995. *Critical Social Theory: Culture, History, and the Challenge of Difference.* Malden, MA: Blackwell Publishers.

Campbell, James. 1999. *Recovering Benjamin Franklin.* Chicago: Open Court.

Cannon, Katie G. 1988. *Black Womanist Ethics.* Atlanta: Scholars Press.

Carastathis, Anna. 2013. "Identity Categories as Potential Coalitions." *Signs* 38 (4): 941–965.

Carastathis, Anna. 2014. "The Concept of Intersectionality in Feminist Theory." *Philosophy Compass* 9 (5): 304–314.

Carastathis, Anna. 2016. *Intersectionality: Origins, Contestations, Horizons.* Lincoln: University of Nebraska Press.

Carbado, Devon W., Kimberle Williams Crenshaw, Vickie M. Mays, and Barbara Tomlinson. 2013. "Intersectionality: Mapping the Movements of a Theory." *Du Bois Review* 10 (2): 303–312.

Carby, Hazel V. 1992. "The Multicultural Wars." In *Black Popular Culture,* edited by Michele Wallace and Gina Dent, 187–199. Seattle: Bay Press.

Carmichael, Stokely, and Charles V. Hamilton. 1967. *Black Power: The Politics of Liberation in America.* New York: Vintage.

Carruthers, Charlene A. 2018. *Unapologetic: A Black, Queer, and Feminist Mandate for Radical Movements.* Boston: Beacon Press.

Castells, Manuel. 2000. *The Rise of Network Society.* 2nd ed. Malden, MA: Blackwell.

Caygill, Howard. 2013. *On Resistance: A Philosophy of Defiance.* London: Bloomsbury.

Centre for Contemporary Cultural Studies. 1982. *The Empire Strikes Back: Racism in 70s Britain.* London: Routledge.

Cherki, Alice. 2006. *Frantz Fanon: A Portrait*. Ithaca, NY: Cornell University Press.

Cho, Sumi, Kimberle Crenshaw, and Leslie McCall. 2013. "Toward a Field of Intersectionality Studies: Theory, Applications, and Praxis." *Signs* 38 (4): 785–810.

Choo, Hae Yeon, and Myra Marx Ferree. 2010. "Practicing Intersectionality in Sociological Research: A Critical Analysis of Inclusions, Interactions, and Institutions in the Study of Inequalities." *Sociological Theory* 28 (2): 129–149.

Clarke, Cheryl. 1995. "Lesbianism: An Act of Resistance." In *Words of Fire: An Anthology of African-American Feminist Thought*, edited by Beverly Guy-Sheftall, 241–251. New York: New Press.

Cohen, Anthony P. 1985. *The Symbolic Construction of Community*. London: Tavistock.

Cohen, Bill. 2001. "The Spider's Web: Creativity and Survival in Dynamic Balance." *Canadian Journal of Native Education* 25 (2): 140–148.

Cohen, Cathy J. 1996. "Contested Membership: Black Gay Identities and the Politics of AIDS." In *Queer Theory/Sociology*, edited by Steven Seidman, 362–394. Malden, MA: Blackwell.

Cohen, Cathy J. 1999. *The Boundaries of Blackness: AIDS and the Breakdown of Black Politics*. Chicago: University of Chicago Press.

Cohen, Cathy J., and Tamara Jones. 1999. "Fighting Homophobia versus Challenging Heterosexism: 'The Failure to Transform' Revisited." In *Dangerous Liaisons: Blacks, Gays, and the Struggle for Equality*, edited by Eric Brandt, 80–101. New York: New Press.

Collier, Jane, Michelle Z. Rosaldo, and Sylvia Yanagisako. 1992. "Is There a Family? New Anthropological Views." In *Rethinking the Family: Some Feminist Questions*, edited by Barrie Thorne and Marilyn Yalom, 31–48. Boston: Northeastern University Press.

Collins, Patricia Hill. 1995. "Reflections on Doing Difference." *Gender and Society* 9 (4): 505–509.

Collins, Patricia Hill. 1998a. *Fighting Words: Black Women and the Search for Justice*. Minneapolis: University of Minnesota Press.

Collins, Patricia Hill. 1998b. "It's All in the Family: Intersections of Gender, Race, and Nation." *Hypatia* 13 (3): 62–82.

Collins, Patricia Hill. 1998c. "The Tie That Binds: Race, Gender and U.S. Violence." *Ethnic and Racial Studies* 21 (5): 918–938.

Collins, Patricia Hill. 2000. *Black Feminist Thought: Knowledge, Consciousness, and the Politics of Empowerment*. 2nd ed. New York: Routledge.

Collins, Patricia Hill. 2001. "Like One of the Family: Race, Ethnicity, and the Paradox of US National Identity." *Ethnic and Racial Studies* 24 (1): 3–28.

Collins, Patricia Hill. 2002. "Introduction to *On Lynchings*." In *On Lynchings*, edited by Ida B. Wells-Barnett, 9–24. Amherst, NY: Humanity Books.

Collins, Patricia Hill. 2004. *Black Sexual Politics: African Americans, Gender, and the New Racism*. New York: Routledge.

Collins, Patricia Hill. 2006. *From Black Power to Hip Hop: Essays on Racism, Nationalism, and Feminism*. Philadelphia: Temple University Press.

Collins, Patricia Hill. 2009. *Another Kind of Public Education: Race, Schools, the Media and Democratic Possibilities*. Boston: Beacon Press.

Collins, Patricia Hill. 2010. "The New Politics of Community." *American Sociological Review* 75 (1): 7–30.

Collins, Patricia Hill. 2013. *On Intellectual Activism*. Philadelphia: Temple University Press.

Collins, Patricia Hill. 2015. "Intersectionality's Definitional Dilemmas." *Annual Review of Sociology*, no. 41 (August): 1–20.

Collins, Patricia Hill. 2017a. "The Difference That Power Makes: Intersectionality and Participatory Democracy." *Investigaciones Feministas*, no. 8: 19–39.

Collins, Patricia Hill. 2017b. "On Violence, Intersectionality and Transversal Politics." *Ethnic and Racial Studies* 40 (9): 1–14.

Collins, Patricia Hill. 2017c. "Simone de Beauvoir, Women's Oppression and Existential Freedom." In *A Companion to Simone de Beauvoir*, edited by Nancy Bauer and Laura Hengehold, 325–338. New York: Blackwell/Wiley.

Collins, Patricia Hill. 2018. "Controlling Images." In *50 Concepts for a Critical Phenomenology*, edited by Gail Weiss, Ann Murphy, and Gayle Salamon. Evanston, IL: Northwestern University Press.

Collins, Patricia Hill, and Sirma Bilge. 2016. *Intersectionality*. Key Concepts. Cambridge, UK: Polity.

Combahee River Collective. 1995 [1975]. "A Black Feminist Statement." In *Words of Fire: An Anthology of African-American Feminist Thought*, edited by Beverly Guy-Sheftall, 232–240. New York: New Press.

Connell, Raewyn. 2007. *Southern Theory: The Global Dynamics of Knowledge in Social Science*. Cambridge, UK: Polity.

Coontz, Stephanie. 1992. *The Way We Never Were: American Families and the Nostalgia Trap*. New York: Basic Books.

Cooper, Anna Julia. 1892. *A Voice from the South; By a Black Woman of the South*. Xenia, OH: Aldine.

Cooper, Brittney. 2017. *Beyond Respectability: The Intellectual Thought of Race Women*. Champaign: University of Illinois Press.

Cooper, Brittney, Susana M. Morris, and Robin M. Boylorn, eds. 2017. *The Crunk Feminist Collection*. New York: Feminist Press at CUNY.

Craven, Christa, and Dana-Ain Davis, eds. 2013. *Feminist Activist Ethnography: Counterpoints to Neoliberalism in North America*. Lanham, MD: Lexington Books.

Crenshaw, Kimberlé Williams. 1989. "Demarginalizing the Intersection of Race and Sex: A Black Feminist Critique of Anti-Discrimination Doctrine, Feminist Theory and Anti-Racist Politics." *The University of Chicago Legal Forum* 1989, article 8.

Crenshaw, Kimberlé Williams. 1991. "Mapping the Margins: Intersectionality, Identity Politics, and Violence against Women of Color." *Stanford Law Review* 43 (6): 1241–1299.

Crenshaw, Kimberlé Williams. 1992. "Whose Story Is It Anyway? Feminist and Antiracist Appropriations of Anita Hill." In *Race-ing Justice, En-Gendering Power*, edited by Toni Morrison, 402–440. New York: Pantheon Books.

Crenshaw, Kimberlé Williams, Neil Gotanda, Gary Peller, and Kendall Thomas, eds. 1995. *Critical Race Theory: The Key Writings that Formed the Movement.* New York: New Press.

Crowell, Steven. 2015. "Existentialism." In *The Stanford Encyclopedia of Philosophy*, edited by Edward N. Zalta. Palo Alto, CA: Stanford University Press.

D'Avigdor, Lewis. 2015. "Participatory Democracy and New Left Student Movements: The University of Sydney, 1973–1979." *Australian Journal of Politics and History* 61 (2): 233–247.

Davidson, Maria Del Guadalupe, Kathryn T. Gines, and Donna-Dale L. Marcano, eds. 2010. *Convergences: Black Feminism and Continental Philosophy.* Albany: State University of New York Press.

Davis, Angela Y. 1978. "Rape, Racism and the Capitalist Setting." *Black Scholar* 9 (7): 24–30.

Davis, Angela Y. 1981. *Women, Race, and Class.* New York: Random House.

Davis, Kathy. 2008. "Intersectionality as a Buzzword: A Sociology of Science Perspective on What Makes a Feminist Theory Successful." *Feminist Theory* 9 (1): 67–85.

de Jesus, Carolina Maria. 2003 [1960]. *Child of the Dark: The Diary of Carolina Maria de Jesus.* Translated by David St. Clair. New York: Penguin.

De Waal, Cornelis. 2005. *On Pragmatism.* Belmont, CA: Wadsworth Press.

DeVault, Marjorie L. 1999. *Liberating Method: Feminism and Social Reseach.* Philadelphia: Temple University Press.

Denzin, Norman K., and Yvonna S. Lincoln, eds. 1994. *Handbook of Qualitative Research.* London: SAGE.

Dewey, John. 1954. *The Public and Its Problems.* Athens: Ohio University Press.

Dhaliwal, Sukjwant, and Nira Yuval-Davis, eds. 2014. *Women Against Fundamentalism: Stories of Dissent and Solidarity.* London: Lawrence and Wishart.

Dieleman, Susan, David Rondel, and Christopher J. Voparil, eds. 2017. *Pragmatism and Justice.* New York: Oxford University Press.

Dill, Bonnie Thornton. 2002. "Work at the Intersections of Race, Gender, Ethnicity, and Other Dimensions of Difference in Higher Education." *Connections: Newsletter of the Consortium on Race, Gender, and Ethnicity*, 5–7.

Dill, Bonnie Thornton. 2009. "Intersections, Identities, and Inequalities in Higher Education." In *Emerging Intersections: Race, Class, and Gender in Theory, Policy, and Practice*, edited by Bonnie Thornton Dill and Ruth Zambrana, 229–252. New Brunswick, NJ: Rutgers University Press.

Dill, Bonnie Thornton, and Marla H. Kohlman. 2012. "Intersectionality: A Transformative Paradigm in Feminist Theory and Social Justice." In *Handbook of Feminist Research, Theory and Praxis*, edited by Sharlene Hesse-Biber, 154–174. Thousand Oaks, CA: Sage.

Dill, Bonnie Thornton, and Ruth Zambrana, eds. 2009. *Emerging Intersections: Race, Class, and Gender in Theory, Policy, and Practice.* New Brunswick, NJ: Rutgers University Press.

Dotson, Kristie. 2011. "Tracking Epistemic Violence, Tracking Practices of Silencing." *Hypatia* 26 (2): 236–257.

Dotson, Kristie. 2014. "Conceptualizing Epistemic Oppression." *Social Epistemology* 28 (2): 115–138.

Douglas, Kelly Brown. 1999. *Sexuality and the Black Church: A Womanist Perspective.* Maryknoll, NY: Orbis.

Douven, Igor. "Abduction." In *The Stanford Encyclopedia of Philosophy*, summer 2017 ed., edited by Edward N. Zalta. https://plato.stanford.edu/archives /sum2017/entries/abduction/.

Duffy, Mignon. 2007. "Doing the Dirty Work: Gender, Race and Reproductive Labor in Historical Perspective." *Gender and Society* 21 (3): 313–336.

Duster, Alfreda M. 1970. *Crusade for Justice: The Autobiography of Ida B. Wells.* Chicago: University of Chicago Press.

Duster, Troy. 2003. *Backdoor to Eugenics.* New York: Routledge.

Duster, Troy. 2015. "A Post-Genomic Surprise: The Molecular Reinscription of Race in Science, Law and Medicine." *British Journal of Sociology* 66 (1): 1–27.

El Saadawi, Nawal. 2015. *Woman at Point Zero.* London: Zed.

Emirbayer, Mustafa. 1997. "Manifesto for a Relational Sociology." *American Journal of Sociology* 103 (2): 281–317.

Emirbayer, Mustafa, and Matthew Desmond. 2015. *The Racial Order.* Chicago: University of Chicago Press.

Fanon, Frantz. 1963. *The Wretched of the Earth.* Translated by Richard Philcox. New York: Grove Press.

Fanon, Frantz. 1967. *Black Skin, White Masks.* New York: Grove Press.

Farmer, Ashley D. 2017. *Remaking Black Power: How Black Women Transformed an Era.* Chapel Hill: University of North Carolina Press.

Ferguson, Roderick A. 2004. *Aberrations in Black: Toward a Queer of Color Critique.* Minneapolis: University of Minnesota Press.

Fischer, Nancy L., and Steven Seidman, eds. 2016. *Introducing the New Sexuality Studies.* 3rd ed. New York: Routledge.

Fonow, Mary Margaret, and J. A. Cook. 2005. "Feminist Methodology: New Applications in the Academy and Public Policy." *Signs* 30 (4): 2211–2230.

Foucault, Michel. 1979. *Discipline and Punish: The Birth of the Prison.* New York: Vintage.

Foucault, Michel. 1980. *Power/Knowledge: Selected Interviews and Other Writings, 1972–1977.* Translated by Colin Gordon. New York: Pantheon.

Foucault, Michel. 1990. *The History of Sexuality,* Vol. I: *An Introduction.* New York: Vintage.

Foucault, Michel. 1994. *The Birth of the Clinic: An Archeology of Medical Perception.* New York: Vintage.

Foucault, Michel. 2003. *Society Must Be Defended: Lectures at the College de France, 1975–1976.* New York: Picador.

Fraser, Nancy. 1998. "Another Pragmatism: Alain Locke, Critical 'Race' Theory, and the Politics of Culture." In *The Revival of Pragmatism: New Essays on Social Thought, Law, and Culture,* edited by Morris Dickstein, 157–175. Durham, NC: Duke University Press.

Fraser, Nancy. 2009. *Scales of Justice: Reimagining Political Space in a Globalizing World.* New York: Columbia University Press.

Gandhi, Leela. 1998. *Postcolonial Theory: A Critical Introduction.* New York: Columbia University Press.

Garcia, Alma M. 1997. "The Development of Chicana Feminist Discourse." In *Feminist Nationalism,* edited by Lois A. West, 247–268. New York: Routledge.

Giddings, Paula J. 1984. *When and Where I Enter: The Impact of Black Women on Race and Sex in America.* New York: William Morrow.

Giddings, Paula J. 2008. *Ida: A Sword Among Lions.* New York: Amistad.

Gilkes, Cheryl Townsend. 2001. *If It Wasn't for the Women: Black Women's Experience and Womanist Culture in Church and Community.* Maryknoll, NY: Orbis.

Gilroy, Paul. 1987. *"There Ain't No Black in the Union Jack": The Cultural Politics of Race and Nation.* Chicago: University of Chicago Press.

Gilroy, Paul. 1993. *The Black Atlantic: Modernity and Double Consciousness.* Cambridge, MA: Harvard University Press.

Gines, Kathryn T. 2010. "Sartre, Beauvoir, and the Race/Class Analogy: A Case for Black Feminist Philosophy." In *Convergences: Black Feminism and Continental Philosophy,* edited by Maria Del Guadalupe Davidson, Kathryn T. Gines and Donna-Dale L. Marcano, 35–51. Albany: State University of New York Press.

Gines, Kathryn T. 2015. "Anna Julia Cooper." In *The Stanford Encyclopedia of Philosophy,* summer 2015 ed., edited by Edward N. Zalta. https://plato.stanford.edu/archives/sum2015/entries/anna-julia-cooper/.

Glaude, Eddie S. 2007. *In a Shade of Blue: Pragmatism and the Politics of Black America.* Chicago: University of Chicago Press.

Glenn, Evelyn Nakano. 2002. *Unequal Freedom: How Race and Gender Shaped American Citizenship and Labor.* Cambridge, MA: Harvard University Press.

Goering, Sara. 2014. "Eugenics." In *The Stanford Encyclopedia of Philosophy,* fall 2014 ed., edited by Edward N. Zalta. https://plato.stanford.edu/archives/fall2014/entries/eugenics/.

Goldberg, David Theo. 1993. *Racist Culture: Philosophy and the Politics of Meaning.* Cambridge, MA: Blackwell.

Goldberg, David Theo. 2002. *The Racial State.* Malden, MA: Blackwell.

Goldberg, David Theo, and Ato Quayson. 2002. *Relocating Postcolonialism*. Malden, MA: Blackwell.

Gordon, Linda. 1994. *Pitied but Not Entitled: Single Mothers and the History of Welfare*. Cambridge, MA: Harvard University Press.

Gqola, Pumla Dineo. 2015. *Rape: A South African Nightmare*. Johannesburg, South Africa: Jacana Media.

Gramsci, Antonio. 1971. *Selections from the Prison Notebooks*. London: Lawrence and Wishart.

Grant, Jacqueline. 1989. *White Women's Christ and Black Women's Jesus: Feminist Christology and Womanist Response*. Atlanta: Scholars Press.

Gross, Neil. 2007. "Pragmatism, Phenomenology, and Twentieth-Century American Sociology." In *Sociology in America: A History*, edited by Craig Calhoun, 183–224. Chicago: University of Chicago Press.

Grossberg, Lawrence. 1996. "On Postmodernism and Articulation: An Interview with Stuart Hall." In *Stuart Hall: Critical Dialogues in Cultural Studies*, edited by David Morley and Kuan-Hsing Chen, 131–150. New York: Routledge.

Grossberg, Lawrence, Cary Nelson, and Paula A. Treichler, eds. 1992. *Cultural Studies*. New York: Routledge.

Grzanka, Patrick R., ed. 2014. *Intersectionality: A Foundations and Frontiers Reader*. Boulder, CO: Westview Press.

Guidroz, Kathleen, and Michele Tracy Berger. 2009. "A Conversation with Founding Scholars of Intersectionality: Kimberlé Crenshaw, Nira Yuval-Davis, and Michelle Fine." In *The Intersectional Approach: Transforming the Academy Through Race, Class and Gender*, edited by Kathleen Guidroz and Michele Berger, 61–78. Chapel Hill: University of North Carolina Press.

Guillaumin, Colette. 1995. *Racism, Sexism, Power and Ideology*. New York: Routledge.

Hall, Stuart. 1996a. "The After-Life of Frantz Fanon: Why Fanon? Why Now? Why *Black Skin, White Masks*?" In *The Fact of Blackness: Frantz Fanon and Visual Representation*, edited by Alan Read, 12–37. Seattle: Bay Press.

Hall, Stuart. 1996b. "For Allon White: Metaphors of Transformation." In *Stuart Hall: Critical Dialogues in Cultural Studies*, edited by David Morley and Kuan-Hsing Chen, 287–305. New York: Routledge.

Hall, Stuart. 1996c. "The Meaning of New Times." In *Critical Dialogues in Cultural Studies*, edited by David Morley and Kuan-Hsing Chen, 223–237. New York: Routledge.

Hall, Stuart. 1996d. "The Problem of Ideology: Marxism without Guarantees." In *Critical Dialogues in Cultural Studies*, edited by David Morley and Kuan-Hsing Chen, 25–46. New York: Routledge.

Hall, Stuart. 2017. *Familiar Stranger: A Life Between Two Islands*. Durham, NC: Duke University Press.

Hanchard, Michael G. 1994. *Orpheus and Power: The Movimento Negro of Rio de Janeiro and Sao Paulo, Brazil, 1945–1988*. Princeton, NJ: Princeton University Press.

Hanchard, Michael G. 2003. "Acts of Misrecognition: Transnational Black Politics, Anti-Imperialism, and the Ethnocentrisms of Pierre Bourdieu and Loic Waquant." *Theory, Culture and Society* 20 (4): 5–29.

Hancock, Ange-Marie. 2016. *Intersectionality: An Intellectual History*. New York: Oxford University Press.

Harding, Sandra. 1986. *The Science Question in Feminism*. Ithaca, NY: Cornell University Press.

Harding, Sandra. 1987. "Introduction: Is There a Feminist Method?" In *Feminism and Methodology*, edited by Sandra Harding, 1–14. Bloomington: Indiana University Press.

Harding, Sandra. 1991. *Whose Science? Whose Knowledge? Thinking from Women's Lives*. Ithaca, NY: Cornell University Press.

Harris, Cheryl I. 1993. "Whiteness as Property." *Harvard Law Review* 106, no. 8 (June): 1707–1791.

Harris, Leonard. 1999. *The Critical Pragmatism of Alain Locke*. Lanham, MD: Rowman and Littlefield.

Hartsock, Nancy. 1983. "The Feminist Standpoint: Developing the Ground for a Specifically Feminist Historical Materialism." In *Discovering Reality*, edited by Sandra Harding and Merrill B. Hintikka, 283–310. Boston: D. Reidel.

Hechter, Michael. 2017 [1975]. *Internal Colonialism: The Celtic Fringe in British National Development*. New York: Routledge.

Hesse, Barnor, ed. 2000. *Un/Settled Multiculturalisms: Diasporas, Entanglements, Transruptions*. London: Zed.

Held, David. 1980. *Introduction to Critical Theory: Horkheimer to Habermas*. Berkeley: University of California Press.

Hengehold, Laura, and Nancy Bauer, eds. 2017. *A Companion to Simone de Beauvoir*. Hoboken, NJ: Wiley Blackwell.

Hickman, Larry A. 2007. *Pragmatism as Post-Postmodernism: Lessons from John Dewey*. New York: Fordham University Press.

Higginbotham, Evelyn Brooks. 1993. *Righteous Discontent: The Women's Movement in the Black Baptist Church 1880–1920*. Cambridge, MA: Harvard University Press.

Hine, Darlene Clark. 1989. "Rape and the Inner Lives of Black Women in the Middle West: Preliminary Thoughts on the Culture of Dissemblance." *Signs* 14 (4): 912–920.

Hine, Darlene Clark, Elsa Barkley Brown, and Rosalyn Terborg-Penn, eds. 1993. *Black Women in America: An Historical Encyclopedia*. New York: Carlson.

Hokowhitu, Brendan. 2009. "Indigenous Existentialism and the Body." *Cultural Studies Review* 15 (2): 101–118.

Hokowhitu, Brendan, Nathalie Kermoal, Chris Andersen, Anna Petersen, Michael Reilly, Altamirano-Jimenez, and Poia Rewi, eds. 2010. *Indigenous Identity and Resistance: Researching the Diversity of Knowledge*. Dunedin, New Zealand: Otago University Press.

Hondagneu-Sotelo, Pierrette. 2001. *Domestica: Immigrant Workers Cleaning and Caring in the Shadow of Affluence.* Berkeley: University of California Press.

Horkheimer, Max. 1982. "Traditional and Critical Theory." In *Critical Theory: Selected Essays,* edited by Max Horkheimer, 188–243. New York: Continuum.

Horkheimer, Max, and Theodor W. Adorno. 1969. *Dialectic of Enlightenment.* New York: Continuum.

Hoy, David Couzens. 2004. *Critical Resistance: From Poststructuralism to Post-Critique.* Cambridge, MA: MIT Press.

James, Stanlie M. 1993. "Mothering: A Possible Black Feminist Link to Social Transformation?" In *Theorizing Black Feminisms: The Visionary Pragmatism of Black Women,* edited by Stanlie M. James and Abena P. A. Busia, 44–54. New York: Routledge.

James, Stanlie M., and Abena P. A. Busia, eds. 1993. *Theorizing Black Feminisms: The Visionary Pragmatism of Black Women.* New York: Routledge.

James, V. Denise. 2009. "Theorizing Black Feminist Pragmatism: Forethoughts on the Practice and Purpose of Philosophy as Envisioned by Black Feminists and John Dewey." *Journal of Speculative Philosophy* 23 (2): 92–99.

Joas, Hans. 1993. *Pragmatism and Social Theory.* Chicago: University of Chicago Press.

Jordan, June. 1992. *Technical Difficulties: African-American Notes on the State of the Union.* New York: Pantheon.

Kalsem, Kristin, and Verna L. Williams. 2010. "Social Justice Feminism." *UCLA Women's Law Journal* 18 (1): 131–193.

Keating, AnaLouise. 2009a. "Introduction: Reading Gloria Anzaldúa, Reading Ourselves . . . Complex Intimacies, Intricate Connections." in *The Gloria Anzaldúa Reader,* edited by AnaLouise Keating, 1–15. Durham, NC: Duke University Press.

Keating, AnaLouise, ed. 2009b. *The Gloria Anzaldúa Reader.* Durham, NC: Duke University Press.

Kelley, Robin D. G. 1994. *Race Rebels: Culture, Politics, and the Black Working Class.* New York: Free Press.

Kelley, Robin D. 2002. *Freedom Dreams: The Black Radical Imagination.* Boston: Beacon.

Ken, Ivy. 2008. "Beyond the Intersection: A New Culinary Metaphor for Race-Class-Gender Studies." *Sociological Theory* 26 (2): 152–172.

Kidd, Ian James, Jose Medina, and Gaile Pohlhaus Jr., eds. 2017. *The Routledge Handbook of Epistemic Justice.* New York: Routledge.

Kim-Puri, H. J. 2005. "Conceptualizing Gender-Sexuality-State-Nation: An Introduction." *Gender and Society* 19 (2): 137–159.

Kim, Kyung-Man. 2005. *Discourses on Liberation: An Anatomy of Critical Theory.* Boulder, CO: Paradigm.

King, Richard H. 1996. *Civil Rights and the Idea of Freedom.* Athens: University of Georgia Press.

Klaw, Barbara. 2006. "The Literary and Historical Context of Beauvoir's Early Writings: 1926–27." In *Simone de Beauvoir: Diary of a Philosophy Student*, edited by Barbara Klaw and Margaret A. Simons, 7–28. Urbana: University of Illinois Press.

Kline, Wendy. 2001. *Building a Better Race: Gender, Sexuality, and Eugenics from the Turn of the Century to the Baby Boom*. Berkeley: University of California Press.

Koopman, Colin. 2011. "Genealogical Pragmatism: How History Matters for Foucault and Dewey." *Journal of the Philosophy of History* 5 (3): 533–556.

Kuhn, Thomas S. 1970. *The Structure of Scientific Revolutions*. Chicago: University of Chicago Press.

Lakoff, George, and Mark Johnson. 2003 [1980]. *Metaphors We Live By*. Chicago: University of Chicago Press.

Lawson, Bill E., and Donald F. Koch, eds. 2004. *Pragmatism and the Problem of Race*. Bloomington: Indiana University Press.

Le Sueur, James D. 2008. *Uncivil War: Intellectuals and Identity Politics During the Decolonization of Algeria*. Lincoln: University of Nebraska Press.

Lee, Richard. 2003. *Life and Times of Cultural Studies: The Politics and Transformation of the Structures of Knowledge*. Durham, NC: Duke University Press.

Lemert, Charles, and Esme Bhan. 1998. *The Voice of Anna Julia Cooper*. Lantham, MD: Rowman and Littlefield.

Lewis, Amanda E. 2004. "'What Group?' Studying Whites and Whiteness in the Era of 'Color-Blindness.'" *Sociological Theory* 22, no. 4: 623–646.

Lewis, David Levering. 1995. *W.E.B. Du Bois: A Reader*. New York: Henry Holt.

Lindblom, Charles E., and David K. Cohen. 1979. *Usable Knowledge: Social Science and Social Problem Solving*. New Haven, CT: Yale University Press.

Locke, Alain LeRoy. 1992. *Race Contacts and Interracial Relations*. Washington, DC: Howard University Press.

Loomba, Ania. 1998. *Colonialism/Postcolonialism*. New York: Routledge.

Lorde, Audre. 1984. *Sister Outsider: Essays and Speeches*. Freedom, CA: Crossing Press.

Lorde, Audre. 1999. "There Is No Hierarchy of Oppressions." In *Dangerous Liaisons: Blacks, Gays, and the Struggle for Equality*, edited by Eric Brandt, 306–307. New York: New Press.

Lutz, Helma, Maria Teresa Herrera Vivar, and Linda Supik. 2011. *Framing Intersectionality: Debates on a Multi-Faceted Concept in Gender Studies. The Feminist Imagination—Europe and Beyond*, edited by Kathy Davis and Mary Evans. Surrey, England: Ashgate.

Mann, Susan Archer. 2012. *Doing Feminist Theory: From Modernity to Postmodernity*. New York: Oxford University Press.

Marable, Manning. 1983a. "Groundings with My Sisters: Patriarchy and the Exploitation of Black Women." In *How Capitalism Underdeveloped Black America*, edited by Manning Marable, 69–104. Boston: South End Press.

Marable, Manning. 1983b. *How Capitalism Underdeveloped Black America*. Boston: South End Press.

Marable, Manning. 1993. "Beyond Identity Politics: Towards a Liberation Theory for Multicultural Democracy." *Race and Class* 35 (1): 113–130.

Marino, Gordon, ed. 2004. *Basic Writings of Existentialism*. New York: Modern Library.

Matsuda, Mari J. 1989. "Public Responses to Racist Speech: Considering the Victim's Story." *Michigan Law Review* 87, no. 8 (August): 2380–2381.

Matsuda, Mari J., Charles Lawrence III, Richard Delgado, and Kimberlé Crenshaw. 1993. *Words that Wound: Critical Race Theory, Assaultive Speech, and the First Amendment*. Boulder, CO: Westview Press.

May, Vivian M. 2007. *Anna Julia Cooper, Visionary Black Feminist: A Critical Introduction*. New York: Routledge.

May, Vivian M. 2015. *Pursuing Intersectionality, Unsettling Dominant Imaginaries*. New York: Routledge.

McCall, Leslie. 2005. "The Complexity of Intersectionality." *Signs* 30 (3): 1771–1800.

McClintock, Anne. 1995. *Imperial Leather: Race, Gender, and Sexuality in the Colonial Contest*. New York: Routledge.

McKee, James B. 1993. *Sociology and the Race Problem: The Failure of a Perspective*. Urbana: University of Illinois Press.

McKenna, Erin, and Scott L. Pratt, eds. 2015. *American Philosophy: From Wounded Knee to the Present*. London: Bloomsbury Academic.

Medina, Jose. 2013. *The Epistemology of Resistance*. New York: Oxford University Press.

Memmi, Albert. 1965. *The Colonizer and the Colonized*. Boston: Beacon Press.

Menand, Louis. 2001. *The Metaphysical Club: A Story of Ideas in America*. New York: Farrar, Straus and Giroux.

Menchu, Rigoberta. 2010. *I, Rigoberta Menchu: An Indian Woman in Guatemala*. Translated by Ann Wright. Edited by Elisabeth Burgos-Debray. London: Verso.

Mendieta, Eduardo. 2016. "Philosophy of Liberation." In *Stanford Encyclopedia of Philosophy*. Stanford, CA: Metaphysics Research Lab, Stanford University.

Mercer, Kobena. 1994. *Welcome to the Jungle: New Positions in Black Cultural Studies*. New York: Routledge.

Mercer, Kobena. 2017a. "Introduction." In *The Fateful Triangle: Race, Ethnicity, Nation*, edited by Kobena Mercer, 1–30. Cambridge, MA: Harvard University Press.

Mercer, Kobena, ed. 2017b. *The Fateful Triangle: Race, Ethnicity, Nation*. Cambridge, MA: Harvard University Press.

Mihesuah, Devon Abbott, and Angela Cavender Wilson. 2004. *Indigenizing the Academy: Transforming Scholarship and Empowering Communities*. Lincoln: University of Nebraska Press.

Mladenov, Teodor. 2016. "Disability and Social Justice." *Disability and Society* 31 (9): 1226–1241.

Mohanty, Chandra Talpade. 2003. *Feminism Without Borders: Decolonizing Theory, Practicing Solidarity*. Durham, NC: Duke University Press.

Molesworth, ed., Charles. 2012. *The Works of Alain Locke*. New York: Oxford University Press.

Morley, David, and Kuan-Hsing Chen, eds. 1996. *Stuart Hall: Critical Dialogues in Cultural Studies*. New York: Routledge.

Morris, Aldon. 2015. *The Scholar Denied: William E. B. Du Bois and the Birth of Modern Sociology*. Berkeley: University of California Press.

Morrison, Toni. 1992. *Playing in the Dark: Whiteness and the Literary Imagination*. Cambridge, MA: Harvard University Press.

Mosse, George L. 1985. *Nationalism and Sexuality: Middle-class Morality and Sexual Norms in Modern Europe*. New York: H. Fertig.

Moya, P. 2001. "Chicana Feminism and Postmodernist Theory." *Signs* 26 (2): 441–483.

Murray, Pauli. 1970a. *Dark Testament and Other Poems*. Norwalk, CT: Silvermine.

Murray, Pauli. 1970b. "The Liberation of Black Women." In *Voices of the New Feminism*, edited by Mary Lou Thompson, 87–102. Boston: Beacon.

Murray, Pauli. 1978 [1956]. *Proud Shoes: The Story of an American Family*. New York: Harper and Row.

Murray, Pauli. 1987. *Song in a Weary Throat: An American Pilgrimage*. New York: Harper and Row.

Murray, Pauli. 2006. *Pauli Murray: Selected Sermons and Writings*. New York: Orbis.

Murray, Pauli, and Leslie Rubin. 1961. *The Constitution and Government of Ghana*. London: Sweet and Maxwell.

Murray, Pauli, and Mary O. Eastwood. 1965. "Jane Crow and the Law: Sex Discrimination and Title VII." *George Washington Law Review* 34 (2): 232–256.

Nagel, Joane. 1998. "Masculinity and Nationalism: Gender and Sexuality in the Making of Nations." *Ethnic and Racial Studies* 21 (2): 242–269.

Nash, Jennifer C. 2008. "Re-thinking Intersectionality." *Feminist Review* no. 89: 1–15.

Nash, Jennifer C., and Emily A. Owens, eds. 2015. "Institutional Feelings: Practicing Women's Studies in the Corporate University." *Feminist Formations* 27 (3): vii–xi.

Negro, Isabel. 2015. "'Corruption is Dirt': Metaphors for Political Corruption in the Spanish Press." *Bulletin of Hispanic Studies* 92 (3): 213–237.

Nelson, Cary, Paula A. Treichler, and Lawrence Grossberg. 1992. "Cultural Studies: An Introduction." In *Cultural Studies*, edited by Lawrence Grossberg, Cary Nelson, and Paula A. Treichler, 1–22. New York: Routledge.

Noble, Safiya Umoja, and Brendesha M. Tynes, eds. 2016. *The Intersectional Internet: Race, Sex, Class, and Culture Online*. New York: Peter Lang.

Norocel, Ov Cristian. 2013. "'Give Us Back Sweden!' A Feminist Reading of the (Re)Interpretations of the *Folkhem* Conceptual Metaphor in Swedish Radical Right Populist Discourse." *Nordic Journal of Feminist and Gender Research* 21 (1): 4–20.

Omi, Michael, and Howard Winant. 1994. *Racial Formation in the United States: From the 1960s to the 1990s*. New York: Routledge.

Ong, Aihwa. 1999. *Flexible Citizenship: The Cultural Logics of Transnationality*. Durham, NC: Duke University Press.

Ordover, Nancy. 2003. *American Eugenics: Race, Queer Anatomy, and the Science of Nationalism*. Minneapolis: University of Minnesota Press.

Ortega, Mariana. 2001. "'New Mestizas,' 'World-Travelers,' and '*Dasein*': Phenomenology and the Multi-Voiced, Multi-Cultural Self." *Hypatia* 16 (3): 1–29.

Ortega, Mariana. 2016. "Speaking in Resistant Tongues: Latina Feminism, Embodied Knowledge, and Transformation." *Hypatia* 31 (2): 313–318.

Outlaw Jr, Lucius T. 2017. "Africana Philosophy." In *The Stanford Encyclopedia of Philosophy*, summer 2017 ed., edited by Edward N. Zalta. https://plato.stanford.edu/archives/sum2017/entries/africana/.

Palacios, Jone Martinez. 2016. "Equality and Diversity in Democracy: How Can We Democratize Inclusively?" *Equality, Diversity and Inclusion: An International Journal* 35 (5–6): 350–363.

Parker, Joe, Ranu Samantrai, and Mary Romero, eds. 2010. *Interdisciplinarity and Social Justice: Revisioning Academic Accountability*. Albany: State University of New York Press.

Parry, Benita. 2002. "Directions and Dead Ends in Postcolonial Studies." In *Relocating Postcolonialism*, edited by David Theo Goldberg and Ato Quayson, 66–81. Oxford, UK: Blackwell.

Passmore, Kevin. 2002. *Fascism: A Very Short Introduction*. New York: Oxford University Press.

Peppard, Christiana Z. 2013. "Democracy, the Verb: Pauli Murray's Poetry as a Resource for Ongoing Freedom Struggles." *Journal of Feminist Studies in Religion* 29 (1): 148–155.

Peterson, V. Spike. 2007. "Thinking Through Intersectionality and War." *Race, Gender and Class* 14 (3–4): 10–27.

Petzen, Jennifer. 2012. "Queer Trouble: Centring Race in Queer and Feminist Politics." *Journal of Intercultural Studies* 33 (3): 289–302.

Phoenix, Ann, and Pamela Pattynama. 2006. "Intersectionality." *European Journal of Women's Studies* 13 (3): 187–192.

Pinn, Anthony B. 2008. *Becoming "America's Problem Child": An Outline of Pauli Murray's Religious Life and Theology*. Eugene, OR: Pickwick Publications.

Posnock, Ross. 1997. "How It Feels to Be a Problem: Du Bois, Fanon, and the 'Impossible Life' of the Black Intellectual." *Critical Inquiry* 23 (2): 323–349.

Posnock, Ross. 1998. "Going Astray, Going Forward: Du Boisian Pragmatism and Its Lineage." In *The Revival of Pragmatism: New Essays on Social Thought, Law, and Culture*, edited by Morris Dickstein, 176–189. Durham, NC: Duke University Press.

Powell, Christopher, and Francois Depelteau, eds. 2013. *Conceptualizing Relational Sociology: Ontological and Theoretical Issues*. New York: Palgrave MacMillan.

Pratt, Scott L. 2002. *Native Pragmatism: Rethinking the Roots of American Philosophy*. Bloomington: Indiana University Press.

Proctor, Robert N. 1988. *Racial Hygiene: Medicine under the Nazis*. Cambridge, MA: Harvard University Press.

Putnam, Lara. 2009. "Nothing Matters But Color: Transnational Circuits, the Interwar Caribbean, and the Black International." In *From Toussaint to Tupac: The Black International since the Age of Revolution*, edited by Michael O. West, William G. Martin and Fanon Che Wilkins, 107–129. Chapel Hill: University of North Carolina Press.

Ramamurthy, Priti, and Ashwindi Tambe. 2017. "Decolonial and Postcolonial Approaches." *Feminist Studies* 43 (3): 503–511.

Ramos-Zayas, Ana Y. 2003. *National Performances: The Politics of Race, Class, and Space in Puerto Rican Chicago*. Chicago: University of Chicago Press.

Ransby, Barbara. 2003. *Ella Baker and the Black Freedom Movement: A Radical Democratic Vision*. Chapel Hill: University of North Carolina Press.

Ransby, Barbara. 2018. *Making All Black Lives Matter: Reimagining Freedom in the 21st Century*. Oakland: University of California Press.

Read, Alan. 1996. *The Fact of Blackness: Frantz Fanon and Visual Representation*. Seattle: Bay Press.

Reisch, Michael, ed. 2016. *The Routledge International Handbook of Social Justice*. New York: Routledge.

Richie, Beth. 2012. *Arrested Justice: Black Women, Violence and America's Prison Nation*. New York: New York University Press.

Rollins, Judith. 1985. *Between Women: Domestics and Their Employers*. Philadelphia: Temple University Press.

Rorty, Richard. 1999. *Philosophy and Social Hope*. New York: Penguin.

Rosenberg, Rosalind. 2017. *Jane Crow: The Life of Pauli Murray*. New York: Oxford University Press.

Roth, Benita. 2004. *Separate Roads to Feminism: Black, Chicana, and White Feminist Movements in America's Second Wave*. New York: Cambridge University Press.

Said, Edward. 1978. *Orientalism*. New York: Vintage.

Said, Edward. 1993. *Culture and Imperialism*. New York: A. A. Knopf.

Said, Edward. 1994. *Representations of the Intellectual*. New York: Vintage.

Sandoval, Chela. 2000. *Methodology of the Oppressed*. Minneapolis: University of Minnesota Press.

Santos, Boaventura de Sousa, ed. 2007. *Another Knowledge Is Possible: Beyond Northern Epistemologies*. New York: Verso.

Santos, Boaventura de Sousa, João Arriscado Nunes, and Maria Paula Meneses. 2007. "Opening Up the Canon of Knowledge and Recognition of Difference." In *Another Knowledge Is Possible: Beyond Northern Epistemologies*, edited by Boaventura de Sousa Santos, xvix–lxii. New York: Verso.

Sartre, Jean-Paul. 1963. "Preface." In *The Wretched of the Earth*, edited by Frantz Fanon, xliii–lxii. New York: Grove Press.

Sartre, Jean-Paul. 1995 [1948]. *Anti-Semite and Jew: An Exploration of the Etiology of Hate*. Translated by George J. Becker. New York: Schocken Books.

Sartre, Jean-Paul. 2006 [1964]. *Colonialism and Neocolonialism*. New York: Routledge.

Scanlon, Jennifer. 2016. *Until There Is Justice: The Life of Anna Arnold Hedgeman*. New York: Oxford University Press.

Schalk, David L. 2005. *War and the Ivory Tower: Algeria and Vietnam*. Lincoln: University of Nebraska Press.

Schulz, Kathryn. 2017. "The Many Lives of Pauli Murray." *New Yorker* (April 17).

Scott, Anne Firor, ed. 2006. *Pauli Murray and Caroline Ware: Forty Years of Letters in Black and White*. Chapel Hill: University of North Carolina Press.

Seigfried, Charlene Haddock. 1993. "Shared Communities of Interest: Feminism and Pragmatism." *Hypatia* 8 (2): 1–14.

Seigfried, Charlene Haddock. 1996. *Pragmatism and Feminism: Reweaving the Social Fabric*. Chicago: University of Chicago.

Sen, Amartya. 2009. *The Idea of Justice*. Cambridge, MA: Harvard University Press.

Shelby, Tommie. 2005. *We Who Are Dark: The Philosophical Foundations of Black Solidarity*. Cambridge, MA: Harvard University Press.

Sherratt, Yvonne. 2006. *Continental Philosophy of Social Science: Hermeneutics, Genealogy, and Critical Theory from Greece to the Twenty-First Century*. New York: Cambridge University Press.

Simons, Margaret A. 1999. *Beauvoir and the Second Sex: Feminism, Race, and the Origins of Existentialism*. Lanham, MD: Rowman and Littlefield.

Simons, Margaret A. 2006. "Beauvoir's Early Philosophy." In *Simone de Beauvoir: Diary of a Philosopher*, edited by Barbara Klaw and Margaret A. Simons, 29–50. Urbana: University of Illinois Press.

Sirianni, Carmen. 2009. *Investing in Democracy: Engaging Citizens in Collaborative Governance*. Washington, DC: Brookings Institution Press.

Sithole, Tendayi. 2016. "Frantz Fanon: Africana Existentialist Philosopher." *African Identities* 14 (2): 177–190.

Slack, Jennifer Daryl. 1996. "The Theory and Method of Articulation in Cultural Studies." In *Stuart Hall: Critical Dialogues in Cultural Studies*, edited by David Morley and Kuan-Hsing Chen, 112–127. New York: Routledge.

Smith, Barbara. 1983. *Home Girls: A Black Feminist Anthology*. New York: Kitchen Table Press.

Smith, Linda Tuhiwai. 2012. *Decolonizing Methodologies*. 2nd ed. London: Zed Books.

Smith, Valerie. 1998. *Not Just Race, Not Just Gender: Black Feminist Readings*. New York: Routledge.

Somerville, Siobhan B. 2000. *Queering the Color Line: Race and the Invention of Homosexuality in American Culture*. Durham, NC: Duke University Press.

Stanley, Jason. 2018. *How Fascism Works: The Politics of Us and Them*. New York: Random House.

Steele, Catherine Knight. 2016. "Signifyin' Bitching, and Bloggins: Black Women and Resistance Discourse Online." In *The Intersectional Internet: Race, Sex, Class, and Culture Online*, edited by Safiya Umoja Noble and Brendesha M. Tynes, 73–94. New York: Peter Lang.

Stepan, Nancy. 1990. "Race and Gender: The Role of Analogy in Science." In *Anatomy of Racism*, edited by David Goldberg, 38–57. Minneapolis: University of Minnesota Press.

Stepan, Nancy. 1991. *"The Hour of Eugenics": Race, Gender, and Nation in Latin America*. Ithaca, NY: Cornell University Press.

Stoetzler, Marcel, and Nira Yuval-Davis. 2002. "Standpoint Theory, Situated Knowledge and the Situated Imagination." *Feminist Theory* 3 (3): 315–333.

Stoler, Ann Laura. 1995. *Race and the Education of Desire: Foucault's History of Sexuality and the Colonial Order of Things*. Durham, NC: Duke University Press.

Story, Kaila Adia, ed. 2014. *Patricia Hill Collins: Reconceiving Motherhood*. Bradford, ON, Canada: Demeter Press.

Stuhr, John J. 2000. "Introduction: Classical American Philosophy." In *Pragmatism and Classical American Philosophy: Essential Readings and Interpretive Essays*, edited by John J. Stuhr, 1–9. New York: Oxford University Press.

Sullivan, Shannon. 2000. "Reconfiguring Gender with John Dewey: Habit, Bodies, and Cultural Change." *Hypatia* 15 (1): 23–42.

Sullivan, Shannon. 2015. "Intersections Between Pragmatist and Continental Feminism." In *The Stanford Encyclopedia of Philosophy*, spring 2015 ed., edited by Edward N. Zalta. https://plato.stanford.edu/archives/spr2015/entries/femapproach-prag-cont/.

Swedberg, Richard. 2014. *The Art of Social Theory*. Princeton, NJ: Princeton University Press.

Takagi, Dana. 2015. "First Precepts for Democracy and Research Practices in Ethnic Studies." *Cultural Studies, Critical Methodology* 15 (2): 100–111.

Takaki, Ronald T. 1993. *A Different Mirror: A History of Multicultural America*. Boston: Little, Brown.

Tavory, Iddo, and Stefan Timmermans. 2014. *Abductive Analysis: Theorizing Qualitative Research*. Chicago: University of Chicago Press.

Taylor, Keeanga-Yamahtta. 2016. *From #BlackLivesMatter to Black Liberation*. Chicago: Haymarket Books.

Terriquez, Veronica. 2015. "Intersectional Mobilization, Social Movement Spillover, and Queer Youth Leadership in the Immigrant Rights Movement." *Social Problems* 62 (3): 343–362.

Thomsen, Carly. 2015. "The Post-Raciality and Post-Spatiality of Calls for LGBTQ and Disability Visibility." *Hypatia* 30 (1): 149–166.

Thorne, Barrie. 1992. "Feminism and the Family: Two Decades of Thought." In *Rethinking the Family: Some Feminist Questions*, edited by Barrie Thorne and Marilyn Yalom, 3–30. Boston: Northeastern University Press.

Thurman, Judith. 2011 [1949]. "Introduction." In *The Second Sex*, edited by Simone de Beauvoir, ix–xvi. New York: Vintage.

Tomaskovic-Devey, Donald, and Kevin Stainback. 2012. *Documenting Desegregation: Racial and Gender Segregation in Private Sector Employment Since the Civil Rights Act*. New York: Russell Sage Foundation.

Tomlinson, Barbara. 2013. "To Tell the Truth and Not Get Trapped: Desire, Distance, and Intersectionality at the Scene of Argument." *Signs* 38 (4): 993–1017.

Torgovnick, Marianna. 1990. *Gone Primitive: Savage Intellects, Modern Lives*. Chicago: University of Chicago Press.

Torres, Carlos A. 2012. "Critical Social Theory: A Portrait." *Ethics and Education* 7 (2): 115–124.

Trout, Lara. 2010. *The Politics of Survival: Peirce, Affectivity, and Social Criticism*. New York: Fordham University Press.

Tucker, William H. 1994. *The Science and Politics of Racial Research*. Urbana: University of Illinois Press.

Turner, Stephen T. 2006. "British Sociology and Public Intellectuals: Consumer Society and Imperial Decline." *British Journal of Sociology* 57 (2): 169–188.

Urry, John. 2005. "The Complexity Turn." *Theory, Culture and Society* 22 (5): 1–14.

Van Deburg, William L. 1997. *Modern Black Nationalism: From Marcus Garvey to Louis Farrakhan*. New York: New York University Press.

Vaughn, Diane. 2014. "Analogy, Cases, and Comparative Social Organization." In *Theorizing in Social Science: The Context of Discovery*, edited by Richard Swedberg, 61–84. Stanford, CA: Stanford University Press.

Wailoo, Keith, Alondra Nelson, and Catherine Lee, eds. 2012. *Genetics and the Unsettled Past: The Collision of DNA, Race, and History*. New Brunswick, NJ: Rutgers University Press.

Walby, Sylvia. 2007. "Complexity Theory, Systems Theory, and Multiple Intersecting Social Inequalities." *Philosophy of the Social Sciences* 37 (4): 449–470.

Wasserman, David, Adrienne Asch, Jeffrey Blustein, and Daniel Putnam. 2015. "Disability and Justice." In *The Stanford Encyclopedia of Philosophy*, summer 2015 ed., edited by Edward N. Zalta. https://plato.stanford.edu/archives/sum2015/entries/disability-justice/.

Wasserman, David, Adrienne Asch, Jeffrey Blustein, and Daniel Putnam. 2016. "Disability: Definitions, Models, Experience. In *The Stanford Encyclopedia of Philosophy*, summer 2016 ed., edited by Edward N. Zalta. https://plato.stanford.edu/archives/sum2016/entries/disability/.

Weindling, Paul. 1999. "International Eugenics: Swedish Sterilization in Context." *Journal of Scandinavian History* 24 (2): 179–197.

Wells-Barnett, Ida B. 2002. *On Lynchings*. Amherst, NY: Humanity Books.

West, Candace, and Sarah Fenstermaker. 1995. "Doing Difference." *Gender and Society* no. 9 (1): 8–37.

West, Cornel. 1989. *The American Evasion of Philosophy: A Genealogy of Pragmatism*. Madison: University of Wisconsin Press.

Wiegman, Robyn. 2012. *Object Lessons*. Durham, NC: Duke University Press.

Willett, Cynthia. 2001. *The Soul of Justice: Social Bonds and Racial Hubris*. Ithaca, NY: Cornell University Press.

Williams, Brackett F. 1995. "Classification Systems Revisited: Kinship, Caste, Race, and Nationality as the Flow of Blood and the Spread of Rights." In *Naturalizing Power: Essays in Feminist Cultural Analysis*, edited by Sylvia Yanagisako and Carol Delaney, 201–236. New York: Routledge.

Williams, Patrick, and Laura Chrisman, eds. 1994. *Colonial Discourse and Post-Colonial Theory: A Reader*. New York: Columbia University Press.

Winant, Howard. 2000. "Race and Race Theory." *Annual Review of Sociology* 26: 169–185.

Wingfield, Adia Harvey, and Renee Skeete Alston. 2012. "The Understudied Case of Black Professional Men: Advocating an Intersectional Approach." *Sociology Compass* 6 (9): 728–739.

Yeğenoğlu, Meyda. 1998. *Colonial Fantasies: Toward a Feminist Reading of Orientalism*. Cambridge, UK: Cambridge University Press.

Young, Iris Marion. 1990. *Justice and the Politics of Difference*. Princeton, NJ: Princeton University Press.

Young, Iris Marion. 2011. *Responsibility for Justice*. New York: Oxford University Press.

Yuval-Davis, Nira. 1997. *Gender and Nation*. Thousand Oaks, CA: Sage.

Yuval-Davis, Nira. 2011. *The Politics of Belonging: Intersectional Contestations*. London: Sage.

Zuberi, Tukufu. 2001. *Thicker Than Blood: How Racial Statistics Lie*. Minneapolis: University of Minnesota Press.

Zuberi, Tukufu, and Eduardo Bonilla-Silva, eds. 2008. *White Logic, White Methods: Racism and Methodology*. Lanham, MD: Rowman and Littlefield.

Index

abductive analysis, 147–51, 309n18, 310n21; dialogical engagement, 147–49; ethnography, 147–48; methodology for studying Pauli Murray, 202–4; participatory action research, 149–51

ability/disability, 10, 259, 323n7; eugenics, 271; normality/abnormality, 257

Addams, Jane, 177, 179

additive frameworks, 227–32

Adorno, Theodor, 57–58

African American social and political thought, 90, 92, 96–97, 204–5; Africana philosophy, 90; Black feminism, 96–98; intellectuals, 92, 93, 303n8; LGBTQ intellectual production, 24, 97, 106, 171. *See also* Black feminism; Black feminist thought

age, 10, 190–91, 195–96, 204

Alexander, M. Jacqui, 105

Althusser, Louis, 295n9

American pragmatism, 172–75, 291n3, 310n2, 312n11, 314n14; community, 14, 181–82; creative social action, 172–80; experience, 172–73, 186–87; experimentalism, 174; feminism, 176–77, 314n16; indigenous peoples, 179; influence of, 314n14; phenomenology, 313n12; power analytic of, 182–83; racial criticism within, 177–78; social inequality within, 175–76

analogical reasoning, 316n6; binary thinking, 100, 103, 218; use in critical thinking, 316n6; metaphors within, 316n7; methodology, 201–2; normality/abnormality, 257; race/gender analogy, 194; sexuality, 257; Simone de Beauvoir, 194–98; stereotypes, 257–58

Anzaldúa, Gloria, 32–33, 105, 106, 111, 129, 134, 138–39, 202, 244–46, 292n6

apartheid, 90, 94

Arendt, Hannah, 129, 190, 239

articulation, 232–40; compared to co-formation, 241; dialogical engagement as methodology, 71–72; dual meanings of, 232–33; eugenics projects, 270; intersectional theorizing, 233–34; mode of relational thinking, 71–72; and Oliver Cox, 319n8; social change, 321n13

Bauman, Zygmunt, 129, 190, 239, 265; on social engineering, 324n10

Beauvoir, Simone de, 14, 76, 190–91, 228–29, 314n15; ambiguity and freedom, 193; analogical reasoning, 190; on age and oppression, 196; on Blacks as slaves, 194; on class, 197; existential freedom, 192–94; experience and freedom, 193; on feminism, 199–200; oppositional difference, 219; use of race/gender analogy, 194–98; relationship to Jean Paul Sartre, 315n2; social action and freedom, 193. *See also Ethics of Ambiguity, The; Second Sex, The*

Bhabha, Homi, 110

binary thinking, 100, 103, 212, 218, 260; essentialism, 319n5

Black feminism, 158–60, 170–72, 311n5; within Black communities, 96–98; identity politics, 137; motherwork as reproductive labor, 168–69; significance of violence, 311n5

Black feminist thought, 14, 158–72, 180–81; community work, 167–72; experience, 185–86; epistemology, 166; historiography, 311n4; ideas and actions within, 159–60; intersectionality and, 310n2; political activism, 107, 139, 140–41, 312n9; as resistant knowledge project, 159, 310n2; scholarship, 311n6; visionary pragmatism, 188, 216–17

Black Lives Matter movement, 171, 306n25

Black Skin, White Masks (Fanon), 73

body politics, 103, 235, 258–61, 323n6

borderlands as metaphor: co-formation, 244–46; spatial metaphor, 33; way of theorizing, 33. *See also* co-formation; metaphors

Bourdieu, Pierre, 77–78, 128, 296n10, 296n15, 302n7; influence on sociology, 299n27; perspective on liberation struggles, 299n28

British cultural studies, 56, 65–72, 82, 83, 88, 231; intersectionality and, 68–69; multiculturalism in Britain, 296n11; treatment of popular culture, 67

Butler, Judith, 100, 102, 128, 232, 292n7; existentialism, 304n13; *Gender Trouble,* 100, 102; on identity, 37; poststructuralism, 304n14

capitalism, 10, 66–67, 212–13, 239; violence, 163–64

Carastathis, Anna, 28, 123, 135

Centre for Contemporary Cultural Studies (cccs), 56, 65. *See also* British cultural studies

Chicana feminism, 32–33, 104. *See also* Anzaldúa, Gloria; Latinas

class analysis, 229–32, 317n14; Angela Y. Davis, 231; intersectional theorizing, 231–32; Pauli Murray, 205–6, 212–13; Simone de Beauvoir, 197

co-formation, 241–49; ability/disability, 323n7; co-causality, 321n16; compared to articulation, 241; contrapuntal motion in music, 322n18; discourse analysis, 243; within humanities and social sciences, 241–44; metaphors of, 244–49

collaboration, 149–50; British cultural studies, 66–67; power relations, 129–30. *See also* dialogical engagement

Combahee River Collective, 97, 106, 137

community, 14, 181–85, 310n1; academic and activist epistemologies, 125–26; community work, 158, 167–68; imagined community, 264; intersectional theorizing, 187–88; power relations, 181–85; symbols, 315n19. *See also* interpretive communities

complexity, 47, 242

conceptual metaphor theory, 29, 292n4

conjuncture, 234, 235, 320n9; articulation, 234–37; example of family 235–36; example of violence, 237–40; saturated sites of power, 235

creative social action, 172–80, 182, 204–8; Wells-Barnett and, 173–74. *See also* American pragmatism

equality, 2, 141–42, 281
ethics, 280–85, 289; in the academy, 281–82; de Beauvoir and, 193; faith-based and secular ethics, 282–84
Ethics of Ambiguity, The (de Beauvoir), 192–94, 198, 315n4
ethnography: abductive analysis, 147–48; as methodology, 309n19
eugenics projects, 254–68; ability/disability, 271; articulation, 270; evolution, 258; immutable difference, 258–59; intersectionality and, 268–73; population control, 254, 265–66; relational logic of, 16, 254–58; saturated site of intersecting power relations, 269; as science, 256, 271; social engineering, 264–68; white nationalism, 94, 95
existential freedom, 75–77, 88, 192–94
experience, 12–13, 157–58, 173, 185; within American pragmatism, 186–87; within Black feminist thought, 158, 185–86
experimentalism in pragmatist philosophy, 174, 313n13, 316n5

faith-based ethics, 191, 207, 216, 282–84
family, 235–36, 261–64
Fanon, Frantz, 73–75, 110, 114, 129, 130, 189, 190, 298n20
fascism, 58–59, 295n6. *See also* eugenics projects
feminism, 89, 98–107, 231
feminist philosophy, 4, 30, 99–101, 306. *See also* Butler, Judith; Carastathis, Anna; Fraser, Nancy; Harding, Sandra; Seigfried, Charlene
feminist theory, 11, 14, 98–107; queer of color critiques, 105–6; queer theory, 103
Firebrand and the First Lady, The (Bell-Scott), 208, 209, 210–11
flexible solidarity, 167–72. *See also* Black feminism; Black feminist thought
Foucault, Michel, 79, 291n2; subjugated knowledges, 84

Francophone intellectual production, 72–81; Algerian War for liberation, 72–73, 76–77; intellectuals, 297n17; social theory, 56–57
Frankfurt School of Critical Theory. *See* Critical Theory (Frankfurt School)
Fraser, Nancy, 178; philosophy of social justice, 326n16
freedom, 2, 14, 191–96, 281; Black freedom struggle, 13, 203, 317; social justice, 315n1

Gandhi, Mahatma, 114, 204
Gender Trouble (Butler), 100, 102
genealogy, 1–3, 88, 291n2; of intersectionality, 123–26
Global South, 87, 109, 300n1
Great Chain of Being, 100, 260, 262
Guillaumin, Colette, 234–35

Habermas, Jürgen, 295n5; dialogic process, 80–81
Hall, Stuart, 27, 65, 69, 110, 129, 189, 190, 232–33, 270; articulation, 68–72; culture, 296n15; identity, 37; paradigm shifts and social theory, 50
Harding, Sandra, 30, 306n4
heteropatriarchy, 103, 227, 239, 304n16
Hill, Anita, 131–33
Horkheimer, Max, 57–64

identity: American pragmatism, 173; coalitional politics, 37; collective identities, 138; identifications and subjectivity, 103; intersectionality as heuristic, 37; Pauli Murray, 317n11; political analysis, 307n11
identity politics, 136, 308n13; Black feminism, 137; Combahee River Collective, 97; criticisms of, 137–38; epistemic agency and resistance, 137–39; lesbian identity politics, 102, 106
indigenous peoples, 24, 114, 260; American pragmatism, 179–80; criticism of

"indigenous worldview," 322n20; methodology, 142–43; Okanagan peoples, 247–48; social thought of, 179–80, 247–48, 260; women, 107, 139
Institute for Social Research: *See* Critical Theory (Frankfurt School)
intellectual activism, 2, 10, 17–18, 167, 221; Ida B. Wells-Barnett, 160–67; intellectuals in exile, 58, 112; Pauli Murray, 201–8
interdisciplinarity, 98–100, 325n13
internal colonialism, 115, 305n24
interpretive communities, 6, 128, 182, 310n1; epistemic power, 127–30; intellectuals within, 128, 130; intersectionality and, 128; social context, 46; social justice, 254; truth, 131–32. *See also* community
intersecting power relations, 16, 26, 30–31, 33
intersectionality and epistemology, 11–12, 122; epistemic authority, 140; ethics, 281–85; logic of segregation, 227–28; meaning through use, 23; relational logic of, 16
intersectionality and resistant knowledge, 10, 87–89, 96, 116–20; British cultural studies, 68–69; critical race theory, 89–97; feminism, 98–107; postcolonial theory, 108–15. *See also* Black feminism; Black feminist thought
intersectionality as discourse, 2–6, 8, 23, 48; categories within, 39–48, 218; cognitive architecture of, 49, 52, 15; coining narrative within, 123–24, 152, 306n1; compared to race/class/gender studies, 39–40; critical commentary on, 13, 22–23; genealogy, 122–26; interpretive communities, 128; queer Black and Latina feminist theorists, 106; significance of naming, 125–26; social justice, 16, 145, 215; as a theory of identity, 37
intersectionality as metaphor, 8, 23, 124; core conceptual metaphor for social

inequality, 29–30; limits of metaphor, 32; of social transformation, 27; as a spatial metaphor, 27–28. *See also* metaphors
intersectionality as methodology, 11–12, 144; context of discovery of, 145–46; core constructs, 45–48; saliency of categories, 270–71
intersectionality's cognitive architecture, 23–24, 49–50, 153; core constructs, 43, 45–48; guiding premises, 43–44, 48–50; heuristic use, 8, 24, 28, 34–41, 124, 167; metaphoric use, 8, 23, 124, 244–49; paradigmatic use, 8, 25, 42–45
intersectionality's core constructs. *See* complexity; power relations; relationality; social context; social inequality; social justice
intersectional theorizing: articulation, 233–34; borderland metaphor, 245–46; class analysis, 231–32; co-formation, 244

Jane Crow (Rosenberg), 208, 209, 211–12
jazz as metaphor, 246–47. *See also* co-formation; metaphors
Jewish people: analogical reasoning, 195–96, 198; Sartre and anti-Semitism, 57–58
journey as metaphor. *See* metaphors; Murray, Pauli; reflexivity

Kuhn, Thomas, 42–43

Latinas, 24, 107, 139–41; theorizing and, 138–39; Latina feminism, 32–33, 104. *See also* Anzaldúa, Gloria
liberation theory, 87, 88, 125, 231; concept of liberation, 76, 77, 298n22; critical theory, 113; *Discourses on Liberation*, 80–81, 113; Frantz Fanon, 75; philosophy of, 298n23; social transformation, 83
Locke, Alain, 92, 177–78, 314n18; racial theory of, 177–78

logic of segregation, 227–28; essentialism, 319n5

Lorde, Audre, 106, 307n8

Marxist social theory, 60, 88, 125, 230–31; in Francophone context, 77, 295n9; labor power, 235; liberation struggles, 299n26; social transformation, 83

matrix of domination, 239

McCall, Leslie: categorical analysis, 242, 321n15

Medina, Jose, 127–28

Memmi, Albert, 306n2

metaphors, 29–33; abductive analysis, 317n12; as centers and margins, 31; of co-formation, 244–49; cognitive thinking, 316n9; conceptual metaphor theory, 30–31; epistemic resistance, 249; of journey, 202, 217, 221; normality/abnormality, 257–59; partial perspectives, 317n15; perspectives on the web, 247–49; of power 31; of sight, 246; social theorizing, 30; social transformation, 27; of sound, 247; of the Spider's Web, 247–48; as thinking tools, 26

methodology, 122, 142–52; context of discovery, 15, 64, 249; epistemology, 11–12; ethnography, 309n19, 310n20; participatory action research, 149–51; power relations, 31, 142; reflexivity, 63–64, 67–68; resistant knowledge projects, 117. *See also* abductive analysis; dialogical engagement

Methodology of the Oppressed (Sandoval), 31

Mob Rule in New Orleans (Wells-Barnett), 161–62

Mohanty, Chandra Talpade, 105

Murray, Pauli, 14, 129, 190–91, 201–16, 229, 234, 243, 306n3, 3316n8; class exploitation, 205; critical praxis, 215; gender oppression, 206; metaphor of journey, 204–8, 217, 221; methodology, 202–3; racism, 205; relational difference, 219; scope of writings, 207;

sexuality as oppression, 206; social action, 190; social justice, 215; transgendered, 206

nationalism, 10, 12, 37–38, 213–14; family rhetoric, 263; fascism, 58–59, 295n6; imagined community, 264; white nationalism, 94, 95. *See also* eugenics projects

Native Pragmatism (Pratt), 179–80

naturalized hierarchy, 258

neocolonialism, 114, 115, 239; formal colonialism and, 115; internal colonialism, 115

oppositional difference. *See* difference

oppression, 10, 12, 14

Orientalism (Said), 111–13

paradigm, 41–42; as heuristic device, 293n9; paradigm shifts, 42–43, 179; within philosophy, 179–80; social theory, 50

performativity, 102

postcolonial theory, 89, 108–15, 305n19; postcolonial versus decolonial feminism, 108–9; related terminology, 108, 305n23

postmodern social theory, 78–79, 143, 300n29

poststructuralism, 72, 77–80, 88, 117, 299n25

power relations, 10, 16, 31, 46, 288–89; within American pragmatism, 182–83

Pratt, Scott L.: *Native Pragmatism*, 179–80

praxis, 89, 117–18

primitivism, 260, 324n8

Proud Shoes (Murray), 211, 214

queer theory, 102–3; feminist theory, 103; queer of color critiques, 105–6

race, 9, 260–61, 263; treatment of within Western academic disciplines, 91–92 race, class, and gender, 8, 35, 39–40; saliency of categories, 203

racial formation theory, 93–96; creative social action, 303n10; implications for intersectionality, 96; influences on, 303n9

Racial Order, The. See Bourdieu, Pierre

racial project, 94–95, 302n6, 303n11

racial segregation, 90, 94, 107, 169

racism, 10, 28, 90–91, 238–39

reflexivity, 63–64, 67–68, 152–54; journey as metaphor, 202, 217, 221; participatory action research, 150. *See also* dialogical engagement; methodology

relational difference, 218, 283, 318n2. *See also* difference

relationality, 15–16, 45–46, 225, 226, 293n10; adding into versus adding together, 227; articulation within British cultural studies, 71–72; master categories, 227, 228; significance, 16, 250–52

resistance, 11, 25, 88, 239–40

resistant knowledge projects, 10, 24, 88, 116–20, 303n10; antiracism, 116; antiviolence, 239; critical ethnic studies, 149–51; critical disability studies, 259; critical race theory, 89–98; experience, 117–18; feminism, 98–107; freedom, 190; internal criticism within, 96; methodology, 117; minority studies, 116; postcolonial theory, 108–15; relationships among, 119–20; social theorists, 129; standpoint epistemology, 139

Said, Edward, 110–12, 129

Sandoval, Chela, 31–32

Sartre, Jean-Paul, 73, 75, 76, 77, 190; anti-Semitism and, 298n24; neocolonialism, 298n24

saturated sites of power: as conjunctures, 235; eugenics as, 324, 12; family as, 235–36; resistance and, 324n12; violence as, 237–40

Second Sex, The (de Beauvoir), 99, 192, 197–201, 315n3

secular ethics, 282–84. *See also* ethics

Seigfried, Charlene, 177, 180

sexage, 234–35

sexuality, 10, 102

silencing: within African American communities, 97; as epistemic violence, 133

Smith, Linda Tuhiwai, 142–43, 151

Smith, Valerie, 229, 243

social action, 4, 12–13, 183, 185–88, 193, 202, 279

social change, 126; the changing same, 61–62, 286; critical social theory and, 4–5; critical theorizing and, 89; eugenic explanations of, 267; racial formation theory and, 95

social class, 229–32; nation, ethnicity as substitutes, 35; within intersectionality, 229–32

social context, 12, 46–47, 310n3

Social Darwinism, 258

social engineering, 264–68

social inequality, 46, 233; intersectionality as metaphor, 29–30; systems of oppression, 239; within American pragmatism, 175–76, 183–85

social justice, 2, 47, 126, 275–76; in the academy, 273–75, 280; backlash against, 125; challenges for intersectionality, 277–78; comparison to freedom, 315n1; competing views of, 325n14; critical social theory, 274; Critical Theory, 62–63; epistemic power, 127; institutional incorporation, 325n13; interdependence, 279; intersectional projects, 253; Nancy Fraser, 326n16; Pauli Murray, 209, 215

social problem solving, 25, 28, 186

social theory, 4, 6, 8–9; abstract language, 300n30; compared to social theorizing, 51; humanities versus social sciences, 8–9, 51–53; paradigms, 50; theorizing co-formation, 243; theorizing versus theory, 51; underemphasis on race, 91–92

social transformation, 25, 27, 75, 81–84

social world. *See* social change; social inequality; social justice; social problem solving

sociology: emphasis on social order, 302n7; eugenics, 323n2

spatial metaphors, 32–33, 244–45

Spider's Web, The (Okangan people), 247–48. *See also* co-formation; metaphors

standpoint epistemology, 100, 136, 139–40, 293n11; criticisms of, 139–40; situated standpoints, 139; as theory of truth, 140

Stuhr, John, 291n3

Swedberg, Richard, 51

Takagi, Dana, 149–51

testimonial authority, 90, 131–36, 152; Global South, 307n10

testimonial quieting, 133–34, 138

testimonial smothering, 134, 308n14

Thomas, Clarence, 131–33

traditional social theory, 59–60

transgendered, 106, 103, 304n17

transnational feminism, 104–5

truth, 131–32, 288

violence: capitalism, 163–64; conjunctures, 236–37; eugenics, 257; gendered, 162–63; intersectional theorizing, 238–40, 320n12; lynching and structural power relations, 162; as a saturated site of power, 35, 237–40; systems of oppression, 237–39

visionary pragmatism, 188, 216–17

Wells-Barnett, Ida B., 93, 129, 189–90, 231, 311n6; anti-lynching crusade, 160–61; counternarrative of lynching, 160–67; as feminist, 167; methodology, 165–66; testimonial authority, 161–62

white nationalism, 94, 95

woman of color, 104, 136, 140

work, 35–36, 205; capitalism and labor markets, 36; motherwork as reproductive labor, 168–69; Pauli Murray as underemployed, 205, 208, 210

Wretched of the Earth, The (Fanon), 73, 76, 77

Yeğenoğlu, Meyda, 112–13